ROCK IN THE LATE SIXTIES
TURNING ON

ROCK IN THE TURNING ON LATE SIXTIES

ORBIS · LONDON

Editors
Ashley Brown
Michael Heatley

Executive Editor
Adrian Gilbert

Production Editor
Annette Kennerley

Chief Sub-Editor
Tom Hibbert

Sub-Editors
Chris Schüler
Alastair Dougall

Picture Editors
Sarah Smith
Dave Kent
Jonathan Reed

Editorial Secretary
Clare Witherden

Departmental Assistant
Darren Crook

Editorial Director
Brian Innes

Production Co-ordinator
Peter Taylor-Medhurst

Art Editor
John Heritage

Designer
Wayne Léal

Consultant Editors
Charlie Gillett
Phil Hardy
Bill Millar
Peter Brookesmith

Volume Editors
Graham Fuller
Lorrie Mack

Acknowledgements
Pictures were supplied by Cyrus Andrews, BBC Hulton Picture Library, Roy Burchell, CBS, Colour Library International, Commerce Studio, Daily Telegraph Colour Library, Arnold Desser, Electra Records, EMI Records, Joel Finler, David Gahr, Mick Gold, Phil Hardy, Bob Hoffindon, Dezo Hoffman, Island Records, Alan Johnson, Yoram Kahana/Shooting Star, Peter Kanze, Graham Keen, Keystone Press Agency, Kobal Collection, Elliot Landy/Star Files, JP Leloir, London Features International, Jim Marshall, Melody Maker, David Morosoli, Chris Morris, National Film Archive, Michael Ochs, Jan Persson/Melody Maker, Pictorial Press, John Pidgeon, John Platt, Barry Plummer, Polydor Records, Popperfoto, Pye Records, Nick Ralph, Rare Pics, David Redfern, Jonathan Reed, Rex Features, Rolling Stone, Shooting Star, Stephen Shore, Syndication International, Tate Gallery, John Topham, UPI, WEA Records, Val Wilmer, Fred Woods Folk Review, Graham Wright.

First published in Great Britain by Orbis Publishing Limited, London 1985

ISBN 0-85613-625-5

Printed in Italy

Contents

INTRODUCTION

In 1967, the Beatles released their eighth album, *Sgt Pepper's Lonely Hearts Club Band*. From the diverse blend of musical and lyrical elements – druggy ragas, music hall whimsy, images of suburbia, ornate nonsense, expansive experiment – to the Pop Art sleeve, which depicted the group, in antique gear from Carnaby Street, rubbing shoulders with their former selves and other stars, the record reflected the optimistic, somewhat self-conscious spirit of the times. Pop devotees and 'intellectual' critics alike acclaimed the LP a masterpiece – true 'art'. Just four years after the Beatles had risen to the top, shaking their fringes for the delight of screaming teenage girls, the correlation between pop and idiocy had been dispelled. The music that cellist Pablo Casals had called 'poison put to sound', that Frank Sinatra had described as a 'rancid-smelling aphrodisiac', had come of age. The late sixties were to witness the emergence of a whole range of innovative performers and styles; this book traces the story of rock's most turbulent and creative era – the years of the 'rock revolution'.

'The sound is the sound of the electronic age, a dissent from older forms.' wrote the late journalist Ralph Gleason of the new rock in 1968. 'The costumes are a dissent from the Ed Sullivan slick. These performers *never* have a nose-bob or cap their teeth.' If it had not been for the Beatles, the story of sixties pop might have consisted entirely of gleaming smiles and bland, sanitised ballads. But in 1964, the Liverpudlians arrived in America to oust the super-clean, teen crooners from the charts and reintroduce excitement and verve into rock and roll. Soon after, the Rolling Stones – described by the New York Post in 1965 as 'five unfolding switchblades' – brought back aggression while American folk singer Bob Dylan turned electric (to the disgust of many of his purist fans) to mix rock forms with a new lyricism and elegant cynicism. The influence of these artists on the development of rock is incalculable: previously, it had been unusual for pop acts to compose their own material but the Beatles and Dylan had changed the rules. By 1966, pop music, on both sides of the Atlantic, boasted more variety and colour than ever before. In the UK, three veterans of the British R&B boom – bassist Jack Bruce, drummer Ginger Baker and guitarist Eric Clapton – had formed Cream, the first of the 'supergroups', and were pioneering 'progressive' rock with demonstrations of instrumental expertise while Pink Floyd, with their novel light shows and studies in experimental sound, were becoming the darlings of London's 'underground' scene. In the US, the jug-band hums of the Lovin' Spoonful and the jangling, cerebral excursions of the Byrds were challenging the market dominance of British beat. And in San Francisco, youth was beginning to 'turn on, tune in and drop out' to the meandering mind-expansion of the Grateful Dead and the drug-riddled political naivety of Jefferson Airplane. The ready availability of hallucinogenic drugs had combined with anti-Vietnam war sentiments, born of traditional youth rebellion, to create a 'counter-culture'. For a few short months, media interest in, and exploitation of, 'flower power' kept San Francisco's psychedelic generation in the public eye.

In January 1967, a 'Human Be-In' – 'a new concert of human relations – a joyful face-to-face beginning of the new epoch', according to the organisers – was held in San Francisco's Golden Gate Park; painted, joyful hippies celebrated 'togetherness' by grooving to poetry and nose-flute music and dancing to the Grateful Dead, Quicksilver Messenger Service and other stars of the Bay Area. In April, Pink Floyd, Soft Machine and 39 other groups of the underground performed at London's Alexandra Palace before 10,000 people, in an attempt to raise funds for the recently 'busted' alternative paper, *International Times*. In June, *Sgt Pepper* was released; that same month, a music festival took place in Monterey, California.

In many ways, Monterey was the culmination of the hippie dream and rock's new age. In the sunshine, before an audience determined to radiate 'vibes' of peace, top acts from Britain and the West Coast of America demonstrated how far rock had progressed since the Beatles had appeared on 'The Ed Sullivan Show' three years before. Country Joe and the Fish, with flower motifs daubed on their cheeks, emanated gentleness through melanges of floating raga; Janis Joplin wailed and stomped through raw blues-rock with a disturbing nervous energy; the Who, dressed in chic English frills, trashed their equipment with practised venom; Jimi Hendrix set fire to his guitar and made onlookers gawp with his overt sexual antics. The diversity of musical styles on display at Monterey was staggering and the crowd – there to share an experience rather than support individual acts – lapped up all proceedings.

The Monterey Festival appeared on film in 1968 and by then, it was evident that pop and rock were becoming separate entities. Teen pop and bubblegum continued to assail the singles charts, courtesy of such hunky beatsters as Tommy James and the Shondells and the Monkees in America, and the Marmalade and Dave Dee, Dozy, Beaky, Mick and Tich in Britain, but albums were generating more and more capital and the new breed of 'serious' rock musician was ascending from the 'underground' to assume star status.

Rock stars didn't talk – as teen idols did, and always had – of how they wished to buy luxury homes for their parents or what kind of girls made ideal wives. They talked of the sins of war, of spirituality, drugs, the influence of dead blues guitarists and intentions of 'getting heads together in the country'. While fans analysed the most banal lyrics, searching for hidden truths and secrets of the cosmos, and argued about which guitar hero could play the fastest 'licks', rock musicians became frighteningly aware of their own importance.

In August 1969, farmer Max Yasgur stood on a stage erected at his farm near Bethel in upstate New York and declared: 'I think you people have proven something to the world – that a half a million kids can get together and have fun and music and nothing *but* fun and music.' This was Woodstock, as celebrated in Joni Mitchell's song and in the slogan 'Woodstock Nation' which, supposedly, symbolised a new utopia based upon the shared love and tolerance of the young generation. But as Tim Hardin, one of the performers at the festival, was moved to comment: 'What do they want? Some of the music is great, some of it ain't and some of it is just an insult. None of it's gonna save our souls. Woodstock's just another show, like Caesar's Palace, and "Woodstock Generation" is just a line for selling more records.'

Four months after Woodstock, the Rolling Stones appeared in the open air at Altamont, California. The event ended in tragedy with a black youth stabbed to death by Hell's Angels; in March 1970, Charles Manson, hippie-weirdo, Beatles fan and Beach Boys collaborator, was charged with the brutal murder of Sharon Tate and others. Already, Haight-Ashbury – San Francisco's hippie quarter – had been annexed by con-men, pushers and thieves. And the Beatles had broken up in acrimony. In short, the hippie dream had gone sour.

But despite all the pretensions, the naive (and occasionally preposterous) ideals, the rock music of the late sixties remains unrivalled in terms of variety and depth of invention; the spirit of the era can never be repeated. Acts such as Pink Floyd, Jimi Hendrix, Love and the Byrds set new standards of technical excellence and musical imagination, while others – the Velvet Underground, the Doors, the Fugs and Iggy and the Stooges – flew in the face of prevailing trends, pioneering a darker, more seamy, sinister and sleazy side of rock which would be an inspiration to the punk rockers of the coming decade. And, of course, it was in the late sixties that the Beatles and Bob Dylan, who had sparked off rock's revolution, produced their best work and redefined the art of contemporary music. As Pete Ham, of Badfinger said in 1974: 'The Beatles, the Byrds, the drugs and the philosophy turned everything around. Rock music became something else – an experience that shivered the spine, shook the windows and made you feel real. Today, it's business as usual – and there's no going back.' Except on the record player and within the pages of this book . . .

TOM HIBBERT

The performances of artists like Joe Cocker (left) made Woodstock the final eruption of the optimism which emerged in the 60s.

ROOTS OF THE NEW ROCK

The musical revolution of the late sixties was crucially influenced by a number of traditional forms. In America, many of the stars-to-be emerged from the well-established folk, blues and country circuits and often took a 'progressive' political stance derived from the wider protest movements. British groups took up the mood of optimism ushered in by the Beatles, and mixed in their own folk and blues traditions

Times A-Changin'

How folk brought new perspectives to the music of the late Sixties

FROM THE MID SIXTIES onwards, the involvement of folk musicians in rock had a revolutionary impact on both the music's direction and youth culture in general. Besides broadening rock's stylistic base, folk singers and songwriters brought a new degree of social and political awareness to rock in the music's post-1967 left-wing leaning, the egalitarian ideology and anti-commercial perspective of the counter-culture, the concept of the music festival as an expression of community, the idea that rock could constitute a popular art form, the new emphasis on lyrics and 'meaning'. All these ideas had antecedents in the American folk movement of the late Fifties and early Sixties.

The folk influence on rock began to be felt as early as 1964. Bob Dylan was important as both a figurehead and a catalyst, bringing 'protest' to the record charts for the first time via 'The Times They Are A-Changin'' and transforming the audience's conception of folk from that of a rustic, harmless novelty to something challenging, even subversive. Folk-style records had often figured in the charts before – the New Christy Minstrels, Harry Belafonte and Peter, Paul and Mary were folk music's chief popularisers – but never with *this* level of invective. Folk and pop musicians took Dylan's cue, some simply for commercial reasons, and the charts were temporarily flooded with protest efforts from the likes of Donovan, P. F. Sloan, the Turtles and Barry McGuire. Finally, Dylan's switch from acoustic accompaniment to rock backing and the Byrds' electrified version of his 'Mr Tambourine Man' gave the pop world both a new stylistic term – 'folk-rock' – and a new marketing platform.

Folk-rock was a short-lived commercial fad, but one that had long-term significance. It was a hybrid form, a crossroads at which various musical roads converged and took off from. It fused elements of the American folk scene, which had been enjoying a boom in the early Sixties, with the emerging wave of protest – an influence which brought a new sincerity and integrity of expression to the lyrics of rock music, introducing more personalised themes. Folk-rock also provided folk with a ticket into the popular mainstream, as it began to draw upon the musical influences of the British invasion. The potential of each genre was thus able to progress in a number of different directions: political, personal, mind-expanding or commercial. Folk-rock encouraged the younger generation of folk singers (Dylan's contemporaries) to examine rock afresh, inducing a mass re-conversion; many folkies, like John Sebastian (founder of the Lovin' Spoonful) and Jim (later Roger) McGuinn (of the Byrds), forsook the customary solo orientation of folk performers and joined or formed folk-rock bands.

The music these artists played differed from conventional folk in more than just instrumentation. Folk music had previously been equated with traditional material or songs written to traditional models; the subject-matter of folk songs had often been political, celebrating class solidarity, workers' struggles or the fight for civil rights; the language of the songs was plain, direct and simple, and most could be sung communally. Dylan introduced to folk a more personal mode of songwriting, taking his own relationships, feelings and atti-

The old and the new: Pete Seeger (inset above) represented the old breed of socially committed folk commentators, while Paul Simon (above) was typical of the new folk-rockers who came to fame in Dylan's wake, and whose lyrics dealt with more personal preoccupations.

EPENDENT
WAY SYSTEM
PATH
PORT AUTHORITY
TRANS-HUDSON
NO LEFT TURN
ONE WAY
NO RIGHT

tudes as his subjects. He did not ignore political concerns but preferred to internalise them and, in so doing, made self-expression the keynote – not just in the new folk music, but throughout rock itself.

Village jug bands

With the emphasis shifting to more complex and personalised lyrics, the singer-songwriter moved into the limelight. Of the singer-songwriters with folk backgrounds, four in particular emerged through folk-rock to produce some of the best music of the genre. Phil Ochs, Tom Paxton, Tim Hardin and Paul Simon first made their names in New York's Greenwich Village – for so long the spiritual home of American bohemianism and the nerve-centre of the American folk scene. The district's folk clubs served as training grounds for innumerable folk musicians, and it was here that the Lovin' Spoonful, the Mamas and the Papas, the Holy Modal Rounders and the Even Dozen Jug Band first formed. The latter two bands specialised in a form of folk – jug-band music – akin to British skiffle in its use of basic instruments like acoustic guitars, washboards, broom-handle basses and empty beer jugs. Equipped with amplifiers and rock instruments, such outfits produced a form of dance music that had some of the outgoing, crowd-pleasing quality of British beat. The Lovin' Spoonful were by far its most successful practitioners, but their approach rubbed off on other bands like the Turtles, the Boston-based Jim Kweskin Jug Band, Spanky and Our Gang and the Critters.

If folk-rock was born in Greenwich Village – and Dylan himself long regarded it as his home – it was in California that the style truly crystallised. By the beginning of 1967, many had followed the example of Roger McGuinn and David Crosby (both of the Byrds), the Lovin' Spoonful, the Mamas and the Papas and others by leaving their New York base for the freer atmosphere and bigger record deals of Los Angeles. Neil Young and Steve Stills moved there and formed Buffalo Springfield, one of the most accomplished of the folk-rock groups yet curiously unrecognised as such at the time; they later became the creative nucleus of Crosby, Stills, Nash and Young, supergroup of the late Sixties and symbols of folk-rock's lasting commercial legacy. Others to take the New York to California route included Scott McKenzie of 'San Francisco (Be Sure To Wear Flowers In Your Hair)' fame and Peter Tork, who was picked for the Monkees on the recommendation of Steve Stills (who was himself turned down).

While the New York/Los Angeles brand of folk-influenced rock quickly entered the pop mainstream, a quite different version of this hybrid style was evolving elsewhere in California, in the musically-isolated city of San Francisco. The record companies' complete lack of interest in the city's rock and folk scenes meant that both could thrive and develop at their own pace, unhindered by the expectations of a record-buying audience and free of media attention. Musicians there were affected by changes in folk music – especially the shockwaves caused by Bob Dylan's venture into rock – but they had neither the need nor the desire to conform to them. The growth of an 'alternative' intellectual community in the city's Haight Ashbury district and the widespread use of LSD made SF music idiosyncratic.

San Franciscan bands with folk roots included the Warlocks, later to become the Grateful Dead, whose music was a self-conscious representation of the 'mind-expanding' effects of LSD; Jefferson Airplane, who sang about those effects, couching their disturbing fantasy lyrics in a more conventional folk-rock setting, and Country Joe and the Fish, who were the most obviously political of all the city's groups. Country Joe Macdonald was something of an oddball on the SF scene, a polemicist with a savage satirical streak who sought constant audience involvement and eschewed the introspective, self-questioning stance of Dylan's followers. The sneering anger of his music – notably the blackly comic 'Feel I'm Fixin' To Die Rag' – and his commitment to the alternative cause marked him as a folk singer in the traditional, purist sense.

While the achievements of the SF groups should not be undervalued, their actual influence was over-rated; their commercial impact was minimal when compared with LA bands like Crosby, Stills, Nash and Young and the Byrds, while their music was too obscurely expansive (and too identified with LSD) to have

Some of the new folk-rockers carried on the old traditions of protest, such as Tom Paxton (inset left), Phil Ochs (below) and, in a more psychedelic context, Country Joe and the Fish (opposite). Others, like John Sebastian of the Lovin' Spoonful (inset far left), moved into pop.

more than transitory importance. Of far greater significance was their role as propagators of hippie philosophy and politics and the way in which they brought the contradictions of the counter-culture into focus. Both they and their audience offered a variation on the age-old tendency of educated middle-class kids to adopt radical causes and construct their lives according to an egalitarian model. In this respect, San Franciscan hippies were the folkniks of the Fifties in new clothes: the *message* of the music was still basically the same, even if the sound had changed.

Flower child

Folk-rock became a passé term as it outgrew its novelty value, but one-time folk singers continued to appear or resurrect themselves in other guises. The flower-power craze of 1967 claimed some of them, notably a beads-and-bells-bedecked Scott McKenzie and the man once pushed as Britain's answer to Bob Dylan, Donovan. He began his pop career on ITV's 'Ready Steady Go!' as a copycat Dylan but avoided being pigeon-holed as a protest singer by constantly refining his 'folk' perspective. Thanks partly to the shrewd management of Mickie Most (who chose the songs most suitable for single release), Donovan always seemed to be one step ahead of the folk pack – playing the protest game on 'Universal Soldier' and 'The War Drags On', wryly commenting on the excesses of swinging London in 'Sunny South Kensington' and 'Museum', and flirting with psychedelia in 'Sunshine Superman'. The problem was that he took his 1967 persona – the artist as flower child – rather too seriously, dropping Mickie Most as his producer. The hits dried up almost completely and he was never able to live down his flower-power image.

The musical atmosphere after 1967 did not favour solo performers, and those who had arrived with folk-rock – original Villagers like Hardin and Ochs and West Coast contemporaries like Bob Lind – seemed unable to attract an audience beyond their established band of followers. The folk world that had nurtured them had changed: the American folk scene that had once been so well-defined with its circuit of clubs and venues, its hierarchy of artists, its own press outlets and record labels, was thrown into turmoil by the intrusion of rock. With its key performers and its young audience lost, there were no artists coming through to maintain American folk's link with its past. Older folk artists like Pete Seeger and Oscar Brand could retreat into the supper clubs and be sure of a receptive clientele, but both the folk-club circuit and folk-based record labels had to adapt in order to survive, and this meant making compromises with rock.

Judy Collins (top) and Fairport Convention (below left) continued to include traditional material in their repertoire, while others moved into soft rock. Carly Simon (above) and Bread, seen here with Bobby Darin (below right) were notable examples.

The major American labels had creamed off much of the best folk and folk-rock talent; the entry of Warner Brothers, A&M and Columbia into the rock arena in 1967 also opened up the folk field, with each signing up the most promising talent from the smaller folk-based labels of New York. Ochs went from Elektra to A&M, Gordon Lightfoot from a United Artists subsidiary to Warners, while Columbia – with Dylan out of action for well over a year after his 1966 motorcycle accident – gave massive promotion to a folk duo who had previously lived in Dylan's shadow, Simon and Garfunkel. Of all these artists, only Simon and Garfunkel lived up to their label's sales expectations in the short term, but the major labels' investment in well-known folk stars as well as relative unknowns was part of a long-term strategy. That investment paid off in the early Seventies when singer-songwriters like Joni Mitchell, James Taylor, Jackson Browne and Englishman Ralph McTell sprang to national (and in some cases international) prominence.

The smaller folk labels could never compete on the same terms as the majors. The most important were Folkways, Prestige, Vanguard and Elektra: the former two survived by keeping faith with the established folk market and continuing to specialise in vintage blues and folk material, while Vanguard became absorbed into the RCA Victor set-up. Elektra, however, prospered by cleverly maintaining its 'folk' identity while broadening its roster to include rock artists. Judy Collins and Tom Paxton were the label's figureheads in the mid Sixties but, by 1969, owner Jac Holzman had also signed the Paul Butterfield Blues Band, Love, the Doors, Clear Light, the MC5 and Lonnie Mack. Holzman's reputation among musicians and Elektra's long-established artistic credibility resulted in the label being

viewed as one that both folk and rock artists could trust. Carly Simon, Mickey Newbury, Harry Chapin and Tim Buckley – all children of the folk-rock scene – strengthened Elektra's image in the Seventies and brought in massive profits, and in 1973, Holzman incorporated the label into the larger Warner Communications organisation, becoming its vice-president.

Elektra's success symbolised the commercial assimilation of folk into rock, but the trend had other manifestations. One was the unprecedented chart run of Simon and Garfunkel's *Bridge Over Troubled Water*, an album of exquisitely crafted modern 'folk' songs that reflected the vulnerability, tensions, insecurities and liberal concerns of late-Sixties middle-of-the-road student America. Yet although Paul Simon's introspective lyrics were the initial focus of attention, it was the *sound* of *Bridge Over Troubled Water* – the album's acoustic ambience, the harmonies and the immaculate production by Jimmie Haskell – that captured the imagination of musicians and producers and proved so ultimately influential. The album created the climate in which not only singer-songwriters but soft-rock groups like Bread and the Eagles could flourish in the Seventies.

The most significant development in folk-rock since the late Sixties had been the music's evolution into a kind of 'hip easy listening' sound tailor-made for America's AOR (adult-oriented rock) radio stations. Linda Ronstadt, Andrew Gold, Styx, America and even the once jazz-based Chicago have specialised in this sound, although its true 'stars' have been astute record producers like Peter Asher, Lenny Waronker and Ted Templeman. The mellow, soporific quality of these records points to a calculated misuse of the folk idiom – folk songs were once written and sung to stir emotion, not to soften it – and one must look elsewhere for a more creative interpretation of folk's legacy.

In the early Seventies, folk singers like Ralph McTell (below) benefited from the singer-songwriter boom. His gritty, heart-wrenching piece of social realism, 'Streets Of London', was a hit in 1974.

One of the most creditable features of Seventies music was the interest that songwriters and musicians took in different aspects of America's musical heritage. This movement began in the late Sixties, when Bob Dylan emerged, after a long lay-off, with *John Wesley Harding*, and the Byrds issued their *Sweetheart Of The Rodeo* album, both of which pointed in the unfashionable direction of country music. The Band, too, produced *Music From Big Pink*, an album that effectively synthesised country, Baptist hymn, folk, soul and rock influences; their music had a distinct sense of history at a time when the ideology of 'progression' seemed to dominate rock. The Nitty Gritty Dirt Band, Randy Newman and Ry Cooder all followed a similar musical route. The work of these and other artists was paralleled in Britain by groups like Fairport Convention, the Albion Band and Steeleye Span, who likewise sought to recreate the *spirit* of traditional music in a modern rock setting. STEPHEN BARNARD

Bringing It All Back Home

The influences on Dylan and those he inspired

ANY CONSIDERATION of the influence of Bob Dylan on the history of rock music has to take into account the formative influences on Dylan himself. Throughout his career, there has been a two-way traffic of ideas between Dylan and other individual performers and areas of popular music. Running parallel to Dylan's love of the folk tradition of Woody Guthrie was his devotion to early rock'n'roll; his formative years were a rich mix of Hank Williams, the Everly Brothers, Leadbelly, James Dean, Johnny Ace, Jack Kerouac and Lord Buckley. A heady combination of comics, rock'n'rollers, country stars and R&B singers.

Indeed, Dylan's first projected single, recorded in 1962, was a healthy slab of rockabilly called 'Mixed Up Confusion', which was withdrawn shortly after its release as CBS felt it didn't fit their image of Dylan as a troubled troubadour. His first LP, entitled simply *Bob Dylan*, drew heavily on the folk and country blues traditions; while 'Highway 51' came from the blues tradition, 'Gospel Plow' was an old spiritual and 'House Of The Rising Sun' a traditional number learned from fellow folk singer Dave Van Ronk. 'Song To Woody' was, of course, dedicated to Dylan's idol Woody Guthrie, while the album's closing number, 'See That My Grave Is Kept Clean' was a powerful blues by Blind Lemon Jefferson.

From blues to the Beatles

It is a measure of Dylan's innovative talent that the successive fields of music, such as folk, electric rock and country and western, which he entered at each stage of his career, were transformed by his contribution to them. In his early songs, he relied on simple acoustic guitar accompaniment and focused on specific incidents, as in 'The Ballad Of Donald White' and 'The Death Of Emmett Till'. It was his later, more abstract protest songs like 'Blowin' In The Wind', 'When The Ship Comes In' and 'Only A Pawn In Their Game' that exerted such a strong influence on his Greenwich Village contemporaries.

Although Dylan himself didn't hit the charts until 1965, his influence was apparent long before. Peter, Paul and Mary's version of 'Blowin' In The Wind' reached Number 2 in America in 1963, and Joan Baez made a point of including many Dylan songs in her repertoire. Dylan's influence on the Beatles was apparent early in their career. John Lennon particularly was impressed with the honesty Dylan incorporated in his lyrics, and began to include 'Dylanesque' sentiments in songs like 'I'm A Loser' and 'Baby's In Black' on the 1964 *Beatles For Sale* album. Lennon's interest continued on the *Help!* and *Rubber Soul* albums with songs like 'You've Got To Hide Your Love Away' and 'Norwegian Wood'.

Talented writers like Phil Ochs, Tom Paxton, Richard Farina, Paul Clayton and David Blue were amazed at Dylan's precocious ability to translate topical incidents into songs of lyrical beauty. The prolificity of that material was only matched by its high quality. But Dylan was always too much of a chameleon to stay in any one place for too long. While others – such as Barry McGuire, Donovan and Sonny Bono – edged their way onto the 'protest' bandwagon, Dylan had moved on. A willingness to experiment and a refusal to be pigeonholed have remained constant in an otherwise mercurial career.

Dylan plugs in

Dylan realised the possibilities of 'folk-rock' as early as 1964 when he heard how the Animals had treated the traditional 'House Of The Rising Sun'. The Byrds weren't slow off the mark to realise the commercial potential of Dylan's material. Their truncated version of 'Mr Tambourine Man' was a global hit, a timeless summer anthem that ensured the composer's name was on every hip lip.

With his classic *Bringing It All Back Home* album in 1965, Dylan took one giant leap for rock'n'roll, fusing vivid, surreal lyrics with the raw power of rock rhythms. During that incredibly fertile period, bordered by *Bringing It All Back Home* and *Blonde On Blonde*, Dylan's influence was

Insets, clockwise from bottom: Eric Burdon of the Animals, whose 'House Of The Rising Sun' made Dylan realise folk-rock's potential; Dire Straits' Mark Knopfler, who borrowed his vocal style from Dylan; James Dean, a prime influence on Dylan's image; and Willie Nelson, whose 'Outlaw' country was inspired greatly by Nashville Skyline.

universal. His young disciples gazed awe-struck at his progress – Paul Simon, Neil Young, Van Morrison, Jackson Browne, James Taylor and Joni Mitchell were only some who were overwhelmed by Dylan's style, and began their imitative efforts.

In electrifying his music, Dylan did more than just set a fashion for other musicians; he conferred a legitimacy on a form of music still regarded with profound suspicion by the aficionados of 'serious' music such as folk. Into a dream world of beach parties and surfing safaris, Dylan proffered the reality of genuine emotion, persecution and segregation. His example was to be crucial for the musical upheavals of the late Sixties and for the new generation of rock fans who saw their music as sharply distinct from 'pop', and demanded intelligent music and literate lyrics rather than chirpy celebrations of teenage love.

The Band's last concert in 1978 united Dylan with several disciples. Joni Mitchell, Neil Young and Van Morrison joined Dylan, Dr John (left) and Band bassist Rick Danko (third from right) on stage.

Travellin' on . . .

But Dylan, as usual, was one step ahead of his fans. While they were assimilating his new 'rock' phase, and while rock itself was going psychedelic, Dylan was spending his convalescence from a motorcycle accident recording a large body of country music with the Band at their house in upstate New York. Bootlegs aside, this material didn't surface until *The Basement Tapes* was released in 1975, but the fruits of this musical exploration were apparent on the 1968 LP *John Wesley Harding*. Tracks like 'I'll Be Your Baby Tonight' helped pave the way for the remarkable Gram Parsons/Byrds *Sweetheart Of The Rodeo* country-rock album. The following year, Dylan plunged deeper into C&W with his own *Nashville Skyline*, an album that was an unashamed celebration of the then unfashionable country music. It set the seal of approval on C&W for a whole new, young generation, laying a foundation for the country-rock of the Eagles, Linda Ronstadt, Commander Cody, Joe Ely and the 'Outlaw' country of Waylon Jennings and Willie Nelson.

A three-year period of near-silence followed *New Morning* in 1970. With the advent of the singer/songwriter vogue of the early Seventies, personified by the success of James Taylor and Carole King, Dylan was regarded as one of rock's elder statesmen. His name was never far from the headlines, particularly during the music press's quest for 'the new Dylan'.

Such performers as Bruce Springsteen, John Prine, Steve Goodman, Steve Forbert and Loudon Wainwright III were lumbered with this unpromising epithet. For nearly all, it did more harm than good, and few sustained their early promise. Even Springsteen's 1973 debut album, *Greetings From Asbury Park NJ*, had Dylan stamped all over it – particularly 'Blinded By The Light', which bore an uncanny resemblance to Dylan's 'Subterranean Homesick Blues' of eight years before.

By the mid-Seventies, it was arguable that Dylan's influence was negligible. But, true to form, he was continuing to look around him, absorbing new influences and synthesising older ones. *Blood On The Tracks* (1974) and *Desire* (1975) saw him fusing folk, country, Tex-Mex and even traditional Jewish religious music into a subtle and mature vehicle for personal expression. Although the introspective cast of these albums seems to reflect the singer-songwriter boom that Dylan himself did so much to spark off, they stood aside from the work of many of his contemporaries in their harrowing honesty and avoidance of self-pity.

The next generation

As part of the rock establishment, Dylan could not remain immune from the punk backlash of the mid to late Seventies. Nevertheless, his influence on a younger generation of musicians was still noticeable. A young Elvis Costello could be heard crooning 'Knocking On Heaven's Door', a song also included in the live set of New York new wave band Television; Dire Straits' Mark Knopfler borrowed much of his vocal phrasing from Dylan – and later played guitar on *Slow Train Coming* – and the militant Tom Robinson Band included 'I Shall Be Released' at virtually every gig. (The song was later adapted as the official anthem of Amnesty International.)

Dylan then turned his attention to gospel music on his 1978 LP *Street-Legal*. With a big backing band and a trio of female vocalists echoing his lyrics, call-and-response style, this testifying album prefigured Dylan's conversion to Christianity the following year. A series of desultory evangelistic albums which followed displayed Dylan's continuing preoccupation with soul music: for *Slow Train Coming*, he called in the services of Jerry Wexler, who had produced many of Atlantic's great soul artists of the Sixties, while Donald 'Duck' Dunn, the famous Stax bassist, contributed to *Shot Of Love*.

Although it is his earlier work which has had the most impact on the course of rock music, that impact has been incalculable. Indeed, a survey of the artists who have recorded Dylan songs provides an indication of his standing. A random selection reveals Elvis Presley, Rod Stewart, Eric Clapton, Bryan Ferry, Johnny Cash and Manfred Mann. The Hollies, Joan Baez and Coulson, Dean, McGuinness, Flint have recorded entire albums of Dylan songs. David Bowie put his own tribute, 'Song For Bob Dylan', on 1971's *Hunky Dory*, and Jimi Hendrix proved how far a Dylan song could be stretched when he transformed 'All Along The Watchtower' into a seething electric vision of the Apocalypse.

Dylan's durability is evident in the scope of his influence and the breadth of his musical vision; the scope of his song styles has been an inspiration to countless musicians, and rock music has been irrevocably changed by his input. PATRICK HUMPHRIES

TAMBOURINES & TWELVE-STRINGS

The timeless flight of the Byrds

OF ALL THE FOLK-ROCK bands of the mid Sixties, the Byrds were perhaps the most innovative and influential. For a brief period in 1965, they stemmed the tide of the English invasion and dominated the American music scene. More importantly, they pushed back the frontiers of rock further than many better-known groups.

In many ways, the Byrds set the pattern for the bands of the late Sixties. They left in their wake a number of lasting (and some more ephemeral) categories, such as folk-rock, acid-rock, space-rock and country-rock, and had a profound influence on the way music was produced in the studio. They were an early example of a rock band seeing themselves as serious artists. And, with the cynicism and world-weariness that set in through endless touring and unresponsive audiences, they became a prototype for the late-Sixties image of the rock performer as victim, the band as a self-destructive mechanism.

If the demise of the Byrds was symptomatic of the pressures of a career in rock, their beginnings were of equal interest. For they were the first significant rock group to have bypassed Fifties rock 'n'roll as an influence, serving their apprenticeships on the folk circuit. Jim McGuinn (born 14 July 1942) started backing the Limeliters, and then joined the Chad Mitchell Trio. In 1962 he began session work as a banjoist before joining Bobby Darin, who had introduced a folk spot into his night-club act to expand his

Above: The original Byrds, with Gene Clark on vocals. Right: After he left; from left, David Crosby, Michael Clarke, Jim McGuinn and Chris Hillman.

repertoire. Gene Clark (born 17 November 1941) was a one-time New Christy Minstrel, while Dave Crosby (born 14 August 1941) had been a Les Baxter Balladeer before becoming a solo coffee-house singer.

The folk circuit in the early Sixties, however, was not the cosy corner of earnest, non-commercial music-making it might appear in comparison with the cut-throat world of rock'n'roll. Folk was business, and the music of the coffee houses was already being prettied up for the night-clubs. And the sweetened harmonies of the New Christy Minstrels were giving way in their turn to the totally saccharine confections of performers like Peter, Paul and Mary. Chris Hillman (born 4 December 1942) quit the coffee house and campus folk circuit to work in the purer field of bluegrass music.

The musicians who were later to become the Byrds might well have achieved a certain degree of success individually on the folk circuit had they drifted with the trend. But then, just as the record industry was about to swallow folk wholesale, along came the Beatles and the English invasion. The effect was instantaneous. After hearing the Beatles, Jim McGuinn began introducing their songs into his act at a Greenwich Village folk club, and looked around to form a group.

Above: Following Gene Clark's departure, the Byrds recorded their classic Fifth Dimension *album. Below: The original band on stage with Bob Dylan.*

Opposite top: The final line-up. Opposite: A short-lived line-up; from top, White, McGuinn, Hillman and Kelley.

Jet Set Beefeaters

Thus, in the summer of 1964, McGuinn, Clark and Crosby started rehearsing in Los Angeles under the name the Jet Set. A trio might have been all very well for vocal harmonies, but with no bass or drums it wasn't exactly a rock group. They then ran into a producer called Jim Dickson, who had recorded and was attempting – with great difficulty – to sell an album he'd produced for Chris Hillman's bluegrass group, the Hillmen. Dickson persuaded Hillman to join the Jet Set and trade in his mandolin for a Japanese bass guitar – which was to become almost a member of the group in its own right, so often was it featured in Columbia's press releases. Michael Clarke (born 3 June 1944) was press-ganged into the group as a drummer because, in the time-honoured phrase, he 'looked the part'.

Dickson had the run of World Pacific studios, so the group rehearsed there, and recorded a tape which Dickson hawked round the major record companies. These tapes, which eventually saw commercial release as *Preflyte* in 1969, saw the group constructed firmly in the image of the Beatles; but then that was only to be expected of a group whose leader, McGuinn, had gone back to see *A Hard Day's Night* a second time to learn what kind of guitar George Harrison was playing.

In the autumn of 1964, Jim Dickson got them a record deal with Elektra. Under the explicitly British name of the Beefeaters, they released a song by Gene Clark, 'Please Let Me Love You'. The single flopped, but Columbia, just moving into the rock market, signed the band, now rechristened the Byrds, to a long-term contract.

The Byrds were, first and foremost, Jim McGuinn's band. He later rechristened himself Roger after his conversion to Subud, a variant of Hinduism with the emphasis on self-fulfilment. The sound of his jangling 12-string Rickenbacker guitar and gruff yet dreamy vocals became the band's trademark. Other members wrote songs and made distinctive contributions – notably Gene Clark with his sad love songs and later Chris Hillman, whose background was bluegrass, a kind of music where content was subdued in the form. All the songs became part of a kaleidoscopic pattern of shifting rhythms, something that was to become an integral part of the Byrds' sound. Later, Gram Parsons was to intensify the country influence.

All these influences, though, worked in relation to McGuinn. He would assess and utilise the other members' interests and abilities according to how well they fitted with the sounds in his head. Their first hit single, 'Mr Tambourine Man', was recorded by Roger McGuinn and sessionmen including such luminaries as Hal Blaine, Leon Russell and Larry Knetchel in 1964. And throughout the band's history, up to and including his 1973 solo LP *Roger McGuinn*, he managed to coax this characteristic sound from a variety of band members and session musicians.

After six months, 'Mr Tambourine Man' soared to the top of the British and American charts in 1965, signalling the arrival of folk-rock and ending the British dominance of the music scene. The record was distinctive enough with its chiming guitar and its sense of weary resignation; but the Byrds, like the Beatles before them, suggested that they were unusual rock stars as well. McGuinn's public statements seemed to catch the arrogance and skewed insights of John Lennon.

'I think the difference is in the mechanical sounds of our time,' he observed. 'Like the sound of the airplane in the Forties was a rrrrrrooooooaaaaaaahhhhhhhhhhh sound and Sinatra and those people sang with those sort of overtones. Now we've got the krrriiiiissssssssshhhhhhh jet sound . . . It's the mechanical sounds of the era: the sounds are different and so the music is different. I trust everything will turn out all right.'

From imitators to explorers

Sadly it didn't for the Byrds. Their success was short-lived; the group's second record, 'All I Really Want To Do' (another Dylan song), was beaten in chart ranking by Cher's version, and their records struggled in the charts after the success of their third single, 'Turn! Turn! Turn!', a biblical passage set to music by folk pioneer Pete Seeger that reached Number 1 in September 1965 and proved an ambiguous anthem at a time when hostilities in Vietnam were escalating dramatically. Leon Russell and Larry Knetchel in 1964. And throughout the band's history, up to and including his 1973 solo LP *Roger McGuinn*, he managed to coax this characteristic sound from a variety of band members and session musicians.

'Mr Tambourine Man' and the release of 'Eight Miles High' saw the Byrds developing from imitators to explorers. Columbia allowed the group to play the instruments as well as sing on their debut album, *Mr Tambourine Man* (1965), which was an unusual mixture of Dylan, traditional folk songs and their own Beatles-influenced pop songs. But if the material was unusual, their treatment of it was even more so. Song by song, in the manner of bluegrass musicians, they stylised their material, experimenting with sound textures and three-part harmonies to create a sound that engulfed the whole album. By the next album, *Turn! Turn! Turn!* (1966), the Byrds had folk-rock down pat, and from material like Dylan's 'Lay Down Your Weary Tune' and Gene Clark's 'Set You Free This Time' they created diamonds of formal perfection that lacked only a sense of excitement.

Their third album, *Fifth Dimension* (1966), saw them tire of folk-rock and begin experimenting with electronics. In part this was a reaction to the loss of Gene Clark, whose sad love songs and plaintive lead vocals had been almost as distinctive as McGuinn's 12-string.

Henceforth, though McGuinn would still define the Byrds' sound on singles, the other members were to achieve greater prominence on albums. *Younger Than Yesterday* (1967), which brought the electronic experimentation of *Fifth Dimension* to absolute perfection, saw Crosby and Hillman develop into superb songwriters, Crosby writing 'Everybody's Been Burned' and 'Renaissance Fair' and Hillman contributing 'Thoughts And Words' and 'Time Between'.

Bitterness in the band

On record the group had never sounded tighter; in performance, however, they were as ragged as ever. Incessant touring (the result of chart failure) was causing increasing tension within the band, a tension aggravated by McGuinn's autocratic leadership and the other members' growing desire to express themselves. The crisis came to a head during the recording of *The Notorious Byrd Brothers* (released in 1968). Crosby refused to sing the Goffin-King 'pop songs' 'Goin' Back' and 'Wasn't Born To Follow', demanding the inclusion of more political songs on the LP. Dissatisfied, Crosby finally quit for a cash payment (with which he bought a yacht) and formed Crosby, Stills and Nash, leaving the Byrds with a half-completed album.

The bitterness in the band was such that when the album was released, the cover depicted the three remaining Byrds looking out of the windows of a barn; where David Crosby's picture would have been, Roger McGuinn had substituted a horse. The group finished the album as a trio, and amazingly it was superb, one of the first and best high technology studio albums, a hymn to phasers and limiters. It sold well, its sound being perfect for the age of stereo headphones. For a while it seemed as if the Byrds might find favour with a more sophisticated audience.

Instead, the group took a radically different direction. Gram Parsons was recruited from the International Submarine Band, and Michael Clarke was replaced by Kevin Kelley; the band headed off to Nashville where they recorded *Sweetheart Of The Rodeo*, virtually creating country-rock and alienating their new audience at the same time.

The failure of *Sweetheart Of The Rodeo* virtually destroyed the group. Roger McGuinn felt that it wasn't essential Byrds, and that he had been sidetracked into country music by Parsons and Hillman. Then Parsons quit rather than tour South Africa – a roadie named Carlos impersonating him to fulfil the commitment – and Hillman threw down his bass after the tour and walked out too. The pair were to form the Flying Burrito Brothers. With their departure, McGuinn came to own 100 per cent of the band; from then on, the other band members would be his employees, hired for a fixed wage. At the same time he decided to take on the management of the band himself.

The new group consisted of Gene Parsons on drums, John York on bass and Clarence White, a flat-pick guitarist who had worked in bluegrass groups such as the Kentucky Colonels and had guested on earlier Byrds albums. Now that he had established his control over the group, however, McGuinn seemed to lose the sense of purpose and direction shown on the earlier albums. The new Byrds album, *Dr Byrds And Mr Hyde* (1969) had a country feel like its predecessor, but the sound was uncharacteristically muddy.

But touring, always a problem for the Byrds, was beginning to look up. Playing at the Boston Tea Party in February 1969 on a bill with other musicians who had been in or played with the Byrds – including Parsons and Hillman's Flying Burrito Brothers – the band maintained their energy and clarity throughout a long set: 'For the first time,' McGuinn said afterwards, 'the Byrds are better live than on record.'

There was an unexpected bonus as well in the phenomenal success of the film *Easy Rider*, which used one of the old Byrds songs on its soundtrack. With a new album, better than its predecessor and craftily titled *The Ballad Of Easy Rider* (1969), the Byrds seemed to be on the way up again. Later that year Skip Battin – who had been half of Skip and Flip, an early Sixties Everly Brothers imitation – replaced York on bass. The touring continued to go well, so well that, to everyone's surprise, one record of the

Top right: McGuinn's Thunderbyrd, 1976. Above right: Gene Clark, McGuinn and Chris Hillman together again, 1976. Right: In the early Seventies, the Byrds included bluegrass in their set. Far right and top: The same line-up electrified.

double album *Untitled* (1970) consisted of live recordings. What was equally important was that the studio set saw McGuinn back on form as a writer.

With lyricist Jaques Levy, with whom he'd been commissioned to write a musical version of Ibsen's 'Peer Gynt' (which never appeared), McGuinn produced songs like 'Chestnut Mare' (a UK Top Twenty hit) and 'Just A Season', songs which fitted perfectly into the classic Byrds mould of weary melancholy. It seemed that McGuinn had once again recaptured the sound and feel of the original group. But it wasn't to be; *Untitled* was the exception rather than the rule, and after two more desultory albums, *Byrdmaniax* (1971) and *Farther Along* (1972), McGuinn folded the group to – of all things – re-form the original Byrds line-up.

Solo together

Of the original Byrds, only Crosby had achieved real success outside the Byrds. Hillman and Clark had made critically acclaimed if commercially neglected albums, and McGuinn had marked time since *Sweetheart Of The Rodeo*. Presumably he hoped that back together – especially in the climate of revived oldies – they could take off again. Sadly, the resulting album, *Byrds* (1973), was an artistic disaster, demonstrating that the original Byrds had grown away from each other and completely lost any sense of balance. Where before they had played together as a group, *Byrds* (with the possible exception of the songs on which Clark sang lead) saw them acting as each other's session men, which they would continue to do on various individual projects throughout the Seventies and into the Eighties.

For a while it looked as though McGuinn, who of all the group had most assiduously cultivated Dylan, might find further success through his association with him, but after the Rolling Thunder Review in 1975 he, too, turned back to gigging with his fellow former Byrds. The last such album, *McGuinn And Hillman* (1981), saw both Hillman and McGuinn in decidedly low key, going through the paces of soft, empty LA country-rock to little purpose.

If the Byrds lacked the ability to stay the course that, say, the Rolling Stones have displayed, they were in their time one of the most influential and assured of groups. They were memorable both for the doors they opened in their experimental and innovative albums and for achievements like 'Eight Miles High'. Well after the event, McGuinn – speaking of 'Mr Tambourine Man' – said: 'I tried to make my voice sound like a cross between Dylan and John Lennon's.'

Precisely; the Byrds' success was that they yoked together the pop of the Beatles with the visions of Dylan. It was a staggering achievement, and one which seemed to burn out the group and its members before their time. PHIL HARDY

THE BYRDS
Discography

Singles

Mr Tambourine Man/I Knew I'd Want You (Columbia 43271, 1965); All I Really Want To Do/I'll Feel A Whole Lot Better (Columbia 43332, 1965); Turn! Turn! Turn!/She Don't Care About Time (Columbia 43424, 1965); It Won't Be Wrong/Set You Free This Time (Columbia 43501, 1965); Eight Miles High/Why (Columbia 43578, 1966); 5D (Fifth Dimension)/Captain Soul (Columbia 43702, 1966); Mr Spaceman/What's Happening (Columbia 43766, 1966); So You Want To Be A Rock 'n' Roll Star/Everybody's Been Burned (Columbia 43987, 1967); My Back Pages/Renaissance Fair (Columbia 44054, 1967); Have You Seen Her Face/Don't Make Waves (Columbia 44157, 1967); Lady Friend/Old John Robertson (Columbia 44230, 1967); Goin' Back/Change Is Now (Columbia 44362, 1967); You Ain't Goin' Nowhere/Artificial Energy (Columbia 44499, 1968); Pretty Boy Floyd/I Am A Pilgrim (Columbia 44643, 1968); Bad Night At Whiskey/Drug Store Truck Drivin' Man (Columbia 44746, 1969); Lay Lady Lay/Old Blue (Columbia 44868, 1969); Ballad Of Easy Rider/Oil In My Lamp (Columbia 44990, 1969); Jesus Is Just Alright/It's All Over Now (Columbia 45071, 1970); Chestnut Mare/Just A Season (Columbia 45259, 1970); Glory Glory/Citizen Kane (Columbia 45440, 1971); America's Greatest National Pastime/Further Along (Columbia 45514, 1971); Jesus Is Just Alright/Mister Spaceman (Columbia 45761, 1973); Full Circle/Long Live The King (Asylum 11016, 1973); Cowgirl In The Sand/Long Live The King (Asylum 11019, 1973).

Albums

Mr Tambourine Man (Columbia CS 9172, 1965); *Turn! Turn! Turn!* (Columbia CS 9254, 1966); *Fifth Dimension* (Columbia CS 9349, 1966); *Younger Than Yesterday* (Columbia CS 9442, 1967); *The Byrds Greatest Hits* (Columbia CS 9516, 1967); *The Notorious Byrd Brothers* (Columbia CS 9575, 1968); *Sweetheart Of The Rodeo* (Columbia CS 9670, 1968); *Preflyte* (Together 1001, 1969); *Dr Byrds And Mr Hyde* (Columbia CS 9755, 1969); *Heavy Hits* (Columbia CS 9840, 1969); *The Ballad Of Easy Rider* (Columbia CS 9942, 1969); *Untitled* (Columbia G 30127, 1970); *Byrdmaniax* (Columbia KC 30640, 1971); *Farther Along* (Columbia KC 31050, 1972); *Best Of The Byrds – Vol 2* (Columbia KC 31795, 1972); *Byrds* (Asylum 5058, 1973).

THE BEATLES
HELP!
REVOLVER
LET IT BE
Love

Classic Sounds Northern Songs

How the Beatles stayed in tune with the Sixties

Few aspects of the history of rock have been explored as relentlessly as the Beatles' musical development. The traditional view has been that they began in Liverpool as enthusiastic amateurs copying what they heard around them, moulded these influences into a style all their own and then set off on an artistic route, expanding the horizons of rock on their way. In fact, they were popularisers rather than innovators. They matured as songwriters and musicians because they never stopped listening to and learning from what other rock artists were doing: their music, even as late as the *Abbey Road* album, was derivative in the most positive sense of the word.

In the early part of their career they performed, wrote and recorded what was essentially *dance* music, best experienced at first hand in the sweaty atmosphere of a club or dance-hall. The songs they played were almost exclusively American and drawn from the same rock'n'roll and R&B repertoire that every Merseyside group plundered; this beat club ambience pervaded their first album, *Please Please Me*.

If their style of performance and choice of covers was drawn from black American music, Lennon and McCartney's earliest songwriting efforts were modelled on the work of Gerry Goffin and Carole King, master suppliers of girl group material. From them, John and Paul learned not only the craft of pop songwriting – how to construct a song, how and when to repeat lines, the importance of a middle eight in rounding off the song and where to place the hook in the melody – but also how to rework conventional pop subject-matter. Their lyrics followed the conventional form used so ably by Gerry Goffin in such songs as 'It Might As Well Rain Until September' and 'Don't Say Nothing Bad About My Baby': early Beatle songs were almost conversations in themselves, addressed to some anonymous third person rather than a partner: 'And I Love *Her*', '*She* Loves You', 'I Saw *Her* Standing There', 'I'm in love with *her*/And I feel fine'. This made for a curious sense of distance in Beatle lyrics, a trait apparent even in one-to-one songs like 'I'm Happy Just To Dance With You', 'I Should Have Known Better' and 'If I Fell', which found the protagonists shrugging off the prospect of getting emotionally involved. If nothing else, such songs presented an accurate, if non-romantic, reading of adolescent temperament.

Left: Each successive Beatles LP from Help! *to their final release,* Let It Be, *showed a continuing experimentation which even took in classical strings.*

Finding the formula

The Beatles' distinctive vocal and instrumental style was already fully developed well before they went into a recording studio, but the change in career emphasis from 'live' to recording work inevitably had an effect on the tone and character of their music. The early success of 'Love Me Do' and 'Please Please Me' established a commercial format, and their next few releases were little more than clever variations on a theme – 'From Me To You' had almost the same melody as 'Please Please Me' and took the form of a message to the fans, a classic hitmaker's ploy, while 'She Loves You' showed to what extent the Beatles' commercial style had crystallised in a few short months. The 'yeah, yeah, yeah' phrase, first used by the Beatles (as by girl groups) for decorative effect, here became the song's pivotal feature – its hook. Yet more cunning was the way the McCartney-Harrison falsetto was strategically placed at the end of the *third* verse rather than the first, to build up anticipation. The record bordered on self-imitation and yet still contrived, successfully, to sound irresistibly fresh.

Both *With The Beatles* and the album that followed it, *A Hard Day's Night*, were perfect realisations of a peculiarly British form of beat music – a form no longer dependent solely on American sources but to a great extent self-generating. Lennon and McCartney continued to write in a beat group context to suit their own vocal strengths and known limitations. A collective process, it left little room for truly individual expression, but this pattern began to change as circumstances altered and the range of the Beatles' own influences began to broaden.

Having established their own sound, the Beatles could so easily have remained in the same commercial rut, giving the public only what it seemed to want. There was no pressure from anybody to modify their style, but they were simply too *interested* in the pop scene and the innovations being made by others to isolate themselves. There were signs of an expanding musical outlook on *A Hard Day's Night*, on which George Harrison could be heard playing his 12-string Rickenbacker guitar for the first time. Its rock application had hitherto been limited (though former Liverpool rivals the Searchers had made tentative use of it on their hit singles) and the guitar sound of the LP was a crucial influence on the Byrds. Much of the material on the album was familiar, mainstream Beatles, lyrically unremarkable, but 'Can't Buy Me Love' and 'You Can't Do That' were both nods in the direction of soul music while McCartney's lilting 'And I Love Her' echoed the compositions of Latin American composer Antonio Carlos Jobim.

Such tracks could hardly be called innovatory, but the Beatles had an exceptional knack for absorbing different elements of current rock styles and making them work in the context of their own music. 'I Feel Fine', a very ordinary song in every other respect, opened to the sound of Yardbirds-inspired feedback; the *Long Tall Sally* EP, released in June 1964, contained such R&B classics as the title track and Larry Williams' 'Slow Down' – both songs reminders to fans of the Rolling Stones, Yardbirds and Animals of the Beatles' own R&B credentials. The *Beatles For Sale* album, released in November 1964, was also rooted in R&B; but on 'Ticket To Ride', they expanded the rich, dense guitar sound of the Searchers with Harrison and McCartney sharing the lead guitar line in the most complex Beatles arrangement to date. Lyrically, too, 'Ticket To Ride' found the Beatles exploring new ground – it was one of the first comments on female independence to appear on record during the Sixties, a cynical counterpoint to the macho sentiments of the Rolling Stones' 'Yesterday's Papers'.

A personal voice

The song, released as a single in April 1965, appeared later that year on the *Help!* album, which displayed further evidence of the Beatles' diversification in the shape of three key tracks. Through Bob Dylan, Lennon in particular learned that popular songs could be vehicles for self-expression, not just vehicles for a kind of generalised romantic sentiment. 'Help!' and 'You've Got To Hide Your Love Away' were his first attempts at writing in this personal mode, though the pointers at insecurity in the album's title song were obscured by the upbeat arrangement; the latter song, meanwhile, was sung by Lennon in a deliberately Dylanesque voice to a suitably simple guitar accompaniment. The song that won all the critical plaudits was, however, Paul McCartney's 'Yesterday', which was the first Beatle track to use strings – actually a string quartet – and the one track to point towards increasing elabora-

tion in the Beatles' music. Beneath George Martin's impressive string scoring, however, was a very conventional ballad that could have been written at any time during the past 40 years.

Disciplined experimentation

Live concerts had long been mass orgies of adulation, where fans came to scream rather than listen, and by the time *Rubber Soul* was recorded, the Beatles were concentrating all their music-making energies on studio work. The contemporary influences here were unmistakable – 'Nowhere Man' was Dylan-inspired social comment, 'Norwegian Wood' featured the sitar (an Indian instrument introduced to British pop by the Yardbirds), 'Drive My Car' had a soul tinge and 'Michelle' was a rather pretentious attempt to emulate French composer Jacques Brel – but the real strength of both this album and the singles that immediately followed was that they reflected so precisely the concerns of the time. By now, the Beatles had adopted the role of commentators, telling a wry tale of Swinging London promiscuity in 'Norwegian Wood', spreading a mystic message in 'The Word', playing with the drug vocabulary in 'Day Tripper' and satirising the media and mass culture in general in 'Paperback Writer', complete with Beach Boy-type harmonies.

If the subject-matter of Beatle songs had broadened immeasurably, in many ways, their musical development consisted of simply applying their professional approach to new areas, producing technically sophisticated songs in a variety of contemporary idioms. The 1966 LP *Revolver* confirmed this: 'Eleanor Rigby' was a stylised piece of Dickensian social com-

Above: By the time Revolver *came out, Lennon's songwriting had become more individual and iconoclastic, while Harrison was developing his own compositional talents. The technical expertise of producer George Martin (inset) complemented the songs perfectly.*

mentary that expressed concern without commitment – not only was the imagery in the lyrics self-consciously stark, but George Martin's arrangement in the manner of Haydn accentuated the detachment between singer and subject. 'For No One' betrayed McCartney's predilection for musical frills with an ornate horn solo by Alan Civil; 'Love You To' was an aimless piece of Indian doodling by George Harrison, apparently included to highlight his new proficiency on the sitar, while 'She Said, She Said' and 'Tomorrow Never Knows' were LSD-influenced songs most notable for George Martin's ingenious production. Lennon took the lyrics of the latter song almost word for word from Timothy Leary's drug bible, *The Tibetan Book Of The Dead*. Even the more lyrically conventional 'Got To Get You Into My Life' sounded like an exercise in writing and arranging in the soul idiom. All in all, the album lacked an identifiable stylistic base, though the craftsmanship was superb.

Workshop pop

The Beatles were by now no longer a beat group but a musical workshop, with George Martin acting as their factotum. Their next project, for which both 'Penny Lane' and 'Strawberry Fields Forever' were originally intended, was the ultimate demonstration of their ability to fashion something accessible, even mainstream out of the more esoteric trends in British and American pop. The musical references on the *Sgt Pepper's Lonely Hearts Club Band* LP were numerous – they included fairground sounds, LSD-influenced acid-rock, English music-hall, Indian music and classical pieces – while the lyrics drew on random newspaper stories for 'A Day In The Life' and 'She's Leaving Home', odd pieces of ephemera (an Edwardian poster inspired 'Being For The Benefit Of Mr Kite'), colloquial phrases in 'Getting Better' and 'With A Little Help From My Friends', images of suburban life ('Fixing A Hole', 'Lovely Rita' and 'When I'm Sixty-Four'), and even TV commercials ('Good Morning, Good Morning' was inspired by a breakfast cereal). From such randomly-chosen elements, the Beatles fashioned a superficially optimistic yet faintly paranoid vision of youth obsessions circa 1967. If the album's music was ornate, grandiose and adorned with orchestral trappings, then this was precisely because of the circumstances in which the Beatles now found themselves. Kings of the EMI castle, they now had the time, the money and – most importantly – almost unlimited musical and technological resources to be as idiosyncratic as they liked.

If *Sgt Pepper* was a monument to excess, *The Beatles* was an exercise in simplicity, a return to musical basics. The plainness of the album's title and packaging – a double sleeve in pure white – underlined this, while George Martin was obliged to step back from his role as 'musical fixer' and restrict himself to supervising the mixing process. Paul's contributions followed a familiar, unchanging pattern: they included a typical McCartney rocker with Beach Boy allusions, 'Back In The USSR', vaudeville-style throwaways like 'Honey Pie', 'Martha My Dear' and 'Rocky Raccoon', and ballads in the 'Yesterday' and 'I'll Follow The Sun' mould, namely the pseudo-sentimental 'Goodnight', 'Mother Nature's Son' and 'I Will'. Alone among the quartet, Paul seemed intent on keeping his Beatle persona alive. John Lennon's songs, by contrast, were his most personal yet, curious mixtures of despair, vitriol and satire – 'Sexy Sadie' was a disguised dig at the Maharishi ('Sexy Sadie, what have you done/You made a fool of everyone'), while 'Julia' was an intense love song to his long-dead mother. Much was made in the press of George's contribution, but while he was improving vastly as an instrumentalist, his composing talent was still comparatively undeveloped.

The album could be described as a product of its time – the downbeat mood of the set, the creeping paranoia of tracks like 'Happiness Is A Warm Gun' and 'Bungalow Bill', reflected the realism abroad in youth politics during 1968 – but keeping up with rock trends was not a Beatle priority any more. Only the singles released at this time (all of them, significantly, McCartney compositions) showed how completely in tune they still were with rock. 'Lady Madonna', a tribute to Fats Domino, hit the chart just as a full-scale rock'n'roll revival was gathering momentum, while 'Get Back' was a hard-core rock track that echoed the work of the Band, the Byrds and Creedence Clearwater Revival in the States.

Phil's final fling

The *Let It Be* and *Abbey Road* albums were the Beatles' swansong, though only the latter gained a special place in Beatle fans' affections. *Let It Be* was a schizophrenic affair consisting of sessions as they happened and a handful of tracks re-mixed and polished up by producer Phil Spector, brought in by Lennon especially for the occasion. The title song, 'Get Back', John's 'Across The Universe' and Paul's 'The Long And Winding Road' – despite Spector's addition of a heavenly choir and a violin and horn section – were the pick of the tracks, though much of the album found the Beatles going nowhere in particular.

Abbey Road, actually recorded after *Let It Be*, was a much more fitting finale, in that it kept very closely to the established Beatle pattern. It included additions to the Beatle gallery of characters ('Polythene Pam' and 'Mean Mr Mustard' following 'Lovely Rita' and 'Rocky Raccoon'), featured songs of 'Good Day Sunshine'-like optimism in 'Here Comes The Sun' and 'Because', and even had a children's song, performed by Ringo, that recalled the watery pleasures of 'Yellow Submarine': 'Octopus's Garden'. The album presented little that was really new – except perhaps George Harrison's emerging qualities as a songwriter, with 'Here Comes The Sun' and the ballad, 'Something' – but it offered *confirmation* of the Beatles' continuing importance as singers, musicians, songwriters and rock figureheads at a time when it was most needed. STEPHEN BARNARD

GARAGE BANDS

Dreams of glory in the backyard of rock

FLICK THE LIGHT, suddenly illuminating a scene that lies at rock'n'roll's moment of conception. The room reveals an amplifier or two. They are not large; one, in fact, is contained in the top lid of a guitar case with the word 'Silvertone' embossed on its surface. A new drum kit stands off to the side, catching and reflecting the light in a red sparkle myriad of tiny stars. A sax and microphone 'borrowed' from the school marching band lie on the floor.

It might have been a basement, or an empty social hall, a back yard or anywhere. In America in the Sixties it was the garage, the car carefully backed out into the street by a kid too young to have his driver's licence, assorted family antiquities heaped nearby, all to make room for what might just be another adolescent infatuation like collecting street signs. The location implied many things: a culture wealthy enough to supply that which a garage supposedly houses, a restless teenage class with an abundance of leisure and an inspirational music that made the act of counting tempo an affirmation of self, the first tentative steps towards identity and artistry.

By the early years of the decade, rock had developed sufficiently so that even the

SHADOWS OF KNIGHT
CYRUS ERIE
THE SEEDS
COUNT FIVE
THE FIVE AMERICANS
THE CRYAN SHAMES

TERRY KNIGHT AND THE PACK

THE CHOIR (WITH THE YARDBIRDS)

THE KNICKERBOCKERS

rankest of musical amateurs felt confident they could take a shot at its glittering prizes. The country-based rockabilly explosion had placed a guitar in every hand, while the R&B-centred vocal groups had set voices harmonising on urban street-corners through the land. But most bands of the time relied heavily on instrumentals, while the singers – except for a few multi-talented musicians – were content to croon and pose. It took the Beatles-led British invasion of 1964 to provide a new model for American bands.

The sound of a typical garage band was rooted more in attitude than any specific musical form. Its practitioners cheerfully pirated and appropriated rock styles at will, blending blues and folk and surf music with their interpretation of the Mersey beat, learning to hold and play their instruments à la the Ventures and dress themselves in the mode of the Rolling Stones. The only thing that tied them together was an unmistakable spark of life; the exhilaration that comes from ascending a stage, realising its power and possibilities as fantasy moves inexorably into reality.

This triumph of substance over style, however, shouldn't obscure certain musical similarities that make the garage bands of the Sixties instantly recognisable, even today. Inventions such as the portable organ pioneered by Vox and Farfisa, guitar distortion boxes such as the fuzz-tone and the widespread acceptance of the electric bass provided the building blocks of the sound. Though these advances would soon become the norm and even obsolete, there was time for a kind of zany experimentation with these new toys. The best garage bands not only surprised their audiences; they also surprised themselves, and perhaps there lies the secret of their music.

Young lions

As might be expected, the phenomenon was generally confined to local areas; only the most sophisticated combinations would have the drive to look beyond their own state boundaries. One-hit wonders became the rule rather than the exception and, except for occasional package tours, most of these bands seldom travelled. Yet in their particular regions, names like the Rationals (Michigan), the North Atlantic Invasion Force (Connecticut), Kenny and the Kasuals (Texas), the Yellow Payges (Southern California), Richard and the Young Lions (New Jersey) and hundreds of others were forces to be reckoned with, their greatest impact coming not from their own success but from the image they presented to other, even more fledgling musicians. It was rock'n'roll that could be reached out and touched, as exciting as a heated Saturday night dance and as close to home as a driveaway down the street.

Many were called, but few were chosen. If one were to pick one song and one band whose rise and fall typifies the garage sound's transitory, rags-to-riches nature, general consensus would point a finger at '96 Tears' by the aptly-named ? and the Mysterians. With its recurrent rinky-dink organ figure and snarled-sung lyrics, '96 Tears' is rock at its most skeletal.

?'s real name was Rudy Martinez, and along with the other Mysterians – Robert Balderrama on guitar, Frank Lugo on bass, Frank Rodriguez on keyboards and drummer Edward Serrato – he had migrated from Texas to the Saginaw Valley area of Michigan. This cross-cultural blend began to bear fruit in the fall of 1966 when '96 Tears', pressed on the small Pa-Go-Go label in Texas, started being requested at a radio station in Flint, Michigan (also home to Terry Knight and the Pack, later the seeds of Grand Funk Railroad). The song was picked up by a major label, Cameo, and swiftly went to Number 1 in the US charts. Except for a few short-lived follow-ups like 'I Need Somebody' and 'Can't Get Enough Of You, Baby', the group was never heard from again.

This was no cause for mourning in the garage band sweepstakes. For every group that had its fleeting moment of glory, another was ready to take its place. In the end, the Mysterians' success was not so much based on their uniqueness as their universality; their music was so basic that it not only provided a willing invitation to any young hopeful to play it immediately, but it also sent out the message: 'we did it, so can you!'

Suburbs to cellar

In the immediate Michigan area, this resulted in one of the best self-contained local scenes of the American Sixties. Mitch Ryder had already come bursting out of Detroit in 1965 with driving R&B-styled tunes like 'Jenny Take A Ride' and, boosted by a chain of teen nightclubs such as the Hideout and the Hullabaloo circuits, names like Suzi Quatro (who played in a band called the Pleasure Seekers), Bob Seger (whose System had hits like 'Heavy Music' and 'East Side Story' long before he became a Seventies superstar), Dick Wagner and the Frost, SRC, the Rationals, the Henchmen and the Underdogs soon began to gather acclaim. The Michigan (and Detroit) area was not to peak, however, until the late Sixties' onslaught of the MC5 and the Stooges, two groups whose influence would reach well into another decade.

The entire Midwest was a cornucopia of rock Americana, with cities like Cleveland contributing the Choir ('It's Cold Outside') and Cyrus Erie, as well as the nationally syndicated television show 'Upbeat'; the Minneapolis/St Paul twins notching up fraternity-rockers-made-good the Castaways ('Liar, Liar') and the Gestures ('Run Run Run'). Even Canada caught the fever with Toronto's Luke and the Apostles and the Ugly Ducklings both enjoying success.

Chicago's thriving blues scene gained good publicity when the Shadows of Knight found themselves in the national charts with a cover of Van Morrison's 'Gloria', an archetypal Sixties anthem. Jim Sohns (vocals and tambourine), Joseph Kelley (lead guitar), Jerry McGeorge (rhythm guitar), Warren Rogers (bass) and Tom Schiffour (drums) had come out of Chicago's northwest suburbs to star at the Cellar in Arlington Heights, Illinois. They brought a surprising veracity to their renditions of blues standards like 'I Just Want To Make Love To You' and 'Boom Boom', though it's likely they took the long way around by learning as much from the British versions, by the Stones and the Animals respectively, as from the originals. Other bands like the Mauds (who had their own horn section) or the more pop Buckinghams and Cryan Shames picked up further aspects of Chicago's heritage.

Seeds of spontaneity

Midwest garage rock had a spontaneous quality that might have been lost in a more sophisticated business centre like Los Angeles. In fact, the reverse is true, if the Seeds are any indication. Led by the inimitable Sky Saxon, they became a 'flower power' band by calculated design, though it hardly interfered with the tenacious one-dimensionality of their sound. 'Pushin' Too Hard' was their greatest hit, and they kept playing it through the course of five albums and ultimate flame-out for Sky when he changed his name to Sunstar and got a job washing dishes at a Sunset Strip health food restaurant.

Still, with better recording studios and a generally sharper sense of pop structure, many Los Angeles bands could break out of the primitivism that dogged many local groups. A record like the Music Machine's 'Talk Talk', or the Leaves' 'Hey Joe', or even the music of the early Byrds, Doors and Love (as they blossomed through local followings), showed conceptual awarenesses that made their transition to national success easier. The kingpin of the Los Angeles garage sound was producer Ed Cobb, a former member of the Four Preps who guided the careers of the Standells ('Dirty Water') and San Jose's Chocolate Watch Band ('Riot On Sunset Strip') with a keen eye towards pop trends and rebellions.

In northern California's San Francisco Bay area, the emphasis was either on folkish Beatles-influenced harmony or out-and-out fuzz fantasies. The first was well-represented by the Beau Brummels, whose 1965 hits 'Laugh, Laugh' and 'Just A Little' are masterfully understated works of songwriting and singing, discovered in their prime by disc jockey Tom Donahue on his Autumn label and co-produced by Sylvester Stewart (later Sly Stone). At the other extreme, the Syndicate of Sound ('Hey Little Girl') and the Count Five ('Psychotic Reaction' – a true Yardbirds tribute) came up from San Jose to pave the way for the mind-bending sounds of the legendary Summer of Love.

Into the ozone

Along with such important forebears as the Kingsmen and the Ventures, it's often forgotten that the Oregon-based Paul Revere and the Raiders ('Kicks' and 'Just Like Me') helped pave the way for much of the garage sound by presenting daily lessons on Dick Clark's afternoon television rock show, 'Where The Action Is'. Also home to such bands as the Sonics ('The Witch') and Seattle's Electric Prunes ('I Had Too Much To Dream Last Night'), the region held its own on a vibrant West Coast.

The South had more trouble establishing a garage indentity, perhaps because other musical magnets were at work there. Texas had a sharply developed scene with bands like Doug Sahm's Sir Douglas Quintet (scoring a big hit in 1965 with 'She's About A Mover'), the Moving Sidewalk (there '99th Floor' featured a young Billy Gibbons, later to form ZZ Top), Mouse and the Traps (whose 'A Public Execution' is an uncanny Dylan sound-alike), the Five Americans ('I See The Light'), and a bizarre collection of bands centred around the International Artists label in Houston. Highlighted by 'the psychedelic sounds' of the Thirteenth Floor Elevators and their 1966 hit 'You're Gonna Miss Me', these acid-punks might be thought of as the secondary stage of garage evolution, beyond English influence into the ozone. A typical example of their mania would be the Red Crayola's *Parable Of Arable Land,* which interspersed 'free-form freak-outs' with songs.

The East Coast was similarly alive with music. A megalopolis stretched northwards from Washington DC (the Hangmen), Philadelphia (the Nazz with Todd Rundgren, Mandrake Memorial and Woody's Truck Stop), through New Jersey (with the Knickerbockers and the Critters), bypassing New York, crossing Connecticut (the Original Sinners) and Rhode Island (Teddy and the Pandas) and up into the unofficial capital of New England, Boston.

There, bands like the Remains galvanised audiences and even toured with the Beatles, while the Hallucinations gathered the blues-based components for what would become the J. Geils Band. The Barbarians, in turn, asked the musical question 'Are You A Boy Or Are You A Girl?', setting the political implications of long hair into perspective. Their greatest moment came in a song entitled 'Moulty', where the drummer told the true story of how he lost his hand in an explosion by a railroad track, and how playing in a band gave him a reason to go on living: 'Now all I need is a girl . . .'

And what of the Squires, the Floyd Dakil Combo, the Bedlam Four, the Clefs of Lavender Hill, the Balloon Farm, the Lollipop Shoppe, the E-Types, the Stillroven, the Calico Wall, Thee Sixpence . . .? Hopes strung like milestones along rock's glory road, a longing and belonging still providing impetus today. LENNY KAYE

THE SONICS

THE CHOCOLATE WATCH BAND

? AND THE MYSTERIANS

MOUSE AND THE TRAPS

THE STANDELLS

THE LEAVES

Summer Magic

Folk and fashion from the Lovin' Spoonful

On the front: four self-consciously zany young men dressed in striped T-shirts sprawling about and grinning hugely at the camera. On the back: a sleeve-note that began 'They dress like comic book characters. They move like a carton of ping-pong balls on their way to some great party somewhere. It couldn't have happened before now.'

The date was December 1965, and this was the sleeve of *Do You Believe In Magic,* the first album by a New York group called the Lovin' Spoonful. The alert record buyer would immediately have picked up the echoes in the sleeve design of the Beatles LP *Help!* and of the host of high-spirited British beat groups which had invaded the United States in the previous two years. But it would only have taken one listen to the sound of the Lovin' Spoonful to realise that these were no musical copyists of the Merseybeat style. With the Byrds and Buffalo Springfield, the Spoonful were part of the great trio of bands that created an all-American beat music during the mid Sixties.

The range of material on that first album provided a neat summary of the story of the band to that date. Five of the dozen tracks were compositions by John Sebastian, the Lovin' Spoonful's central figure, while five more were traditional blues tunes which had become part of the standard repertoire of jug bands and folk singers in New York's Greenwich Village. There was also one composition by the respected Village folkie Fred Neil and one from the Brill Building in midtown New York, written by pop composers Cynthia Weil and Barry Mann with record producer Phil Spector. So the Lovin' Spoonful's folk roots and pop destination were combined with the major reason for their coming success: John Sebastian's eloquence as a songwriter.

Bad influence

Sebastian (born 17 March 1944) came from a musical background, having a father who was a renowned classical harmonica player. A teenager when the folk revival took off in the early Sixties, John took up the same instrument but pursued a folk-blues style. He was soon able to find jobs accompanying folk singers in coffee houses and eventually on record. His first disc was made as part of the Even Dozen Jug Band when, rather than the family

Above: Eric Jacobsen, producer and mentor of the Spoonful, with leggy friend. Below from left: Zal Yanovsky, Joe Butler, John Sebastian and Steve Boone. Opposite: The band on British TV.

name, he called himself John Benson. 'It was my first recording on the harmonica, and I wasn't too sure of myself,' Sebastian explained later.

He needn't have been so concerned, since he was soon working steadily as a session musician, backing folk singers like Tom Rush and Judy Collins. Meanwhile, the British influence was beginning to be felt in New York. In the late summer of 1964 the first folk-rock band, the Mugwumps, flourished briefly. The guitarist was Zal Yanovsky (born 19 December 1944), a friend of Sebastian, while John himself was briefly associated with the group: 'They fired me because they said I was having a bad influence on Zal.'

At this point, too, John Sebastian had a crucial encounter with record producer Eric Jacobsen. Perhaps more than anyone else in New York, Jacobsen could see the vast potential in a fusion of the imagination and commitment of the folk scene with the sheer exuberance of the British groups. And in John Sebastian he saw the figure around whom such a fusion could be built. Jacobsen not only persuaded Sebastian that he was a singer as well as a harmonica player, but convinced him that his songs were as good as those of the folk 'stars' he accompanied.

The obvious thing to do was to start a group. Fortuitously, the Mugwumps were on the point of splitting up, with Denny Doherty and Cass Elliot setting off for California where they would become part of the Mamas and the Papas. Zal Yanovsky, keen to trade in his acoustic guitar for an electric one, thus joined up once more with Sebastian. Steve Boone (born 23 September 1943) came in on bass guitar, having been selected as much for his fashionably shaggy hair as for his skill. Finally, Eric Jacobsen provided Joe Butler (born 19 January 1943), a drummer from a bunch of Beatles imitators aptly named the Sell Outs, whose records Jacobsen had produced. The new band's name reflected the folk scene background of Yanovsky and Sebastian; 'Lovin' Spoonful' was a phrase from 'Coffee Blues' by the renowned blues singer Mississippi John Hurt.

The Lovin' Spoonful's first performance was less than successful. They played the Night Owl Cafe, a famous folk venue, and were told by the owner to 'go away and practise'. So they retreated to the basement of the Albert Hotel, a haunt of many musicians. According to Eric Jacobsen, this was 'the worst rehearsal hall you could ever imagine. It was just incredible! Cockroaches everywhere, rivulets flowing across the floor into big pools, slime all over the place, mushrooms and fungi growing in the corners, plaster and old flaking paint falling off the ceiling . . .'

The two months of rehearsal paid off, however, and the Spoonful returned to the Night Owl in triumph, playing the mixture of Sebastian originals and blues standards that were to appear on the first album. But it took a while for Jacobsen to get a recording contract for the group. With a demonstration disc of Sebastian's song 'Do You Believe In Magic' he toured the record companies without luck until he bumped into two music business figures called Don Rubin and Charlie Koppelman. They signed the Spoonful to their production company, leasing the recordings to a new label called Kama Sutra which in turn used MGM Records to distribute the discs. As a result, Kama Sutra got 11 per cent of the proceeds from MGM and Koppelman and Rubin received 9 per cent in their turn. Eventually, the Lovin' Spoonful got something too.

Good-time music

Nobody had to wait long to make money from the Spoonful. 'Do You Believe In Magic' was released in the autumn of 1965, rising to Number 9 in the US charts. Nine more hits were to follow in the next 20 months. The band's success was due in equal measure to the originality of their style and to the quality of John Sebastian's songs. The Lovin' Spoonful's sound was perhaps best described as 'good-time music', and their first big hit epitomised the group's approach. Musically, it was dominated by mellow, rippling guitar chords from Yanovsky, while Sebastian's warm, soft singing delivered the memorable lyrics which extolled the pleasures of music itself. It was the first of a line of songs of celebration composed by Sebastian and one which characteristically mixed sentiment and wit.

In 'Daydream', a Number 2 hit, he sang of the delights of laziness and of lying in the sun, in terms which had some listeners reading drug-laden double meanings into the lyrics. 'Summer In The City', an altogether tougher-sounding disc, is for many people the classic Spoonful song and was their only US chart-topper. 'Hot days, summer in the city/Back of my neck getting dirty and gritty' sang Sebastian and went on to a paint a word-picture of oppressive summer days and cool evenings full of promise. On a lighter, more quirky, note, 'Nashville Cats' was an affectionate tribute to John Sebastian's musical heroes, the guitar pickers who 'play clean as country water'. And while John sang those lines, Zal was doing just that behind him.

As a love-song writer, Sebastian was a full-blown romantic, more of a McCartney than a Lennon. But even here, sentiment stopped short of sentimentality because of an unexpected turn of phrase or a precise observation. 'You didn't have to be so nice,' he wrote, 'I would have liked you anyway.' That song plus 'Did You Ever Have To Make Up Your Mind', 'Rain On The Roof' and 'Darling Be Home Soon'

Above: Yanovsky (left) and Butler (right) harmonise in the studio while Sebastian looks on. Below: Zal on stage.

were all big hits for the band.

In addition to their musical innovations, the group took their place alongside such figures as Sonny and Cher as 'way out' fashion leaders. Zal Yanovsky had a penchant for cowboy hats and fur coats, while John Sebastian could claim the credit for popularising the wearing of 'granny' wire-framed spectacles. He even wrote a song about glasses, wryly entitled 'Four Eyes'.

Perhaps because of their general reputation as representatives of the new generation of American youth, the Spoonful also recorded the soundtracks for two films by directors who would later become internationally known. *You're A Big Boy Now* was the first major feature by Francis Ford Coppola, later of *Godfather* fame, while comedian Woody Allen directed *What's Up, Tiger Lily*. But like many individualistic songwriters, John Sebastian found it difficult to adapt to writing for the screen and the two soundtrack albums were disappointing.

The last hit for the band was the haunting 'She Is Still A Mystery', which reached Number 27 in November 1967. By this time, the Lovin' Spoonful were beginning to disintegrate. Zal Yanovsky had already left the group amid accusations from the underground press that he and Steve Boone had given information to the police after being arrested on drugs charges. According to rock authority Lillian Roxon, 'The Spoonful's name was mud. Their albums were used as doormats. Groupies were urged not to ball them.'

In 1968, John Sebastian himself left and, although drummer Joe Butler kept the band going for a few more months, that – to all intents and purposes – was the end. As if to underline Sebastian's predominance within the Lovin' Spoonful, he was the only one of the band to continue to record and give live concerts.

Blissed-out hippie

That quality of optimism, celebration and good humour evident in his pop hits of 1965 to 1967 led John Sebastian just a couple of years later to become one of the early heroes of the 'flower power' generation. He appeared at the famous Woodstock Festival of 1969 as well as the British equivalent at the Isle of Wight a year later. Paradoxically, although this period immediately following the end of the Lovin' Spoonful saw Sebastian acquire the reputation of a classic blissed-out hippie, it also produced two of his more critically attuned songs. 'Money' was a quizzical account of the curious features of a way of life based on the circulation of notes and coins:

'You give money to me
To tickle your whims and blow up
  your mind
I give money to you
And pay you back in kind.'

The other song, 'Younger Generation', took an ironic look at the position of

Sebastian's own rebellious generation when faced with the demands of their own children:

'Hey dad, my girlfriend's only three
She's got her own videophone and
she's taking LSD
And now she wants to give a bit to
me.
What's the matter, daddy
How come you're turning green?
Can it be that you can't live up to
your dreams?

Above: John Sebastian in 1971, in the film Celebration At Big Sur. *Below, from left: Boone, Sebastian, Jerry Yester (Zal Yanovsky's replacement) and Joe Butler.*

Welcome Home

During the Seventies, John Sebastian had a rather low-key career as a solo artist, occasionally touring and cutting only a few albums. The pattern was broken in 1976 when he had a Number 1 hit single in America with 'Welcome Home', the theme from a top television series. His subsequent compositions are of a more relaxed character too, with perhaps only 'Stories We Can Tell' up to the level of the half-dozen or so classic Spoonful songs.

Those songs – 'Summer In The City', 'Daydream' and the rest – stand with the best records of the 1964-67 period in their equal appeal to the heads, hearts and feet of the audience. As rock music fragmented in the years after 1967, dance music seemed to go in one direction, love songs in another and progressive rock in a third. The Lovin' Spoonful, like the Beatles, the Byrds and others, had been in the right place at the right time to reach a mass audience at the three levels of message, feeling and rhythm. Like those other bands, they possessed a source of first-rate songs – in the case of the Spoonful, the prolific John Sebastian. DAVE LAING

Lovin' Spoonful
Recommended Listening

All Of Lovin' Spoonful's Greatest Hits (Pye Golden Hour GH 838) (Includes: Summer In The City, Nashville Cats, Younger Girl, Do You Believe In Magic, Daydream, Darling Be Home Soon).

GROOVIN'

The Young Rascals' superb mastery of black R&B

Musicians based on America's East Coast have long had a reputation for producing music of a grittier, more streetwise kind than that of their West Coast counterparts. If California-made rock is traditionally all harmonies and sophistication, East Coast rock has a more basic quality, an earthiness evident even in the early-Sixties discs of New York groups like the Four Seasons and Dion and the Belmonts. The prime exponent of East Coast rock in the mid Sixties was a four-piece New Jersey-based band named the Young Rascals, all but one of whom shared Dion's and the Seasons' Italian-American background. Arguably the only white rock band of the period to master the black R&B sound, they did more than any other group to establish an East Coast rock 'tradition' to which Eighties acts like Bruce Springsteen, Bob Seger, Steely Dan and Todd Rundgren can all be said to belong.

Mixed-up music

The four musicians who made up the Rascals were Felix Cavaliere (vocals and keyboards, born 29 November 1944), Eddie Brigati (vocals, born 22 October 1946), Gene Cornish (lead guitar, born 14 May 1945), and Dino Danelli (drums, born 23 July 1945). Their particular brand of R&B – which was very close to black 'soul' music – had an authenticity born of the free mixing between black and Italian kids in the working-class areas of the big Eastern cities: Cavaliere, for instance, grew up in the racially-mixed area of Pelham, New York, and took up singing in his teens with the impromptu vocal groups who hung around the street-corners. Often, he was the only white member.

Brigati came from Garfield, New Jersey, and played in various groups before joining his elder brother Dave in the Starlighters, local singer Joey Dee's backing group. Dee and the Starlighters enjoyed massive success in the US charts with one of the big Twist records of 1961, 'Peppermint Twist', made when they were the house band at Manhattan's chic Peppermint Lounge night-spot; both Cavaliere and Cornish joined the line-up some time later. Cornish, a New Yorker of Irish extraction, had previously led a couple of groups of his own and had written and recorded a novelty disc called 'I Wanna Be

Below left: The Rascals in costume, 1965. Above left: By 1967 the group's attire had become more practical. Above: Joey Dee and the Starlighters featuring Eddie Brigati (second from right). Right, from top: Brigati, Gene Cornish, Felix Cavaliere and Dino Danelli.

A Beatle' at the height of American Beatlemania, under the name of Gene Cornish and the Unbeetables.

The Starlighters gave all three the invaluable experience of working with black musicians, but they began to grow restless when Joey Dee's popularity started to fade. Sharing a common love of R&B and an intimate knowledge of each other's playing styles, they left the Starlighters in late 1964 and first performed together as a three-man unit in February 1965 in Garfield, New Jersey.

Dino Danelli, an old friend of Cavaliere's from pre-Joey Dee days, joined shortly after on drums: though only 20, he had several years of playing experience behind him in jazz outfits and house bands in Las Vegas as well as New York. His playing gave the group – now named the Rascals, though they amended this to the 'Young' Rascals just prior to signing their recording contract – an extra edge, and they quickly built up a reputation on the New Jersey club scene for their tight, no-nonsense blend of soul standards, rock-'n'roll and self-written R&B. The fact that they did *not* deliberately set out to ape the Rolling Stones or any of the other then-popular British R&B bands counted in their favour, giving them credibility among those local fans who despised the British sound.

Knickerbocker glory

From the local club scene, the Rascals moved swiftly to gigs further afield. In July 1965, thanks largely to the efforts of agent Walter Hyman, they won a key residency at a floating Long Island night-club called The Barge, where the sweet young things of the New York jet set were known to gather. Their 'live' act – 45 minutes of solid R&B, interspersed with the customary beat and rock favourites – was a sensation and they stayed at the club for weeks. Around this time they also adopted a strong visual gimmick to give their act added interest – each wore choirboy shirts, plus-fours and knickerbockers, as if to mock their Italian backgrounds.

Their growing reputation brought them to the attention of Sid Bernstein, an influential New York promoter. Hearing them at first hand, he was convinced of their potential. 'I looked at these funny-looking guys,' he later told John Lombardi of *Rolling Stone*. 'They don't have sex appeal – who's going to buy those knickers? They looked like Italian kids from a Tremont Avenue poolroom I used to live near. Forty-five minutes later I felt I had heard the greatest group I ever heard in my life. They were so dynamic. They were beautiful. All of a sudden they had sex appeal.'

Appointing himself as their manager, Bernstein's first move was to use the Beatles' appearance at Shea Stadium to the Rascals' advantage: he had the words 'The Rascals Are Here' flashed on to the electronic scoreboard. Next he played the various newly-interested record companies against one another and eventually settled on a deal with Atlantic's Ahmet Ertegun, despite offers from both Phil Spector (on the lookout for another white R&B act for his own label, having lost the Righteous Brothers to Verve) and Leiber and Stoller's Red Bird label. Ertegun gave the group the unusually high advance of 10,000 dollars and their first record, a Rudy Clark-Arthur Resnick composition called 'I Ain't Gonna Eat Out My Heart Anymore', was issued in November 1965.

The disc reached Number 52 in the *Billboard* chart – a respectable showing for a debut effort – and was plugged particularly heavily by New York's black stations. The big chart breakthrough, however, came with 'Good Lovin'' (released in April 1966), which went to Number 1 and featured all the hallmarks of the fast-crystallising Rascals sound. A raunchy, impassioned soul stomper, it revealed their mastery of the music's particular vocal and instrumental demands – the shared vocal work, by Brigati and Cavaliere, could easily have passed for black – while the song itself showed Brigati and Cavaliere's command of the vocabulary of soul in a manner that did not suggest mere imitation.

With this record and subsequent releases – 'You Better Run' (Number 20 in July 1966), 'Come On Up' (Number 43 in

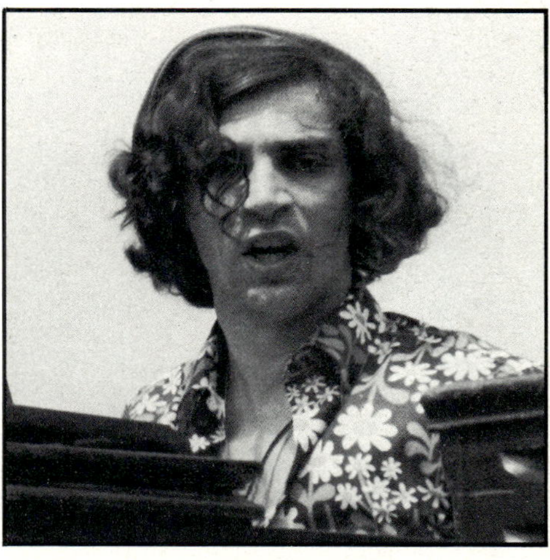

Top: Rascals groovin' on stage. Above: Fotomaker, the band formed by Cornish (right) and Danelli (second from right) in the late Seventies; the group aslo included Wally Bryson (second from left), one-time member of the Choir. Opposite: Late-Sixties Rascals – they espoused the cause of racial harmony.

September 1966) and 'I've Been Lonely Too Long' (Number 16 in March 1967) – the group consolidated their hip status, though their Italian good looks and vaguely punkish image gave them natural teenybopper appeal. Their discs sold as well to black as to white audiences, indicating how – almost alone among white rock groups of the Sixties – they had a real feel for the heart of black music, an exact understanding of its power and style. The fact that Atlantic, a predominantly black label, was prepared to sign them was indicative of their success; in time, however, they would develop a genuinely innovative blend of soul and latin rhythms, causing mixed feelings among some record company executives at the group's change of style.

Shifting sounds

Atlantic's principal aim seemed to be to recapture on record the sheer drive and energy of the Rascals' now legendary 'live' performances – and that meant that the more ethereal qualities of their music tended to be overlooked. The choice of material on their first album, *The Young Rascals,* reflected this: alongside some uncertain rock'n'roll versions of Dylan's 'Like A Rolling Stone', the Beau Brummels' 'Just A Little' and the old Frankie Laine hit, 'I Believe', were a glut of R&B standards like 'Mustang Sally', 'Slow Down' and 'In The Midnight Hour', all of which were stage show favourites. Writing more and more material of their own, the group began moving slowly away from their 'blue-eyed soul' beginnings, although the production work of Tom Dowd tended to obscure this at first. Also the rock scene was itself changing and the group wanted to keep up with events. By 1967, a change of pace was needed.

That change came with 'Groovin'' (released in April 1967), a beautifully-atmospheric summer ballad which gave them their second US Number 1 and their first UK hit. The record was immaculately produced by the Rascals themselves, with Tom Dowd giving technical assistance and Atlantic house arranger Arif Mardin conducting the session, and had a distinctive, open-air quality, full of space and light. The follow-up, 'A Girl Like You', was a more typical Rascals track with vocal punch and the customary Atlantic horn section, but even this featured a cleaner, slicker sound than Rascals fans had been used to. The trend towards greater sophistication reached a logical peak with their fourth release of 1967, 'How Can I Be Sure', a continental-style ballad complete with French accordions and orchestral accompaniment.

All this amounted to a new independence in the Rascals' musical outlook, a desire to experiment with different styles and play a greater role in their own recording and management affairs. Their mid-1967 album *Groovin'* underlined their new approach: again produced by the group, it included three 1967 singles and eight other tracks highlighting a new versatility – among them latin-styled pop ballads with almost Californian-style harmonies ('I Don't Love You Anymore', 'I'm So Happy Now' and 'If You Knew') and a long, laid-back, gospel-flavoured treatment of the Fifties standard, 'A Place In The Sun'.

In the context of 1967, when so many bands were embracing new ideas and rejecting commercial conventions, the Rascals' quest for a new, more progressive identity was easy to understand. Felix Cavaliere became particularly absorbed in eastern mysticism and the trappings of the flower culture, adopting an Indian philosopher named Swami Satchidananda as his guru, and their next album (released in June 1968) reflected it. Called *Once Upon A Dream,* this was a concept album replete with symbolism and sound effects. Tom Dowd for one was disappointed with the shift from their early style. 'If they hadn't left that earthy sound,' he said later, 'there'd never have been a need for Steppenwolf, Three Dog Night, the Flaming Ember. The Rascals could do that better than anybody.'

The price of harmony

To make a point of their new maturity and their desire to be taken seriously as rock musicians, the group dropped the 'Young' from their name in 1968 and reverted to their old name. Their interviews became more meditative and their statements more openly political, but they at least paid more than lip service to the ideals of brotherhood and racial harmony at the heart of post-1967 hippie thinking. A first-hand experience of anti-rock hostility on tour in Florida during the early months of 1968 left a mental scar on each of them, when their trailer broke down outside the town of Fort Pierce and the group had to run the gauntlet – without effective police protection – of redneck hatred. After that episode the group announced that they would no longer play on bills that didn't feature at least one black act – no token gesture, this, because it meant that the group were suddenly no longer welcome at certain key venues. Financially, the decision cost them considerably.

The Rascals also played more benefit gigs than virtually any other late Sixties band or artist, usually for black or left-wing causes, and made particularly notable appearances at a Martin Luther King tribute concert at Madison Square Garden in 1968 and at a UNICEF concert in London in 1969. The full extent of their commitment was yet more evident in their music, not so much in their rather meandering albums but in their exhilarating 1968 single, 'People Got To Be Free'. A classic (if only temporary) return to the soul idiom, the record had an almost fiery passion – due in part, no doubt, to its being recorded on the night of Robert Kennedy's shooting. It was, however, the Rascals' last major American singles hit; like most of their contemporaries, they concentrated most of their attention on ablums: *Freedom Suite* was issued in March 1969 and *See* later that year.

Internal dissensions and personal problems led to the group cutting back on recording and performing during 1970 and few were surprised when Eddie Brigati announced his decision to leave. The remaining three recorded one more album for Atlantic, *Search And Nearness,* before leaving the label for Columbia in a one million dollar deal that also guaranteed the Rascals 250,000 dollars per album. With Brigati gone, however, the band lost considerable momentum and increasingly became the vehicle for Felix Cavaliere's jazz-rock ideas. Gene Cornish left before work on their first album for Columbia, *Peaceful World,* was completed and Cavaliere carried on with jazz musicians Robert 'Pops' Popwell (later of the Crusaders), Ann Sutton and Buzzy Feiten. One more album, *Island Of Real,* resulted before Cavaliere formally brought the Rascals story to an end by dissolving the group.

Cavaliere went into production work, notably with Laura Nyro, and made two excellent solo albums – again in the jazz-rock style – for the Bearsville label. Brigati drifted into the relative obscurity of session work, while Gene Cornish and Dino Danelli teamed up again in a band called Fotomaker, who released a rather neglected album of the same name in 1978. With their best collective work behind them, it is too much to expect that the four former Rascals should continue to make an impact on contemporary rock: their greatest period of influence was in the middle years of the Sixties, when they not only inspired a so-called 'East Coast sound' – the Vanilla Fudge and the Vagrants were just two groups who emerged soon after, from the same environment – but gave American rock a new impetus in the face of the British invasion.

STEPHEN BARNARD

Young Rascals Recommended Listening

The Young Rascals (Atlantic 588012, 1966) (Includes: I Ain't Gonna Eat Out My Heart Anymore, Good Lovin', Slow Down, Mustang Sally, Like A Rolling Stone, Do You Feel It); *Groovin'* (Atlantic 588074, 1967) (Includes: You Better Run, A Place In The Sun, Sueno, Groovin', How Can I Be Sure, A Girl Like You).

WHEELS OF FIRE

Top: Cream. Insets, from left: The Graham Bond Organisation with Bruce (left) and Baker (right), Manfred Mann with Bruce (right) and Clapton's Yardbirds.

Cream: at the Crossroads as rock turned progressive

IN A CAREER lasting a mere two-and-a-half years, Cream redefined the musical possibilities of rock groups and raised the expectations of their listeners, selling long-playing records in such prodigious quantities that the album outstripped the single as pop's prime product.

In many ways, Cream were the first of the 'progressive' album-oriented groups; as such they helped to establish a strand of rock music that many observers have come to consider tedious and reactionary. The syndrome had certainly become over-indulgent by the time punk arrived in 1976, but the fact that album sales and technical virtuosity prevailed as the principal yardsticks of 'serious' music for nearly a decade after Cream's demise is testimony to their great influence.

In musical circles, Jack Bruce, Ginger Baker and Eric Clapton were all acknowledged as masters of their chosen instruments, though in 1966 Clapton was the only one to have built a substantial public following – 'Clapton Is God' was already familiar graffiti around London. Born in Ripley, Surrey, on 30 March 1945, Clapton had listened with awe to the master American R&B and blues guitarists, progressing from Chuck Berry to B. B. King and Buddy Guy. His delinquent tendencies – 'I was an undesirable influence on the other students' – served to get him thrown out of Kingston Art College, and he joined his first serious group the Roosters in January 1963. Originally an R&B group from Oxford, the Roosters only lasted till August of that year. Next Clapton played with Casey Jones and the Engineers, a fruitless engagement that he left after only seven gigs.

October 1963 saw a change in fortunes when Clapton joined the Yardbirds. Here he got his first taste of success as the group followed the Stones into a residency at the Crawdaddy Club, and he was soon laying the foundations of his formidable reputation, both on stage and on the *Five Live Yardbirds* album. However the change of direction from 'pure' R&B towards a more commercial format, which afforded the group their first Top Ten record, 'For Your Love', upset Clapton, a staunch blues purist. He served notice and quit, choosing to go and work on a building site just as the record entered the charts. This was generally held to be a courageous and principled move and further enhanced his standing. In April 1965 he joined John Mayall and firmly consolidated his reputation both live and by his inspired and widely-applauded contribution to Mayall's milestone 1966 album *Bluesbreakers*. Prior to the recording of this classic set, bassist Jack Bruce had also done a brief tour of duty with Mayall's Bluesbreakers.

In contrast to Clapton's self-taught background, Bruce (born 14 May 1943) had won a scholarship to the Royal Scottish Academy of Music but left after three months, dissatisfied with the teaching methods. A multi-instrumentalist, he arrived in London in 1962, proficient on cello, electric and upright bass, harmonica and piano. One of his early gigs in the capital was with Alexis Korner's Blues Incorporated, at that time holding down an enormously popular residency at the Marquee Club. Other members of the group at various times included organist Graham Bond, and drummer Ginger Baker; in 1963 these two left, with Bruce, to form the Graham Bond Organisation. In August 1965 Bruce left the Organisation for his brief sojourn with John Mayall's Bluesbreakers, where he made a lasting impression on the lead guitarist. 'From then on, he was a natural choice in any group I might dream about forming,' Clapton commented. But Bruce, at this time newly married and impelled by the usual financial exigencies, left Mayall's Bluesbreakers after only six weeks to join Manfred Mann, contributing bass to their Number 1 record 'Pretty Flamingo'.

Ginger-haired Peter Baker was born in Lewisham on 19 August 1939 and began his musical career at the age of fourteen as a trumpeter with the band of the local branch of Air Training Cadets. His first drumming job was at age 16 with the Storyville Jazzmen, and he went on to play with numerous jazz acts, including Acker Bilk's Paramount Jazz Band and Terry Lightfoot, as well as serving a spell as resident drummer at Ronnie Scott's Soho jazz club. He first played with Jack Bruce in the Bert Courtley Band at a gig at Cambridge University, and then they played together in Blues Incorporated and the Graham Bond Organisation. While Bruce was playing with Mayall and Manfred Mann, Baker remained with Graham Bond.

Wrapping riffs

Cream, then, were a product of the unashamedly incestuous and polygamous British R&B/blues scene of the mid Sixties. The spark for their formation came one night in June 1966 when Ginger Baker turned up unannounced at a Bluesbreakers gig and asked to sit in on drums. He and Clapton formed a mutual admiration society on the spot. In a subsequent discussion Baker suggested they form a group; Clapton agreed, and nominated Jack Bruce as bass player and vocalist.

Above: Ginger Baker takes to the bottle.
Below: Eric Clapton takes to the floor.
Opposite: Cream pose for the camera.

Baker had some misgivings over the choice of Bruce because the two musicians had not got on during their time together in the Graham Bond Organisation – eventually Baker and Bond had joined forces to sack Bruce from the group. It is significant, then, that Baker and Bruce were both prepared to waive these personal differences out of respect for each other's musical abilities. For the new group was to be no old pals' organisation like the Beatles or the Rolling Stones. Their desire to play together stemmed from the need to eliminate any weak musical links and to give each of them as individuals a satisfactory outlet for their virtuoso talents.

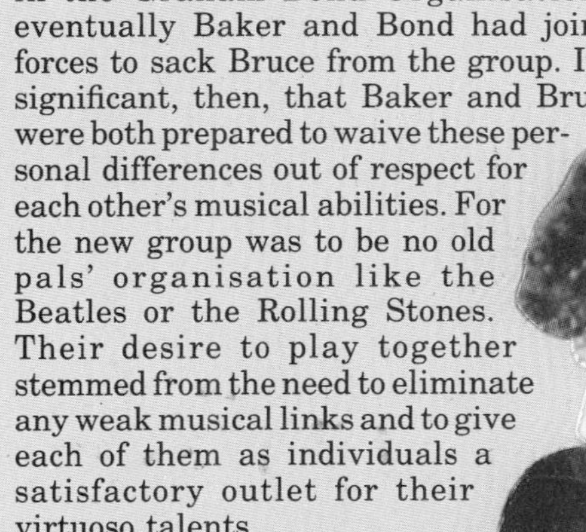

Before meeting the public's gaze, however, they had to prove that Baker's jazz background, Bruce's classical leaning and Clapton's obsession with the blues were compatible influences. So one day in June Clapton and Bruce hauled their amplifiers into the front room of Ginger Baker's house in the north London suburb of Neasden, where the drummer's kit was set up, switched on and without preamble played non-stop for about two hours. Subsequent rehearsals proved that the chemistry was there and Cream found themselves with a management deal (with Robert Stigwood) and major press interest even before they had played a gig. The group first performed in front of an audience at the Twisted Wheel club in Manchester, and on 3 July 1966 played their first major gig at the Windsor Jazz and Blues Festival, where they were received with great enthusiasm.

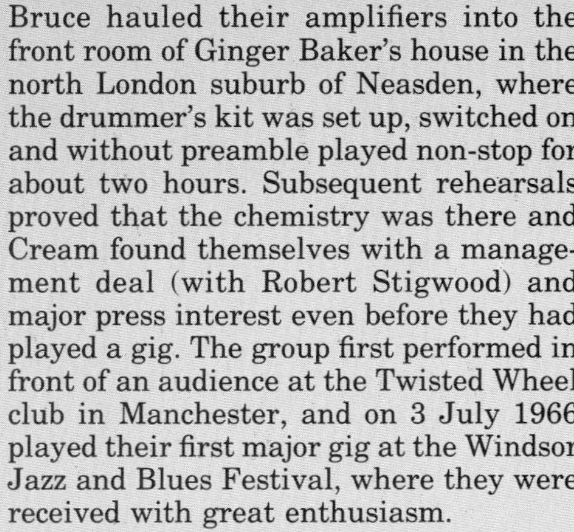

From the start, Cream showed themselves to be a musical unit of stunning power and ingenuity. Ignoring the conventional pop/rock code of three to four-minute songs with any improvisation occurring in fairly structured solo breaks, Cream turned the format on its head. Their trick was very often to play the song as written for only a couple of verses and chorus before branching out into long exploratory pasages of improvisation. No-one was tied down or cast in the role of

timekeeper – they were all free to express themselves fully, and of course flaunt their not-inconsiderable technical prowess. It was to be some time before this live approach was committed to disc, however, and at first the group were uncertain how to approach the requirements of studio recording. For one thing they still felt under considerable pressure to come up with the all-important three-minute hit. Their first single, despite Clapton's apparent distaste for out-and-out commerciality, was 'Wrapping Paper', a rather lightweight whimsical offering dominated by airy quasi-falsetto harmonies which reached Number 34 in the charts and provided a useful bridgehead to public awareness. The follow-up, 'I Feel Free', was an altogether tougher offering with a catchy vocal riff and a powerful Clapton solo. The record reached Number 11 in December.

An unblinking eye

Despite their singles' success, it was with *Fresh Cream*, the first album released on Robert Stigwood's newly-created Reaction label, that the group were to showcase their talents. On this powerful and timely debut statement, half the cuts were originals – mostly Bruce feeling his way as a songwriter – and the other half were radically restructured blues standards. The musical ability of the trio was never in doubt, but beyond this they showed a courageous willingness to take chances. On 'Sweet Wine', for instance, Clapton made use of feedback and heavy guitar distortion in a free-form solo well ahead of its time. The Muddy Waters classic 'Rollin' And Tumblin'' was stripped down to bare essentials and delivered without any bass guitar in a raucous surge of near-anarchic treble noise. 'I'm So Glad' and 'Spoonful' both featured extended instrumental workouts, nowhere near as extensive as their live counterparts but still considerably longer and more improvisatory than people were used to hearing. And of course there was Baker's remarkable *tour de force*, 'Toad', a drum solo of a magnitude and dexterity unheard-of in rock circles. *Fresh Cream* was an immediate success, reaching Number 6 in the album charts in January 1967 just six months after the group had formed.

In April Cream made their first visit to America, playing on US television's 'Murray The K Show' for 10 days. While there, they went into Atlantic studios in New York to record tracks for their second album. They toured Britain, and 'Strange Brew', their third single entered the Top Twenty in June. In September they began their first full-scale American tour at Bill Graham's San Francisco Fillmore West. Although aware of their healthy record sales in America, Cream were not prepared for the intensity of reaction that greeted their performance. It was the pinnacle of the group's career.

Musically, as has already been indicated, Cream were in the vanguard of the progressive movement and they became altogether more important than a mere rock group. They were looked up to as heroes and leaders of the counter culture of psychedelia and hippiedom. Along with their rival and friend Jimi Hendrix, they pioneered the wearing of outlandish and flamboyantly colourful clothes (including enormous bell-bottom trousers) and Clapton had his hair permed into an outrageous Afro frizz of unrivalled circumference.

Cream's second album *Disraeli Gears*,

Left: Lyricist Pete Brown. Below: Cream's farewell performance at the Albert Hall, 26 November 1968. Insets: The group's first and second albums, Fresh Cream *(left) and* Disraeli Gears.

CREAM
Discography

Singles
Wrapping Paper/Cat's Squirrel (Reaction 591007, 1966); I Feel Free/N.S.U. (Reaction 591011, 1966); Strange Brew/Tales Of Brave Ulysses (Reaction 591015, 1967); Anyone For Tennis/Pressed Rat And Warthog (Polydor 56258, 1968); Sunshine Of Your Love/Swlabr (Polydor 56286, 1968); White Room/Those Were The Days (Polydor 56300, 1968); Badge/What A Bringdown (Polydor 56315, 1969).

Albums
Fresh Cream (Reaction 593001, 1966); *Disraeli Gears* (Reaction 593003, 1967); *Wheels Of Fire* (double album) (Polydor 582031/2, 1968); *Wheels Of Fire* (in the studio) (Polydor 582033, 1968); *Wheels Of Fire* (Live at the Fillmore) (Polydor 582040, 1968); *Goodbye* (Polydor 583053, 1969); *Best Of Cream* (Polydor 583060, 1969); *Live Cream* (Polydor 2383 016, 1970); *Full Cream* (Polydor 2447 010, 1970); *Live Cream Vol 2* (Polydor 2383 119, 1972); *Heavy Cream* (Polydor 2659 022, 1973); *Cream* (Polydor 2384 067, 1975).

released in November 1967, reflected the group's position of cultural influence. Martin Sharp, who did many of the graphics for the celebrated and highly notorious underground magazine *Oz*, designed the cover. A wash of glaring colours, flowers, horses, swirls, bubbles, peacocks and spacey motifs round an unblinking eye, the sleeve remains the paradigm of psychedelic art. The majority of the tracks were originals and lyricist/poet Pete Brown, with whom Bruce had formed a songwriting partnership, produced suitably mystical, hip lyrics that – even for those hazy days – had a slight tendency towards pretentious vacuity but nevertheless matched the stoned mood of the Summer of Love. Produced by Felix Pappalardi, the album was a definite progression away from the blues. If the heavy riff was born when the Kinks recorded 'You Really Got Me', then it came of age with 'Sunshine Of Your Love', probably Cream's best-remembered anthem. Clapton and Bruce made a fine vocal team and never more so than on this track. The album went into the Top Five in both the UK and the US.

Gears and wheels

Disraeli Gears was released in the midst of a string of highly-successful dates in Britain. But the financial incentives apparent on the other side of the Atlantic were more compelling. Their live reputation was such that, by undertaking long US tours, Cream could realise a money-making potential hitherto unknown in rock group history.

In February 1968 they returned to the States and embarked on a tour due to last several months. Under the sustained pressures of playing night after night, however, they began to lose their love of performing together. The music they produced on stage was largely a result of inspiration and spontaneity of approach and it just could not be purveyed ceaselessly gig after gig. Though the audiences were as wild as ever, a key factor in the group's onstage chemistry, that of bouncing ideas backwards and forwards, playing for and against each other, was gone. All that was left were three huge egos competing for space.

Cream returned to Britain, and in July it was announced that the group was going to split up at the end of the year. The following month they became the first rock act to issue a double album of previously-unreleased recordings. *Wheels Of Fire* also belatedly brought the musical essence of their stage act across to a wider audience, incorporating both a studio album and a live album. It reached Number 3 in the UK and was a Number 1 hit in America. As with their previous work, it was a trail-blazing album. Clapton played possibly his finest recorded guitar solo ever on 'Crossroads', Bruce demonstrated his peerless technical mastery of the harmonica on 'Traintime', and Baker took his art to the limit (and beyond for some people) with 15 minutes of 'Toad'. On 'Spoonful', all three musicians peaked with what may be *the* definitive recorded statement of rock improvisation.

In October 1968 Cream commenced their farewell tour of America, playing to capacity crowds. They did some recording in New York at the end of the tour and in London on their return to lay down tracks for a final album. On 26 November 1968 they played their farewell British concerts to two packed houses at London's Albert Hall, and formally disbanded.

A posthumous album, *Goodbye*, was released in March 1969. A fitting conclusion, it again contained a mixture of studio and live tracks and provided the group with their only UK Number 1 in the LP charts. A Number 18 hit single also resulted in 'Badge', a song written by Clapton and George Harrison. *Best Of Cream* appeared later in the year.

Despite Cream's limited lifespan, the group had achieved far more than they ever expected to. The three individual talents had met, fulfilled their needs at the time, and moved on once they could perceive no further musical progression from their collaboration. While many contemporary critics were moved to hyperbole in trying to sum up the achievements of Cream, it is worth remembering the attitude that made what they did possible. Perhaps the last words here should be those of Jack Bruce: 'The way I feel about it is we'd a few good plays and made a bit of bread, and it's finished.' DAVID SINCLAIR

WINWOOD

From Traffic control to solo stardom

STEVE WINWOOD has attracted endless superlatives as a child prodigy, multi-instrumentalist and superstar during a career which has spanned several bands and substantial solo work. Stephen Philip Winwood (born 12 May 1948) was raised in the Birmingham suburb of Great Barr. His family was musical, although neither parent was a professional musician. In a *Musician* interview Winwood recalled jamming as early as 1961 with trombonist Rico and a little later with Owen Grey, Tony Washington and Wilfred 'Jackie' Edwards (the author of 'Keep On Running' and 'Somebody Help Me'). By the age of 14 he was playing in the Muff Woody Jazz Band, which was where Spencer Davis first clapped eyes on him; that led to the formation of the Spencer Davis Rhythm and Blues Quartet with Davis, Muff and Steve Winwood and Pete York – a line-up that soon became the Spencer Davis Group.

Musical maturity

Steve left school at 16 to concentrate on the band. His musical influences encompassed blues, jazz, folk, ska, bluebeat and pop, in particular Buddy Holly, Carl Perkins, Elvis Presley and Ray Charles. From these diverse sources Steve fashioned his riveting vocal style, widely proclaimed as the finest white R&B voice of his generation. His style was strong, his voice original and mature. His keyboard playing was direct, buoyant and perfect for fleshing out the sound; over the years it became increasingly more articulate. And although he was modest about his prowess on guitar, he was an accomplished player.

Steve Winwood was the star of the Spencer Davis Group, his instrumental and vocal talents attracting the attention of fellow musicians as well as the audience. After hearing Winwood's version of the jazz standard 'Nobody Knows You When You're Down And Out' on the 1966 album *Autumn 66*, Al Kooper (session musician for Dylan, the Rolling Stones and Hendrix and founder of the Blues Project) wrote in *Rolling Stone*: 'I regard Stevie as the finest white blues singer I have ever heard, regardless of age or environment.' The teenager's musical talents were being exercised in other directions outside the confines of the Spencer Davis Group, however. He worked on a short-lived studio project, Powerhouse, with Eric Clapton (guitar), Jack Bruce (bass), Paul Jones (harmonica), Pete York (drummer with the Spencer Davis Group) and Ben Palmer (keyboards). At producer Joe Boyd's instigation, the project contributed three tracks – 'I Want To Know', 'Crossroads' and 'Steppin' Out' – to Elektra's *What's Shakin'*. The anthology, rechristened *Good Time Music* in the UK, also included rare performances by the Paul Butterfield Blues Band, Al Kooper and the Lovin' Spoonful.

The seeds of Traffic were also being sown at this time, as Steve Winwood began jamming with Dave Mason (guitar and vocals), Chris Wood (flute and sax) and Jim Capaldi (drums and vocals) in 1966 in a late-night Birmingham club called the Elbow Room. The three also played session on the Spencer Davis Group's third hit single 'I'm A Man' which made the Top Ten on both sides of the Atlantic early in 1967. Mason (born 10 May 1945) and Capaldi (born 8 February 1944) had played with Winwood in the Birmingham-based band Deep Feeling; Wood (born 24 June 1944) came from art school and a number of blues bands including Locomotive. Despite the chart success that was being enjoyed at this time by the Spencer Davis Group, Winwood saw the potential in the new venture and quit the Spencer Davis Group in 1967.

Country music

Traffic then retreated into the Berkshire countryside at Aston Tirrold to 'get things together' in a cottage, something which subsequently became a 'hip' thing to do. The country setting is echoed in songs like 'Berkshire Poppies', 'Little Woman' and 'House For Everyone', peppered also with references to drugs. The quartet took shape in the first few months of their rustic seclusion. Winwood played guitar, keyboards and occasionally electric bass, Mason played guitar and Indian instruments such as the sitar, Capaldi played drums and Wood played organ, flute and sax; all contributed vocals.

Traffic's debut single 'Paper Sun', released on Chris Blackwell's Island label in June 1967, reached Number 5 in the UK charts (and just crept into the US Hot Hundred). It featured Winwood's throaty vocals and Mason's sitar. The follow-ups, 'Hole In My Shoe' and 'Here We Go Round The Mulberry Bush', were in the same psychedelic vein – ideal for the Summer of Love. Based on a dream of Mason's, 'Hole In My Shoe' was the band's most successful single, reaching Number 2 in the UK charts, while 'Here We Go Round The Mulberry Bush' made it to Number 8.

The band's first LP, *Mr Fantasy*, was released late in 1967 and perhaps showed the direction in which Traffic was heading – namely the division that was growing between the talents of Mason and Winwood. The two apparently disagreed about the choice of singles material, Mason's inclination towards light melodies being at odds with the rest of the band's orientation towards jazz. Rumoured disagreements over royalties further aggravated the situation. He left in December 1967, returning a few months later for a US tour; the band were met off the plane in San Francisco by acid king Owsley Stanley and later jammed on stage with the Grateful Dead's Jerry Garcia and Jefferson Airplane's Jack Casady.

Mason also contributed to the second album, *Traffic* (1968), which continued in the same vein as *Mr Fantasy* but with fewer gimmicky sound effects. Mason left again later that year, and the band's farewell album, *Last Exit*, featured him only on the studio side, the remaining trio recording the Fillmore West concert side. Traffic continued for a while, the trio shifting from one instrument to another on stage, until a new project lured Winwood away in early 1969 when he went off into the wilds of Surrey to form Blind Faith with Clapton. Chris Wood went on to do session work with Dr John.

Blind Faith was a short-lived supergroup which emerged out of the ashes of other mega-bands and in this case brought together Winwood, Clapton and Ginger Baker (both from Cream), and Rick Grech from Family. The band was a showcase for individual talents: Baker's percussion solo on 'Do What You Like', Grech's violin solo on 'Sea Of Joy', Clapton's wah-wah technique, Winwood's songwriting, singing

Opposite: Steve Winwood in the Eighties working in his home recording studio. After leaving the Spencer Davis Group in 1967, Winwood formed Traffic (above), moving into the ranks of supergroup Blind Faith (top) two years later.

and instrumental achievements. Blind Faith suffered a lot from all the hyping they received: Winwood and Clapton have both since stressed the disillusionment caused by gigs where the response from the audience was equally ecstatic, irrespective of the quality of the performance. The band's legacy to the world of music was their one eponymous album, and the memories of their one tour (which included an open-air concert in London's Hyde Park), after which the superstars went their separate ways.

In January 1970 Winwood joined the line-up of Ginger Baker's Airforce, a 10-piece band which included Traffic's Chris Wood, Rick Grech, Graham Bond, Denny Laine, Remi Kabaka and Phil Seaman. Winwood started work in 1970 on a solo album *Mad Shadows* which developed into a Traffic album when Wood and Capaldi were brought in as session men. The album eventually came out in July as *John Barleycorn Must Die*; this included 'Stranger To Himself', on which Winwood overdubbed all instruments.

Shoals and heels

The album merged jazz, R&B, rock and traditional folk. It was difficult to perform live, however, so the trio was augmented by Grech and, later, percussionist Reebop Kwaku-Baah, ex-Domino Jim Gordon on drums and – intermittently – old faithful Dave Mason. The line-up embarked upon a summer tour of Britain, recorded the live album *Welcome To The Canteen* and the studio album *Low Spark Of High Heeled Boys* (both 1971) and toured America. Grech and Gordon then quit, Winwood took time off to recover from peritonitis and Capaldi worked on a solo LP at Muscle Shoals Studios *Oh! How We Danced*. Session musicians David Hood (bass) and Roger Hawkins (drums), both from Muscle Shoals, augmented the line-up of Traffic for the band's next album *Shoot Out At The Fantasy Factory* (recorded in Jamaica in 1972). Another Shoalsman Barry Beckett joined on keyboards for the band's 1973 world tour; the live double album *On The Road* was recorded in Germany, after which the Shoalsmen departed.

For their final tour in 1974 and the last album, *When The Eagle Flies*, Traffic were joined by bassist Rosko Gee from Gonzales, an able player. Winwood concentrated mainly on organ, piano and synthesiser on the album which contained the Winwood-Viv Stanshall composition 'Dream Gerrard'. The collaboration with Stanshall (formerly of the Bonzo Dog Band) continued, with Winwood working on Stanshall's *Men Opening Umbrellas Ahead* (1974) and *Sir Henry At Rawlinson's End* (1978). Traffic had run its course and the band finally disintegrated in 1975. Capaldi went on to pursue his solo career; Rosko Gee and Reebop joined the German-based band Can.

Winwood was in no hurry to forge a solo career and played sessions, appearing on albums by Sandy Denny, the Fania All Stars, Jim Capaldi, Toots and the Maytals, George Harrison and Stomu Yamashta's *Go* project, a mixture which typified his desire to play in a variety of styles and

Steve Winwood's fellow musicians in the original Traffic were Chris Wood (below), Dave Mason (centre) and singer/sometime drummer Jim Capaldi (far right).

Inset bottom: Traffic 'get their heads together' outside their cottage, 1967. In keeping with the spirit of the times, their early work was in a psychedelic vein.

different contexts. His first solo album *Steve Winwood* (1977) was a surprise in some ways. Like *When The Eagle Flies* it contained a number of Winwood-Capaldi compositions, of which 'Time Is Running Out' and the wistful 'Let Me Make Something In Your Life' were perhaps the best, even if not equal to 'Walkin' In The Wind' or 'When The Eagle Flies'. Viv Stanshall's lyric for 'Vacant Chair', however, was everything that 'Dream Gerrard' had promised and Winwood's music had soared to meet the challenge. Session musicians on *Steve Winwood* included Reebop, Andy Newmark and Willie Weeks.

Winwood was doing selective live work, too; the Steve Winwood Band played the Rough Hill Festival in Cirencester; for that engagement the only personnel member on both *Steve Winwood* and in the live band was his wife, Nicole, on vocals. Other musicians included two ex-Uncle Dog members, guitarist John Porter and drummer Terry Stannard, and a percussionist called Demelza. Rumours of impending tours or one-off gigs appeared periodically in the music press but his audience was denied the opportunity to see Winwood play his own music. Nevertheless he did perform with Stomu Yamashta on *Go Live From Paris* (1976) – on which his vocal on 'Crossing The Line' was a highlight – and another concert saw him guesting with Georgie Fame. His second LP, *Arc Of A Diver*, was released in 1980. Between the two he worked on Marianne Faithfull's LP *Broken English* (1979) for which he devised the title track's menacing bass figure.

Arc Of A Diver was the product of much work; Winwood had assembled the entire thing himself. Described as an album of songs by Will Jennings, George Fleming and Viv Stanshall (the three lyricists involved), it contained some powerful performances. His use of synthesisers and electronic keyboard instruments was his most accomplished to date and built on the foundations of *When The Eagle Flies* and *Steve Winwood*. The album's *tour de force* was its title track which married his music to Stanshall's mysterious, tongue-twisting lyrics. The other songs were made by Winwood's vocal energies but lyrically they were much slighter; they attracted criticism, even if it was easy to bathe in their sound (at the expense of their meaning) on songs like 'While You See A Chance', 'Slowdown Sundown' and 'Night Train'.

Night talk

At the end of 1979 there was even talk of Robert Hunter, the Grateful Dead's lyricist, then living in Great Britain, contributing some lyrics but this never got beyond the 'ideas' stage. *Arc Of A Diver* was welcomed, however, and the hours of seclusion in the studio were showing their importance. *Talking Back To The Night* (1982) also made innovative use of Multi-moog and polysynthesiser, former Crusaders lyricist Will Jennings and Winwood having composed all the material. There were still lyrical weaknesses; the reviewer in *Rolling Stone* expressed disquiet that one song had a female's name in the title ('Valerie') calling it 'always a bad sign'.

Despite being proclaimed a superlative singer and musician, Winwood often gives the impression that there is still something within him which should have been nursed out. A musician who has always worked at his own pace, his track record proves that he is more than just a superlative craftsman; he has consistently moved forward, sometimes barely perceptibly, and his use of the studio and its facilities has been increasingly more innovative as technology progresses. He is one of rock music's elder statesmen and one who will continue to develop. KEN HUNT

Traffic in the early Seventies with the Muscle Shoals musicians and percussionist Reebop.

STEVIE WINWOOD
Discography

With Traffic
Singles
Paper Sun/Giving To You (Island WIP 6002, 1967); Hole In My Shoe/Smiling Phases (Island WIP 6017, 1967); Here We Go Round The Mulberry Bush/Coloured Rain (Island WIP 6025, 1967); No Face, No Name, No Number/40,000 Headmen (Island WIP 6030, 1968); Feeling Alright/Withering Tree (Island WIP 6041, 1968); Medicated Goo/Shanghai Noodle Factory (Island WIP 6050, 1968); Walking In The Wind/Walking In The Wind (Instrumental) (Island WIP 6207, 1974).

EPs
Traffic (Island IEP 7, 1978).

Albums
Mr Fantasy (Island ILPS 9061, 1967); *Traffic* (Island ILPS 9081, 1968); *Last Exit* (Island ILPS 9097, 1968); *Best Of Traffic* (Island ILPS 9112, 1969); *John Barleycorn Must Die* (Island ILPS 9116, 1970); *Welcome To The Canteen* (Island ILPS 9166, 1971); *Low Spark Of High Heeled Boys* (Island ILPS 9180, 1971); *Shoot Out At The Fantasy Factory* (Island ILPS 9224, 1973); *On The Road* (Island ILSD 2, 1974); *When The Eagle Flies* (Island ILPS 9273, 1974).

With Blind Faith
Album
Blind Faith (Polydor 583 059, 1969).

Steve Winwood solo
Singles
Time Is Running Out/Penultimate Zone (Island 12-WIP 6394, 1977); While You See A Chance/Vacant Chair (Island WIP 6655, 1980); Spanish Dancer/Hold On (Island WIP 6680, 1981); Night Train/Night Train (Instrumental) (Island WIP 6710, 1981); There's A River/Two Way Stretch (Island WIP 6747, 1981); Still In The Game/Dust (Island WIP 6786, 1982); Valerie/Slowdown Sundown (Island WIP 6818, 1982).

Albums
Steve Winwood (Island ILPS 9494, 1977); *Arc Of A Diver* (Island ILPS 9576, 1980); *Talking Back To The Night* (Island ILPS 9777, 1982).

ENGLAND KEEPS SWINGING

In the wake of the Beatles-led British invasion of the music scene, many different talents were given the opportunity to establish themselves, some through the auspices of the Beatles' own ill-fated Apple venture. While the Stones and Pink Floyd have consolidated their success to become institutions in their own right, others proved less enduring with the fickle public. In their time, however, all contributed significantly to the mood of the era, giving evidence that, by night or by day, England was a super-hip place to be

THROUGH THE PAST *Darkly*

The longest-running success story in rock

'Mick Jagger is the perfect pop star,' Elton John once said. 'He's rude, he's ugly attractive, he's brilliant. The Rolling Stones are the perfect pop group – they don't give a shit.' Forgetting for a moment Jagger's undoubted personal charisma, the Stones' pop perfection stems from their success in embracing the mainstream musical direction of the moment, often gracing it with some glib but appropriate social comment. In their heyday at the end of the Sixties they did actually direct the musical status quo, but by the mid Seventies they had again become derivative, as they had been in their early days covering black R&B numbers.

Like their music, their image management has moved astutely with the times, from raggedy long-hairs in an era of smart suits and fixed smiles to sexual ambiguity, male chauvinism and druggy innuendo in a variety of guises. When flower-power bloomed, the Stones wore *de rigeur* paisley and velvet flares, but perverted the image with an aura of sorcery and decadence; when glam-rock glittered, Jagger wore sequinned jumpsuits but had 'It's Only Rock'n'Roll' spray-painted all over London.

The Stones began to roll early in 1962 when Keith Richards, Brian Jones, Charlie Watts and Ian Stewart were all members of a loose-knit collection of bands associated with Alexis Korner's Blues Incorporated. They had come together the previous year, although Jagger and Richards had spent time together at Maypole County Primary School when they were both about six or seven.

The catalyst was Dick Taylor, later to become guitarist with one of the Stones' less successful but almost as long-lived contemporaries, the Pretty Things. Taylor was at Dartford Grammar School with Jagger, encountering Richards at Sidcup Art School where almost everybody seemed to be forming beat groups. Taylor brought Jagger into his band, the Blue Boys, and Richards was soon there too, after a chance meeting that Keith describes thus: 'So I get on this fucking train one morning and there's Jagger and under his arm he has four or five albums. I haven't seen him since I bought an ice-cream off him . . . we recognised each other straight off . . . and under his arm he's got Chuck Berry, Little Walter, Muddy Waters. . . .'

In those days the names of these obscure black American musicians were passports to a vibrant netherworld of smoky basement clubs and art school dances. Blues and R&B were just emerging in a peculiar Anglicised form, initially promoted by jazzmen like Chris Barber and quickly taken up by students. One of these was Brian Jones, studying at Cheltenham Art College but playing sax and clarinet with local jazz bands at night. After enthusing over this new music with Alexis Korner when the latter was gigging in Cheltenham, Brian persuaded himself that if he wanted to pursue a career in R&B, he'd have to move to London. This he did and, supporting himself by working in department stores, he regularly played guitar with Alexis' band (which at the time included Charlie Watts and harmonica virtuoso Cyril Davies).

It was at one of the Korner band's resident gigs at the Ealing Blues Club that Jones met the Blue Boys. By this time Jones had become sufficiently confident in his direction to put a 'musicians wanted' advertisement in *Jazz News*, and through this had discovered pianist Ian Stewart and singer Paul Jones (also known as P. P. Pond and later to become front-man for Manfred Mann and then the Blues Band). But at Ealing Blues Club the die was cast.

Jagger began rehearsing with Jones and Stewart, later bringing along Richards and Taylor. Another guitarist, Geoff Bradford, was introduced to the team by Stewart, who had extensive jazz connections; Stewart was also responsible for securing the services of any drummer who could or would play R&B. After months spent starving together in a Fulham bedsitter, Jones, Jagger and Richards eventually found themselves a regular drummer, Tony Chapman, and began promoting their own gigs because no one else would book them. Jagger was still earning a few pounds singing with Blues Incorporated at the time and that, together with unused luncheon vouchers donated by Stewart and food parcels from Richards' mother, sustained them through 1962.

Chapman was a travelling salesman who never made it to practice sessions and, in any case, they'd only enlisted him in the

Top far left: The Stones before psychedelia. Top left: In the shade of Sgt Pepper. Above left: Brian Jones (left) at the beggars' banquet. Below left: Mick Taylor (back row) in the navy. Below right: Ron Wood (left) joins the boys in the band.

absence of anyone better. The fledgling Stones had left an open invitation to Charlie Watts, but since he'd already left Blues Incorporated because the gigs were getting too frequent and he had a lucrative day job in advertising, he wasn't overly keen to join Jagger and company. (Jagger soon left the Korner band after one of those famous 'differences of musical opinion'.) Eventually Watts decided to throw in his lot, but not before his predecessor, Tony Chapman, had introduced the band to one Bill Wyman (né Perks), who played bass guitar for a band called the Cliftons. Wyman passed the audition on the strength of his ownership of a good amplifier rather than for his musical ability.

Crawdaddy to Chelsea

With the British R&B fraternity rapidly becoming as cliquey and hidebound as the jazz world from which it had emerged, the Rolling Stones were already trading on the rebel image and finding a ready audience. They secured a residency at Giorgio Gomelsky's Crawdaddy Club in Richmond, generating a buzz that extended far beyond the art college and Chelsea sets into the music business – at that time overburdened with nice young people singing about nice young things. It was at the Crawdaddy that they met their future

Getting their act together: the Stones in rehearsal (above). Bill Wyman (left) and Keith Richards (far right) practise their licks; Brian Jones (right) listens in. Below right: An unusual early shot of Jagger playing guitar with Richards.

manager Andrew Loog Oldham. What Oldham saw in the band can be deduced from his famous aphorism: 'Pop music is sex, and you have to hit them in the face with it.'

As a result, Oldham told the group that Ian Stewart didn't fit in with the image he was about to promote for them; he was just too straight. To this day, Stewart remains an essential adjunct to the Stones' music, playing on recording sessions and on their tours. In May 1963, Oldham produced his and the band's first record, a revved-up version of Chuck Berry's 'Come On', backed with Willie Dixon's 'I Want To Be Loved'. The Stones were promptly spruced up and put into houndstooth check jackets for an appearance on ABC-TV's 'Thank Your Lucky Stars', along with such squeaky-clean outfits as the Cadets Showband, the Viscounts and Helen Shapiro.

Their performance clearly made some impact; 'Come On' was in the pop charts for 14 weeks, reaching the dizzy heights of Number 21. The Stones consolidated this success by gigging any and everywhere. They played small clubs, managed to get a place low on the bill of the prestigious Third National Jazz Festival and were added to the bill of one of those six-act, 20-minutes-a-set packages that toured the cinemas of Great Britain during the Sixties. In these, the halcyon days of Merseybeat when everyone was forming beat groups and claiming to come from Liverpool, joining a bill with the Everly Brothers, Julie Grant and Bo Diddley might have seemed an odd move. But Diddley was one of their idols (they had already backed him on his 'Saturday Club' radio appearance) and when promoter Don Arden flew in Little Richard to boost flagging attendances, the tour suddenly became a real rock'n'roll show.

By this time, Oldham had persuaded John Lennon and Paul McCartney to write 'I Wanna Be Your Man' for the Stones. With an added banshee guitar riff and Jagger's coarsest vocal, it was in the charts within a month of its November release. Aided no doubt by the fact that they'd bashed the song out to 60 cinema-sized audiences in the space of a month, the record reached Number 12 and stayed in the best-seller lists for 16 weeks.

In those days it was unusual for a group to make an album after only one or two hit singles, but EPs were a popular tactic to capitalise on such successes while allowing an act to show its versatility. The Stones were to release two of these in 1964, and the first, *The Rolling Stones*, coincided with the band's first headlining tour. Although Keith and Mick were making their first, tentative steps toward original composition, they decided to play safe with American R&B material, most notably a ballad, in Arthur Alexander's anguished 'You'd Better Move On'. This EP also included a stab at 'Money', Barrett Strong's US hit which had been recorded by the Beatles for the *With The Beatles* album released in November 1963.

Fuelled by the achievements of the tour and EP, the Stones quickly put out a cover of the Crickets' 'Not Fade Away' as a heavily Bo Diddley-riffed single. The subject of much speculation about production credits, the session was attended by Phil Spector and Gene Pitney. While it's not clear if Spector had a hand in the knob-twiddling, he did co-author the B-side, a thinly disguised re-hash of Jimmy Reed's 'Shame, Shame, Shame' called 'Little By Little'. Pitney played piano on this, and maracas on 'Not Fade Away'.

The single soon shot to Number 3, and long before it finally disappeared from the charts, the Stones had already released their first album. Titled – like the first EP – with the band's name, it contained just one and a half self-penned numbers – the steady, marching crescendo of 'Tell Me', and half of 'Little By Little', which was co-written by Phil Spector and Keith Richards, hiding under his pseudonym 'Phelge' (Jagger's was Nanker). The two main Stones were not very confident of their writing abilities then, and their early efforts went to other artists; 'As Tears Go By' was recorded by Marianne Faithfull, and 'That Girl Belongs To Yesterday' by Gene Pitney, for example. The Stones preferred to rely on black soul and R&B material like Chuck Berry's arrangement of 'Route 66', and Marvin Gaye's 'Can I Get A Witness'.

In June 1964, the band went to Chicago and recorded in the legendary Chess Records studio, where many of the records they had covered had originally been created. They cut a radically different version of the Valentinos' near-acappella 'It's All Over Now', and five tracks for the *Five By Five* EP which represent possibly the best work of these early years. The single was their first to hit the Number 1 spot, and the EP caused a small stir in its inclusion of a lengthy instrumental jam, '2120 South Michigan Avenue' (the address of Chess Records).

Rock'n'roll rumpus

Back in Britain, the Stones began developing their notoriety. After topping the bill at the National Jazz and Blues Festival, they toured as headliners over Charlie and Inez Foxx, causing riots almost everywhere. The mayhem extended to Europe, where audiences were even more ebullient and frequently trashed the venues the Stones played at. Preceded by this bad reputation, the band flew off for an autumn tour of America, caused a rumpus during a television appearance on the staid 'Ed Sullivan Show' (Sullivan subsequently announced a ban on rock'n'roll) and established themselves as a major weapon in the current British invasion.

This was something of a paradox, for most of the British bands then making it in the US were blatantly pop. The Stones had little wish to compromise their R&B heritage for the sake of further fame and fortune and, despite pressure from both their British (Decca) and American (London) labels, they next released a moody, suggestive version of Willie Dixon's 'Little Red Rooster'. It went to Number 1, and from then on it seemed as though the Rolling Stones could do exactly as they liked. By mid-1965, this included urinating on garage forecourts, an incident which led to the celebrated prosecution against Jagger, Wyman and Jones, for 'insulting behaviour' on 22 July that year.

Earlier in 1965, the band had released their second album, recorded hastily in London, Chicago and Los Angeles. The package followed Oldham's audacious practice of having no name on its cover, and included more original material. In June that same year they put out their third EP, the raucous, screaming *Got Live If You Want It*, a highly-successful recorded testimony to the Stones' live impact.

In August 1965 Allen Klein took on the management of the band and Oldham's business affairs, and in September the Stones' third album, *Out Of Our Heads*, was released. This was the first to be produced entirely in the United States, and one distinguished by little except an obvious softening of their approach, presumably in deference to American markets. The R&B was still there – the raw edge wasn't.

The same could not be said of their next offering, *Aftermath*, which had Phil Spector's arranger, Jack Nitzsche, on hand to flesh out the relationship between the musicians. This particularly benefited Brian Jones, already the *enfant terrible* of the band but a natural musician who could quickly turn his hand to almost any instrument. Jones added dulcimer, sitar and organ to *Aftermath*, his artistry most notable on 'Goin' Home', an 11 minute 35 second track that completes the first side. This loping, mesmeric number foreshadowed much of what was to come on *Their Satanic Majesties*, *Beggars Banquet* and *Let It Bleed*: raga rock with R&B roots.

Aftermath also exhibited the growing confidence of Jagger and Richards' songwriting, a phenomenon unfortunately steeped in chauvinism, even misogyny; the strongest tracks – 'Stupid Girl', 'Under My Thumb' and 'Out Of Time' – all disparage women to varying degrees. The Stones have often attracted criticism on this level – the sadistic advertising for the *Black And Blue* album and the lyrics of 'Some Girls' being the most blatant example of their disdain for womankind. Jagger himself made his attitude clear: 'There's really no reason to have women on a tour unless they've got a job to do. The only other reason is to screw.'

Perform!

1968 saw the first of many attempts by the Stones to emulate the Beatles' success in the cinema. *Only Lovers Left Alive*, a projected multi-million dollar enterprise to be co-produced by Oldham and Klein, never materialised. Nor did 'Rock'n'Roll Circus', a planned 1967 TV extravaganza which was to have starred Cream, Marianne Faithfull, and John Lennon and Yoko Ono. Of the Stones' films that did materialise, *Ned Kelly* (1969) was an embarrassment to all concerned while *Michael Kohlhaas* (1969), a historical costume drama with David Warner, Anita Pallenberg and Keith Richards, was quickly withdrawn.

The Stones' reputation has always been dependent on a display of sexual bravado; lyrics bragged of their prowess, while the press reinforced the image, photographing them with a succession of women. Anita Pallenberg (top left) with Keith, Bianca Jagger (left), Marianne Faithfull (below left) and Jerry Hall (below) with Mick, were all caught in the eye of the lens.

More successful was *Performance*. Made in 1969 but delayed by a nervous Warner Brothers until 1971, it featured Jagger as a decadent, androgynous pop recluse who shelters gangster James Fox and offered a tantalising glimpse of Sixties rock excess. This was also captured in the Maysles brothers' *Gimme Shelter* (1970), a documentary about the carnage at the Stones' concert at Altamont, and in *Cocksucker Blues*, Robert Frank's 1972 documentary about the sexual antics and drug abuse surrounding the Stones on tour that he was legally restrained from screening.

1967 saw the Rolling Stones cast as scapegoats for the drug culture that was spreading far and wide in the wake of flower-power. In February Keith's home in West Wittering was raided by 15 policemen and various substances were confiscated; Jagger was subsequently charged with possession of pep pills, while Richards was accused of allowing his house to be used for pot smoking. When the case reached court in June, they were both given absurdly heavy fines *and* prison sentences. This prompted the famous leader in *The Times*, 'Who Breaks A Butterfly On A Wheel?', in which editor William Rees-Mogg eloquently questioned the quality of British justice. The two Stones were released from prison on bail and their sentences quashed on appeal.

Brian Jones, meanwhile, had been arrested for possession of drugs at his London flat. Soon afterwards he had a nervous breakdown and, after being sentenced in court to nine months' imprisonment, he again collapsed prior to an appeal being heard. A team of three psychiatrists assessed him as 'a very frightened young man', and the appeal judge dismissed the sentence against him.

The traumas continued throughout 1967, with the sacking of Andrew Oldham as Stones manager. Klein himself got the boot in 1970, some time before he fell foul of his other superstar clients, the Beatles. As might be expected, the Stones' recording output suffered in 1967, and also reflected their troubles. *Between The Buttons*, released in January, was Oldham's final production credit and betrayed a weariness and a paucity of good material. The familiar themes of sex and drugs mingled uneasily with vestiges of fey English pop music. There was, however, a little more force behind 'We Love You', the single released to celebrate the dropping of prison sentences (complete with a slamming cell door, Lennon and McCartney on backing vocals and Brian Jones all over the place on Mellotron). In spite of the public support the band marshalled during their ordeals following the bust, the single only went as high as Number 8.

In December, the album *Their Satanic Majesties Request* came out in an expensive laminated 3-D cover, and consisted of quasi-cosmic rock dirges and space chants. This was a radical new musical direction for the Stones, one in which they committed the rare mistake of making their experiments in public. But as Charlie Watts said afterwards: 'Sometimes I think it was a miracle that we produced *anything* under the pressures and emotional upheavals within the group.' The album reached Number 3 in the UK charts.

The embodiment of evil

It was the end of an era, both for pop music and the Stones. In 1968, the beleagured Brian Jones was again busted, three days before the release of the group's classic Number 1 single, 'Jumping Jack Flash'. The song was a menacing dance for the Devil, with Jagger at his most arch and the chiming guitars of Jones and Richards casting an appropriate spell. It embodied all the evil the Stones had been confronted with and, of course, generated themselves; 'Jumping Jack Flash' became the Stones' new and abiding alter ego.

But Jones was fading fast; he couldn't stand the legal and personal pressures, and his contribution to their next album, *Beggars Banquet*, was minimal. The album is a masterpiece, a musical antidote to the vacillations of *Satanic Majesties* and full of brooding, anarchic images, yet still spattered with Jagger-ish whimsy like 'Factory Girl'. Now under the firm production guidance of American and former Spencer Davis Group producer Jimmy Miller, the LP begins with one of the ultimate Stones anthems, 'Sympathy For The Devil', replete with jungle-ish conga, devilish yelps and powerhouse guitar work from Keith. 'Sympathy' is a tour de force only equalled by 'Gimme Shelter' off the subsequent album, *Let It Bleed*, in 1969. The Stones never recovered the pulsating, manic form of these two tracks until 1972 and *Exile On Main Street*.

Sadly though, Brian Jones couldn't cope any longer, and officially left the group on 9 June 1969. Less than a month later he was found unconscious in the swimming pool of his Sussex home, but by the time a doctor arrived he was dead. Jones' replacement was Mick Taylor, a rather shy but highly-respected guitarist from that veritable nursery school of British R&B, John Mayall's Bluesbreakers. His first public appearance with the Stones was at a free concert in London's Hyde Park, two days after Brian's death; Jagger read an epitaph from Shelley, wore a frock and released several thousand butterflies into the air. A tropical breed unaccustomed to the climate, they all died within minutes. It was a strange and sad occasion.

Mick was again busted for drugs in 1969, along with his girlfriend Marianne Faithfull. *Let It Bleed* was released, continuing the image of the Stones as benign agents of the Devil, and containing some of their best music, and the ill-fated Altamont concert ended the year on a low note. Hastily arranged after the original venue had been cancelled, Altamont was a day of unease and violence culminating in the fatal stabbing of a young Negro, Meredith Hunter, by the Hell's Angels hired as 'security guards' on the advice of the Grateful Dead. The Stones were visibly shaken by this experience; their flirtation with the Antichrist had perhaps become too close to reality and backfired on them.

Despite European and UK tours and the release of their first live album, *Get Yer Ya-Ya's Out!* (fulfilling their expiring Decca contract), the following year was a quiet one for the Stones while 1971 was notable for the press hoopla over Mick's wedding to Bianca Perez Moreno de Macias in St Tropez and the group's establishment of their own record label, distributed by Kinney. *Sticky Fingers* was the first fruit from that union, an abundantly decadent album but one that rocked with a vengeance. As Bill Wyman put it: 'With *Sticky Fingers* we are going back to the public with the blues that made us.'

Blues it most certainly was, and it fairly sizzled with the sax and trumpet of Bobby Keyes and Jim Price, an addition they decided to take on the road with them in 1972. This infamous, gruelling three-month trek, filmed by Robert Frank and chronicled in book form by Robert Greenfield, involved every excess and almost every incident known in rock'n'roll mythology. Having hardly recovered from this massive troop movement, Keith and Anita faced more drug charges on the French Riviera, and Mick and Bianca rushed to try and find Bianca's mother after the devastation of the Nicaraguan earthquake.

Halfway through the following year, Keith Richards and Anita Pallenberg were busted again, this time in London and for illegal possession of a .38 revolver as well as the inevitable collection of narcotics. With them at the house in Cheyne Walk were the exotically-titled Prince Stanislaus Klossowski and Baron de Watteville, ironically confirming the Stones' gradual absorption into the jet-set elite which was to become their natural habitat for the rest of their career. Indeed, 1973 was in many ways the year the Stones ceased to be the big, bad boys of rock'n'roll and became celebrities instead. The Stones were now moving beyond the acceptable boundaries of rock-star ostentation, and it's hard to be a street fighting man when you've got a villa in France and an estate in England.

The whip comes down

Debilitated by their excesses, demoralised by their busts (and Keith still had a big one ahead of him in Canada), the Stones began a slow but perceptible retreat. *Goat's Head Soup*, their 1973 album, contains some fine rocking dance tunes, but it didn't do anything the band hadn't already tried. The album that followed it, *It's Only Rock 'n'Roll*, was more of the same – good, workmanlike rock that was unmistakably the Stones, but not much more. Even its title track failed to become the anthem it perhaps should have done, reaching only Number 9 in the UK charts and staying in them just seven weeks. Something was wrong, and when Mick Taylor left the group in December 1974, there was speculation that it was either the end of the Stones as a performing band or a recognition that some hot new blood was needed.

In April 1975, after much auditioning, Faces' guitarist Ron Wood 'temporarily' joined the band for an American tour, their first since 1972. A contemporary of the band back in the R&B days of 1964 and 1965 when he gigged in several London bands, Wood had the wasted looks and cavalier temperament of a true Stone. More of a showman and less of a technician than Mick Taylor, he had already worked with Keith on solo projects and he fitted in just fine, but it wasn't until December 1975 that he was finally admitted into the inner sanctum. Wood only played on two tracks on the next LP, *Black And Blue*, as the lads had cannily tried out various guitarists for possible enlistment during its recording, including Wayne Perkins (who nearly got the job), and Harvey Mandel, formerly of Canned Heat.

Black And Blue was the Stones' last studio album for two years, and from then on similar intervals punctuated their LP releases, and they stopped recording material specifically for singles. Of course there was, as there always had been, the inevitable compilations, live albums and a plethora of bootlegs. There were also tours, sometimes on the grand scale, seemingly bent on recreating the halcyon days of the Major Event, sometimes merely lightning raids on small European halls. Having reached a peak of musical originality in the 1968-70 period, the Stones found it hard – or even inconceivable – to revert to what they'd once been so adept at: taking other musical forms and absorbing them into their own material. By the mid Seventies they were essentially recycling a groove that had long since run out.

But in 1978, *Some Girls* indicated that they could still suss out the predominant influence of the pop scene – in this case, disco – and make something of their own from it (something they'd wisely avoided with punk, which would *really* have been an embarrassment). *Some Girls* is a pretty decent assemblage of music, as are the albums they made subsequently (*Emotional Rescue* and *Tattoo You*), each of which reflect contemporary trends as much as the Stones probably dare without risking parody or anachronism. But how long can it go on? Ask Mick Jagger: 'I'd rather be dead than singing "Satisfaction" when I'm forty-five.' MARK WILLIAMS

Look, no leads! As their stages got bigger (inset far right), the Stones abandoned cable microphones (inset right) for radio mikes (centre).

THE ROLLING STONES
Discography

Singles
Come On/I Want To Be Loved (Decca F11675, 1963); I Wanna Be Your Man/Stoned (Decca F11764, 1963); Not Fade Away/Little By Little (Decca F11845, 1964); It's All Over Now/Good Times, Bad Times (Decca F11934, 1964); Little Red Rooster/Off The Hook (Decca F12014, 1964); The Last Time/Play With Fire (Decca F12104, 1965); (I Can't Get No) Satisfaction/Spider And The Fly (Decca F12220, 1965); Get Off Of My Cloud/The Singer Not The Song (Decca F12263, 1965); 19th Nervous Breakdown/As Tears Go By (Decca F12331, 1966); Paint It Black/Long Long While (Decca F12395, 1966); Have You Seen Your Mother Baby/Who's Driving Your Plane (Decca F12497, 1966); Let's Spend The Night Together/Ruby Tuesday (Decca F12546, 1967); We Love You/Dandelion (Decca F12654, 1967); Jumping Jack Flash/Child Of The Moon (Decca F12782, 1968); Honky Tonk Women/You Can't Always Get What You Want (Decca F12952, 1969); Street Fighting Man/Surprise Surprise (Decca F13203, 1970); Brown Sugar/Bitch/Let It Rock (Rolling Stones RS19100, 1971); Tumbling Dice/Sweet Black Angel (Rolling Stones RS19103, 1972); Sad Day/You Can't Always Get What You Want (Decca F13404, 1973); Angie/Silver Train (Rolling Stones RS19105, 1973); It's Only Rock'n'Roll/Through The Lonely Nights (Rolling Stones RS19114, 1974); I Don't Know Why/Try A Little Harder (Decca F13584, 1975); Out Of Time/Jiving Sister Fanny (Decca F13597, 1975); Honky Tonk Women/Sympathy For The Devil (Decca F13635, 1976); Fool To Cry/Crazy Mama (Rolling Stones RS19121, 1976); Miss You/Faraway Eyes (Rolling Stones EMI2802, 1978); Respectable/When The Whip Comes Down (Rolling Stones EMI2861, 1978); Emotional Rescue/Down In The Hole (Rolling Stones RSR105, 1980); She's So Cold/Send It To Me (Rolling Stones RSR106, 1980); Start Me Up/No Use In Crying (Rolling Stones RSR108, 1981);

Waiting On A Friend/Little T&A (Rolling Stones RSR109, 1981); (I Can't Get No) Satisfaction/Under Assistant West Coast Promotion Man (Decca F12220, 1982); Going To A Go Go/Beast Of Burden (Rolling Stones RSR110, 1982).

EPs
The Rolling Stones (Decca DFE8560, 1964); *Five By Five* (Decca DFE8590, 1964); *Got Live If You Want It* (Decca DFE8620, 1965).

Albums
The Rolling Stones (Decca LK4605, 1964); *The Rolling Stones No 2* (Decca LK4661, 1965); *Out Of Our Heads* (Decca SKL4773, 1965); *Aftermath* (Decca SKL4786, 1966); *Big Hits (High Tide And Green Grass)* (Decca TXS101, 1966); *Between The Buttons* (Decca SKL4852, 1967); *Their Satanic Majesties Request* (Decca TXS103, 1967); *Beggars Banquet* (Decca SKL4955, 1968); *Through The Past Darkly (Big Hits Vol 2)* (Decca SKL5019, 1969); *Let It Bleed* (Decca SKL5025, 1969); *Get Yer Ya-Yas Out!* (Decca SKL5065, 1970); *Stone Age* (Decca SKL5084, 1971); *Sticky Fingers* (Rolling Stones COC59100, 1971); *Milestones* (Decca SKL5098, 1972); *Exile On Main Street* (Rolling Stones COC69100, 1972); *Gimme Shelter* (Decca SKL5101, 1972); *Rock'n'Rolling Stones* (Decca SKL5149, 1972); *Goat's Head Soup* (Rolling Stones COC59101, 1973); *No Stone Unturned* (Decca SKL5173, 1973); *It's Only Rock'n'Roll* (Rolling Stones COC59103, 1974); *Made In The Shade* (Rolling Stones COC59104, 1975); *Metamorphosis* (Decca SKL5212, 1975); *Rolled Gold* (Decca ROST1/2, 1975); *Black And Blue* (Rolling Stones COC59106, 1976); *Get Stoned* (Arcade ADEP32, 1977); *Love You Live* (Rolling Stones COC89101, 1977); *Some Girls* (Rolling Stones CUN39108, 1978); *Time Waits For No One* (Rolling Stones COC59107, 1979); *Emotional Rescue* (Rolling Stones CUN39111, 1980); *Sucking In The Seventies* (Rolling Stones CUNS39112, 1980); *Tattoo You* (Rolling Stones CUNS39114, 1981); *Still Life* (Rolling Stones CUNS39115, 1982).

From Dylan imitation to pure psychedelia

THE HUGELY-POPULAR and all-too shortlived 'Ready Steady Go!', which brought so many groups and artists to the attention of British television viewers in the mid Sixties, attempted to recreate a live, club atmosphere. In keeping with this aim, it was decided to accord certain acts the status of resident performers, providing these combos or individuals with almost unprecedented public exposure. The first such to be chosen was a (for the time) quite outrageously scruffy young expatriate Scot with a snub nose, a birdsnest of curly black locks, a Dylan cap and a breathy, reedy voice tinged with an affected Celtic lilt and laced with a curious but entirely natural vibrato.

Donovan suddenly popped up in millions of households during the early months of 1965 singing an insistently catchy, self-penned folkie ballad called 'Catch The Wind' to his own solo accompaniment of a battered and weatherbeaten acoustic guitar prominently emblazoned 'This Machine Kills', a bowdlerisation of Woody Guthrie's more pointed original 'This Machine Kills Fascists'. Donovan's guitar didn't actually kill anyone, but he succeeded in stunning the masses.

Right: Donovan's early image was modelled closely on Dylan, and for a while he sat on the fence between protest-folk and flower-power whimsy. Below: Launching his career on 'Ready Steady Go!'

Sunshine Superman

Donovan Leitch was born on 10 May 1946 in Glasgow, but the Leitch household quit Scotland while he was still a child and settled in the ancient and picturesque Hertfordshire market town of St Albans. There Donovan whiled away his teens dreaming of unfettered horizons and hanging out with other local disaffected post-Beat poets, pre-hippie types like his close friend Gypsy Dave and future songwriter Mick Softley. Legend has it that they were a talented crew but rather lacking in motivation and only Donovan could bestir himself enough to make the 30-mile excursion to London to seek his fortune.

For a while the Dylan parallel was enough to sustain the young singer, who stuck to his mysterious hobo persona through 1965. Donovan had been snapped up by Pye Records in the wake of his 'Ready Steady Go!' appearances; 'Catch The Wind' was his first release on the label. The single reached Number 4 in the UK charts in April. 'Colours', the similar-sounding follow-up, hit the Top Thirty two months later, eventually achieving the same position as its predecessor. The year also saw two hastily assembled albums *What's Bin Did And What's Bin Hid* and *Fairytale*, both of which were all-acoustic pot-pourris of sub-Zimmerman satiric protest, Woody Guthrie songs, folk-club standards and engaging originals that exposed the fertile, if hopelessly romantic imagination of a questing, questioning visionary.

Dylan himself was now evolving from a starcrossed folkie into the original rock 'n'roll intellectual poet; on his *Bringing It All Back Home* LP in 1965 he employed electric instruments on one of its sides and Donovan, keeping tabs on his hero (and never much of a loyalist folkie anyway), was delighted. With vague desires towards setting sail for uncharted electric possibilities he ran into pop producer Mickie Most, who had proved his commercial acumen in 1964 by producing the Animals' 'House Of The Rising Sun'. Most succeeded in luring Donovan out of his Dylan impersonation and into the guise with which he has stuck to this day since it mirrors Mr Leitch's character so exactly, that of the psychedelic mystic and eternal child.

The growing hippie scene in San Francisco had brought on an age of euphoria and optimism and the Most/Donovan camp set out to supply some psychedelic candyfloss. A string of inimitable classic singles followed, beginning with the hazy drone of the influential 'Sunshine Superman'/'The Trip' – a UK Number 3 and US charttopper – and continuing through the paisley whimsies of 'Mellow Yellow' (a UK Number 8 and US Number 2) and 'There Is A Mountain', another UK Number 8 which reached Number 11 in the US. But whereas Dylan had emerged as a serious, driven subversive, an icon for the alternative society, Donovan, always less in touch with real life, instead went for the immediate and enormous commercial rewards yielded by flower power.

Donovan's first Mickie Most-produced album, *Sunshine Superman*, seemed to encapsulate the whole hippie/flower child vision while the singer's statements, often quoted in the press, were equally in step with the hopeful, celebratory times: 'Pop is the perfect religious vehicle,' he told *Queen* magazine in 1967. 'It's as if God had come down to earth and seen all the ugliness that was being created and chosen pop to be the great force for love and beauty.'

Celtic dreams

But with the winter of 1967 came the first signs of hippie disillusionment. While others, such as Jefferson Airplane and Country Joe and the Fish, turned their attentions to more active anti-establishment musical forms, Donovan retained his kaftan and his vague dreams of spiritual bliss. *A Gift From A Flower To A Garden*, an expensive double album released in 1968, came in a classical music-type box adorned with the image of Maharishi Mahesh Yogi, the Eastern guru. It contained two vividly contrasting records, one a round-up of ten excessively twee flower power songs, the other a captivating collection of all-acoustic material that exuded spiritual power and Celtic mystery. 'Isle Of

Islay' was proof of Donovan's sincere commitment to his muse and fascination with his ancestral homeland, but – unfortunately – the depth of feeling and clarity of the second disc was largely ignored in favour of the quaint imagery of the first, with numbers like 'Wear Your Love Like Heaven'; in a way, Donovan's fate was thereby sealed.

However Donovan, with Most still producing, still managed to turn out hits in 1968 with the bubbly 'Jennifer Juniper', a UK Number 5 and US Number 26, the churning 'Hurdy Gurdy Man' (Numbers 4 and 5 respectively), the ethereal 'Atlantis' (Numbers 23 and 7) and the skip-beat tongue-twister 'Barabajagal', a Number 12 UK hit in 1969 on which the singer was backed by the Jeff Beck Group. The two further 1968 albums, *Hurdy Gurdy Man* and *Barabajagal*, ran the gamut from light cocktail jazz to string-drenched meditations and buzzsaw rock, from the lascivious strut of 'Superlungs My Supergirl' (later superbly covered by Terry Reid) to such infantile idiocy as 'I Love My Shirt'. Strangely, Pye declined to release either LP in the UK where Donovan's popularity was on the decline. In the States, however, where the records were released on Epic, Donovan remained as popular as ever.

Along the open road

His next release in his home country was *Donovan In Concert* which featured some very spare, jazz-flecked readings of audience favourites performed by the late Harold McNair (flute), Danny Thompson (acoustic bass) and Tony Carr (drums). The album showed that Donovan was attempting to leave rock behind in order to emulate the success of the much hipper Incredible String Band.

Donovan now became obsessed with the idea of a mutant strain of music he called Celtic Rock, and in order to realise it (and perhaps incidentally in order to revive a flagging career) he formed a group known as Open Road with John Carr and Mike Thompson, a democratic unit in which the whole group sang and composed. Following a brief interlude on the Leitch estate near Dunvegan in the Isle of Skye to soak up the timeless atmosphere and sling a set together, almost apologetically unleashed an LP *Open Road* on Pye's new 'progressive' Dawn label.

Artistically *Open Road* was a success, a direct and honest bootleg-style production by Don himself who flew directly in the face of the 1970 trend of over-elaborate and baroque 'progressive' values by recording the group as if they had just set up in the listener's living room. He supplied a dozen of his most varied, heartfelt and committed songs for the occasion, from the irresistible minor US hit 'Riki Tiki Tavi' to the scathing 'Poke At The Pope' and the icy beauty of 'Roots Of Oak'. Unfortunately it was a resounding commercial failure.

Donovan had still not managed to shake off his hippie/flower child image and thus seemed a natural choice to play the Pied Piper of Hamlyn in David Puttnam's 1971 film *The Pied Piper*. The disappointing fantasy featured Donovan flitting across the pastures in garish robes, blowing down a recorder and contributing little dialogue.

The film made a negligible impact and, perhaps because of his increasingly low profile, Donovan's next album – his last for Dawn – leaked out rather like a guilty secret with little or no publicity. *HMS Donovan* saw Leitch revisiting both his roots and the mists of childhood. A two-record, almost totally solo set comprised of quiet, self-penned vignettes and lullabyes peppered with Don's musical settings of poems by the likes of Lewis Carroll and Edward Lear and the occasional masterpiece like his luminously lovely reading of Yeats' 'Song Of The Wandering Aengus' and the traditional shanty 'Henry Martin', *HMS Donovan* was effectively the swansong of a unique artist. Arresting and intimate, it sold virtually no copies, although it did sire a US hit single in its one electric track, 'Celia Of The Seals'.

Nothing more was heard until late 1972 when the Most-produced *Cosmic Wheels* appeared on the UK Epic label amid much media gabble about a Donovan revival. The LP had its moments (particularly the stirring title cut) but mainly seemed to underline Don's reputation as a spent force, difficult to deny in the face of the puerile jokes of 'The Intergalactic Laxative', a song concerning the lavatorial activities of astronauts. An endless parade of ever more redundant product followed in a steady stream throughout the Seventies as Donovan flitted from one producer and set of session men to another.

Albums like 1973's Andrew Loog Oldham-produced *Essence To Essence* and Donovan's 1976 offering, *Slow Down World* came and went in a welter of clumsy production, lacklustre performances and dangerously thin material. An exception was 1974's *7-Tease*, an ambitious 'concept' album cut in Nashville under producer Norbert Putnam which was chiefly notable for its portrayal of the artist haplessly adrift outside his own era and bewildered by the cynicism of the modern world and its cruel rejection of his homilies which it once seemed so ready and eager to embrace. But it was product like *7-Tease* – which took a year to record and cost enormous sums of Epic money – that finally led the label to drop Donovan in the late Seventies. He vanished into obscurity, living in America with his wife Linda on the edge of the Mojave desert and, in his own words, 'raising babies in the sun'.

Donovan weathered the late Seventies new wave by remaining determinedly invisible but in 1981 he showed signs of stirring from the torpor he had sunk into, with an acoustic album released only in Europe called *Neutronica* and with an increased willingness to perform in public.

By the end of the year, Donovan Leitch had settled in Windsor, Berkshire and was displaying a marked desire to continue to perform and record. As an artist, he had had more revivals than anyone is really entitled to but a talent such as his can never be spent or written off completely. Conceivably the mood of the times may one day change and the man who signed himself 'Thy humble minstrel' may once more play the Pied Piper for a whole new generation.

STEVE BURGESS

Donovan's castles in the air (inset top) were given substance by his link-up with producer Mickie Most. The astute Most helped transform Donovan from just another folkie (right) to gold disc status (inset right, Most holding record).

DONOVAN
Recommended Listening

Donovan's Greatest Hits (Pye NPL18283) (Includes: Sunshine Superman, Hurdy Gurdy Man, Mellow Yellow, Catch The Wind); *Golden Hour Of Donovan* (Pye Golden Hour GH506) (Includes: Hey Gyp (Dig The Slowness), Sunny Goodge Street, Turquoise, Remember The Alamo, Ballad Of A Crystal Man, War Drags On).

WHO
20

THRESHOLD OF SUCCESS

The symphonic sounds of the Moody Blues

If someone staged a poll to determine the band most likely to possess the key to the mystery of the cosmos, America would probably vote for the Moody Blues. The group would undoubtedly get a sizeable vote throughout the rest of the world, too. Since they released their second album, *Days Of Future Passed*, in 1967, the Moodies have inspired a loyalty in their massive army of fans that amounts to near-fanaticism. And, at the same time, they have been accused by a large body of critics of being both pretentious and boring.

The opinion of those who hold the latter view may have been coloured by the band's enormous success and by a nagging feeling that they have had it easy. The success is true enough: it is almost certain that they had earned more platinum albums worldwide than any other band, bar the Beatles, by the end of 1982. But their route to such status was probably as strewn with problems and pitfalls as any more critically fashionable contender.

The original Moody Blues took shape in June 1964 and comprised members of three Birmingham bands – Denny Laine and the Diplomats, Gary Levene and the Avengers and El Riot and the Rebels. The band consisted of Denny Laine (lead guitar), Mike Pinder (keyboards), Graeme Edge (drums), Ray Thomas (harmonica) and Clint Warwick (bass); vocals were shared between the band members.

Lose your money

Bass guitarist John Lodge had been a member of the band for a short period before that line-up was finalised, but had decided not to go full-time with a band until he had passed his City and Guild examinations. Warwick had been recruited on the understanding that he would be a temporary member of the band. The first Moodies line-up was very much an R&B-based band, playing the circuit of

The young Moodies, with Denny Laine on guitar, hold up rush-hour commuters.

small clubs and pubs around Birmingham and the West Midlands that they had all played in their previous groups.

However, a chance sighting of them by a domestic appliance salesman – who also happened to be a friend of the management team of Alex Murray and Tony Secunda – at a Brum nightclub led to an audition and a contract with the said managers. 'They wanted a band because Tony had been in Seltaeb, the Beatles merchandising company, and had seen how lucrative the music business could be', Graeme Edge recalled years later.

In mid 1964, the Moody Blues landed a contract with Decca, who were possibly hoping to do with Brumbeat what they'd missed out on with Merseybeat. The band's first single was written by Laine and Pinder; aptly titled 'Lose Your Money', it was a flop. They decided to try a different approach and, on sifting through a pile of records, they came across a demo by American blues singer Bessie Banks called 'Go Now'.

They altered the tempo and added a haunting middle eight to round it off. The single was released in January 1965 and was an immediate success. One of the greatest admirers of the song was Paul McCartney, who spent much of his time raving about the record when the Beatles were in Austria filming for *Help!* The single made Number 1 in Britain, Number 10 in the US and did well elsewhere.

Above: The Moody Blues on the threshold of success. Overleaf: Their best-known line-up – Graeme Edge (top left), Mike Pinder (top right), Justin Hayward (centre), John Lodge (bottom left) and Ray Thomas (bottom right).

Tea time blues

Aside from giving them immediate celebrity status in the pop media, however, 'Go Now' didn't do much else for the band. Follow-up singles were flops and they lost their management following an argument about £200 for a celebration party. 'Ironically enough,' recalled Edge, 'we found ourselves with more problems after the record was a hit than before. Paul McCartney helped us out, though, by introducing us to Brian Epstein, who took over our management. This was some time after we'd ended up on the chicken-in-the-basket circuit and after flogging our guts out on the Continent. We never really got a chance to find out what we might have done with him, though; I remember going to his house trying to have a talk with him and being told to go away. I only found out later that that was the day he'd died.'

The Moodies had retired to live in Belgium and work mainly in France. Clint Warwick had left in the summer of 1966 and Denny Laine followed soon after to pursue a solo career that eventually led him to join Paul McCartney in Wings. Lodge came in to replace Warwick, as originally planned, and a young guitarist from Swindon, Justin Hayward, replaced Laine.

Hayward was a songwriter and a session guitarist, earning some of his daily bread by playing on TV jingles: 'There was one I did with Jimmy Page and Clem Cattini, who had been the drummer in the Tornados. It was for Ty-Phoo Tea. We were getting £9 apiece and we didn't think that was enough so I got elected to go to the producer and ask for £12 each. I was told in very short and succinct words to get back into the studio otherwise the only thing we'd get was the sack.'

The addition of Lodge and Hayward, plus a growing dissatisfaction with playing two 40-minute sets a night in northern clubs performing cover versions of hits, gave the band a renewed sense of determination. They had been writing their own material and came up with the idea of a song cycle that would reflect the passage of a day. The climax to the collection of songs was Justin Hayward's 'Nights In White Satin'.

The Moodies got their chance to reveal their new stage show to a major audience when Tom Jones was booked to play the Paris Olympia. The bookers expected Jones to have a full show with him, but the Welshman only had about half an hour's worth of material. The Moodies, then in France, were contacted via agent Colin Berlin. They played their set, got an en-

thusiastic response and felt they had something to offer.

Around the same time Decca's Deram label were anxious to promote a so-called new system of stereo recording called Deramic Super Sound. They were keen to find a whole variety of different musical combinations to record in it and thereby promote this 'breakthrough'. Tom Jones' admiration for the band and Colin Berlin's recommendation of them both led to Deram contracting the Moodies to record a version of Dvorak's 'New World Symphony' with the London Festival Orchestra. Through some miracle of persuasion and diplomacy the Moodies managed to convince producer, arranger and conductor Peter Knight not to record Dvorak's work but their own instead.

'You've got to hand it to Peter Knight!' said Edge. 'He obviously had a lot of faith in us and our music. But it must have taken a hell of a lot of nerve to decide to record *Days Of Future Passed* and present it to the Decca executives when they were expecting Dvorak's "New World Symphony".'

The brave Knight did exactly that, however, and the verdict of Decca's head office was pessimistic; they felt that the recording didn't stand a chance. However, an executive from the American branch of the company heard the demo tape and pronounced emphatically that it would most certainly sell in the States.

The album was by no means an instant success, although it sold well enough to indicate to the Moodies that their style had commercial possibilities. In addition 'Nights In White Satin' gave them their first Top Twenty single in three years, reaching Number 19 in the UK in early 1968. (When re-released in 1972 'Nights' made Number 9 and made a third chart appearance in 1979, peaking at the Number 14 position.)

Passing time profitably

Days Of Future Passed was an impressive album both of its time and outside of it. It was a 'concept' album – still a pejorative phrase in many minds – and was executed with immense style and clarity. Although it was mildly criticised at the time of its release for failing to fuse rock band and symphony orchestra successfully, it has outlasted such similar efforts as Deep Purple's *Concerto For Group And Orchestra* (1970) and *Procol Harum In Concert With The Edmonton Symphony Orchestra* (1972).

By the end of 1968 the album had proved to be a massive seller on both sides of the Atlantic; US sales had topped 150,000 copies, while it sold about 25,000 in Britain. That same year saw the release of the next Moodies album *In Search Of The Lost Chord* which consolidated the band's success. It vaulted into the Top Ten in Britain and America with ease and set the Moody Blues firmly on a musical course – combining complex structures with melodic fluency – from which they have subsequently deviated little.

Aside from the sheer precision of their music – the symphonic arrangements, the sense of dynamics and indeed the very quality of the band's musicianship – allied to the immaculate production of longtime collaborator Tony Clarke, the Moodies' style also depended strongly on their lyrics, which were always perfectly enunciated. Whether by accident or design, these seemed to appeal enormously to vast legions of people by being vaguely-formulated philosophies about such weighty matters as life and the universe.

Universal lyricism

To their credit, however, the Moodies have never claimed that they had a philosophical answer to anything. 'All we've ever done is write how we feel,' said Justin Hayward. 'If people want to read anything extra into the lyrics that's fine.' Ray Thomas was more succinct and consciously more self-deprecating: 'I don't know what half of them are about myself.'

What the Moody Blues have demonstrated more than adequately since the end of the Sixties is that they certainly do know about business. Having released *On The Threshold Of A Dream* in April 1969 – their most successful album, making Number 1 on both sides of the Atlantic – they decided to form their own record company, Threshold. They had started talking to Decca about their own label at the beginning of 1969, the way their records were selling giving them adequate bargaining power. When they announced the formation of Threshold in October of that year they were able to report that they had sold 10 million dollars' worth of albums in the previous two years.

The first release on Threshold was the Moodies' own album *To Our Children's Children's Children*. Inevitably it was a huge seller. Unfortunately the same couldn't be said for fellow Threshold artists like the Justin Hayward discovery Timon – a Liverpool solo singer – or John Lodge protégés Trapeze. Like other artist-owned

labels, Threshold was started with the best possible intentions; the Moodies wanted control over their own artistic creations, of everything from album artwork to singles releases.

Threshold did not pose the Moodies as many problems as Apple did the Beatles, for example. Nonetheless it could have been a contributory factor to the group's later extended 'holiday' which lasted from 1973 to 1978. Complained Thomas: 'I started to worry when I found myself travelling on the Tube at rush hour with a briefcase full of papers which I had to do my homework on. That wasn't why I'd originally joined a band.'

From the formation of Threshold and the release of *Children*, the Moodies released an indefatigable series of mega-platinum albums – *A Question Of Balance, Every Good Boy Deserves Favour* and *Seventh Sojourn*, in 1970, 1971 and 1972 respectively. They also had Top Thirty hit singles on both sides of the Atlantic in the shape of 'Question', 'Isn't Life Strange?' and 'I'm Just A Singer (In A Rock And Roll Band)'.

Top: The Moodies shake their moneymakers. Above: Hayward and Lodge as the Blue Jays. Overleaf: Out of retirement, minus Mike Pinder.

Long distance voyagers

Around the release of *Seventh Sojourn*, the Moody Blues set off on their most extensive tour yet – a true world excursion. It was after that they ceased functioning as a band. 'It seemed a natural thing to do,' said Lodge. 'I think it was just a sort of subconscious decision for us. In fact there was a clue, albeit subconscious, in the title *Seventh Sojourn*. It had obviously come to a time when we needed a sojourn, a rest.'

Both Graeme Edge and Justin Hayward suggested the individual members of the band had a need to play with different musicians, but as usual Ray Thomas had the pithiest explanation: 'After all those albums, all those tours and living practically next door to each other I don't think we had anything left to say to each other. You couldn't say "Guess what I did yesterday?" because everyone knew what you'd done yesterday already.'

Whatever the reason for the hiatus, it certainly wasn't a desire to escape from work, as the individual members of the band showed by launching themselves into a flurry of solo projects. Graeme Edge teamed up with Adrian Gurvitz and brought out *Kick Off Your Muddy Boots* (1974), Mike Pinder recorded *The Promise* (1976), Ray Thomas *From Mighty Oaks* (1975), while Justin Hayward and John Lodge teamed up to form Blue Jays.

The latter duo had by far the most media attention of the Moody Blues offshoots, helped considerably by the spectacular launch of their eponymous first album in March 1975. They hired Carnegie Hall in New York and filled it with 300 writers and DJs plus 2500 fans; the assembled multitude heard the record through the band's own PA system. 'We were in the dressing room,' recalls John Lodge, 'and it was the most bizarre experience hearing people cheering after each track. It was like doing a gig and being in the audience at the same time.'

Further solo successes followed, the greatest being Justin Hayward's participation in Jeff Wayne's *War Of The Worlds* project; a single, 'Forever Autumn', made the UK Number 5 position in 1978. By then, it seemed obvious to most people that the Moody Blues had broken up. In that year, however, they got back together to discuss a compilation project that Decca was proposing. John Lodge: 'I don't know who suggested it but eventually we agreed it would be better to record a new album rather than spend time worrying about track selection, running order, artwork and all that on an old one.'

By this time, however, Mike Pinder had decided enough was enough. He had decided to stay in America and continue a life of domestic bliss; as *Melody Maker*'s Chris Welch once remarked: 'If I'd sold 42 platinum albums I'd probably do the same.' The band recorded *Octave* as a four-piece and, following its release in 1978, were joined for stage performances by Patrick Moraz, a Swiss keyboard player originally with Refugee and formerly a replacement for Rick Wakeman in Yes. The *Octave* album sold a million copies in America alone, and a lengthy US tour that followed in 1979 was a sell-out.

In 1981 the Moodies brought out *Long Distance Voyager*, which repeated the success of its predecessor. In addition they played an extensive series of concerts worldwide which amply demonstrated both the extent and the loyalty of the band's fans. The end of 1982 saw the group working on another album and showing no signs of giving up. 'I can't see any reason why we should,' said John Lodge. 'We enjoy what we do, we're still creative and people still seem to like us.' Quite an understatement . . .

BRIAN HARRIGAN

MOODY BLUES
Discography

Singles
Lose Your Money/Steal Your Heart Away (Decca F 11971, 1964); Go Now/It's Easy Child (Decca F 12022, 1964); I Don't Want To Go On Without You/Time Is On My Side (Decca F 12095, 1965); From The Bottom Of My Heart/And My Baby's Gone (Decca F 12166, 1965); Everyday/You Don't (Decca F 12266, 1965); Boulevard De La Madelaine/This Is My House (Decca F 12498, 1966); Life's Not Life/He Can Win (Decca F 12543, 1967); Fly Me High/Really Haven't Got The Time (Decca F 12607, 1967); Love And Beauty/Leave This Man Alone (Decca F 12670, 1967); Nights In White Satin/Cities (Deram DM 161, 1967); Voices In The Sky/Dr Livingstone I Presume (Deram DM 196, 1968); Ride My See-Saw/Simple Game (Deram DM 213, 1968); Never Comes The Day/So Deep Within You (Deram DM 247, 1969); Watching And Waiting/Out And In (Threshold TH 1, 1969); Question/Candle Of Life (Threshold TH 4, 1970); Isn't Life Strange/After You Came (Threshold TH 9, 1972); I'm Just A Singer (In A Rock And Roll Band)/For My Lady (Threshold TH 13, 1973); Stepping In The Slide Zone/I'll Be Level With You (Decca F 13790, 1978); Driftwood/I'm Your Man (Decca F 13809, 1978); Meanwhile/22,000 Days (Threshold TH 26, 1981); Gemini Dream/Painted Smile (Threshold TH 27, 1981); The Voice/22,000 Days (Threshold TH 28, 1981); Talking Out Of Turn/Veteran Cosmic Rocker (Threshold TH 29, 1982).

EP
The Moody Blues (Decca DKE 8622, 1965).

Albums
The Magnificent Moodies (Decca LK 4711, 1965); *Days Of Future Passed* (Deram SML 707, 1967); *In Search Of The Last Chord* (Deram SML 711, 1968); *On The Threshold Of A Dream* (Deram SML 1035, 1969); *To Our Children's Children's Children* (Threshold THS 1, 1969); *A Question Of Balance* (Threshold THS 3, 1970); *Every Good Boy Deserves Favour* (Threshold THS 5, 1971); *Seventh Sojourn* (Threshold THS 7, 1972); *This Is The Moody Blues* (Threshold MB 1-2, 1974); *Caught Live Plus Five* (Threshold MB 3-4, 1977); *Octave* (Decca TXS 129, 1978); *Out Of This World* (K-Tel NE 1051, 1979); *Long Distance Voyager* (Decca TXS 139, 1981).

WELCOME TO THE MACHINE

How Pink Floyd set the controls for success

PINK FLOYD was formed by Roger Keith (Syd) Barrett, George Roger Waters, Richard William Wright and Nicholas Berkeley Mason in London during the latter part of 1965. Syd Barrett and Roger Waters both attended Cambridge High School for Boys, where Dave Gilmour, who would subsequently replace Barrett on guitar in the group, had been a fellow pupil. On leaving Cambridge, Barrett enrolled at Camberwell School of Art in London, the classic type of establishment for any aspiring Sixties pop star. There he applied a certain amount of paint to canvas, but became increasingly interested in playing the guitar. Gilmour was also in London at the time and ironically taught Barrett many of his early chords.

Waters also left Cambridge for London, but he opted for the rather more prosaic environs of the Regent Street Polytechnic and a course in architecture. There he met Nick Mason and Rick Wright on the same course and the three quickly discovered a mutual interest in forming a group, the first version of which was called Sigma 6 and had no success in securing a recording contract. At this point, Wright could already play piano, harmonium, harpsichord and cello, while Mason, an accomplished tympanist, was of more immediate practical use in providing the money for the group's early equipment.

Other names and line-ups followed, including the T-Set, the Abdabs and the Screaming Abdabs and all met with the same fate. Eventually, Waters on bass, Mason on drums and Wright on keyboards made one final attempt to make it work, bringing in two new members, a jazz guitarist called Bob Close and Syd Barrett, who was still friendly with Waters from Cambridge days. Barrett, in a typical burst of lateral thinking, named the group the Pink Floyd Sound after a pair of old bluesmen called Pink Anderson and Floyd Council. Barrett and Close did not get on

Right: At the gates of fame – the psychedelic Pink Floyd in 1967. Clockwise from top left: Nick Mason, Rick Wright, Syd Barrett and Roger Waters.

together and shortly afterwards Close left the group as a result of one of the earliest recorded examples of 'musical differences'.

Games on the underground

The four-piece line-up now secured their first regular dates on Sunday afternoons at the Marquee Club in London's Wardour Street during a series of concerts with the generic title of 'Spontaneous Underground', which commenced in February 1966. The group's set at this time was a weird mixture of straight R&B tunes such as 'Roadrunner' and interludes of imaginative instrument abuse as the group explored the possibilities of feedback. Later that year the group discovered the other element that was to transform their stage shows and make them the house band of underground London. During a series of dates at the London Free School's Sound/Light Workshop, held in All Saint's Church Hall in Notting Hill Gate, Pink Floyd met an American couple called Joel and Toni Brown, both of whom were students of Timothy Leary. Together they conceived the idea of using a rudimentary lightshow during the performance with brightly coloured slides projected on the group.

On 15 October 1966, Pink Floyd consummated its affair with the underground by playing at the launch party for *International Times*, the first newspaper to be produced specifically for the alternative culture. The Floyd played to an audience of over 2000 and the response confirmed that the group had found an identity and a following which was to be the stepping stone to future success. At the end of that same month, the four members of the group together with then-manager Peter Jenner and Andrew King formed Blackhill Enterprises as a partnership to run the group's business affairs. The upswing in their fortunes was confirmed on 23 December 1966 when the legendary UFO club first opened its doors in Tottenham Court Road. Given the experimental sights and sounds of Pink Floyd's new stage act, they were a natural choice as the resident group.

The next step was to release a single to capitalise on the band's popularity. This duly appeared at the beginning of 1967, produced by UFO co-founder Joe Boyd. Released on EMI's Columbia label, to whom the group had signed for a reputed £5000 advance, the single was called 'Arnold Layne'. It was written by Barrett and, far from being some vague experiment in feedback, it turned out to be a pithy ditty concerning the activities of a young man who steals ladies' underwear from washing lines, and it was promptly banned by a number of radio stations. This affected sales to an extent, but the single still reached Number 20 in the charts.

Meanwhile the group were using numerous live dates as a testing ground for an increasingly ambitious range of material. Dates varied from small clubs to another *IT* extravaganza at London's Alexandra Palace, 'The 14 Hour Technicolor Dream Free Speech Festival', and most ambitiously a solo concert at the Queen Elizabeth Hall. The event was entitled 'Games For May', and it saw the group make their first tentative step to improving the dire standards of sound prevalent at the time by installing speakers at the back of the hall to give a primitive version of quadrophonic sound. As well as being the title of the event, 'Games For May' was also a new Syd Barrett song and with a change of name and lyrics it became their second single.

At the gates

On 22 June 1967, 'See Emily Play' hit the charts and spent 12 weeks there, peaking at Number 6. Although again on Columbia, the group had undergone a change of producer, Joe Boyd having been replaced by staff man Norman Smith at EMI's insistence. The fact that Pink Floyd did not have another hit single for 12 years after this gives an indication of the change of direction that was already imminent. On 5 August of that year, Pink Floyd released their debut LP, *The Piper At The Gates Of Dawn*; the title had been culled by Barrett from one of the most popular underground reading manuals, Kenneth Grahame's *The Wind In The Willows*.

The material on the LP reflected Syd Barrett's dominance of the group at this stage in its development; of the 11 tracks on the record Barrett had wholly or co-written 10 – the only exception was a minor effort from Waters called 'Take Up Thy Stethoscope And Walk'. Not content with this, Barrett also provided the artwork for the back of the cover. The first track on the first side spelled out the direction in which Pink Floyd were heading and was in marked contrast to the group's first two singles; 'Astronomy Domine' was a dynamic space anthem that was to remain one of the highlights of the Floyd's repertoire for years to come. On 24 October 1967 Pink Floyd began their first tour of the US,

taking British psychedelia to an amazed and then appreciative audience in the country where it had all started. The focal point was inevitably Barrett, whose deranged stage presence was pushed to manic extremes by his constant intake of large amounts of LSD. Barrett's erratic behaviour was making it increasingly difficult for his fellow group members to work with him, and his days with the Floyd were numbered.

Another symptom of the growing malaise was the delay in releasing the group's third single. Another Barrett composition, entitled 'Apples And Oranges', it took an inordinately long time to record and, following its eventual release on 18 November 1967, flopped disastrously. The failure of the single, together with Barrett's general state of mind, made a change of musical policy inevitable. It duly arrived in the shape of Dave Gilmour who, since teaching Barrett the rudiments of the guitar, had pursued a nomadic existence in Europe with his own group. He spent some time in Paris where he learned French and also worked for a time as a male model. Gilmour joined the group in February as second guitarist, although it was widely realised what the eventual outcome would be. Barrett's mental state made it impossible for him to carry on and a matter of weeks after Gilmour's arrival Syd was asked to leave the group.

On stage, the Floyd members have always played second fiddle to spectacular effects. Opposite: The band play before film of prime minister Edward Heath, 1972. Above: Amid smoke the same year.

During the Barrett period, Pink Floyd had been a distinctly schizophrenic outfit, with a devoted but relatively small underground following for their live performances and their more ambitious musical output. They also enjoyed a more general appreciation among young pop fans for their quirky singles and appearances on BBC-TV's 'Top Of The Pops'. The group deliberately turned its back on the latter (potentially more lucrative) market and devoted its energies solely to LPs, a policy it resolutely maintained thereafter.

Pink Floyd continued to enhance their live reputation by playing a wide range of dates. The equally legendary Middle Earth club had superseded UFO, and the band played this venue several times to general acclaim. Although Blackhill Enterprises had became divorced from Pink Floyd's management during the upheaval of Barrett's departure (he remained with Blackhill), the company was busily engaged in promoting the first of what would become traditional London events: the Hyde Park free concerts. On 29 June 1968 Pink Floyd headlined the first free concert in the park on a bill that included Jethro Tull and Roy Harper. June was a significant month for the group in that it also marked the release of their second album, *A Saucerful Of Secrets*. Playing without the charismatic Barrett on stage in front of a large audience and producing an LP without his songwriting abilities represented a doubly searching test of the new formation's strengths, and the confidence they gained by passing both ordeals bolstered the group immeasurably. In fact the LP did contain one Barrett composition, 'Jugband Blues', but it was, to all intents and purposes, a triumph for the new line-up – and in particular Waters, whose 'Set The Controls For The Heart Of The Sun' became another live favourite, with its simple repeated phrase providing the launching pad for sundry instrumental pyrotechnics.

Azimuth and Auximenes

Another extensive bout of touring followed, with visits to all parts of Europe and then a further assault on the American concert circuit later in 1968. The group spent a lot of time and money in developing a sound system that could accurately reproduce their increasingly sophisticated musical effects. The results of this research were formally unveiled in London's Festival Hall on 14 April 1969 in the shape of the Azimuth Co-ordinator. The event was entitled, with a suitable flourish, 'More Furious Madness From The Massed

Inset top: Roger Waters. Above: Nick Mason. Below: The Floyd take France by storm, 1974.

Gadgets Of Auximenes'. The Azimuth device was basically a rotating control stick, and while the basic drum and bass sound thundered out of the main PA system, the control stick was used to send a barrage of electronic effects whirling from speaker to speaker around the audience.

With this concert and the subsequent tour with a show called more simply 'The Journey', Pink Floyd broke out of the restricting confines of being a psychedelic band and reached a larger audience. With the exception of Syd Barrett, the group had never espoused the philosophy of LSD. The group was later quoted as saying: 'Our attitude to freak-outs is that we would not play at one again unless they paid us three times our normal fee.' Roger Waters was even more scathing: 'There was so much dope and acid around in those days that I don't think anyone can remember anything about anything.'

Cymbaline in the cinema

Given the extended atmospheric pieces for which Pink Floyd were becoming renowned, it was a logical diversification for the group to get involved in producing film music – so when Barbet Schroeder offered them a considerable sum to write the music for a film he was directing called *More*, they were happy to accept. And it was a number entitled 'Cymbaline', from the soundtrack LP released in 1969, that first gained a radio breakthrough for the group in the United States and brought them to the attention of a wider audience.

It was the group's next album that established them as a major force in 'progressive' music. Released in October 1969 on EMI's newly-formed underground label, Harvest, *Ummagumma* was a double LP, half of which had been recorded live earlier that year on dates in Manchester and Birmingham. The live album perfectly captured the atmospheric intensity of the Floyd's electric stage performances as they ran through their space anthems, 'Astronomy Domine' and 'Set The Controls For The Heart Of The Sun', as well as 'A Saucerful Of Secrets' and the truly chilling 'Careful With That Axe, Eugene'.

The second record saw the group in an experimental vein, with each band member given an equal amount of room for compositions; although such contributions as Wright's 'Sysyphus' or Waters' 'Several Species Of Small Furry Animals Gathered Together In A Cave And Grooving With A Pict' seem self-indulgent in retrospect, they were quite in keeping with the nature of the 'progressive' era. *Ummagumma*'s cover, meanwhile, gave some indication as to how the group – who always maintained a low public profile, the members never parading themselves as 'stars' – viewed itself. On the front were mysteriously changing mirror images of the group members, while the reverse showed their barrage of equipment laid out on the tarmac of a runway – suggesting, or so it seemed, that the electric tools of the Floyd's trade were as important as the personalities within the group itself.

During much of 1970 the group remained out of the public eye until the release in October of *Atom Heart Mother*, complete with a striking Hipgnosis cover depicting a cow. The title track was an extended piece that included choral and orchestral segments alongside guitar solos. This was balanced by a more conventional second side that contained some of the band's most relaxed work, including

Inset top: Guitarist Dave Gilmour, who took over from Syd Barrett in 1968. Above: Rick Wright at the keyboards.

the wry humour of 'Alan's Psychedelic Breakfast'; in subsequent live dates, tea was made on stage during this number. The group took the work to America at the end of the year, accompanied by a 10-piece orchestral group and a choir of 20. Together with the 360-degree sound system, the show made quite an impression on audiences. The *LA Free Press* noted in astonishment that, rather than dancing, the 'freaks' in the audience actually sat down and listened to the music, while Roger Waters commented: 'Our idea is to put the sound all around the audience with ourselves in the middle. Then the performance becomes more theatrical – it can include melodrama, literary things, music and lights.'

Obscured by the moon

15 May 1971 saw the group in action at a Crystal Palace Garden Party, complete with a giant inflatable octopus which rose from the lake in front of the stage. The set featured a new piece called 'Return To The Sun Of Nothing'; on 13 November this was to surface as 'Echoes', forming the second side of the band's new LP *Meddle*.

Although 'Echoes' was a beautifully constructed, seductive and atmospheric piece, it gave signs that the Floyd's development might be slowing down. As Nick Mason commented: 'There are similarities between *Atom Heart Mother* and *Meddle* and there are various things in the construction [of 'Echoes'] that have a Pink Floyd flavour but are also very dangerous Pink Floyd clichés. One is the possible tendency to get stuck into a sort of slow four tempo. And the other thing is to take a melody line and flog it to death.'

Much of the year was taken up by a mammoth world tour, while 1972 found the Floyd again lying low; their only activity was to release another soundtrack album, *Obscured By Clouds*, from another Barbet Schroeder film, *La Vallée*. The American public again took to Pink Floyd's film music and, although *Atom Heart Mother* had reached Number 1 in the UK, it was only with this LP that the group started to sell records in great quantities in the US.

This relatively quiet period was fully explained the following year with the release of *Dark Side Of The Moon*, which burst upon an unsuspecting rock press at a preview held in the London Planetarium in March 1973. The group was now producing itself and the result of nearly a year's painstaking efforts was an LP of startling clarity and power. The ultimate technical compliment was paid when it was revealed that hi-fi buffs were buying the record simply to test the quality of their equipment. The songs on the LP – titles included 'Brain Damage', 'Money' and 'Time' – dealt with a very dark side of life and this indicated the Floyd's growing interest in doomy themes. 'We sat in a rehearsal room and Roger came up with the specific idea of dealing with all the things that drive people mad,' Wright later said.

The subsequent tour featuring the material was suitably epic, with a soul vocal group called the Blackberries used on the US dates. By the time Pink Floyd played at London's Earl's Court in May, they had perfected a show with a dazzling array of special effects, including a flaming gong, a creature with green laser eyes and an aeroplane that swooped from the back of the hall and crashed on stage in blinding light and smoke.

Pink Floyd performing The Wall *in 1980. Right: The grotesque figure of the teacher wields his cane as the band play on regardless. Below: The group line up with Pink Floyd 'doubles'.*

The band then spent over two years attempting to produce a worthy successor to *Dark Side Of The Moon*, such were the pressures its worldwide success had created. The outcome was *Wish You Were Here*, released in September 1975, and it was rather predictably given a lukewarm reception. The LP had some fine moments, however, notably the tribute to Syd Barrett called 'Shine On You Crazy Diamond'. It was only with the release of *Animals* in February 1977 that Pink Floyd regained critical favour. As on *Dark Side Of The Moon*, Waters' songs dealt with the unacceptable facets of life, and his view of the human condition is reflected both in the song titles – 'Pigs', 'Dogs' and 'Sheep' – and in uncompromisingly bleak lyrics. The tours were given added power by the ex-

tensive use of film, projected on a circular screen behind the band, additional musicians to boost the sound and an inflatable pig which was very much the album's symbol. The cover featured one flying over Battersea power station and caused endless problems when it was photographed on a windy day.

While the other three members of the group had produced solo efforts relatively quickly – David Gilmour's eponymous album and Wright's *Wet Dream* were both released in 1978, while Mason had done production work for Principal Edwards' Magic Theatre, Unicorn, Robert Wyatt and others – Roger Waters' effort was longer in gestation. It eventually appeared as a double LP credited to the group, but was in most respects Waters' own creation.

Up against The Wall

As *The Wall*, it was released on 30 November 1979. The songs were linked by the presence of a central character called Pink who, through a series of trials and tribulations, becomes a powerful symbol of society's oppression of the individual. The single 'Another Brick In The Wall (Part Two)', taken from the LP, soared into the UK charts on 1 December 1979 and subsequently became the band's first Number 1 single despite its unlikely content – a savage indictment of the educational system. The live performances of *The Wall* were dominated by the construction of an enormous wall during the course of the set that gradually obscured the group from view. A band of Pink Floyd doubles then took the stage, while the real group played on invisibly. At the climax of the performance, the wall crashed down and the group emerged with acoustic instruments.

Reaction of critics to *The Wall* was mixed to say the least – some thought it the Floyd's finest production yet, others considered it depressingly self-indulgent – but the public proved Pink Floyd were as bankable as ever. After *The Wall*'s enormous success, however, the group went back into hibernation. Waters worked with director Alan Parker on the film of *The Wall* (which was released in 1982) but the hiatus between the original album's release and the appearance of 1983's *The Final Cut* underlined the problems in following such a creation. As *The Final Cut* came out, it was announced that keyboardist Rick Wright had left the band.

Aside from the lasting power and beauty of much of their music, one of the main achievements of Pink Floyd lies in their uncompromising search for perfection in sound and presentation. After the chaos of the psychedelic era, the group pioneered a sound of the highest quality in both their recorded and live work. Both albums and concerts have been characterised by an attention to detail that has made them monumental experiences and the group was to influence a new generation of artists of the Seventies – Yes, Mike Oldfield, Genesis *et al* – who valued musicianship and presentation above all else.

Following the development of the late Seventies new wave, critics began to dismiss the group as self-indulgent hasbeens, accusing them of distancing themselves quite cynically from their audience. But, in their own way, Pink Floyd have been as harsh critics of society as any socially-conscious punk band. And the fact remains that they continue to experiment and explore – and their enormous following across the globe bears witness to their continuing durability.

PETER CLARK

PINK FLOYD
Discography

Singles
Arnold Layne/Candy And A Currant Bun (Columbia DB 8156, 1967); See Emily Play/Scarecrow (Columbia DB 8214, 1967); Apples And Oranges/Paintbox (Columbia DB 8310, 1967); It Would Be So Nice/Julia Dream (Columbia DB 8410, 1968); Point Me At The Sky/Careful With That Axe, Eugene (Columbia DB 8511, 1968); Another Brick In The Wall (Part Two)/One Of My Turns (Harvest HAR 5194, 1979); When The Tigers Broke Free/Bring The Boys Back Home (Harvest HAR 5222, 1982).

Albums
The Piper At The Gates Of Dawn (Columbia SCX 6157, 1967); *A Saucerful Of Secrets* (Columbia SCX 6258, 1968); *More* (Columbia SCX 6345, 1969); *Ummagumma* (Harvest SHDW 1/2, 1969); *Atom Heart Mother* (Harvest SHVL 781, 1970); *Relics* (Starline SRS 5071, 1971); *Meddle* (Harvest SHVL 795, 1971); *Obscured By Clouds* (Harvest SHSP 4020, 1972); *The Dark Side Of The Moon* (Harvest SHVL 804, 1973); *Wish You Were Here* (Harvest SHVL 814, 1975); *Animals* (Harvest SHVL 815, 1977); *The Wall* (Harvest SHDW 411, 1979); *A Collection Of Great Dance Songs* (Harvest SHVL 822, 1981); *The Final Cut* (Harvest SHPF 1983, 1983).

Procol Harum

Classic rock that captured the mood of 1967

PROCOL HARUM will be remembered for their chart-topping 'A Whiter Shade Of Pale', if nothing else. Hitting the Number 1 slot in the UK in May 1967, and Number 5 in the US in July, it was a dreamy, fantasy-laden sound which drifted easily into the atmosphere which pervaded the summer of 1967. It hogged the Number 1 position for six weeks and even in 1972, when it was re-released, it climbed to Number 13 in the UK.

But behind the one-hit-wonder label, the history of the band with the strange, exotic name spanned almost 20 years and encompassed a wide progression of musical styles. They had their beginnings at the time of the beat and R&B booms, reached their chart zenith in the height of flower power in the Summer of Love, and worked as one of the main bands on the American tour circuit in the Seventies. The history is a chequered one and the line-up changed constantly, the stable core of Gary Brooker and lyricist Keith Reid ensuring a certain continuity of style despite changing trends.

The story begins with the Paramounts, a Southend R&B group that was formed in 1960, when a schoolboy band called the Raiders was re-christened by a local dance hall manager. The line-up at the time revolved around pianist Gary Brooker (born 29 May 1945) and guitarist Robin Trower (born 9 March 1945) and included drummer B. J. Wilson (born 18 March 1947) and bassist Chris Copping (born 29 August 1945). Their sporadic public appearances were split between playing dates on their own, doing cover versions of American rock'n'roll and Shadows instrumentals, and backing solo artists visiting the Southend area.

Gary Brooker recalls the period thus: 'We backed Tommy Bruce on a thing called 'Rock Across The Channel' on the boat to Calais. It was us, Gerry and the Pacemakers, Duffy Power, the Dreamers and the Shadows . . . they would turn up five minutes before they were due to go on for their 20-minute sets. They would bring charts, with the chords scribbled down, so anybody who could follow a chord chart used to get the job of backing them.'

By 1963, the group had settled down with a personnel of Brooker, Trower, Wilson and bassist Diz Derrick. In that year, soon after leaving school, they got a recording contract with Parlophone, who were busy signing up provincial groups in the wake of the Beatles. The Paramounts' first effort for the label was a version of 'Poison Ivy', the old Coasters hit from 1959, which sneaked into the Top Fifty in January 1964. It was to be the high-point of the Paramounts' career, however. Despite constant touring, TV appearances on shows like 'Ready Steady Go!' and 'Thank Your Lucky Stars', *and* the accolade of being dubbed 'the best R&B group in England' by the Rolling Stones, they got nowhere. Five further singles for Parlophone flopped – including 'Bad Blood', which was banned

Before and after: the Paramounts (below left) became Procol Harum (below right). Robin Trower (right) later went solo.

when the BBC decided it was about syphilis – and by 1966 they were once more reduced to backing other artists – first Beryl Marsden on the Beatles' final British tour, then with Sandie Shaw in Paris, and finally behind Chris 'Yesterday Man' Andrews in Germany. Robin Trower refused to go on this last expedition, and when they returned home, the Paramounts called it a day.

Copy cats

Having been among the handful of groups who could reasonably claim to have started the R&B bandwagon rolling in this country, they had found themselves still pushing for success, while later (and lesser) arrivals rode to the top in comfort. Gary Brooker explains: 'In the early days of the group, we were doing unusual numbers which people enjoyed hearing. But then a lot of bands started doing them – people like Zoot Money and the Animals – and I reckon that's one of the reasons our popularity declined.' Another reason may have been that, while many of their contemporaries had moved on to writing their own material, the Paramounts never did, apart from the occasional spur-of-the-moment B-side. Brooker aimed to set this right. Before the Paramounts had split up, he had met lyricist Keith Reid through producer Guy Stevens. While the rest of the group went their separate ways, Brooker and Reid began songwriting in earnest.

Their original intention was to get other people to perform their songs, but several months of hawking their work around publishers came to nothing. Brooker considered joining Dusty Springfield's backing group, but eventually decided to form another band.

A 'Musicians Wanted' ad in *Melody Maker* brought them guitarist Ray Royer (born 8 October 1945) and bassist David Knights (born 28 June 1945). In the 'Musicians Available' column they found organist Matthew Fisher (born 7 March 1946). They also acquired a name, from the pedigree name of a cat belonging to a friend of Guy Stevens (apparently it should have been Procol Harun, which supposedly means 'beyond these things'), and signed a contract with Denny Cordell's Straight Ahead Productions.

Still lacking a drummer, the band recorded their first single using session drummer Bill Eyden. By coincidence, old acquaintance Bobby Harrison turned up at the same time. He had occasionally played drums with the Paramounts, and he was promptly offered the job with Procol Harum.

The group were soon ready to do live dates, and on the day 'A Whiter Shade Of Pale' was released in April 1967, they were playing the UFO club, the focal point of London's burgeoning underground scene. By the first week in June, the record had entered the charts, and the following week it made Number 1. All summer long, the song floated out of radios and open windows, capturing the surreal, magical mood of the times. The inspiration for the work came from one of Bach's cantatas.

Things were not going so well behind the scenes, however. When it came to making an album, Royer and Harrison didn't work out, so they got the elbow and went off to form Freedom. Almost immediately, the group's manager, Jonathan Weston, departed, too. 'After three weeks it was obvious Jonathan didn't work out,' said Brooker. 'When the Rolls Royce called for me for the seventh time to take me to the shops, I got a bit pissed off. He was just wasting my money. If we were going to the studio across at Barnes, I'd be getting ready to catch the bus and I'd find a uniformed chauffeur at the door.'

Ex-Paramounts Trower and Wilson returned to replace Royer and Harrison and the band had to return to the rehearsal room to complete their first album when they should have been out capitalising on their sudden success. To make matters worse, new manager Tony Secunda's approach to handling media enquiries was apparently less than subtle. Just about the only publicity Procol Harum got at the peak of their fame was when Bill Eyden revealed his role in the recording of 'A Whiter Shade Of Pale' and demanded a fifth of the royalties. The press promptly accused Procol Harum of being a bogus group whose records were made by studio session men. Despite all this, the group's second single, 'Homburg', made the Number 6 position in October 1967. But thereafter success in their homeland was sporadic, due largely to problems with management and their record company: after Tony Secunda was ousted at the end of 1967, the band were without proper representation in the UK for three years, while their production company lumbered the group with Regal Zonophone, one of the world's less dynamic labels.

US to the rescue

These problems also meant that in their first few years, Procol Harum lurched from one financial crisis to the next. They were by no means the first or last group to suffer from poor business deals, but it does seem tragic that the proceeds from something as magnificent as 'A Whiter Shade Of Pale' should fail to find their way to its creators. From worldwide sales of over eight million copies, which should have left writers Brooker and Reid, at least, quite comfortably off, they were left with nothing. 'It did all seem to get absorbed,' Brooker has confessed. 'We had a terrible contract with the

Right: Procol Harum in a later incarnation, with B. J. Wilson on drums, Alan Cartwright on bass and Mick Grabham on guitar. Lyricist Keith Reid (above) and composer Gary Brooker (inset far right) remained the mainstay of the band, while Chris Copping (inset right) switched from bass to organ and back.

production company, and it always cost a lot of money to get rid of all these managers and other people. In fact, we did a tour of the States and all the money went to people we'd never signed a contract with.'

What saved Procol Harum from going the same way as the Paramounts was the US. 'A Whiter Shade Of Pale' had been a huge (Number 5) hit there, as it was all round the world, but the Americans seemed keen to hear what else the band were doing, and were given plenty of opportunity to do so, since Procol Harum toured there eleven times in under four years! That work rate, allied to a rather more efficient record company in A&M, kept the group well to the fore across the Atlantic, during three or four years when they were all but forgotten at home. They also worked regularly in Europe, where they had considerable success, and it wasn't until early 1972 – after they had switched to the fast-growing Chrysalis label – that they did their first proper tour of the UK as support to Jethro Tull.

In what little time remained between these travels, the band made three albums. The 1967 debut, *Procol Harum* (a restrained title for such over-the-top times) was hastily and rather poorly produced by Denny Cordell, but not bad for all that. It was a sombre, stately work with a classical dignity, the despair of Reid's cryptic lyrics set in contrast to the deliberate architecture of the music, the religiosity of Fisher's organ-playing and Brooker's gospel-tinged piano and vocals.

Cordell did little better with *Shine On Brightly*, recorded through late 1967 and early 1968, though what emerged was arguably a greatly under-rated album. At this point Cordell got side-tracked by Joe Cocker, and Matthew Fisher took over for *A Salty Dog* (1969).

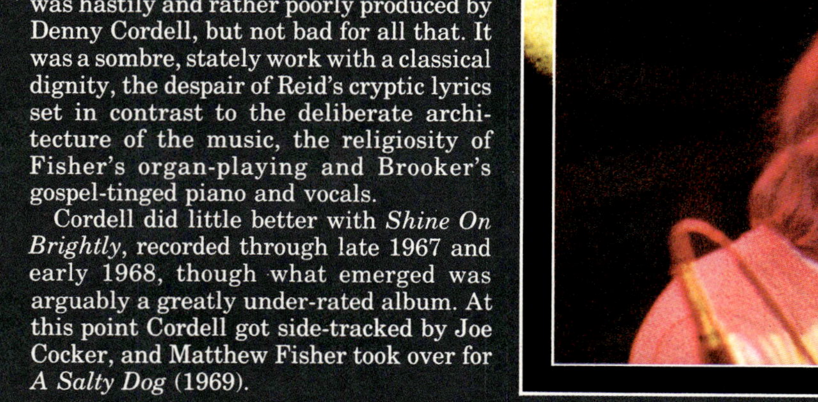

Having been bitten by the production bug, Fisher left to concentrate on that and to make a couple of solo albums during the Seventies. David Knights also departed to take up management – he probably decided that's where the money was – and both were replaced by Chris Copping. Chris had left the Paramounts to go to college, where he had learned to play the organ, as well as bass. With Fisher gone, Chris Thomas was called on to produce their fourth album, *Home*, and this proved to be the start of a fruitful combination which lasted for four years and five albums.

The group personnel was rather less consistent. Robin Trower left, after discovering a songwriting talent during the making of the album *Broken Barricades*, and formed a sub-Hendrix trio which has done noticeably better commercially than Procol Harum. He was replaced briefly by Dave Ball, and then more permanently by Mick Grabham, who had previously been with Cochise. Chris Copping eventually concentrated on organ when Alan Cartwright came in, from Brian Davison's Every Which Way, on bass. When Cartwright left in 1976, Copping moved back to the bass and Pete Solley – previously a member of Snafu with original Procol drummer-turned-vocalist, Bobby Harrison – joined to play keyboards. Throughout these comings and goings, Procol Harum trundled on, never making bad records, while never threatening to rekindle the flames of 1967. They had one memorable moment, however, when they played a concert in Edmonton, Canada, with the Edmonton Symphony Orchestra in November 1971. The concert was recorded for a live album, and the version of 'Conquistador' gave them their first hit single for nearly five years on both sides of the Atlantic, reaching the US Number 16 and UK Number 22 positions.

They were in the British charts again three years later at Number 16 with 'Pandora's Box' from *Procol's Ninth* (1975), which was produced for them by Leiber and Stoller. In 1977, probably worn down by their consistent failure to make a significant commercial breakthrough, Procol Harum split up, leaving *Something Magic* as an inappropriately-titled farewell. Lyricist Keith Reid went into management and some of the others turned their hands to session work, while Gary Brooker combined the keyboard-playing role in Eric Clapton's band with a solo career which in the early Eighties yielded two albums, *No Fear Of Flying* and *Lead Me To The Water*. On its US release, the latter was accompanied by publicity shrieking 'A Whiter Shade Of Success'. Some folks just won't let a chap forget. PAUL KENDALL

Procol Harum
Recommended Listening

A Whiter Shade Of Pale/A Salty Dog (Cube TOOFA 7, double album) (Includes: A Whiter Shade Of Pale, Conquistador, Kaleidoscope, Salad Days, Salty Dog, Wreck Of The Hesperus).

SHEFFIELD STEEL

Joe Cocker: casualty or chart survivor?

DESPITE THE FACT that Joe Cocker had to wait until 1968, when he was 24 years of age, before achieving his first major hit, the singer is rightly considered part of the early Sixties British R&B movement. The relative lateness of Cocker's appearance in the charts may be attributed to his unsteady temperament, which has revealed itself throughout his career in excessive drinking, periodic lay-offs and frequent comebacks and a general aura of neurotic instability. On stage, Cocker's arms flail about, his voice is hoarse and ragged and his whole stance suggests palsy or, more accurately, a man trapped between the desperate need to express himself and the recognition of his inability to do so. Disillusion and depression have plagued Cocker's career as he swings between a genuine commitment to rock's expressive power and a persistent desire to exploit its commercial potential.

It was commerciality which informed the choice of Cocker's 1968 hit – a cover of the Beatles' *Sgt Pepper* track, 'With A Little Help From My Friends' – for Cocker had been performing since the Fifties and had made his first, unsuccessful, record (as Vance Arnold backed by the Avengers) in 1963. Ironically, this debut disc was a cover of an earlier Beatles' song, 'I'll Cry Instead', while the B-side was 'Georgia On My Mind'. It was Ray Charles who had turned this Stuart Gorrell-Hoagy Carmichael standard into a US chart-topper in 1960, and it was Charles who most accurately represented Cocker's musical aspirations.

Joe Cocker was born in England's steel town, Sheffield, on 20 May 1944. Like many other provincial centres in the late Fifties and early Sixties, Sheffield saw the rise of a musical underground based on an appreciation of black American styles. Cocker entered this underground through skiffle – a route he shared with many others, including the embryonic Beatles.

'When we were kids, we were constantly bored,' Cocker once recalled. 'Then skiffle came along, Lonnie Donegan and that stuff. So when I was about 13 I bought a cheap drum kit and began messing about with some kids who'd bought guitars.' By the time his schooling ended at the age of 16, Cocker had moved on to rock'n'roll and blues – working as a gas-fitter by day and playing by night. 'I was especially attracted to the blues,' he said, 'which seemed to have great honesty compared to all the bullshit English pop amounted to then.'

Feeling bluesy

Ray Charles was the major influence on Cocker's singing style, his inspiration lying in his ability to blend blues feeling with unashamedly commercial songs. By 1963, Cocker had given up his regular job and won a recording contract for Vance Arnold and the Avengers. The group toured with the Rolling Stones and the Hollies, but there was little or no interest in them and, after 'I'll Cry Instead', the option on their contract was dropped. The group played American air bases for a while and Cocker recalled how they 'went down sensationally with the blacks, and the white guys didn't want to know us'.

Jerking and twitching like a puppet, Joe Cocker's shambolic stage presence (above and opposite) belied his terrific vocal energy and flair. After splitting from the Grease Band (inset opposite), his groups generally included a horn section (below).

For the first but not the last time, Cocker's career went into a sharp decline. He was broke, worked as a casual labourer and spent most of his money drinking. By 1967, however, the rock scene had moved on. Black music had become established; blues feeling – transmuted by hallucinogenic drugs – underpinned much of the work of new bands then emerging and the record-buying public were more open to a wider range of styles and approaches than ever before.

Cocker and a pianist friend from Sheffield, Chris Stainton, worked on some new material – including a Stainton composition called 'Marjorine'. A demo attracted the interest of producer Denny Cordell, who had worked with the Moody Blues, the Move, Georgie Fame and Procol Harum. 'Marjorine' was released as a single and entered the British Top Fifty in May 1968. The wave of interest in Cocker's powerful style was helped along by his stage performances (with Joe Cocker's Big Blues Band). He sang like a demented string-puppet, eyes half-closed, limbs jerking while his vocal performance possessed an energy completely at variance with his slovenly appearance.

With the success of 'With A Little Help From My Friends', which went to Number 1 in November 1968, Cocker's future seemed assured – anyone who could transform the jolly Ringo Starr-sung number

from *Sgt Pepper* into a song of anguish and triumph had to have *something*.

Under Denny Cordell's guidance, Cocker now recorded his first album, *With A Little Help From My Friends* (1969) – the friends in this case being a host of sidemen including Jimmy Page, Albert Lee, Steve Winwood and Spooky Tooth drummer Mike Kellie. Following the LP's release, a group, named the Grease Band, was formed to back Cocker on stage. The band comprised Chris Stainton, Alan Spenner (bass), Bruce Rowland (drums) and Henry McCullough (guitar) and in the early summer of 1969 Cocker and band left for America, where they played at Woodstock.

Grease in the delta

It was in Los Angeles that Cocker made the acquaintance of session musician-cum-producer Leon Russell, who had played on the records of such diverse artists as Frank Sinatra, Jerry Lee Lewis and the Byrds. It was with a Russell song, 'Delta Lady', that Cocker had his third hit – the record reached Number 10 in Britain in October – while Russell also helped to supervise the recording of a second album. Recorded in LA, *Joe Cocker* boasted the talents of such musicians as Sneaky Pete Kleinow of the Flying Burrito Brothers and Clarence White of the Byrds and their playing gave the album a lighter, countryish feel to the rougher, bluesy soul sound of its predecessor. This disparity in styles highlighted Cocker's major problem: relying solely on his feeling, energy and interpretative originality, he was far too susceptible to the control of arrangers, producers and those better able to formulate a musical policy than himself. Joe Cocker's talent was always an eccentric one and seemed unable to define and control itself.

In 1970, the Grease Band – overlooked in all the high-powered session-work – left Cocker on the eve of another American tour to strike out on their own. Russell immediately stepped in and organised a

Joe Cocker might have been the official star of the show (above left), but out in the midday sun (right) of the 'Mad Dogs And Englishmen' tour, he found himself eclipsed by Leon Russell (below). In 1982, however, his duet with Jennifer Warnes (inset above right) finally put them 'Up Where We Belong' – at the top of the US charts.

group of 42 men, women and children, including the Delaney and Bonnie Band, Rita Coolidge, Cocker and Russell himself, to play the dates. The tour was billed as 'Mad Dogs and Englishmen' and was a huge success. A live double album of the same title was released in 1970 and a film in 1971. Cocker, ostensibly the star, emerged – so he has said – with 2000 dollars and a drug habit at the end of it, while Russell emerged as the actual star, continuing to tour with a smaller group of 'Mad Dog' survivors and rake in the money long after Cocker had run back to Sheffield.

Cocker down under

The singer spent the next 18 months in virtual retirement before making a comeback in 1972 with a tour which opened in America and closed, disastrously, in Australia. In October 1972, the Australian courts convicted Cocker and six members of the tour party on drugs charges. They were ordered out of the country, but before they left Cocker appeared at one final show so drunk that he fell over, and later managed to get himself evicted from his Melbourne hotel after a brawl.

Throughout the Seventies, Cocker's career continued to be erratic. A cover version of the Box Tops hit 'The Letter' had been his final UK chart entry in 1970, though he reached Number 5 in America with 'You Are So Beautiful' in 1975. During the decade, the singer made repeated attempts to take to live performance again, but failed signally to approach the heights of his achievements of 1968 and 1969 and although he released several albums on a variety of labels, all were marked by lack of decision and direction, uncertainty in choice of material and a shifting mass of session players. Though Cocker's voice remained, on occasion, as soulful and expressive as ever, the arrangements, the musicians' performances and many of the songs themselves did it little justice.

By the Eighties, critics, and the majority of the public too, had written Cocker off as a wasted talent – one couldn't help but feel that the image of a puppet or a Frankenstein monster which seemed once to counterpoint his all-too-human vocals had become ironically appropriate. But then, in November 1982, such theories were confounded when the aptly-titled 'Up Where We Belong' – on which Cocker duetted with Jennifer Warnes, a past collaborator with Warren Zevon and Leonard Cohen – rose to the top of the US charts. It seemed that, at last, Joe Cocker might have shrugged off his personal problems to come up trumps once again. GARY HERMAN

Joe Cocker
Recommended Listening

With A Little Help From My Friends/Joe Cocker (Cube TOOFA 1/2, 1975) (Includes: With A Little Help From My Friends, Marjorine, Delta Lady, I Shall Be Released, Dear Landlord, She Came In Through The Bathroom Window, Something).

APPLE

The rise and fall of the Beatles' business empire

FROM THE START, it had always been Brian Epstein and the Beatles. If any one person had the right to call himself the fifth Beatle is was Epstein, the apparently self-possessed, smart Jewish businessman from Liverpool. Epstein had dragged the Beatles from the gutter – from basement clubs on Merseyside and seedy bars in Hamburg's red-light district – dressed them in suits and ties, cut their hair, defined them as rascally, quick-witted and ever-so-slightly bohemian and pushed them into the hearts and minds of millions of record-buyers, TV viewers and concert-goers around the world.

Epstein was their manager, but he was also their surrogate father: he ruled them sternly, but with affection – mindful of their happiness more, perhaps, than their material wealth. It became fashionable, after Epstein's death, to devalue his achievements. The self-aggrandisement of those who sought to take his place, the revelations of discord within the Beatle camp and the eventual acrimonious break-up of the group all conspired to diminish Epstein's reputation and tarnish the image of the Beatles as a happy and workable democracy.

Subsequent fashion has tended to vindicate Brian Epstein and to suggest that any deficiencies in his business practice were the result not so much of his ineptitude as of the novelty of his position. Nobody had sailed such a remarkable entertainment phenomenon as the Beatles through such a stormy and changeable sea as the music business in the Sixties. It was inevitable that mistakes would be made, and Epstein was remarkable for making so few. Compared to the variety of people who tried to steer the Beatle ship after Epstein's death (including the Beatles themselves), Epstein was a paragon of managerial talent.

By early 1967, things were getting bad for the Beatles. The group had stopped touring in August 1966, largely because they hated it. They were, as Lennon later said, little more than 'performing fleas', unable to play anything other than their old hits which were impossible to hear above the screaming. But live performance had always been Brian Epstein's domain.

He could have little influence over the group's music, but his hand had guided their appearance, their public manner and the organisation of their performances. The vacuum that was left by the group's huge success and the cessation of touring needed to be filled, but no other performers in his stable matched the success of the Beatles. He bought the Savile Theatre in Shaftesbury Avenue, London, in 1965, staging rock shows which, though creating some interest among the rock cognoscenti, succeeded largely in losing money.

Klein and cash

In January 1967, the Beatles renegotiated their recording deal with EMI. This ensured that, for the first time, they would be likely to make more money from records than from live performance. The group, in particular McCartney, were getting increasingly interested in the financial arrangements that would allow them to indulge their artistic fantasies. McCartney even suggested bringing in a business adviser, having been impressed by the handling of the Stones' financial affairs by New York accountant Allen Klein. Epstein's interests turned towards his company NEMS (North End Music Stores – the name of his family's record shop in Liverpool) and he busied himself discussing business with American lawyer Nat Weiss and Robert Stigwood, the Australian whom Epstein had brought in as joint managing director of NEMS Enterprises; meanwhile the Beatles were becoming a partnership in law.

Their original company, Beatles Ltd, started in 1963 to handle their joint earnings from recording and performing, was joined by the partnership of the group's four individual members to form the Beatles & Co in April 1967 – a move that released £800,000 in cash to each of the partners. While NEMS would continue to collect its 25 per cent of the Beatles' record royalties, the group now had money of their own and an institutional instrument

After the death of Brian Epstein (above left), the Beatles set up Apple (right). The goods in the Apple shop (left) were easy pickings for freeloaders.

Borough of St. Marylebone
PADDINGTON
STREET, W.1.
CLAS

with which to pursue their own aims. They would also receive a large tax bill if they didn't spend some of their and the partnership's money – around £2 million of it – and quickly. And that, with or without Brian Epstein's advice, was precisely what they intended to do.

Writing on the wall

Epstein died of a drugs overdose in August 1967, and the Beatles, despite an army of hangers-on and advisers, were very much on their own. McCartney, always the most ambitious and money-oriented of the group, seemed to ease himself into a position of authority. It was not so much that he wished to lead the group, but that his ambitions were the most acute and the best-articulated. When McCartney argued that the group should go ahead with their 'Magical Mystery Tour' project, writing, directing and producing the film themselves, the others agreed. When he suggested that they should call their organisation Apple after a painting by Magritte, the others agreed. When McCartney envisioned Apple as a haven for new musicians, writers, artists and creative talents in general, the others agreed.

The seeds of the Apple republic took root in an 18th century Georgian corner house in London's Baker Street where a large chunk of the partnership's money went into setting up a lavish and exotic boutique called The Fool, run by three Dutch clothes designers and English publicist Barry Finch. The designers – Marijke Koger, Simon Posthuma and Josje Leeger – spent £100,000 on the shop, which opened with a fashion show and party in December 1967.

The side wall had been decorated with psychedelic murals painted by art students; inside the dark musk-scented shop were garments in rich velvets and sequins, feather boas and swinging assistants (who included Pattie Harrison's sister, Jennie). There were plans for laser beams and a giant artificial sun. The Apple empire was full of familiar faces – one of John Lennon's old schoolfriends, Pete Shotton, who managed a supermarket John had bought him on Hayling Island, was brought in to administer Apple Retail. It turned out to be one of the less successful ventures of the Apple Corps, however. Its contents had a habit of disappearing without any profit being made, and it eventually closed in July 1968 with a massive give-away at which a dozen policemen fought to control the rush for Afghan coats, Indian beads and all removable fittings.

Above: The Lennons with Magic Alex (second from right). Below: 'Santa' Lennon with Mary Hopkin. Right: Allen Klein.

Apple Corps Ltd was established in January 1968 and soon expanded to occupy a suite of offices in Wigmore Street. The dream was to have something the Beatles actually controlled themselves – away from the 'men in suits' – a democracy to prove how artistic freedom could be achieved within a business structure. The Apple cart became a bandwagon for a host of people – old friends and hangers-on – and the branches of the Apple tree spread in a number of different directions – most of them bearing little fruit. Out of all the various divisions, only Apple Records was really successful. With Jane Asher's brother, Peter, as A&R man, its other artists included Mary Hopkin, James Taylor, Billy Preston, Jackie Lomax, Grapefruit and the Iveys. In August 1968, four singles were released – Mary Hopkin's 'Those Were The Days', Jackie Lomax's 'Sour Milk Sea', Black Dyke Mills Brass Band's 'Thingummybob' and the Beatles' 'Hey Jude'. The latter (with 'Revolution' on the B-side) sold over three million copies and reached Number 1 in the UK charts; Mary Hopkin's single also made Number 1 in the UK and Number 2 in the US Hot Hundred.

The record division released all the Beatles singles from 'Hey Jude' on and all the albums from *The Beatles* ('White Album') on. Later it also released work by individual members of the group – much of it uncommercial, like John and Yoko's experiments in avant-garde electronic music which included the *Two Virgins* LP with its controversial sleeve picture of John and Yoko in the nude which was eventually distributed by Track Records inside brown paper envelopes. Apple Records' output dried up considerably through 1968, as did that of Apple Films. The first production credited to this division was the universally panned 'Magical Mystery Tour', released, on TV only, in December 1967. Other plans which never materialised included a film featuring model Twiggy and a version of *Lord Of The Rings*. It wasn't until January 1969 that work began on *Let It Be*, with Michael Lindsay-Hogg directing.

Other divisions included Apple Music, run by Terry Doran, Apple Publicity, run by Derek Taylor, and Apple Electronics. The latter was run by a young blond Greek called Alexis Mardas – a self-styled inventor who earned the nickname 'Magic Alex' for his inventive ideas – none of which seemed to get much further than his imagination. He was ever demanding vast sums of money to work on such gadgets as an electric apple which lit up and played music, a telephone which dialled its own numbers in response to the human voice, a 'nothing box' which had 12 red lights turning on and off at random and a spoiler-signal device to prevent illegal taping of records. He also promised to update the equipment at EMI to provide 72-track recording facilities. None of these projects materialised.

Perhaps the most shortsighted and short-lived venture was McCartney's plan for an Apple Foundation for the Arts – a scheme which invited worthy creative artists to apply for financial assistance to enable them to realise their dreams. This brought an avalanche of mail and a motley crowd of people to the Apple offices which soon began to resemble a holiday camp for all and sundry. All sorts of people wandered into and hung out at the Apple offices, which moved in June 1968 to bigger premises at 3 Savile Row, a five-storey Georgian house (formerly the Albany Club) in an elegant setting amid high-class tailors and dealers in hand-made cigarettes.

A day-long vigil was kept up outside the premises by fans, waiting for a white Rolls Royce to draw up and a glimpse of the Fab Four. Apple green carpet spread throughout the building, and framed gold discs lined the staircase walls. Staff and visitors were greeted with a constant supply of food from the *cordon bleu*-trained chefs, and drink and drugs flowed freely. In the press office, psychedelic lights swirled over soft sofas on which visitors could await an interview with Derek Taylor. Security was at a minimum and television sets, typewriters, lamps, records, cameras, the lead off the roof and even pay packets had a habit of disappearing.

The rot sets in

In little over a year, the rot had set in at Apple. The Corps had lost the Beatles over £1 million, and all four partners were overdrawn by tens of thousands. In October 1968 accountants warned the Beatles that their personal finances, and those of Apple, were in a mess. That Christmas, the fun went on, with a kids' party in Savile Row, with a 42-pound turkey and John and Yoko dressed as Father and Mother Christmas. But early in 1969 the axe came down on the Apple in the hands of Allen Klein. Klein had had his eye on the Beatles for some time. The stocky little accountant had built up a reputation for himself as a tough operator in the music business, renowned for extracting money from record companies for performers. His clients included Bobby Darin, Sam Cooke, the Stones, Herman's Hermits, the Animals, Donovan and the Dave Clark Five.

Klein had enriched Bobby Darin's pocket by tens of thousands of dollars in unpaid royalties and fees and secured an advance royalty deal for the Stones to the tune of 1.25 million dollars. In 1967, he took over Cameo-Parkway Records and used it to build up a new company ABKCO Industries Inc (Allen and Betty Klein Company), attracting much criticism for the way in which Cameo shares rose in price following the company's acquisition. Lennon, Starr and Harrison were impressed with Klein; McCartney was not so keen. His associations with American photographer Linda Eastman's family firm of lawyers led him to suggest employing her brother John. For a while Klein and John Eastman worked somewhat uneasily in harness. They were mainly concerned with gaining money and control over the various Beatle-associated companies on behalf of their clients – but without total success.

Klein was instrumental in releasing the Beatles from their ties with NEMS which, in early 1969, was taken over by a merchant bank-controlled investment house, Triumph, and in releasing Lennon and McCartney from their association with their original publishing company, Northern Songs, which was taken over in 1969 by Lord Grade's ATV company. But these manoeuvres were hardly about winning control: in fact, they were an admission of the Beatles' inability to be their own bosses in a world run by large-scale financial institutions. Most of the money Klein gained for the Beatles was essentially the result of liquidating their assets, a fact which the Eastmans continued to emphasise throughout the last period of the Beatles' disintegration.

Klein did, however, succeed in simplifying the Beatles' affairs in the first few months of 1969 and was confirmed as business manager in May of that year. A ruthless operator, he mopped up all the excesses at the Apple headquarters, sacking people at a moment's notice – even such a long-standing servant as Alistair Taylor who had acted as general manager. Magic Alex got the chop, as did Apple Retail, Apple Publishing, Apple Foundation for the Arts and Zapple (an offshoot from an idea of McCartney's to produce recordings of the spoken word). Expense accounts were trimmed and a clocking-in system introduced. The halcyon days for the hangers-on at Savile Row were over.

By 1970, Apple had become a profitable organisation, if a pale shadow of its former, fun-loving self. Its main business was as a record label and agent for the Beatles and a handful of other performers. Few of the label's releases by people other than the Beatles (jointly or individually) made any impact at all, and Apple's release policy reflected the taste of individual Beatles rather than commercial sense. While Klein could claim to have made the Beatles over £4 million in 1970, doubling the previous year's earnings, he could hardly claim that Apple without the Beatles would be a viable organisation.

McCartney happily accepted the

bounty that Klein's management brought (even doing some private share-dealing to the dismay of his fellow Beatles), but he never liked the man. The Eastmans insisted that Klein had actually lost the group potential earnings, notwithstanding the improved royalty deal he had negotiated with EMI, Apple's distributors. It later came out that Klein had indeed liberally interpreted his agreement with the Beatles in order to rake off a higher percentage of those royalties than he was strictly entitled to. The Beatles themselves rarely came to the office any more; they were preoccupied with their individual careers and private relationships.

The final straw came in early 1970 when the four fell out over the timing of the release of the last Beatles' album, *Let It Be*. The tapes, produced by Phil Spector, had been around since early 1969; nobody liked the session well enough to release them, but there was a film tie-in to the album and George Martin had been brought in to relieve the album of its worst Spectorian excesses – it was, after all, an asset. Meanwhile, Paul had readied his own first solo album for release and the scheduled dates coincided too closely for his personal or the Beatles' collective liking.

Paul McCartney's announcement that the Beatles no longer existed – issued at the time of his solo album release – was followed a few months later by his legal suit to dissolve the Beatles & Co partnership. Lennon gave his 'working-class hero' interview to *Rolling Stone* and, between that and the court case, a great deal of dirty linen was washed in public. Beatles & Co was eventually dissolved in the spring of 1971. Apple was reduced to a skeleton record company, releasing individual work

Above: McCartney and step-daughter take control during Let It Be. *Below: Up on the roof – the Beatles' final performance.*

by the Beatles until the time for the renegotiation of contracts with EMI came up in 1976.

An empire crumbles

Allen Klein went back to the United States to face charges relating to the illicit sale of promotional Apple albums and each of the Beatles (especially McCartney) ended up making more money in the next eight or nine years than they had probably dreamed of during the Beatlemania period. They became an empire – but one whose territories were so far-flung that, rich as the Beatles might be, only the 'men in suits sitting on their fat arses in the City' of whom Lennon had complained in 1969 had any idea of what the empire was about. It was, of course, about money – as it always had been.

The film *Let It Be* (released in 1970) records those final years at Apple, culminating in the famous scene on the rooftop of the Savile Row offices one afternoon. The traffic was brought to a standstill by four long-haired chaps playing 'Get Back', the cold wind blowing in their faces, as an era drew to its close. In the words of John Lennon: 'Everybody had a good time'.

GARY HERMAN

GOING UNDERGROUND

The London club scene took off with UFO

THE STORY OF THE CLUBS and musical events associated with the underground scene in London is, in many ways, the evolution of the underground itself – the two are inextricably bound up with each other. By common agreement, the first public manifestation of the phenomenon was the International Poetry Festival at the Albert Hall in June 1965, which brought together poets from the English alternative arts scene, like Pete Brown, and Americans such as Allen Ginsberg. The audience that day was full of strangely clad figures, bedecked with flowers and carrying joss-sticks – hippies were making their first public appearance in the UK.

Hazy Sunday afternoons

A number of the Americans who helped organise the event remained in London and became prime movers on the scene. One was Steve Stollman, brother of the owner of the avant-garde ESP label in New York. In February 1966 he organised the first of a series of events known as 'Spontaneous Underground', which were held at the Marquee Club on Sunday afternoons. In retrospect these events seem oddly parochial, decidedly naive and having more in common with early Sixties beatnik happenings than anything else; they were, nonetheless, the first link in the chain that led to the UFO club and beyond. The early ones featured people like Cream lyricist Pete Brown performing conjuring tricks, and strange avant-garde orchestras that utilised transistor radios, not to mention a girl playing a Bach fugue accompanied by African drummers. Then in March, Spontaneous Underground was enlivened by the appearance of an unknown band dubbed the Pink Floyd Sound. They were loud, weird and unique – and they fitted perfectly.

Over the weeks at the Marquee things developed, plans were hatched and the characters who were to become major

Below far left: John 'Hoppy' Hopkins, co-founder of IT *and UFO. Bottom far left: Pedestrian art at the* IT *launch party, 1966. Bottom centre: Soft Machine play at the same event. Below left: Flesh and lights at the Arts Lab, Drury Lane, 1967. Below: Pink Floyd at Middle Earth. Bottom: A hippie at Alexandra Palace, 1967.*

forces in the underground – John Hopkins, Miles (who ran Indica Books), Andrew King and Pete Jenner (who became the Floyd's managers) and Joe Boyd – all came together. The scene shifted from the Marquee to the London Free School in Notting Hill Gate, a community self-help establishment run primarily by 'Hoppy' (as Hopkins was universally known). One of its early classes was the Sound/Light Workshop, at which Pink Floyd often provided music. The group soon became the centre of interest, and All Saints Hall in Powis Square was swamped every week. The stage was set for something new and exciting involving all the various components: lights, films, dance and music.

The first big event of this 'new' underground was a party to launch *International Times* (England's first underground paper and the brainchild of Miles and Hoppy), held at the Roundhouse in Chalk Farm on 15 October 1966. Originally an engine shed, the Roundhouse had been taken over by the Gilbey's Gin concern, which had installed a balcony that stood on wooden pillars. The building had a marvellous, almost romantic atmosphere – it was a monument to nineteenth-century industrial design. Unfortunately it was cold, had almost no lighting, just two lavatories and the only entrance was via an ancient, steep and extremely narrow staircase.

Nonetheless the *IT* party was a memorable event. Some 2000 people turned up and were greeted by Miles handing out sugar-cubes (which turned out not to be of the LSD-coated variety, despite legend to the contrary). What took place set the style for later events – people in bizarre fancy dress rolling in huge jellies, dancing, revelling, tripping and watching films; a Bacchanal of the first order. Paul McCartney showed up dressed as an Arab, the Italian film director Michelangelo Antonioni was there taking a break from shooting *Blow Up* and Marianne Faithfull, wearing a nun's habit, won the prize for the 'shortest/barest' costume. Music was provided not only by Pink Floyd but also Soft Machine, whose instrumentation included a motorcycle with a contact mike attached to the cylinder head – the bike was revved up from time to time to add to the group's euphonious wailing.

Pink Floyd, meanwhile, brought with them the light show they had been using at the Free School – oil dropped on photographic slides pulsated in time with music. Within months that light show was to seem incredibly primitive, but few people had seen one before and the Roundhouse audience was transfixed. Musically the Floyd played one of their best sets, even though the power short-circuited in the middle of 'Interstellar Overdrive'.

Underground freak out

The *IT* party was also the first underground event to garner national press coverage; *The Sunday Times* ran a story on it, including an interview with Pink Floyd's Roger Waters. Over the next few months, further one-off events along the lines of the party took place. Some, like 'Psychodelphia Versus Ian Smith', were held at the Roundhouse; others, like the even more bizarrely-named 'Freak Out Ethel', were held elsewhere. However, none of them quite captured the magic of the *IT* party, especially as many (the 'New Years Eve All Night Rave' at the Roundhouse, for example) were obviously commercially-motivated ventures. But by the end of the year, the underground had found a new centre – at UFO, the Friday night club founded by Hoppy (aided and abetted by Joe Boyd and Miles) that had grown out of the Free School.

Below: An audience sits and 'grooves' to the sounds and lights at UFO. Until its demise in October 1967, the club served as headquarters of the London underground scene. Inset: Granny Takes A Trip, a popular hippie clothes outlet.

Above left: Poster for the 14 Hour Technicolor Dream. With 41 groups on the bill and over 10,000 people in the audience (above), this turned out to be the London underground's biggest event.

UFO was located in an Irish dance-hall called the Blarney Club in the basement of 31 Tottenham Court Road, opposite the Dominion Theatre, and opened on 23 December 1966. At first, the club was titled 'UFO Presents Night Tripper'; the 'Night' part was relevant as UFO always hosted all-night events, a factor that put it out of the reach of many hippies, especially young ones and those with day-jobs.

The UFO legend has grown over the years and, as Roger Waters has said, 'It's got rosier with age, but there is a germ of truth in it.' So what actually happened there? It certainly wasn't just a club in the entertainment sense; it was a genuine meeting/market place for the underground. For the first couple of months virtually everyone knew everyone else who was packed inside and sniffed the overpowering aroma of sweat and dope. Deals were made and projects planned. One could buy hippie paraphernalia from the 'head' shop or a frilly shirt from John Pearce's Granny Takes A Trip stall. Later on, more intense activities took place in backrooms, like black activist Michael X relieving liberals of 'conscience' money for one of his schemes or Michael Henshaw (accountant to the underground and the 'responsible' face of UFO) trying to arrange bail for someone. It was a remarkably relaxed environment, in which the likes of Mick Jagger or John Lennon could sit all night without being pestered for autographs.

And then there was the entertainment itself, with which UFO refined the previous mixed-media attempts into a heady brew that has never been equalled. Some nights it did bear more relation to the early Sixties – tired poets reading their works to the backing of jazz combos – but generally, especially when Pink Floyd played, it was magic. When UFO started Hoppy had given the Floyd the contract to provide music and lights at the club. Although the group didn't play at UFO every week, it's fair to say that the club was home base for the band and it always gave them a chance to play for an audience that understood and loved their music.

Helter-skelter

UFO also attracted many of the new bands who were springing up in the wake of the Floyd. Some went on to some degree of fame and fortune, notably Soft Machine, perhaps the most intellectual of them all. Others included Arthur Brown (he of the flaming head-dress), the Purple Gang (who recorded 'Granny Takes A Trip', a UFO anthem), Tomorrow (featuring singer Keith West, future Yes guitarist Steve Howe and a great line in theatrics) and Procol Harum, who played at UFO the week their 'A Whiter Shade Of Pale' went to Number 1.

Not everyone thought that UFO – or the underground in general – was wonderful, however. There was increasingly abusive coverage in the press, and at the beginning of April 1967 the police raided the offices of *IT* in a calculated attempt to close the paper down. In order to raise money a benefit event was put together. 'The 14 Hour Technicolor Dream', as it was called, took place at Alexandra Palace on 29 April and it turned out to be the biggest single underground event – though it is a curious paradox that something that attracted over 10,000 people could be described as 'underground'. This immense crowd turned up to watch the 41 bands, listen to poetry, see films and ride the helter-skelter. There were two stages with bands playing simultaneously, which with the various light shows was almost too much to take in. Soft Machine were in top form – Kevin Ayers in cowboy hat surmounted by aeroplane wings, Daevid Allen in miner's helmet – but once again it was Pink Floyd who stole the show, coming on as the first light of dawn poured through the high windows, their eerie sounds echoing around the building. In retrospect, the Technicolor Dream was not only the biggest and best underground event but also the last genuine one.

Back at UFO things were starting to go awry; basically it was too small to accommodate the increasing number of visitors. The original 'freaks' and hippies had been largely displaced by unwelcome newcomers; at best, these were 'weekend hippies', at worst they were drunken sailors (who took the idea of 'free love' a little too literally) or hippie-bashing skinheads.

The crunch came in June, when Hoppy was imprisoned for drug offences. Police pressure on the club increased in the following weeks, resulting in the landlords revoking the lease. The club moved into the Roundhouse but, despite the fact that the building was still almost derelict, the rent was exorbitant. When a big name like Eric Burdon or Jeff Beck was playing, UFO broke even, but the club more often lost money. The Roundhouse may have been a good place for special events, but the atmosphere of the club evaporated in the cold emptiness of the building. UFO stuck it out until October and then folded – for many people it was the end of an era.

Part-time hippies

That summer of 1967 had represented the height, in public terms, of the new alternative culture; by the autumn it had sunk, very nearly without trace. From being the property of a committed minority the previous winter, it had spread with remarkable speed throughout the country, falling prey to over-commercialisation; neck-bells tinkled in high streets across the country and by September flower power had become a national joke. The music suffered too. Any band that had been remotely kaftan-and-bell-oriented was in danger of being laughed off stage.

Pockets of resistance held out, however, and a few clubs continued something approximating to a UFO style. UFO had not been the only club with an underground atmosphere and clientele at the time, but the others were without exception more overtly commercial enterprises. One of the best was Happening 44, located at 44 Gerrard Street in Soho and run by Jack Bracelin, who had been part of the Free School Light/Sound workshop where he had developed his own light show. The Social Deviants (with Mick Farren) was virtually Happening 44's houseband.

Better-known than Happening 44, however, was Middle Earth in Covent Garden. This had evolved from the Electric Garden

Above: Dancing and hanging around at the Roundhouse, 1967. Below: Spandau Ballet's Martin Kemp (right) with Steve Strange, whose occasional clubs in the Eighties resurrected the ideals of UFO.

which had opened a few months after UFO but, despite interesting bills, had never taken off. Yoko Ono was supposed to have sensed 'bad vibrations' on the opening night – possibly because the club was run by two East End gangsters. After a couple of months it closed and then reopened as Middle Earth. It was still run on commercial lines but the new owners wisely employed hippies as organisers of the club, notably Dave Howson, who had been one of the organisers of the 'Technicolor Dream'. While UFO was still in operation, Middle Earth diplomatically closed on Friday nights.

After the demise of UFO, however, Middle Earth took over as the main underground music club. The club's policy was, in some ways, less adventurous than that of UFO, but their more commercial nature meant they were able to book a lot of big-name artists, especially from the United States; over the following year Tim Buckley, Captain Beefheart, the Byrds and even the Ike and Tina Turner Revue played in Covent Garden. Also, like UFO, Middle Earth tried out the Roundhouse for a few gigs, including the major coup of putting on Jefferson Airplane and the Doors in September 1968. Shortly after, however, the club folded, another victim of dwindling finances and police pressure. Arguably, Middle Earth was the last genuine underground club, although mention should be made of the Temple, which in 1969 operated out of the basement of the old Flamingo Club in Wardour Street. The Temple was probably the seediest rock venue London has ever had and attracted a clientele to match its sordid decor: acid casualties, speed freaks, shysters and thieves.

By 1969, the underground – superficially, at least – had more adherents than ever before; in reality, however, it simply meant there were more people (particularly in the suburbs) with long hair who took LSD. Any connection they may have had with the early UFO crowd was accidental and their meeting places – the Midnight Court at the Lyceum (run by Mecca) and Implosion at the Roundhouse – lie outside this history.

The underground clubs and events were, of course, a product of their time and thus can never be duplicated. However, the clubs and events arranged by Steve Strange in the early Eighties, with their emphasis on performance art and esoteric atmosphere, resurrected some of the ideas, if not the spirit, of UFO. JOHN PLATT

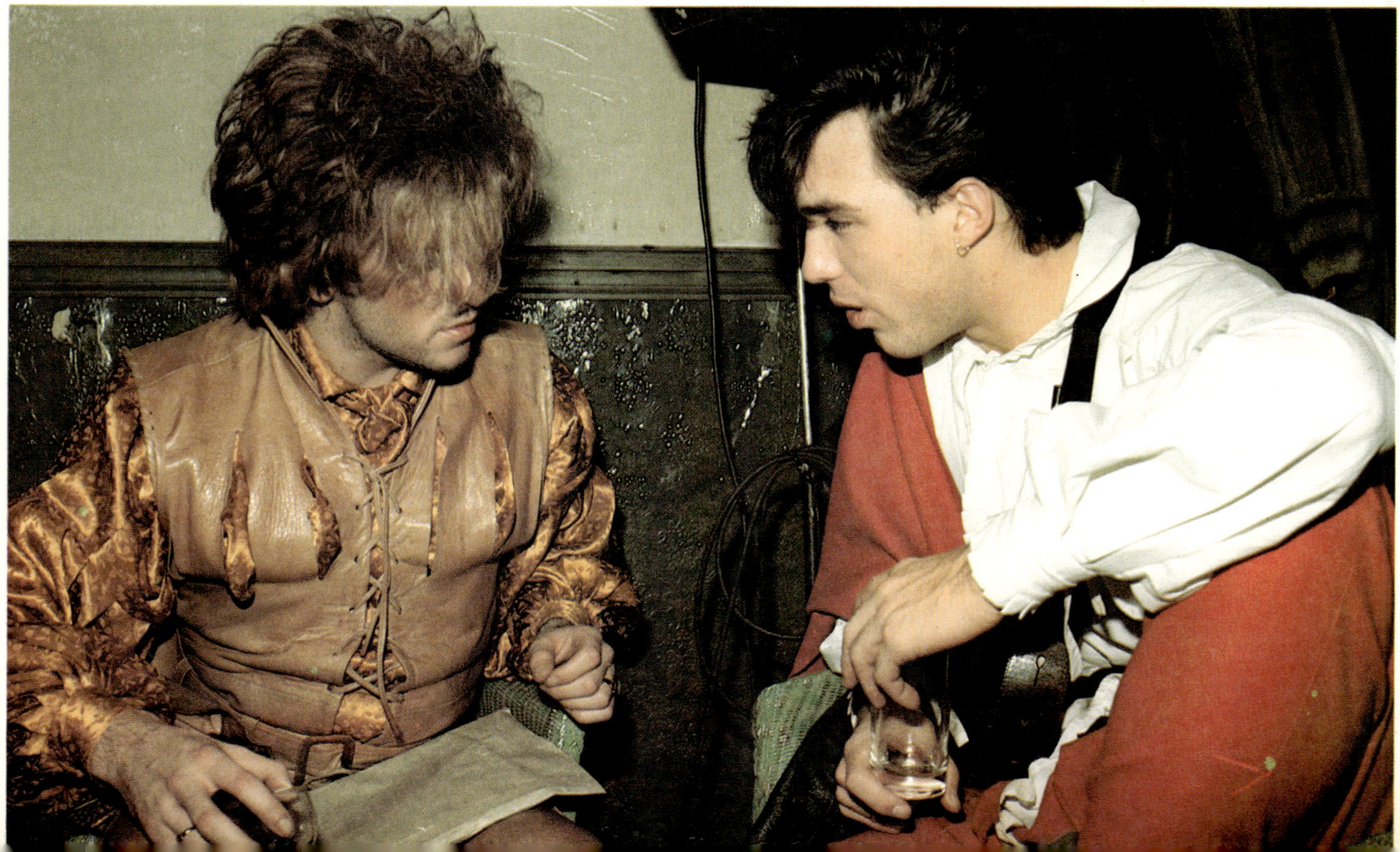

THE SPIRIT OF '67

It was the year of *Sgt Pepper*, of the comic-book antics of the Monkees, of the unbridled optimism of Monterey. It was also the year that the Beatles' mentor, Brian Epstein died, that music stars and the law came into increasing conflict, that protest against 'Yankee imperialism' became more vociferous. In 1967, the idealistic hippie myth reached the height of its influence and, simultaneously, discovered how far it had to fall

THE MOOD OF '67

In 1967 all the elements of rock that had been gathering momentum for over a decade were transformed by the atmosphere of a single extraordinary year, and gave birth to the music we know today. The 'atmosphere' of one year is elusive – impossible to recreate. Perhaps that of 1967 is best summed up in the word optimism. People – young people especially – felt that things could (and would) get better. Youth thought it could take over the world; and music was the mood of the moment.

By 1967, rock was a music with a distinct history. What musicians did in that year was often more ambitious or better-played than what had gone before; but it was part of a tradition that still continues. The power of Janis Joplin on stage was preceded by the charisma of the early Elvis Presley – and was to be followed by the stage pyrotechnics of Bruce Springsteen. The singing style of Smokey Robinson and the Miracles was in the line of Clyde McPhatter and the Drifters; the Beatles could hold audiences spellbound playing Little Richard tunes of 1956. Pete Townshend represented his generation just as Gene Vincent had 10 years before and as Johnny Rotten was to 10 years later. In 1967, rock musicians were more aware of their history than ever before and partly *because* they knew where the music came from there was an unprecedented interaction that led to new forms, new possibilities and new attitudes, and that determined the music to be heard in the Seventies and Eighties. The terms of the mid-Sixties – 'beat', 'surf', 'mod', 'soul', all under the heading 'pop' – were becoming outmoded: a new age was beginning. In 1967, 'rock' was defining itself.

The new excitement and widening relationships spread outside the music. Rock even evolved its own distinct visual sense; not just in the clothes and hairstyles of the performers, but in art. When the Beatles opened their Apple boutique in late 1967 it was covered with a huge mural in the psychedelic style. Clothes, record sleeves, posters, even cars, all bore the characteristic swirling motifs.

Rock is . . .

By 1967 folk-rock, the most striking combination of different traditions, had already become an accomplished fact. But 1967 saw combination and fusion accelerating, and working at all levels. The blues tradition and the expanded consciousness (and self-consciousness) of psychedelia came together in Cream and the Jimi Hendrix Experience to give birth to the heavy metal sounds that dominated the early Seventies; the Seventies punk revolution was prefigured in the work of the Velvet Underground, whose emergence was a result of the interaction between the New York rock scene and Andy Warhol's organisation. Jazz-rock, too, was beginning as Miles Davis experimented with electric keyboards.

Below: Joe Strummer of the Clash: once the embodiment of punk he became the darling of music's radical chic.

It is one thing to identify the various strands present at the beginning of 1967; but quite another to show how and why they were changed. Rock as a music can be defined academically in terms of dynamic repetitive rhythms and certain melodic and harmonic structures, but ultimately it refuses to be pinned down, dissected and analysed. It has to be seen and heard, to be experienced. From 1956 to the present day, the same elements show through – Chuck Berry's guitar on 'Johnny B. Goode', and the sound of Jimmy Page on 'Whole Lotta Love'; the stage performances of Jerry Lee Lewis and David Bowie; Fats Domino's solitary piano and Rick Wakeman's battery of keyboards. They all, in their different ways, make rock music.

Rock is the result of contradictory forces – personal expression versus financial necessity; social comment versus commercial greed; the meticulous standards of the recording studio versus the wild anarchy of stage performance. But it acts as an acute and often liberating expression of generation-wide feelings and emotions. For above all, rock reflects its audience. The musicians are not isolated artists, working alone on something that is uniquely theirs, but neither can they be mere skilled manipulators, working on the orders of a record company. What happened in 1967 was that the audience was changing, at the same time as the musicians themselves were searching

the application of the driving rhythms of rock to the more demanding or 'committed' lyrics of the folk tradition, but also in the development of more expressive instrumental techniques, and the attempt to articulate more complex emotional states in the sound of the music itself.

The Beatles

In 1967, then, people were expecting more, and they were being given more from the music. And in this process, the Beatles held a unique place. They were the undisputed kings of 'pop' music, and their influence on the development of new attitudes was immense – not perhaps so much in what they actually achieved, but because their innovations legitimised the process of reaching out for something new. Unlike Elvis Presley or any of the previous great names, they had not been content to follow a conventionally safe commercial path after their first wave of international success. Their LPs showed a distinct musical progression, cannibalising old styles and evolving new ones: their last LP of 1966, *Revolver*, for example, had a far harder edge than its predecessor, *Rubber Soul*. Their album covers had been influential in changing styles of presentation; even their films were a departure from the norms of previous 'pop' cinema. The Beatles were a catalyst of crucial importance in creating new expectations both in the audience and in other musicians.

In 1967, it seemed the whole world was waiting for something new, and the power of music was beyond doubt. Against this background, the most eagerly-awaited event of the year was the release in the summer of *Sgt Pepper*, the Beatles' new LP.

Above: Mick Jagger, still going strong after all those years. While most of the big groups of the Sixties fell by the wayside, the Rolling Stones carried on, a tribute to Jagger and Keith Richards' continuing inventiveness. Right: Jimmy Page, guitar hero of Led Zeppelin, heavy-metal axeman extraordinary.

for new levels of expression. Neither 'caused' the other – but they coincided and were inextricably linked.

A new audience

In 1967 young people were taking themselves more seriously than ever before. Various factors were at work: the Vietnam War and the growth of political consciousness; riots in the black ghettoes and the civil rights movement in the USA; the extension of university education; growth in teenage purchasing power; and the general dissatisfaction with traditional institutions that was to erupt in Europe, especially in Paris, during the following year.

The centres of a new youth culture were 'swinging London' and California – Carnaby Street and Haight Ashbury. And in both, music – rock music – was all important.

The audience who had welcomed the Beatles three years before had not grown away from the music; but now they expected it to reflect different concerns. No longer was music merely an escape for a frustrated generation; it was becoming the symbol of a generation which felt that it might embody real change – either social, political or personal. Music had to become more expressive to reflect this.

If the audience was changing, so too were the musicians. Many of them wanted to do more than had previously been attempted in popular music, and now they had a golden opportunity to do so. This was not merely in

The Beatles in 1967; all you need is love. They invited their friends along to share in the love, peace and flower-power of the happening. The world looked in.

1967 *The year it all came together*

ALL WE'VE GOT NOW is a collection of well-mannered pop songs in a fading Pop Art sleeve, but at the time *Sgt Pepper's Lonely Hearts Club Band* was an event, the greatest *event*, indeed, that pop had ever known.

The LP was released on 1 June, but had been news for months before. 'Strawberry Fields Forever'/'Penny Lane' was the taster, and we all knew – because the noise was leaking out of the studio, into the press – that the Beatles were making a masterpiece. *Sgt Pepper* was the sign of the summer of love before we'd even heard a note, and it headed the album charts for the rest of the year. Everyone, everywhere, listened to it. *Sgt Pepper* crossed class, age and cultural lines, and the Beatles' evangelical role was fixed finally by television, in the live transmission round the world of 'All You Need Is Love'; the power of the Beatles' music to create community was expressed by a jumble of stoned Beatles' friends chanting their all-embracing love in an eternal fade.

The Beatles' genius was to make music out of such conceits – 'All You Need Is Love' was a genuinely moving song, and *Sgt Pepper* was, at the least, a striking restatement of the Beatles' ability to throw sounds and ideas into a pop swirl and always emerge with instantly accessible, immediately pleasurable *songs*. John Lennon and Paul McCartney's melodic ease and lyrical wit sparkled through the new effects – the sitars and farmyard noises, the electronic devices, the backwards-running tapes, the trumpets and strings. The Beatles' music was, as ever, appealing because of its very cleverness, as, for example, when Lennon turned a found poem, 'For The Benefit Of Mr Kite' into the musical equivalent of the reproduction Edwardian posters that were, by now, lining the King's Road. But *Sgt Pepper* was more than just another good pop LP. In making their own style out of the sounds of 1967 streets, the Beatles gave these sounds a shape, a form. *Sgt Pepper* made 1967 optimism concrete; it defined the year.

The watershed

Sgt Pepper was, according to its producer, George Martin, 'the watershed which changed the recording art from something that merely made amusing sounds into something which will stand the test of time as a valid art form: sculpture in music, if you like.' In fact, *Sgt Pepper* can be seen as the last great pop album, the last LP ambitious to amuse *everyone*. And what made the record so successful an event was, precisely, its ambition. *Sgt Pepper* took 700 hours to record (remarkably, George Martin was still using only a four-track machine) and cost £25,000 to produce; the Beatles' first LP had cost £1,250. Pop artists Peter Blake and Jan Haworth were commissioned to design the sleeve and it cost almost as much – EMI agreed the cover montage of 62 celebrities only when the Beatles guaranteed to cover the possible costs of up to £2 million should any of these famous faces sue. These facts and figures were part of the package – *Sgt Pepper* appealed because it was such an expensive, such an elaborate, playful *product*.

Recognise the faces on the sleeve, read through the lyrics and spot the marijuana plants, unpick the acid language ('Lucy In The Sky With Diamonds'), laugh as the BBC banned 'Day In The Life' ('I'd love to turn you on . . .') – *Sgt Pepper* turned pop fans into cultists and, for a moment, changed people's sense of what pop meant. This was, gushed drama critic Kenneth Tynan, 'a decisive moment in the history of Western Civilisation'. Sgt Pepper's Lonely Hearts Club Band was a new community of the young – classless and ageless too. This was pop's new purpose: to make out of pleasure a cultural, political optimism. Such ambition derived from the Beatles' authority – not just as skilled rock musicians, but skilled pop artists, self-conscious, calculating their entertaining effects. But it derived too from their wonderful responsiveness to the audience itself. The Beatles were not the leaders of 1967 pop but its symbols. They were as fascinated as everyone else by what was happening on the streets; they were as keen as everyone else to be followers of fashion. Their importance in 1967 was to use their position as superstars to express a generation's new concerns. The Beatles had been scruffy teenage rock'n'roll fans in the Fifties. By 1967 they were reworking their adolescence; this time they had money to spend. They were in charge now – ordering up weird sounds, dressing the hired symphony musicians in evening suits and red noses, telling EMI what to do. The company's only contribution to *Sgt Pepper* was to have Gandhi taken out of the cover picture; the company couldn't risk the Asian market.

Sgt Pepper celebrated the Beatles' own success, which they were only now beginning to understand. They had begun, like hundreds of other British musicians in the late Fifties (from Cliff Richard and Tommy Steele to the Animals and the Rolling Stones), by imitating the American sounds of rock'n'roll, rockabilly, skiffle, rhythm and blues, soul music, each dreaming of being the British Elvis Presley. They were the children of rock's first great age. But by 1967 the Beatles had changed what it meant to be a pop star.

John Lennon and Paul McCartney could take their market for granted; they were turning consumption into a culture. This music did indeed articulate most strikingly, most stirringly, the mood of 1967. *Sgt Pepper* marked the triumph of mod, the British way of being young. Rock'n'roll had always been about the teenage experience (just think of the songs of Buddy Holly or Eddie Cochran); mod music was about being young and British.

Swinging London

The Beatles no longer made a Liverpool sound. They had started as just another locally-supported provincial beat group, one among many (the Swinging Blue Jeans, the Hollies, the Fourmost, etc, etc) but they were now the centre of British pop. *Sgt Pepper* was London music, a shopping style: male boutiques (the Beatles' hand-made bandsmen's suits), sitar echoes and the smell of incense amongst the traffic noises of Carnaby Street and the King's Road, advertisements for swinging London, posing for provincial tourists, loitering on the pavements with the consumer élite.

1967's best pop songs were about *London* life and leisure – Jeff Beck's 'Hi Ho Silver Lining', the Small Faces' 'Here Come The Nice' and 'Itchycoò Park', Keith West's 'Excerpt From A Teenage Opera', Cat Stevens' 'Matthew And Son', the Zombies' 'Care Of Cell 44', David McWilliams' 'Days Of Pearly Spencer'. Mod songs in which play is hard work and work is just a

'When it came to putting the record out, the boys were convinced, rightly, that they had done something really worthwhile, which no one else had ever tried. They were determined that the cover should be equally original. So they got a man called Peter Blake to stage it for them. It cost a great deal. They wanted the faces of all the people they had ever admired to be in the photograph with them, together, just for the heck of it, with a lot of people they didn't admire at all. They borrowed wax models of themselves from Madame Tussaud's, together with the effigies of Diana Dors and Sonny Liston. Well, why not? Marlene Dietrich was there as a cardboard cut-out, along with D.H. Lawrence. Then they added all the things that they felt were indicative of their times: musical instruments, a hookah, a television set . . . and marijuana plants. There was a row about that, naturally.' **George Martin**

Top: George Martin, production genius behind the Beatles. They dressed up as theatrical soldiers for Sgt Pepper *(left), the cover of which featured their gallery of personalities. The presentation was jokey: a cut-out moustache and medal were given away with the LP. All in all,* Sgt Pepper *summed up the Beatles' position as the kings of pop who could do no wrong.*

chore; restless, knowing songs. The Kinks' 'Waterloo Sunset' held London in the going-home twilight: what if no-one asked you out to play?

These records marked the turning point of British beat; the music was no longer crude or raucous, but smart in all senses of the word. The established groups – Herman's Hermits, the Hollies, Manfred Mann, the Tremeloes, Dave Dee, Dozy, Beaky, Mick and Titch – grinned, wore bright clothes and sang high, soft harmonies. Even the Troggs, previously known for their uncouth image, chimed in that 'Love Is All Around'.

British beat had become a popular form to be made, artificially, in the studio; it was no longer necessarily bounced off sweaty dance floors or jumping teenage crowds. The roots of Seventies glam and glitter rock lay in 1967's increasingly ironic, distanced approach to record making, to the use of form as content.

These new pop writers weren't just cleverer than the Denmark Street studio pros who'd been turning out teenage hits for years; they showed off their cleverness and weren't concerned to fake angst or intimacy. The game was to apply the form to any content – mining disasters as well as love disorders. The self-conscious performers who were to dominate British pop in the Seventies had arrived.

David Bowie was still singing his London songs in an acoustic, Anthony Newley style, while Marc Bolan was forming Tyrannosaurus Rex. Bryan Ferry had completed his Pop Art studies with Richard Hamilton (who was to design the next Beatles sleeve, the White LP), while Jeff Lynne had already formed Idle Race and Roy Wood was taking the Move into the charts with 'Night Of Fear', 'I Can Hear The Grass Grow' and 'Flowers In The Rain'. As Graham Gouldman left Britain to try his hand at American bubblegum, the Bee Gees arrived back to make their first LP. Elton John and Rod Stewart were singing back-up vocals in blues bands.

The finest of the London bands was the Who, the smartest of the 1967 theorists was Pete Townshend. *The Who Sell Out* was a buoyant, funny record with a sharper concept than Sgt Pepper's sentimental lonely hearts club band. The Who had always been self-conscious about their music, explicit about their role as the spokesmen of 'My Generation'. They had always credited the inspiration of previous teenage pop spokesmen like Eddie Cochran and the Beach Boys; now Townshend's and John Entwistle's songs were about music as commodity. The group took their links and jingles from a real station, Radio London, but they wrote their own ads, and their songs could just as well have been adverts. *The Who Sell Out*, featuring falsetto harmony and jangling guitar, was the Who's long-promised Pop Art LP, a mocking presentation of the group as product. It was, like *Sgt Pepper*, a supremely confident record: the group pro-

Iod London in 1967. A Pre-Space Oddity
David Bowie strums acoustic guitar (inset
eft); Dave Dee, wearing yellow jacket,
poses with his group and female fan
below); while the Herd mime to their
ingle, 'From The Underworld' on 'Top of
he Pops', the television show.
Right: The cover of The Who Sell Out –
mainstream mod meets Pop Art.

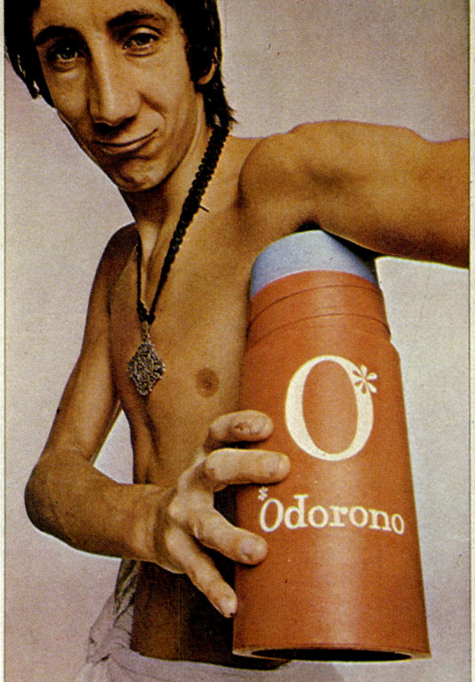

THE WHO SELL OUT

Replacing the stale smell of excess with the sweet smell of success, Peter Townshend, who, like nine out of ten stars, needs it. Face the music with Odorono, the all-day deodorant that turns perspiration into inspiration.

THE WHO SELL OUT

This way to a cowboy's breakfast. Daltry rides again. Thinks: "Thanks to Heinz Baked Beans everyday is a super day". Those who know how many beans make five get Heinz beans inside and outside at every opportunity. Get saucy.

vided their own commercial setting and so distanced themselves from it. Pete Townshend proclaimed his mastery of pop context as well as pop form – *The Who Sell Out*, like all his best work, was an account of a rock'n'roll fan, and looked forward to *Tommy*, the Who's triumphant statement of the power of rock music. Even in 1967, hippy days, Townshend was not anti-commercial. He argued that it was from commercial music that teenage solidarity and excitement derived.

The problem for mod music in 1967 was that it was finally tipping over and losing its balance – becoming just too commercial to embody teenage solidarity. Rock has always had a complex relationship with the established music industry. In 1956, the major record companies only reluctantly recognised rock'n'roll, and did their best to clean up the music; in 1976 they were unwilling to accept punk until forced to. In 1967, the establishment was enthusiastically embracing 'pop' and 'mod' music, which proved unable to resist the seductive lure of a comfortable future. This absorption by the establishment was symbolised by the creation of Radio 1 in the autumn. The BBC now undertook to fuel the youth market – and independent stations were squashed.

Radio in the USA had been essential to the emergence and spread of rock'n'roll (it was a radio DJ, Alan Freed, who popularised the term) and British pop music had suffered from the BBC's neglect – teenage fans were dependent on the erratic reception of Radio Luxembourg or patronising 'youth' programmes like 'Saturday Club'. It had taken pirate radio stations, broadcasting British beat, to challenge the BBC's elderly approach, and by 1967 the pirates, always aimed at youthful consumers, had made their point; their DJs, from Tony Blackburn to John Peel, were now BBC staff.

The success of the establishment in taming large segments of pop music led – inevitably – to reaction. The BBC, for example, had to censor its new DJs, especially where song lyrics concerned drugs. Even the Beatles' tune 'A Day In The Life' could not be played. Drug-culture psychedelia and progressive rock were clearly now the essence of rock as revolt – the sharp edge of the music.

The most distinctive single of 1967 was Procol Harum's 'Whiter Shade Of Pale', which married a white soul vocal and a Bach organ exercise to a flatly obscure lyric. 'Whiter Shade Of Pale' hinted at a vital secret open only to people in the right, drug-determined, state of mind. But the most symptomatic single of the year was the Herd's 'From The Underworld', which took the same beat sound, added a touch of Townshend guitar and Beatle trumpet, and accurately captured the feel of mod going psychedelic. This state of mind could be bought over the counter.

Psychedelia

Psychedelic rock had the mod concern for looking smart, but the shift of drugs, from pills to pot, was paralleled by a shift of aesthetic; there were new means of musical consumption – park concerts, multimedia happenings. Dancing became less important than listening and psychedelia developed its own clubs (UFO, Middle Earth), events (the 24 Hour Technicolour Dream) and radio shows (John Peel's 'Perfumed Garden'). The most obvious signs of psychedelia were not sounds but pictures, posters, sleeve designs. Primary, flowing colours, Asian motifs and fairy-story lines, elaborate symmetries and sci-fi bubbles turned up on the Rolling Stones' *Their Satanic Majesties Request* as well as on Donovan's *Gift From A Flower To A Garden*, on the Bee Gees' first LP as well as on the Incredible String Band's *5000 Spirits Or The Layers Of The Onion*, on Cream's *Disraeli Gears* and *Wheels Of Fire* as well as on Jimi Hendrix's *Axis: Bold As Love*.

Psychedelia was essentially élitist but

the joy of psychedelic pop was that it made everyone part of the élite. The musical implication was that only some people knew the truth of this art, but the social implication was that everyone had access to these musical mysteries. Hippy enlightenment was a state of mind that could be reached by all – through drugs, communes, meditation – and the British hippy cult soon had its own language, its own coded sets of references and attitudes, its own journals, *Oz* and *IT*. Partly because of this articulacy, the sheer weight of hippy words, psychedelia translated generational restlessness into an explicit counter-culture. And counter-culture meant artistic self-consciousness. Hippy musicians laid claim to superior knowledge as well as to superior musical skills, and musicians like Jimi Hendrix and Cream suggested possibilities of musical and artistic expression – though lengthy improvisation, more open harmonies, freer rhythms – that had never been dreamt of in three-minute pop songs. Musicians began to identify themselves with romantic artists generally – writers, painters, poets; they began to assume a culturally well-educated audience. Musicians moved from show biz to bohemia; bohemians seized on music as one more means of self-expression. John Lennon and Mick Jagger showed up in art galleries and books of poetry came out in psychedelic covers.

The self-definition of musicians as artists marked the move from the 'pop' of the mid-Sixties to what we now call 'rock'. At issue was the purpose of music-making – to please and put together a mass audience or to please and put together oneself. In 1967 the Beatles showed most clearly what the move from pop to rock meant. Their year began with 'Strawberry Fields Forever', psychedelic pop. It ended (after the death of Brian Epstein and the Maharishi moment) with the 'Magical Mystery Tour', a wilfully inexplicable TV special which put most of the audience to sleep. The Beatles were no longer in control of their time. Whereas they had once been able to seize on any idea and 'Beatlefy' it, make it common currency, they were now running vainly after a trend that was determined to leave the common audience behind.

The confusion was even more obvious in what happened to the Rolling Stones. Their year began, traditionally, with a TV show row (they had to change the words of 'Let's Spend The Night Together' on the Ed Sullivan Show) but the coy sex and drug references of *Between The Buttons* took on a new meaning when Mick Jagger, Keith Richards and Brian Jones were each convicted in the courts for drug offences. The Stones became, almost despite themselves, hippy heroes; the problem was what this meant musically and, for a moment, Jagger and Richards' detached, selfish rock'n'roll commitment was shaken – 'We Love You' and the *Satanic Majesties* LP were too-obvious attempts to follow the Beatles' psychedelic trip. It wasn't until 1968, when youth politics got rougher, that the Stones made 'Jumping Jack Flash' and became *the* rock group, translating drug culture back into rock-'n'roll terms.

An important source of the new psychedelic sounds was folk music. Donovan's 'Sunshine Superman' and 'Mellow Yellow' were, in one sense, just airy examples of London pop (produced by Mickie Most) but Donovan had begun as a folk club Dylan imitator and what he brought to psychedelia were folk qualities: a gentle voice and intimate acoustic appeal.

Psychedelic Britain: A poster for London's UFO club (above); the 5000 Spirits *cover (left) and an early shot of Pink Floyd (below) with the legendary guitarist Syd Barrett seated centre. Opposite top: Cream (Clapton, Baker, Bruce). Opposite below: Donovan.*

The possibilities of folk-rock were further explored by the much more agile, ambitious and, in folk terms, authentic Incredible String Band, whose second album, the *5000 Spirits*, combined the psychedelic pursuit of innocence and the traditional themes – love and death – of folk bohemia. This combination – songs of innocence and experience – quickly became familiar, and marked the link between the British traditional folk revival of the early Sixties and the singer songwriters of the Seventies (like Roy Harper and Gerry Rafferty). Pentangle was formed in 1967 by the most influential folk bohemian, Bert Jansch, and that summer Fairport Convention, still under the influence of Bob Dylan's 1966 electric tour, began playing their own version of American folk-rock in the Middle Earth and UFO clubs. But the most original and immediately successful folk-rock group was Traffic, whose retreat from city noise to a cottage-in-the-country resulted in *Mr Fantasy*; Steve Winwood's soulful vocals were given a setting of psychedelic folk music.

The Progressives

The second element of British hippie music was 'progressivism'. In 1967 Pink Floyd released their début single, 'Arnold Layne', and their début album, *The Piper At The Gates Of Dawn*. The group were UFO's most regular, most honoured performers. Syd Barrett's songs had the folk-rock combination of naivety and knowledge, but his music also had a menace, a sense that what was unsaid was too unset-

'Strange times – a kaleidoscope of allnighters at the Roundhouse and Middle Earth, La Fenêtre Rose in Paris and the Heliport in Rotterdam. Pink Floyd playing astral Bo Diddley, Tomorrow, Dantalion's Chariot, Mark Boyle's light show, overnight drives in an ancient Commer van.

The year came to a climax with the monster Christmas gig at Olympia – Hendrix, Traffic, Soft Machine and many others. I managed to set up the gear and then retired to bed for a week with flu, missing what was probably one of the best musical events of that famous year.'

Hugh Hopper, Soft Machine roadie

tling to be heard. Barrett had drug nightmares which came out in his guitar style, a free-form exploration of harsh electronic tones (an obvious precursor of the punk guitar style of the late Seventies). The other Floyds set Barrett's private dreads in a public drama – space sounds, galactic life-forms hurtling past the beat. Pink Floyd shows, featuring long, quirky instrumentals, depended as much on the group's technological as their musical imagination. They provided noises and lights to lie back and have visions to, and such soundtracks became the norm of British progressive rock. Steve Howe, for example, was only one of numerous musicians who in 1967 began the move from psychedelic pop (Tomorrow's 'My White Bicycle') to progressive atmospherics (with Yes).

The most influential British avant-garde group in 1967 was Soft Machine, whose first single was released that year. Leading lights were Kevin Ayers, the Terry Riley-influenced Mike Ratledge and Daevid Allen (who soon moved to Gong and European progressive rock).

This music was 'progressive' because it was expected to progress: the musicians were going to get better and technique and expressive skills were equated – the better they could play, the more complicated things they would say. And the rock audience was progressing too: as the music got more profound, the music's listeners were getting more sophisticated. The hippy audience defined itself as different from, superior to, the 'normal' mass audience, the mindless fans of mod and pop, whose music had gone commercial.

Black sounds

The most widespread sound of commercial mod was Motown, the smartest, sharpest dance music around. Motown producers determined the sound of mod music: controlled emotion and a joyous beat, tentative voices with a sure support. The Supremes' 'Baby Love' and 'Where Did Our Love Go' had swept to the top of the British charts in 1964 and from 1964 to 1967 Motown was the sound everyone hoped to hear on the radio, to move to on the dance floor. By 1967 the company's hits had a relaxed sophistication, an emotional depth, that has never been matched. There was Smokey Robinson and the Miracles' 'I Second That Emotion', Jimmy Ruffin's 'What Becomes Of The Broken Hearted', the Four Tops' 'Standing In The Shadows Of Love' and 'Seven Rooms of Gloom', the Marvelettes' 'The Hunter Gets Captured By The Game', the Temptations' '(I Know) I'm Losing You', and the Supremes' 'The Happening', Motown's own sly psychedelic reference.

But if Motown was as important as the Beatles in producing the sound of the Sixties, the company was, by 1967, becoming the victim of its own success. Motown went on having hits (in the next couple of years it was more successful than ever) but these increasingly reflected the company's absorption into the pop mainstream (this was symbolised in 1967 by Diana Ross' separate billing from the Supremes), and Motown became steadily less significant. Rock fans, concerned for 'authenticity' and art, suspicious of craft and calculation, began to set Motown music against deep soul, against the 'spontaneity' of James Brown and the rawer sounds of Stax. By 1967 the king and queen of soul were, for white audiences, Otis Redding and Aretha Franklin.

Otis Redding died in 1967, killed on 10 December in a plane crash just as he was becoming a rock star. His posthumous hit, 'Dock Of The Bay', reflected his move out of soul; the frantic struggle for words was replaced by cool commentary on feelings. But that was to come. In 1967 Otis Redding and the Stax-Volt package toured Europe and their shows weren't about detachment from anything. Stax live was a quasi-religious experience; Stax soul involved an emotional commitment that shook even mod cool; Stax music (celebrated in Arthur Conley's 'Sweet Soul Music' and Sam and Dave's 'Soul Man') was sweaty and public and involving.

Aretha Franklin's *I Never Loved A Man (The Way I Love You)* represented a different sort of soul magnificence – the magnificence of 'Respect', female strength and black pride, music made without concessions, racial or sexual, black music without white frills. Aretha Franklin's music, like Otis Redding's, had a black power that anticipated the great soul years of 1969–72, when musicians like Isaac Hayes (in 1967 still working backstage with David Porter on Sam and Dave), Norman Whitfield, Curtis Mayfield and Marvin Gaye used their musical craft to create not popular community but black consciousness.

There was a similar shift in Jamaican music. In 1967 Desmond Dekker had his first British chart hit, '007', Prince Buster had his only British chart hit, 'Al Capone', and Dandy Livingstone made 'Rudy A Message To You', a chart hit for the Specials many years later. The sound of ska was making its move from mod cult to skinhead youth club, while in Jamaica Bob Marley, Bunny Livingstone and Peter McIntosh, collectively known as the Wailers, were recording 'I'm The Toughest'. Jamaican musicians were enjoying the post-rude boys relaxed rocksteady beat and beginning to develop the more political, spiritual, militant black sound of reggae.

The history of rock is inextricable from the history of Afro-American music – black Americans (and, more recently, Jamaicans) have provided rock musicians with their basic musical language. But the relationship of black music to rock has never been easy. In the Fifties the rock-'n'roll use of R&B songs and sounds often involved straightforward theft and it took the British beat groups of the mid-Sixties to reopen white American ears to music that had come to seem (after the brief success of Chuck Berry, Little Richard and Bo Diddley) 'crude' and 'monotonous'. By 1967 the possibilities of black and white musicians working together were open again, but the white-run music business continued to exploit black sounds as novelties.

During the Seventies, black and white music audiences, particularly in the USA, rarely overlapped. Black musicians had black concerns, and rock fans were hemmed in by their conception of art. Hippies stopped dancing to black music, and the collective excitement of late Sixties' soul was forgotten until the late Seventies rise of disco and rediscovery of funk. The possibilities for the development of a progressive British soul sound, still open in 1967, vanished until the appearance of Dexy's Midnight Runners over ten years later. 1967 was the year of the Foundations' 'Baby Now That I've Found You' and P.P. Arnold's 'The First Cut Is The Deepest' (written by Cat Stevens). P.P. Arnold's backing group went on to be the Nice and, unfortunately, this move (and Keith Emerson's later step from the Nice to ELP) was defined as 'progress'. Black music was honoured only on the dance floor.

The dancing sounds of '67 were those of Motown and soul – provided by stars such as Jimmy Ruffin (opposite top) the Supremes and Stevie Wonder (opposite bottom), Otis Redding (left) Wilson Pickett (right) and Ike and Tina Turner (below).

Back in the USA

By 1967 the USA had developed its own version of mod pop. Los Angeles was London's twin town; in its boutiques and clubs, on its radio shows and records the latest Anglo styles were posed and sold.

Buffalo Springfield's songwriters and singers, Steve Stills and Neil Young, had begun their musical life as folk singers. Their move into pop was an example of the Beatles' most important effect on American music, reclaiming the loyalties of thousands of disillusioned rock'n'roll fans (from Bob Dylan on down), who had abandoned teenage pop at the end of the 1950s for the 'adult' concerns of folk. Elvis Presley became a middle-of-the-road Hollywood star and Chuck Berry, Buddy Holly, Jerry Lee Lewis, Gene Vincent and the rest of the rock'n'roll pioneers had, in one way or another, been silenced and replaced by packaged teenage stars, but the fans were convinced by the new British sound that rock'n'roll was still exciting.

American Beatlemania further suggested that it was precisely its vast popular appeal that made rock'n'roll, compared to folk, an urgent, relevant political medium. As Bob Dylan soon discovered, there's no greater musical power than a Number 1 radio hit, and by 1967 everyone's ambition was to be a rock star – just as it had been in 1957 and was to be in 1977. American towns filled with teenage garage bands and punks making their own versions of the post-Beatle, post-Byrd, post-Yardbird psychedelic sound – fuzz tones, electric guitars, screamed vocals – which was, eventually, to become heavy metal.

It was ironic that the key influences on the British mod sound (which became the USA's mod sound) were also American. They were not much honoured in their own country either. In 1967 Phil Spector and Brian Wilson, their determination sapped by failure, withdrew from their role as America's pop pioneers. Neither ever returned to it.

Phil Spector's biggest pop successes had been with the records he made for the Crystals and the Ronettes but his crowning achievement was Ike and Tina Turner's 'River Deep Mountain High', which came out in 1966 to be a British hit. In the USA, though, it got little radio play and few sales. Spector's final integration of emotional and technological melodrama meant, apparently, nothing. He retired; Philles Records folded. Spector's ambitions for record production as an art form were to be central to the progressive rock of the Seventies; what didn't survive was

The two sides of American rock. The Monkees (top left) were the darlings of teen magazines (centre left) and inspired adolescent demonstrations when Davy Jones was threatened with the draft (left). Bob Dylan (right and inset) was a different phenomenon entirely: the artist as a spokesman for his generation, an independent, often introspective commentator.

his unique combination of megalomania, humour and pre-teen sentimentality.

Brian Wilson, like Spector, moved in the LA pop milieu, but whereas Spector had a commercially conventional role in this milieu, Brian Wilson and the Beach Boys tried to change the system. Wilson wrote his group's songs, recorded them himself, chose his own studios and musicians and engineers. He ignored his record company's usually dominant A&R (artists and repertoire) systems – the Beach Boys' Brother label, formed in 1967, pre-dated the Beatles' Apple by a year. The Beach Boys' independence reflected the position they had built since the 1963 release of 'Surfin' USA' as *the* American teenage group, but they soon showed they were much more than this. *Pet Sounds*, released like 'River Deep Mountain High' in 1966, was a record that the Capitol A&R department would certainly not then have been able to make for themselves; the record's use of painstaking overdubs, its 'non-musical' noises, its extraordinary ethereal atmosphere testified to Brian Wilson's claim to have invented 'art rock'.

Pet Sounds wasn't exactly a commercial failure – its premier track, 'Good Vibrations', was a huge hit on both sides of the Atlantic. Nevertheless, the Beach Boys continued to be regarded by the music world (including Capitol Records) as a party band who'd made a 'weird' record; *Pet Sounds* never got the critical acclaim afforded to *Sgt Pepper*.

By 1967 Brian Wilson was torn between the ideas of his new, strange LA pop cronies like Van Dyke Parks, and the nagging of the rest of his family, who wanted their traditional success. On 2 May it was announced that the Beach Boys had abandoned Wilson's most ambitious project yet, *Smile*. What we got instead was the low-key eccentricity of *Smiley Smile* and the fresh but backward-looking pop of *Wild Honey*. Wilson had lost confidence in his own unequalled utopianism.

Phil Spector's and Brian Wilson's withdrawal from the LA music scene reflected their loss of faith in the mass market's ability to absorb their imaginations; the effect of their withdrawal was to accelerate a rock/pop split that has afflicted American music ever since. 1967 was, in fact, an excellent year for American pop music. There was a spate of Spector/Wilson-influenced hits, such as the Electric Prunes' 'I Had Too Much To Dream Last Night', the Turtles' 'Happy Together', Strawberry Alarm Clock's 'Incense and Peppermints', Tommy James and the Shondells', 'I Think We're Alone Now', Fifth Dimension's 'Up, Up And Away'. But these were isolated hits by ephemeral groups rather than routine offerings from established hit groups. American pop still meant teenage manipulation and, measured by that yardstick, the most successful group of 1967 was the Monkees.

TV and the Monkees

The Monkees were put together, an obvious imitation of the Beatles, for a TV show aimed, like *American Bandstand* 10 years earlier, at teenage girls. Their music was produced according to the traditional rules of teenage pop (rules that Phil Spector had helped to write) by Brill Building veterans Don Kirshner and Jeff Barry, using songs written by professionals like Neil Diamond and John Stewart. The Monkees were designed to be the latest in the long line of TV-made teenybopper stars that began with Fabian and Frankie Avalon in the late Fifties and was to continue with the Osmonds, David Cassidy and the Bay City Rollers in the Seventies. The irony of the Monkees' success was that two members of the group, Peter Tork and Mike Nesmith, were themselves anti-pop ex-folk singers who had been hanging out in the LA scene with many of the people who were to become the 'authentic' rock stars of the Seventies like Steve Stills, who also tried for the Monkees but failed his audition. As it was, the Monkees came to stand for the way of making music against which rock was a revolt.

So, in a different way, did Los Angeles' second most successful group in 1967, the Mamas and Papas. The Mamas and Papas equally represented the LA combination of folk singers and old music biz pros but they wrote their own songs and had a

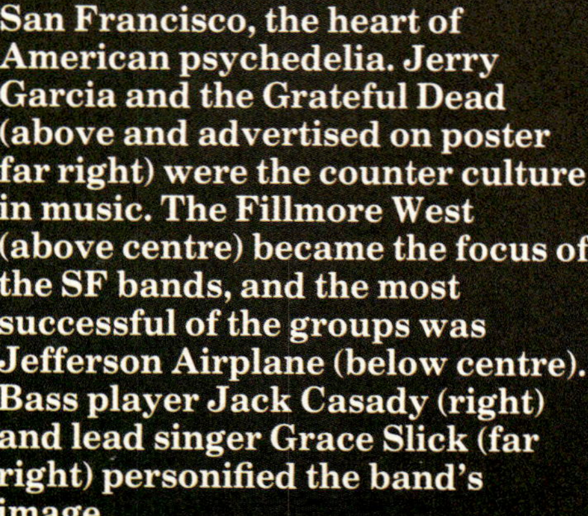

San Francisco, the heart of American psychedelia. Jerry Garcia and the Grateful Dead (above and advertised on poster far right) were the counter culture in music. The Fillmore West (above centre) became the focus of the SF bands, and the most successful of the groups was Jefferson Airplane (below centre). Bass player Jack Casady (right) and lead singer Grace Slick (far right) personified the band's image.

'The rock bands created a tribal, animal energy. We were a religion, a family, a culture, with our own music, our own dress, our own human relationships, our own stimulants, our own media.

And we believed that our energy would turn on the world.'

Jerry Rubin

more grown-up charm. They were in their own way hippies, but their music involved a soft-focus commercialisation of the Californian beach scene and as performers the Mamas and Papas rarely moved out of the middle of the road. Their songs and their sound were exhilirating; but when the American rock revolt began they too, as LA pop stars, were compromised. For American rock arguments came from San Francisco, a self-consciously anti-commercial, anti-pop musicians' community.

San Francisco

By 1967 San Francisco's hippies were being celebrated in song: Scott McKenzie's 'San Francisco', the Flowerpot Men's 'Let's Go To San Francisco', Eric Burdon's 'San Francisco Nights', songs which sold San Francisco as a natural product, like sunshine and flowers, available, like all pop, to the young at heart. The basis of the San Francisco community, though, was the city's artistic tradition. San Francisco music was made out of non-pop forms, blues and folk and jazz, and addressed non-pop issues; the San Francisco sound was, at heart, the sound of beatniks.

The San Francisco sound was, from the beginning, just one of a jumble of artistic activities – the beat/hippy connection was most obvious in Ken Kesey and the Pranksters' Acid Tests: music and lights and dance and drama and LSD were combined to achieve a total transformation of the senses.

The result was a new sort of music show which reached its climax on 14 January 1967 in the Human Be-In, a 'gathering of the tribes' of 20,000 people in Golden Gate Park, a free concert which featured the beat poetry of Allen Ginsberg, Gary Snyder and Michael McClure and the new Bay Area rock bands – the Grateful Dead, Jefferson Airplane, Quicksilver Messenger Service, Moby Grape, Steve Miller Band, Country Joe and the Fish and Big Brother and the Holding Company. The music these bands made reflected the needs of their acid-dropping audiences. It was rambling, loud, multi-textured and raw; with loose melodies and a heavy beat.

In counter-cultural terms, what mattered most about the San Francisco sound was not its content (loosely meaningful lyrics went with the loosely meaningful music) but its form. The SF bands made a new sort of popular music for a new sort of popular audience; they represented a new organisation of American leisure. What emerged from San Francisco was, in fact, a new style of commercialism. The most significant people in the Bay area music community weren't the musicians but the entrepreneurs. The most important rock-'n'roll entrepreneurs previously had been outsiders, seizing on stars opportunistically (Colonel Parker with Elvis Presley, the Chess brothers with Chicago R&B). The San Francisco operators, in contrast, emerged from within the new audience itself.

Concerts, radio and the press

Tom Donahue, a disc jockey and radio businessman, used the newly-freed FM wavelength to develop a new sort of music radio. His station, KMPX, featured album tracks, quiet disc jockeys, long spells of uninterrupted music; its concern (which soon had plenty of advertising support) was to organise the consumption of the Bay Area's hip community. Promoter Bill Graham turned hippy concerts, the trips, festivals and be-ins, into the money-making formula of the Fillmore night out – light shows and posters courtesy of the local artistic community, rock bands offered every technical facility, audiences guaranteed an efficient transcending experience. Journalist Jann Wenner started *Rolling Stone*, a rock fortnightly designed to fill the gap between the music trade press and the teenybop magazines by taking the new musicians and their audiences as seriously as they took themselves. The *Rolling Stone* approach was soon apparent too in the British music press, as *Melody Maker* and the *New Musical Express* began to change from pop papers, identifying with the business, to rock papers, identifying with the audience. These new ideas were symbolised by a single 1967 event: the Monterey International Pop Festival.

Glimpse of a new world

The Monterey Festival was the Los Angeles response to the Human Be-In. It was, in part, a sincere attempt to recreate the San Francisco event and to give the Bay Area bands (and their hippy message) a wider audience. But the Festival's central organisers (John Phillips of the Mamas and Papas, publicist Derek Taylor, entrepreneur Lou Adler) also had a clear sense of the Festival's commercial implications. They sold the film and TV rights in advance and made sure that Monterey was a showbiz gathering as well as a fan event – record company executives were pressured to come and see the wares.

For them the Festival was, in the words of Clive Davis of CBS, 'a glimpse of a new world', and the stampede to sign the Bay Area bands (all the Be-In acts were at Monterey) and give them national promotion accelerated. Jefferson Airplane had signed to RCA for 25,000 dollars in 1966, but now 'Somebody To Love' and 'White Rabbit' were Top Ten hits; so on the strength of their San Francisco base the Steve Miller Band were offered 75,000 dollars by Capitol, who also took Quicksilver Messenger Service. The hottest property at Monterey was Big Brother and the Holding Company or, rather Janis Joplin (managed now by Albert Grossman, Bob Dylan's manager). Clive Davis eventually got her for CBS. Her advance, an astonishing 250,000 dollars confirmed that the rock 'revolution', far from being anticommercial, was going to transform American popular music into an even bigger business.

The festival was a new sort of music-making event and symbolised rock as a new sort of relationship between performers and audience. Unlike the traditional package show tour, put together *for* the fans out there, festivals – in their length, their size, their settings – were attempts to provide materially the experience of community that the music expressed symbolically. Monterey stood too for pop as a multi-national community. The Festival's advisory panel (which included Brian Wilson, Brian Jones, Paul McCartney, Paul Simon and Art Garfunkel) was deliberately broad in its suggestions for performers. The San Francisco musicians on the five-day bill were joined by the Who and Jimi Hendrix from London, by the Byrds, Buffalo Springfield and the Mamas and Papas from LA, by blues bands like Canned Heat and Electric Flag, by the folk singer/songwriters Simon and Garfunkel and Laura Nyro, by Ravi Shankar and Otis Redding. The Festival was a statement of both rock's roots and rock's future.

Hendrix and Joplin

The performers who made the biggest stir at Monterey were Jimi Hendrix and Janis Joplin. Jimi Hendrix's importance for black and white musicians and audiences was immense. Together with Sly Stone (himself a member of the San Francisco scene, who signed to CBS in 1967) Hendrix opened up a place in rock for black musicians and, unlike Chuck Berry, Little Richard, Ray Charles, Muddy Waters or any of the Motown or Stax musicians, he became a teen idol. Also he founcd a place in black music for rock devices – electronics, flamboyance, the rock'n'roll beat. After Hendrix (via Miles Davis) came jazz rock and the funk fusion. But Hendrix's significance at Monterey was as a guitar hero; his amazing technical and imaginative skills were inextricable from his personality and his supposed prowess as lover.

Hendrix's British success ('Hey Joe' and 'Purple Haze' were hits in 1967) was not, at first, easy to translate into American market terms – he was only put on the Monterey bill at Paul McCartney's insistence and had been booked to tour the USA as support to the Monkees! Both Hendrix's Monterey appearance and his Monkees tour proved that American teenage music didn't have to be teenage pop: the idea of rock musicians as artists, as technical virtuosi, had arrived.

Jimi Hendrix wasn't the only source of the heavy metal sound. The Yardbirds – by 1967 on their way to becoming Led Zeppelin – had an equally direct influence on the garage bands, and the evolution of white blues from a purist, historical form (Eric Clapton had left the Yardbirds because they had become too commercial) into a crowd-pleasing technique was pioneered in Britain by Cream, formed by Clapton himself, Jack Bruce and Ginger Baker in 1966. Their music, lengthy electric improvisations and obscure lyrics courtesy of poet Pete Brown, had obvious parallels to that of San Francisco bands like the Grateful Dead. But Cream's music was more disciplined, more imaginative, more assertive and as Cream, following Hendrix, began to tour America they found, like him, a huge market – a market serviced by the new rock institutions: the Fillmore, *Rolling Stone* and FM radio.

Janis Joplin had much less musical influence than Jimi Hendrix, but her symbolic importance was as great – compare, for example, her confident, aggressive energy with the simpering 'sexy' sounds still expected from female pop singers in 1967 (the year of Sandie Shaw's aptly-titled 'Puppet On A String' and Sandy Posey's 'Single Girl') or with the pure tones of a female folk singer like Joan Baez. Joplin was not as good a singer as her fellow San Franciscan Grace Slick but she mattered more to her audiences because she challenged a wider set of assumptions about female glamour and attraction.

Janis Joplin trusted her audiences to such an extent that she held nothing back. Little of this can be heard on recor where Joplin's technical and imaginati weaknesses become obvious, but the i volving impact of her performances ha only ever been matched by Bruce Sprin steen.

Neither Joplin nor Hendrix surviv the confusion of their public and priva lives, but they set the problem th dominated rock musicians' lives for th next decade: how to guarantee the em tional impact of their performances nig after night after night. The answer (mo obvious in the Who's Woodstock perform ance) lay in technology, volume, a gr dually-evolved repertoire of rock signs.

The paradox of Monterey was one of th paradoxes of rock: massive record sal were predicted (and achieved) on the bas of the experience of live performan (Hendrix's and Joplin's in particular). If successful American mainstream LP ha until 1967, sold 300,000 copies, Jimi He drix established two million sales as th target. The most successful company i exploiting the rock boom was CBS, and i lead was followed by Warner Brother which took over Atlantic (and thus th American rights to Cream and Led Zepp lin) and went on to dominate the LA roc business.

'Up there in the festival grounds it was like the greatest show on earth, all life and vigour and health and loud, loud music. It was good to be, it was good to be. There were hassles, but they were about nothing and no one. The Chief of Police said it had been like a dream and we gave him a necklace. There wasn't one arrest and there wasn't one injury and the Mayor said she was very pleased with the young people who had come to her city. Music, love and flowers . . . the motto had come true and next year the city, remembering, decided such a thing must not happen again, and it hasn't since – not in Monterey. But once, it did happen in Monterey, a long time ago.'

Derek Taylor

Scenes at Monterey: the Mamas and Papas (far left), a poster stall and spectator (left and below left), Brian Jones (right) and the one and only Janis Joplin.

The other side of '67

The success of the major record companies with rock meant success too for the numerous independent rock entrepreneurs (like Robert Stigwood, manager of Cream and the Bee Gees, and Chris Blackwell of Island Records) who emerged to service them. The results were new selling systems (LPs, FM radio, serious rock magazines, concert tours and hip record stores as against singles, AM radio, poster magazines and package tours) in both Britain and the USA. In Britain, for example, 1967 was the last year in which singles outsold albums, the last time the major British record companies (Decca, Pye, EMI) dominated the British charts. The year was the turning point of the relationship between English and American music established by the Beatles. In 1967 US record sales topped a billion and in the long rock boom that followed CBS and WEA (Warner Elektra Asylum) slowly but steadily took over world and British sales from EMI and Decca.

What began at Monterey as the exhilarating process of putting together a new open-minded audience soon became the less risky process of servicing particular markets. Rock musicians were happy to make money, but they resisted definitions of their work in terms of pleasing audiences, giving them what *they* wanted. In fact, rock musicians soon found that they could have it both ways – make lots of money by apparently pleasing themselves. Self-indulgence, a contempt for the idea of 'pop', whatever the actual sales figures, became in itself an aspect of rock's popular appeal.

Left: We're Only In It For The Money, *Zappa's satire on* Sgt Pepper.

Personal visions

This sense of self-importance was most obvious in the American singer/songwriters inspired by Bob Dylan to use rock-'n'roll for their own purposes. Bob Dylan himself was notable by his absence in 1967, having withdrawn into domesticity to make the Basement Tapes with the Band, but the shift from folk songwriting to rock songwriting continued apace. It was obvious among women writers (folk was one of the few musical areas where it was possible to be an independent female performer). While Joan Baez was spending 10 days in jail for a draft resistance demonstration, Joni Mitchell was making the break out of the East Coast folk circuit. Her songs were taken up by established singers like Judy Collins, whose LPs *Wildflowers* and *In My Life* (arranged in an American version of Donovan's psychedelic folk by Joshua Rifkin) included not only Mitchell's 'Both Sides Now', but also Leonard Cohen's 'Suzanne'.

There had always been performers in pop who wrote their own songs but they had not previously been regarded as distinctive pop makers, as 'singer/songwriters'. Paul Anka's 'Diana', for example, had never been thought to express *his own* experience. Folk singers were contrasted to pop singers because they wrote and sang about the 'real' world of politics and individual experience.

Joni Mitchell and Judy Collins' music fitted comfortably into the 1967 sound of American pop; folk-rock breeziness had already been made popular by the Byrds and the Lovin' Spoonful. But 1967 also marked a shift of songwriting mood, The Lovin' Spoonful broke up amidst the recriminations that followed Zal Yanofsky's San Francisco drug bust (though John Sebastian's tie-dyed niceness survived in later stars like John Denver) and the Byrds made the ironic, sour single 'So You Want To Be A Rock'n'Roll Star'. 1967 was also the year of Bobbie Gentry's 'Ode To Billie Joe'; the possibilities of the singer/songwriter were now being exploited in Nashville, where Kris Kristofferson was already hard at work. Hank Williams and country boogie had been major influences on early rock'n'roll, and now country was reclaiming its place as a major force in rock.

Zappa and the avant-garde

Country music retained an unself-conscious populism as it took its place on the periphery of rock. Conversely, however, there was, by 1967, a self-proclaimed rock avant-garde concerned to make music about music, to comment on the process by which popular music became popular.

The most explicit rock élitist was Frank Zappa. The Mothers of Invention released *Absolutely Free* and *We're Only In It For The Money* in 1967, records with a sharp and savage sense of humour. Zappa was a nihilist who was rooted (and highly skilled) in avant-garde serious music. The Mothers of Invention used musical montages, tape cut-up techniques that were to influence progressive rock musicians for many years to come, and Frank Zappa was, in addition, an inventive electric guitarist with one of the most distinctive

Radio 1: The Class of '67. Tony Blackburn (1), Jimmy Young (2), Kenny Everett (3), Duncan Johnson (4), Robin Scott (5), David Rider (6), Dave Cash (7), Pete Brady (8), David Symonds (9), Bob Holness (10), Terry Wogan (11), Barry Alldis (12), Mike Lennox (13), Keith Skues (14), Chris Denning (15), Johnny Moran (16), Pete Myers (17), Pete Murray (18), Ed Stewart (19), Pete Drummond (20), Mike Raven (21), Mike Ahern (22) and John Peel (23).

1967, the year of optimism, had its other side. The Beatles' move towards transcendental meditation (above left) coincided with the death of manager Brian Epstein. The arrest of Mick Jagger (seen in the painting by Richard Hamilton, above, and a news photograph, right) was evidence of an irreconcilable conflict of lifestyles. The summer of love was not to generate a new world; the continuing power of the establishment was demonstrated when Radio 1 was founded.

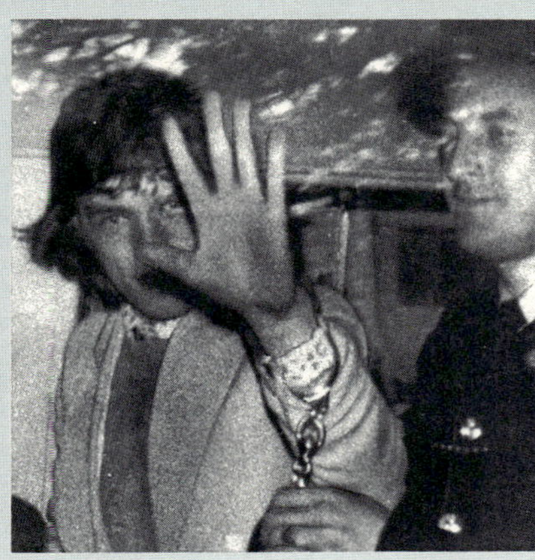

instrumental styles in rock. The most important aspect of his music in 1967, however was its commentary on the hippy/rock community itself; *We're Only In It For The Money*, for example, was packaged as a sharp parody of *Sgt Pepper* – the Beatles were not amused. Zappa's argument was that psychedelia's flower punks and instant hippies were just as dependent on received opinions, on commercial clichés, as the parents of Middle America who had been the Mothers' original target. Long before the Dead Kennedys' 'California Uber Alles', Zappa was describing California as Camp Reagan and instructing his listeners to read Kafka's *In The Colony*.

The Mothers of Invention's early records are still funny, acute and rewarding. Ultimately, however, his contempt for all rock fans, including his own, raised the question of why he made the music in the first place. In the end, it was Zappa's friend Captain Beefheart who made an avant-garde rock sound that was inspiring as well as harsh and weird.

Frank Zappa's contempt for the rock world was shared, in a different musical setting, by another self-styled artist from Los Angeles, Jim Morrison. The Doors took their name from William Blake (via Aldous Huxley) and were the most militant exponents of the counter-culture's romantic individualism. Morrison's image as a poet referred not just to his lyrics but also to his personality, his obsession with his own perceptions. He seized on the romantic ideal of decadence – it was Morrison's experiences of rock performance that mattered, not those of his audience.

Given musical form by Robbie Krieger, Jim Morrison's narcissism was compelling, and 1967 was dominated by the sound of 'Light My Fire', 'The End', the *Strange Days* LP. However, the rock audience became increasingly unimportant to Morrison as a source of sensation and, in the end, his legacy to rock, like Frank Zappa's, was merely a style of contempt.

Velvet Underground & Nico

Looking back, it seems clear that the most extraordinary record released in 1967 wasn't *Sgt Pepper* but *The Velvet Underground & Nico*. Both records made new arguments about what popular music could do, but *Sgt Pepper* was the culmination of a *public* process: the Beatles encapsulated the history of rock in their own careers. The Velvet Underground, by contrast, seemed to come from nowhere. New York doesn't feature much in accounts of 1967. Mod music and psychedelic pop was made in London and Los Angeles, hippy music and rock came from San Francisco. But New York had its own musical and commercial traditions and its own bohemians who were, on the whole more cynical, more political, more aggressive (and more conscious of black culture) than anyone in California. The Fugs, for example, formed by New York beat poets Ed Sanders and Tuli Kupferberg, made angry music about American politics as well as romantic music about love and drugs. And if the Fugs mocked the pop scene, they also marvelled at it.

The Velvet Underground were 'discovered' amidst New York's lofty bohemian activists by Andy Warhol who, long fascinated by the cultural effects of British beat, instantly included them in the Factory's line-up for its own multi-media show, the Exploding Plastic Inevitable. Andy Warhol wouldn't have been seen dead with a flower in his hair and his idea of a rock event was rather different from that of the Grateful Dead's.

Warhol wasn't concerned to inspire a community or to provide a background noise for people tripping out gently among themselves. He wanted to stir people up and see what happened, and was drawn to the Velvets because they made such an unbearable din. His only creative addition to their show was the deadpan German vocalist Nico, who left the group when they left Warhol later in the year.

The Velvet Underground & Nico came

in a distinctive package. The front cover pictured a big banana and the name Andy Warhol; inside the gatefold there were quotes from the critics and information laid out as if in a film's credits list. For Warhol, the Velvet Underground were a work of pop art, not a rock group but a commentary on a rock group. The miracle was (not Warhol's doing) that the Velvet Underground *were* a rock group, to me one of the finest ever.

Lou Reed's songs were intense commentaries on the underside of bohemian city life – drugs as sickness and money, sex as jealousy and pain. His fascination with decadence was full of fears, fears caught up in the scrambled chords of his guitar. John Cale added to this an avant-garde obsession with textural repetition, with the impact amid such monotony of the smallest dissonance. The Velvet Underground's sound was harsh and very loud, its listeners were struck immediately by the feedback, by the band's screeching. But *The Velvet Underground & Nico* also revealed something much more carefully crafted: a demanding music made not out of melodies, hooks and choruses, but out of riffs, repeated phrases that built up their effects in layers, made their rhythmic and harmonic impact simultaneously. Each Velvet Underground song used a small cluster of notes that battered and battered against each other until feedback, a screech, was the only logical place to go. The Velvet Underground's music, unlike everything else in 1967, offered no escape.

Sgt Pepper was the most important LP of the year 1967 because it expressed most pleasingly, most cheerfully, the optimism that was central to the year's experience – the sense that youth was on the move. It encapsulated all that had gone before, and seemed to be opening the way to future delights. But as we lived through the Seventies, the Sex Pistols, the new political aggression, the rioting in the streets, it began to seem as if *The Velvet Underground & Nico* could be a sign not of what had been but of what was still to come.

SIMON FRITH

'... the Velvets played so loud and crazy I couldn't even begin to guess the decibels ... the Velvets played and the different-coloured hypnotic dot patterns swirled and bounced off the walls and the strobes flashed and you could close your eyes and hear cymbals and boots stomping and whips cracking and tambourines sounding like chains rattling.'

Andy Warhol

One music

Sgt Pepper is 1967's optimism incarnate – the summer sunny side up – and *The Velvet Underground & Nico* is its very opposite, in its sound and the ideas behind that sound. But what is ultimately more important than this polarity is the fact that, opposed or not, both albums are part of the same tradition: they are both classic *rock* records. They both spring from the same source: the music revolution of the mid-Fifties, when from a variety of backgrounds a new sound – rock'n'roll – emerged. The cultural changes marked by these two albums set the standards for the music that followed and provided the key to the electrifyingly diverse sounds to be heard all over the world today.

The sound – and look – of the future. In spite of the attempt to contain them in the art avant-garde by Andy Warhol (left) through such devices as the sleeve of the album The Velvet Underground & Nico *(above left) the Velvet Underground (below) were at the heart of rock. From left, they were Lou Reed, Sterling Morrison, Nico, Maureen Tucker and John Cale.*

California Dreamin'

Golden sounds from the Mamas and the Papas

THE MAMAS AND THE PAPAS came together in the Virgin Islands in 1965. They were the brainchild of John Phillips (born August 1935), a folk singer who had been playing in the clubs of Greenwich Village since 1957. He had been a member of the Jouneymen trio (along with Scott McKenzie) and in 1962 had married Michelle Gilliam (born 1944), a Californian model. Phillips had also met up with two other folk musicians in Greenwich Village, Cass Elliot (born 1943) and Denny Doherty (1941); both were members of the Mugwumps, a band which included Zal Yanovsky, later a founder of the Lovin' Spoonful.

Phillips realised that the folk-rock boom spearheaded by Bob Dylan offered unlimited possibilities. During 1966-67, the group were to achieve greater commercial success than their more illustrious contemporaries, mainly because their appeal extended to the MOR tastes of an older audience. Their apparent wholesomeness and family appeal has too often caused them to be dismissed as a short-lived Sixties harmony unit unworthy of attention. Yet their influence could still be heard in the Seventies and Eighties through countless boy/girl groups, such as Abba, Bucks Fizz and Dollar.

The Mamas and the Papas' clean-cut image, however, was merely a publicist's myth, shrouding a sordid world of drug dependence, marital wrangling, nervous breakdowns and an insidious disillusionment that finally overtook them at their creative peak.

Success and tragedy

Once the line-up was shaped, Phillips moved the penniless band to Hollywood where they signed with Lou Adler's Dunhill label and eventually adopted a Beverly Hills lifestyle. Their music was distinctly Californian and celebrated a philosophy that permeated post-Kennedy America. Many of their songs were tinged with sadness, but the predominant sentiments were optimism and exuberance.

In March 1966 the first Mamas and the Papas single, 'California Dreamin'', reached Number 4 in the Hot Hundred and sold a million copies. The song immediately drew attention to the talents of John Phillips as the latest in a series of 'spokesmen for the new generation'. It was quickly followed two months later by 'Monday Monday', another million-seller which reached Number 1 in America and Number 3 in the UK, where its predecessor had only made Number 23.

The band were able to move into Bel Air mansions, drive limousines and entertain with champagne breakfasts, yet they continued to wear kaftans, patched jeans and beads in an attempt to keep their young radical audience. Phillips had proved himself articulate enough to ingratiate himself with the press, who quickly latched on to the group members' eccentricities. Equally important to the press was the fact that the individuals offered the possibility of distinct stereotyped personalities, a precedent set by the Beatles. Michelle was the shy, mysterious girl – blonde, beautiful and 'angelic when she wants to be'; Cass, absurdly overweight yet bubbly and garrulous, the perfect complement; John, a tall, intellectual guru and musical genius and finally Denny, the handsome Canadian humorist.

Their much-publicised lifestyle and lively personalities were sufficient to keep them in the limelight for many years, while the combined talents of the quartet – excellent songs and stunning vocals – looked likely to ensure a profitable career in the Seventies. Sadly, an inability to cope with their sudden and enormous wealth was to prove their undoing.

After the success of the first two singles, their debut album *If You Can Believe Your Eyes And Ears* received rave reviews and sold a million. The preponderance of uninspired covers was a compromise indicating the group's determination to retain a bland mass appeal. In spite of such limitations, the group were loved by their peers and received glowing testimonials from various Byrds, Beatles and Stones. The Phillips' fraternisation with the rock elite increased following the installation of a studio in their Bel Air attic. Jam sessions would sometimes include such luminaries as Paul McCartney and Brian Wilson.

Previous page: The original Mamas and the Papas; Cass Elliot, Denny Doherty, John Phillips and Michelle Phillips. Above: A later line-up, with Spanky McFarlane (far left) and John Phillips' daughter Mackenzie (left).

In spite of their enormous success, the Mamas and the Papas were an unstable unit. The Phillips' marital problems seriously affected their working relationship and at one point late in 1966 Michelle was fired, being temporarily replaced by Gillian Gibson. Amid the increasing tensions their second album, *Cass, John, Michelle And Denny,* released in late 1966, was an effective reminder of their combined talents and a vast improvement on their debut effort. 'No Salt On Her Tail', 'I Saw Her Again' and 'Dancing Bear' demonstrated Phillips' growing maturity as a songwriter/arranger. Although there were enough cover versions to ensure radio play and MOR acceptance, it was clear that the Mamas and the Papas had lost none of their hippie following. The oblique allusions to drugs on 'Straight Shooter' from the first LP were more explicit on 'Strange Young Girls', which told of Hollywood nubiles offering themselves on an acid altar. The Mamas and the Papas were able to champion the counter-culture almost as frequently as the Byrds, Doors and Jefferson Airplane.

The internal problems that almost split the group in 1966 showed little signs of abating in the New Year. Cass's pregnancy prevented them from appearing live for at least six months and sporadic work on a third album meant further delays. Events took a more pleasant turn, however, when Michelle presented the possibility of covering the Shirelles' 'Dedicated To The One I Love' in April 1967. It reached Number 2 on both sides of the Atlantic and the autobiographical 'Creeque Alley' also reached both Top Tens three months later. The third single of 1967, 'Twelve Thirty', got high into the US charts, but did nothing in the UK. At the same time, the third album, *Deliver,* proved their best offering to date. It was clear that the group were no longer relying purely on their distinctive vocal harmonies but were intent upon incorporating different musical styles, including the use of brass and harpsichord; the record also included two purely instrumental tracks.

In June that year, Phillips and producer Lou Adler organised the Monterey Pop Festival which included Jimi Hendrix, Janis Joplin, the Who, Otis Redding and, naturally, the Mamas and the Papas. A full-length feature film of the festival was highly profitable. Meanwhile, John Phillips wrote the anthem of the era, 'San Francisco (Wear Some Flowers In Your Hair)', which he gave to his old friend Scott McKenzie to cover. The song was a Top Ten hit in the summer of 1967 both in the US and UK charts.

Despite resurgent success during 1967, the Mamas and the Papas were living on borrowed time. During a winter tour of Britain, their problems seemed to tear them apart. Cass Elliot was arrested in Southampton, accused of stealing from the Royal Garden Hotel in Kensington, while Michelle assaulted a police officer and was left on the brink of a nervous breakdown. At length, the group decided to complete their fourth album and then revert to solo careers. *The Papas And The Mamas* was released early in 1968 and became one of the most underrated albums of the Sixties. John Phillips' extraordinary songwriting talent was demonstrated in a string of superb songs, including 'Safe In My Garden', 'For The Love Of Ivy' and the single 'Twelve Thirty'. 'Rooms' and 'Mansions' both chronicled the group's downfall as a symptom of the growing alienation of their Hollywood fantasy lifestyle. After three years of undaunted activity and success, the band dissolved in 1968, apparently for Cass Elliot to pursue a solo career.

Disastrous dreams

Elliot had a transatlantic Top Twenty hit later that year with 'Dream A Little Dream Of Me', but her subsequent career was sadly unsuccessful. Three solo albums sold poorly and an optimistic partnership with Dave Mason yielded one unmemorable album. After a brief spell on the cabaret circuit, Mama Cass died in London in 1974 of heart failure.

The ever-adaptable Michelle Phillips finally emerged as an actress, most noted for her part in Ken Russell's *Valentino*. Excessive lifestyles, however, seriously affected the careers of both Denny Doherty and John Phillips. After the release of the *Live At Monterey* album in 1971 amid intense legal wranglings (the group tried to ban its release on account of its poor quality), there followed an abortive attempt at a Mama and the Papas reunion with *People Like Us* (1972). The album was uninspired, lacking all the trademarks that had made the group so successful in the Sixties.

Phillips squandered a potentially brilliant talent through drug abuse and began the Eighties with the possibility of many years' imprisonment for drug offences. Following a rehabilitation course, however, he re-formed the Mamas and the Papas to include his daughter Mackenzie Phillips and former Sixties star Elaine 'Spanky' McFarlane (from Spanky and Our Gang). The motives behind this move may be questionable, but there is no doubt that the wide-ranging talents of the original line-up produced some fine musical memories.

JOHNNY ROGAN

The Mamas and the Papas Recommended Listening

Mamas And Papas 20 Greatest Hits (Music For Pleasure MFP 50493) (Includes: California Dreamin', Dedicated To The One I Love, Monday Monday, Creeque Alley, Dream A Little Dream Of Me, You Baby, Safe In My Garden).

The Mamas and the Papas on stage (below), with Denny Doherty keeping cool in a kaftan. After leaving the group, Cass Elliot (left) attempted to pursue a solo career until her untimely death in 1974, while Michelle Phillips (right) later resurfaced as an actress.

ROCKING EAST & WEST

Bill Graham's Fillmores and the radio revolution

UNTIL THE MID SIXTIES, rock'n'roll had been considered an exclusively teenage music, a belief fostered by the industry's incessant creation of teen idols from the 'American Bandstand' school onwards. The single most influential factor in shattering this 'age barrier' was, of course, the Beatles. Their effect on the listening public was dramatic, especially in the US, where their slow start was followed by overwhelming success; suddenly, older people were listening to rock music. The other trend that went hand in hand with this phenomenon was a gradual shift away from singles towards albums.

Nonetheless, the music business was slow to react to the changes. The way rock was packaged remained virtually unchanged until 1966, and much later than

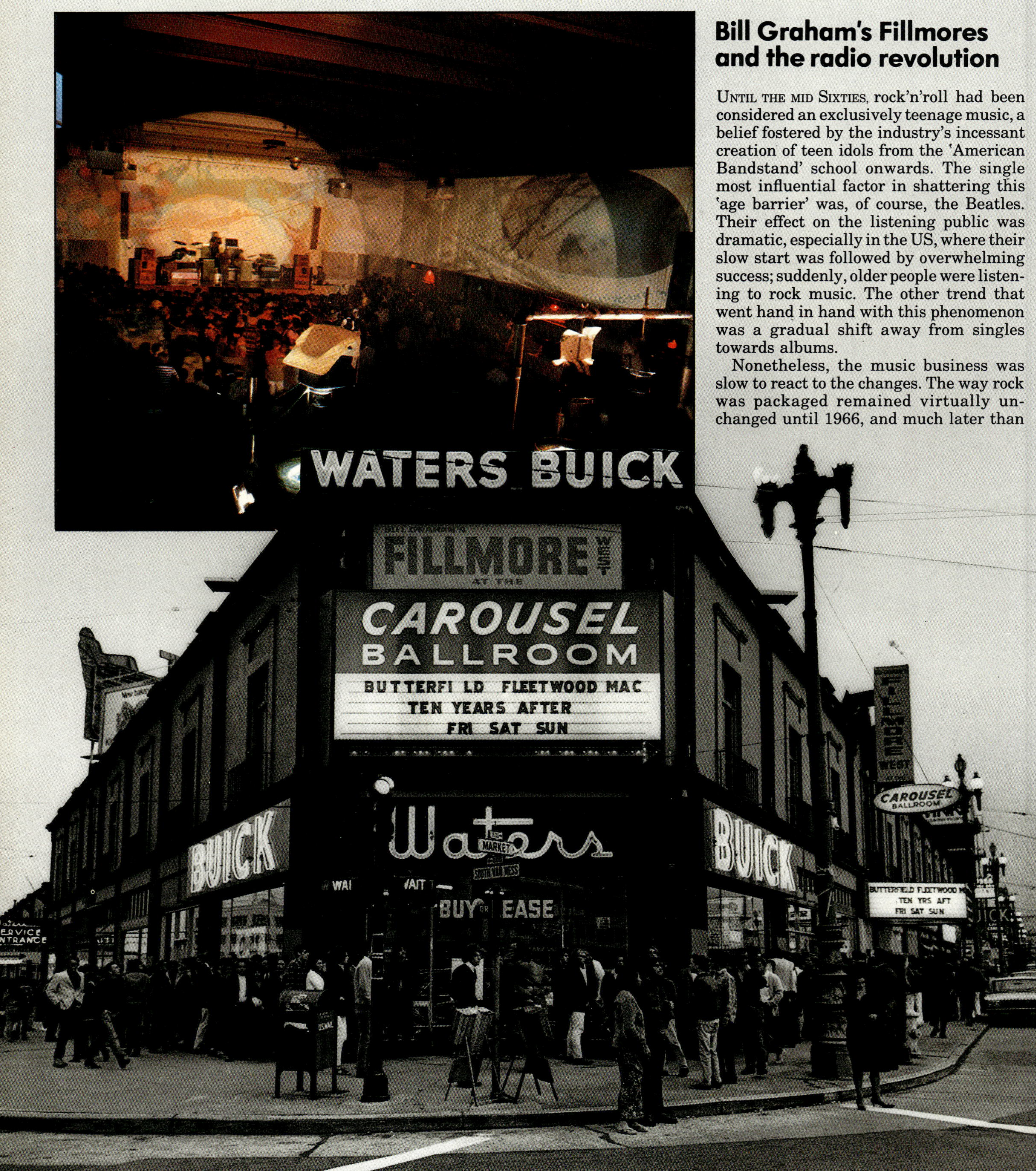

Bill Graham (above) was a shrewd entrepreneur who grasped the mood of the moment; his Fillmore West auditorium (opposite below) provided the perfect setting for the new music, complete with psychedelic light shows (opposite). DJ Tom Donahue (seated right, with a colleague at KMPX) changed the face of FM radio.

that in many areas. Such changes that did take place were often the result of efforts made by individuals outside the corporate structures. And two of the most significant developments – the presentation of live music and radio programming – came out of San Francisco.

Prior to 1966, most live rock music had been confined either to the High School Prom/Battle of the Bands on one level, or the inevitable package tours of top bands on the other. It was designed for kids and everybody knew it; sophisticates went to jazz clubs, folk festivals and classical concerts. But with the growth of new bands and audiences, changes were inevitable; a new environment was required.

The first city that really met the need was San Francisco, where the new Haight Ashbury community had become a significant force as early as 1965. Ironically there were almost no live venues in the city at the time, and certainly nowhere for people to dance. After a few dances in the autumn of 1965, it became apparent that a whole new style of entertainment was being born, and that someone with sufficient skill and insight could give people what they wanted and still run it as a successful business; that person was Bill Graham.

New palaces of rock

Born Wolfgang Grajanka in Berlin in 1931, Graham had emigrated to New York as a teenager. There he had gone through college and worked as an actor and an office manager. He was blunt, shrewd and direct, but also dedicated and hardworking. He wound up in San Francisco in 1965 as manager of the Mime Troupe, a famous radical theatre group, and in order to raise funds for them he organised a benefit on 6 November. Almost by chance, he booked Jefferson Airplane to play; it was an astonishing success. The following January, he attended the 'Trips Festival' that the Family Dogg had put on at the Fillmore Auditorium, and for him the future was obvious. He started to run dances there, alternating with the Family Dogg for the first few weeks. They soon moved out to start a rival ballroom, the Avalon, run on looser, less commercial lines, and from then on Graham was in sole charge of the Fillmore.

Initially, Graham didn't book the new 'adult' rock bands exclusively, but after a few months his policy was clear. The staple fare became local acts like the Grateful Dead and Quicksilver or visitors like the Mothers of Invention and Paul Butterfield, plus the odd play and even an appearance by Lenny Bruce.

The Fillmore and the Avalon were a whole new concept in entertainment. They were called dance-concerts but that was too simple a description for something that created a complete environment, with light shows, films and poetry readings as well as music. Such was the rapid rise of the San Francisco scene that by the end of 1966 'psychedelic' ballrooms were opening up in all the major cities in the States, notably the Shrine in Los Angeles, the Grande and the Aragon in Detroit, and within a year the Electric Circus in New York and Ungamos in Philadelphia.

Back in San Francisco at the end of 1967, the Grateful Dead opened their own venue, the Carousel, but were forced to close down by mid-1968 due to mounting overheads; Bill Graham, feeling increasingly threatened by his location in the Fillmore ghetto, took over the Carousel lease and renamed it the Fillmore West. Earlier in the year he had taken over the old Village Theatre in New York, which became the Fillmore East. For the next three-and-a-half years the Fillmores were the undisputed palaces of the new rock music.

Graham closed both venues in mid-1971, feeling that the Fillmore concept had been an essentially Sixties phenomenon and by his action marking the final passing of an era. Graham felt that what had originally been a subculture had become hopelessly commercialised; his detractors said that Graham himself was largely instrumental in that process. While he certainly provided an environment in which the San Francisco freaks could indulge their alternative lifestyle – on one occasion restraining the police from arresting a performer who decided to take his clothes off on stage – he also alienated many of the musicians who performed there because of his commercial methods, his insistence on punctuality, his reliance on bodyguards and his authoritarian style.

When the Fillmore West was threatened with closure in 1969, the *San Francisco Chronicle* ran an editorial in Graham's defence, claiming that the Fillmore was 'one of the factors for channelling the unrest and dissent of youth away from the destructive activism that has racked many other communities'. Perhaps that double-edged compliment is the most appropriate epitaph for Bill Graham's managership of these venues; he remains today one of the most successful concert promoters in the United States.

Underground FM

The changes that took place in radio programming followed similar lines to the changes in live music, but due to the commercial considerations involved they were harder-fought and more difficult to maintain. The Top Forty format of traditional American rock radio dates back to the late Fifties. As a rigidly-formulated presentation of popular music, it proved extremely successful for a chain of stations in the Midwest owned by Tod Storz and those in the Midwest and South operated by the Plough Corporation, a Southwest pharmaceutical house. The Beatles may have changed some of the underlying principles of this kind of programming, but radio tried to ignore the changes.

In mid-1967 DJ Tom Donahue joined KMPX, one of a number of local FM stations, as Operations Manager and announcer. Previously he'd been a Top Forty DJ on KYA but in mid-1965 had given it up to become involved in the city's nascent rock scene. At the time he joined, KMPX was in a bad way, but they allowed him to shape the programming and the results were astonishing: not only album cuts, blues, jazz, even classical music, but also an absence both of silly jingles and amphetamined, raving DJs. It was a success, but less than a year later the advertisers got cold feet and pulled out.

In March 1968, Donahue moved to KSAN, the most famous station of all, for 10 years synonymous with progressive programming. The concept of 'Underground FM' had arrived. Stations started to specialise; one would play nothing but soul, another jazz, another rock – there were even total oldies stations. And although these later attempts were always a compromise, it was theoretically possible, particularly in major cities, to hear what you wanted, when you wanted. JOHN PLATT

PERFECT PARTNERS

Simon and Garfunkel: bridging folk and rock

IN THE EARLY SEVENTIES, journalist Bob Woffinden worked for a while in the London warehouse of CBS Records. 'The job was routine,' he wrote later, 'just making sure the racks were well supplied with all the records in stock. Pure mindless monotony. We never used to refer to titles of records, just their catalogue numbers, and *Bridge Over Troubled Water*, the album we handled most, was 63699. Probably every army draftee or convict is given a personal number which is a cause of personal bitterness; but 63699 was a number that drove all of us crazy together. Eight million copies, and some days it seemed like we'd handled every one.'

In fact, Simon and Garfunkel's *Bridge Over Troubled Water* album went on to sell over twelve million units worldwide, making it among the handful of bestsellers of its era, alongside *The Sound Of Music* and Carole King's *Tapestry*. It also proved to be the climax of a musical partnership which had begun in very different circumstances many years before.

Tom and Jerry in Wonderland

Art Garfunkel (born in New York, 5 November 1942) and Paul Simon (born Newark, New Jersey, 13 October 1941) were childhood friends. They acted together in a school production of 'Alice In Wonderland' – Paul was the White Rabbit and Art the Cheshire Cat. Art's family had two tape recorders – his parents both sang – and Paul Simon would come round on rainy Sunday afternoons to fool around with the machines. When they were about 13, listening to rock'n'roll on Alan Freed's show, they started rehearsing seriously, writing their own songs and taking them round the record companies in Manhattan.

After nearly three years hawking their songs round the Brill Building, the duo were in a studio cutting a demo of one of their songs when they were overheard by Sid Prosen, a minor wheeler-dealer in the New York record business. He took them to a small label called Big Records, and in November 1957, 'Hey! Schoolgirl' by Tom and Jerry was released.

It was nothing special, and clearly owed much to both the Everly Brothers and to Buddy Holly. The composer credits read 'Garfunkel-Simon', but the lads called themselves Tom Graph (Art) and Jerry Landis (Paul) for recording purposes. 'Hey! Schoolgirl' began to sell, and climbed as high as Number 54 in the charts. Tom and

Simon and Garfunkel's clear, chiming harmonies became the soundtrack for an entire bedsit generation.

Jerry made personal appearances to plug the disc, including one on the prestigious 'American Bandstand' television show.

Like so many teenage artists of the Fifties, however, Tom and Jerry turned out to be one-hit wonders. In the next year they released several singles on three different labels; all were flops, and Paul Simon and Art Garfunkel returned to their studies. 'We didn't plan to go on with music as a career,' Paul recalled later, 'but it wasn't for fun. We were deadly serious about everything we did.' Simon went to Brooklyn Law School, while Garfunkel studied art at Columbia; both continued to release records, Simon under the names Tico and the Triumphs and Jerry Landis – his 'Lone Teen Ranger' reached the dizzy heights of Number 97 in 1963 – and Garfunkel as Artie Garr.

By this time, however, the musical climate in New York was changing. In Greenwich Village and on the college campuses a folk boom was underway; students were listening to Bob Dylan or Peter, Paul and Mary and taking up political causes like black civil rights. A friend of Simon and Garfunkel's was killed on a demonstration in Mississippi, prompting Paul Simon to write the impassioned 'He Was My Brother'.

For a while, Paul Simon lived in the two worlds of Tin Pan Alley pop and Greenwich Village folk. By day he worked for a music publishing house, peddling the company's songs round the record labels. By night he would sing and play – usually with Garfunkel – in coffeehouses like Folk City and Café Wha. 'He Was My Brother' was eventually released as a single on the obscure Triumph label, under the name Paul Kane.

Left: The teenage duo Tom and Jerry. Paul Simon (below left) was Jerry, Art Garfunkel (below right) was Tom.

Both Paul Simon and Art Garfunkel pursued careers in films as well as music. Art acted in movies such as Catch-22 *(above left), while Paul wrote and produced his own semi-autobiographical film,* One Trick Pony *(above right).*

Signs of Simon

Paul used his contacts in the music business to get the duo their first major break. One day, instead of selling his company's songs, he offered his own compositions to producer Tom Wilson at Columbia: 'Would you be interested in hearing them? My friend's uptown; he sings them with me'. Wilson was impressed and set up an audition; the engineer, Roy Halee, was sympathetic. When they came back again to sing some more, they requested that he look after the sound again. Roy Halee was to work with Simon and Garfunkel for the rest of their career, and co-produced their 1981 live reunion album.

For Columbia, the duo recorded their first, acoustic LP *Wednesday Morning 3 A.M.*, which appeared in America in November 1964 and included a new recording of 'He Was My Brother'. In many ways it was typical of the large number of folk albums flooding the market as the major labels caught on to the new musical trend. There was a Bob Dylan song, a couple of tunes with anti-war lyrics by British writers, some traditional songs and five of Paul Simon's own compositions. Among these was a number called 'The Sounds Of Silence'. In time, this would become Paul Simon's most-recorded composition, with around a hundred versions of it by other artists. Initially, however, both song and album made no impact at all.

Meanwhile, Simon spent the summers of 1964 and 1965 travelling and performing in Europe. Sometimes playing solo and sometimes with Art Garfunkel, he busked in Paris and became a well-known figure around the bustling British folk-club circuit. As a result, he recorded some of his compositions for BBC radio and cut a solo album in the London studios of CBS Records. The radio broadcasts were the idea of Judith Piepe, a social worker in the East End of London. Impressed with the character of Paul Simon's lyrics, she presented them along with her own comments on a religious slot called 'Five To Ten'. At the time this association of contemporary folk songs with religious broadcasting was regarded as revolutionary; it is a measure of the aptness of the 'Five To Ten' items that the combination is now regarded as something of a cliché.

Many of the songs used for the radio and on the London album, *The Paul Simon Songbook*, cut in May 1965, had themselves been written in England. Several, too, lent themselves easily to Judith Piepe's moral interpretations. 'A Most Peculiar Man' was inspired by a newspaper report of a suicide, while both 'The Sounds Of Silence' and 'I Am A Rock' expressed that state of personal isolation and distance from society that was fashionably known as 'alienation'. Although the most durable of the other songs written at this time was 'Homeward Bound', conceived by Simon in a fit of homesickness at Widnes railway station, one of the finest was 'Kathy's Song'. Its lyrics had a fluency and quietly melancholic tinge which were to characterise much of Paul Simon's work in the following decade.

The Paul Simon Songbook was released in Britain in August 1965 and sold steadily around the folk-club circuit. Meanwhile, across the Atlantic, a chain of events which was to catapult Simon and Garfunkel to stardom within six months began when a disc jockey in Boston unexpectedly began to feature the album track of 'The Sounds Of Silence'. Students at local campuses immediately began requesting it, and the local promotion man for Columbia Records reported this to New York. It was decided to issue the song as a single: but this was the era of 'folk-rock', so house producer Tom Wilson was told to add electric guitar, bass and drums to the acoustic sound to make it more commercial.

The plan worked, and 'The Sounds Of Silence' began to climb the US charts. In Europe, Paul Simon was totally unaware of his success until, on a tour of Denmark, someone showed him a copy of the American charts. He caught the next plane back to New York, reunited with Art Garfunkel and began touring large halls as the record reached Number 1 at the close of 1965. From that point on, Simon and Garfunkel were set for success.

Herbal sounds

Eager to make the most of their new-found stars, Columbia rushed them into the studio to make an album with the same title as their surprise hit. Although the producer was Bob Johnston, who had supervised Bob Dylan's *Highway 61 Revisited*, the result was something of a musical hotch-potch. Several different rock styles were used, but most sounded as if they had been crudely imposed upon a basic acoustic song. 'Richard Cory', one of only three new songs on the record, had everything from a heavy rock rhythm section to strings.

At this stage of the duo's career, there was a sharp conflict between the pace at which Paul Simon was able to write songs and the hectic recording schedule demanded of the duo by Columbia. Simon worked slowly and meticulously on songs, while the record company was pushing for a new album as soon as *The Sounds Of Silence* was released. So back into the studio they went, to make *Parsley, Sage, Rosemary And Thyme*, which was brought out in September 1966, on the back of a series of hit singles, 'Homeward Bound', 'I Am A Rock' and 'Dangling Conversation'. The first of these was the duo's British chart debut, making the Number 9 position that March.

Although the *Parsley, Sage, Rosemary And Thyme* album had its share of reworked acoustic numbers, it presented a much more unified sound, in a style which would later be termed 'soft rock'. It was also a well-balanced collection of songs, from the comic protest parody 'Simple

Desultory Philippic' through love songs ('Flowers Never Bend With The Rainfall' and 'For Emily') to lightweight but skilful pop like '59th Street Bridge Song (Feelin' Groovy)', which became a US Number 13 hit for the close-harmony group Harper's Bizarre. In addition, there were two interesting experiments in which diverse pieces were played off against each other. In the first, the traditional English song 'Scarborough Fair' (from which the album's title was taken) was interwoven with 'The Side Of A Hill', an anti-war song first recorded on *The Paul Simon Songbook*. The other track, '7 O'Clock News'/ 'Silent Night', had the Christmas hymn intercut with a news bulletin detailing examples of man's inhumanity to man.

These last songs connected with the album's sleevenote. Written by Ralph J. Gleason, a jazz critic who had been converted to rock by Bob Dylan, it concluded: 'There are songs of alienation, but there are songs of love too, and they touch closely the prevailing philosophical current of the New Youth which is that of creativity AGAINST the machine and thus FOR humanity.'

After the frantic activity of 1966, Simon and Garfunkel recorded very little in the following year. They toured heavily in America and Europe and appeared at the Monterey Pop Festival. The two singles released in 1967, 'At The Zoo' and 'Fakin' It', were a foretaste of the major artistic advance which their next album *Bookends* was to represent. In particular, 'Fakin' It', with its dreamlike atmosphere and haunting lyrics, showed Paul Simon had been listening hard to the music that was happening around him.

When *Bookends* did appear, in April 1968, the results were dramatic: on 15 June 1968, Simon and Garfunkel had the top three albums in the US charts. One was *Bookends*, one was the re-activated *Parsley, Sage, Rosemary And Thyme*, while the third, and perhaps the most crucial, was the soundtrack album from the movie *The Graduate*. Ironically, this was a record that Paul and Art had not wanted to come out. The film's director, Mike Nichols, had decided to use only five of Simon and Garfunkel's songs, including just one new one, 'Mrs Robinson'. Realising that this was not enough music for a whole LP, but also that the film's probable success would give the duo a vast new audience, Columbia's wily president Clive Davis had the record padded out with incidental instrumental music from the movie.

He was proved right. Cleverly constructed to take the controversy out of the 'generation gap', the movie was a massive box-office hit. Undoubtedly Simon and Garfunkel's association with the film contributed to the extensive sales of *Bookends*.

One side of the *Bookends* LP consisted of tracks previously released as singles, but the other was clearly intended to be heard as a unified song-cycle, since it opened and closed with the 'Bookends Theme'. It moved from a melodramatic song about a mother and child ('Save The Life Of My Child') through two muted love songs in 'America' and 'Overs' to voices of old people recorded by Art Garfunkel and the nostalgic 'Old Friends'. The project was derided by some reviewers as pretentious and praised by others as proof that rock could be as literate as any other art form. Undoubtedly, however, 'America' stood out as not only Paul's finest love lyric since 'Dangling Conversation', but a song that opened into a wider dimension with the vision of America suggested in its evocative final lines: 'Counting the cars on the New Jersey turnpike/They've all come to look for America.'

A Bridge too far

There had been a gap of 20 months between the release dates of *Parsley, Sage, Rosemary And Thyme* and *Bookends*, and there would be a similar wait for the next Simon and Garfunkel album, *Bridge Over Troubled Water*. Much of it was due to the meticulous attention to detail that was a hallmark of all their records, but this time there was an added factor. Mike Nichols, director of *The Graduate*, had been chosen to film Joseph Heller's novel *Catch-22*, the campus classic of the Sixties, and had offered Art Garfunkel a part. As a result, Art spent several months filming in Mexico while Paul Simon continued to work on the album in New York. The *Bridge* record even included a song about the situation, the gentle 'Only Living Boy In New York' which began, 'Tom, get your plane right on time . . .' Art had, of course, been Tom in Tom and Jerry.

This enforced separation during 1969 meant that several tracks on *Bridge Over Troubled Water* were virtually solo efforts by Paul Simon. They included 'The Boxer' and 'Baby Driver', which were released on either side of a single in April of that year. Both were evidence of Paul's growing sophistication as a songwriter. They were based on lyric ideas common to folk song and blues: the narrative ballad ('I am just a poor boy . . .') and use of auto images to refer to sex ('I wonder how your engine feels').

Towards the end of 1969, progress on the album became slower and slower, and both Simon and Garfunkel realised that their partnership had outlived its usefulness.

Below: Simon and Garfunkel in the studio, where engineer Roy Halee provided the third vital component of their sound.

Paul Simon goes gospel in the mid Seventies (inset far left), Art Garfunkel takes a breather at Central Park (inset left), and the duo together again in 1982 (left).

Art was tiring of what he later described as his 'underdog role': Simon wrote the songs, Garfunkel just sang them. 'I felt envious of Paul's writing and playing, especially onstage, where I had nothing to do with my hands.' That autumn, they toured widely in Europe and America, made a television special and returned to the studio to put the finishing touches to the new album. It was completed early in 1970, but only after Garfunkel had vetoed the final song Simon had wanted to include, a number called 'Cuba Si, Nixon No'.

The exhausted Simon had used up all his musical ideas, and decided it was time to think about an album of material that would be totally personal. Garfunkel had another movie – *Carnal Knowledge* – to make. So, as *Bridge Over Troubled Water* topped singles and album charts on both sides of the Atlantic, the decision to split up was taken.

There Goes Rhymin' Simon

During the Seventies, Paul Simon's recorded output was even smaller than that of his Simon and Garfunkel period, but his ability as a songwriter increased substantially. The first solo album, called *Paul Simon* in Britain and *Mother And Child Reunion* in America, appeared in 1972 and was described by Jon Landau in Rolling Stone as 'a piece of self-expression designed to communicate some very unpleasant but very real truths'.

The following year, 1973, Simon released *There Goes Rhymin' Simon*, an album which showed his increasing involvement with a wide range of musical forms and traditions. It contained the gospel-inspired 'Loves Me Like A Rock', and other songs featuring New Orleans marching band music, as well as the low-key rock background to the album's two consummate lyrics – the love song 'Something So Right' and 'American Tune', in which Simon linked personal feelings with wider social moods of questioning and self-doubt.

During 1973, Simon toured extensively throughout the United States and Europe, releasing *Live Rhymin'* the following year. *Still Crazy After All These Years* appeared in 1976; two further songs, 'Slip Slidin' Away' and 'Stranded In A Limousine' made their debut on his 1977 *Greatest Hits Etc* record. *Still Crazy* contained one track, 'My Little Town', which featured a duet with Art Garfunkel, their first recording together for six years. In the meantime Garfunkel had made three solo albums of his own, and had a US Number 18 and UK Number 1 hit in 1975 with a revamp of 'I Only Have Eyes For You': he equalled the latter position in 1979 with 'Bright Eyes'.

The early Eighties, however, saw both their solo careers take a downturn. Garfunkel's solo LP *Scissors Cut* bombed, and the single off it, 'Heart In New York' did poorly in the charts. Nic Roeg's film *Bad Timing*, in which Garfunkel had played the leading part, vanished without trace in the US, though it was an art-house success in Europe. Paul Simon's venture into the movies, his self-written *One Trick Pony*, also did poorly.

Throughout the Seventies, Simon and Garfunkel had been under frequent pressure to reunite, but apart from a few guest appearances and a series of benefits for George McGovern's presidential campaign in 1973, it was not until after their successful 1981 Central Park concert that they decided to tour together again. Apart from the concerts' nostalgic appeal, the singers' repertoire provided ample evidence of the constant evolution of Paul Simon's writing, from the adolescent naivety of his earliest compositions to the sure evocation of the subtleties of adult relationships in his songs of the Seventies.

The concerts also included a new Paul Simon song, 'The Late Great Johnny Ace', dedicated to John Lennon. It linked Lennon's death with that of the R&B star Johnny Ace in 1954 and that of President Kennedy. In its historical timespan, therefore, it neatly completed the circle that had begun with two high-school kids singing Everly Brothers songs 25 years earlier.

DAVE LAING

SIMON AND GARFUNKEL
Discography

Singles

As Tom and Jerry
Hey! Schoolgirl/Dancin' Wild (Big 613, 1957); Our Song/Two Teenagers (Big 616, 1958); That's My Story/Don't Say Goodbye (Big 618, 1958); Baby Talk/Two Teenagers (Big 621, 1959); I'm Lonesome/Looking At You (Ember 1094, 1963); Surrender, Please Surrender/Fighting Mad (ABC Paramount, 1962):

As Simon and Garfunkel
The Sounds Of Silence/We've Got A Groovy Thing Goin' (Columbia 43396, 1965); That's My Story/Tia-Juana Blues (ABC Paramount 10788, 1966); Homeward Bound/Leaves That Are Green (Columbia 43511, 1966); Dangling Conversation/Big Bright Green Pleasure Machine (Columbia 43728, 1966); A Hazy Shade Of Winter/For Emily, Wherever I May Find Her (Columbia 43873, 1966); At The Zoo/59th Bridge Street Song (Feelin' Groovy) (Columbia 44046, 1967); Fakin' It/You Don't Know Where Your Interest Lies (Columbia 44232, 1967); Scarborough Fair/Canticle: April Come She Will (Columbia 44465, 1968); Mrs Robinson/Old Friends/Bookends (Columbia 44511, 1968); The Boxer/Baby Driver (Columbia 44785, 1969); Bridge Over Troubled Water/Keep The Customer Satisfied (Columbia 45079, 1970); Cecilia/The Only Living Boy In New York (Columbia 45133, 1970); El Condor Pasa/Why Don't You Write Me (Columbia 45237, 1970); For Emily, Wherever I May Find Her/America (Columbia 45663, 1972); Me And Julio Down By The Schoolyard/Wake Up Little Susie (Warner Brothers 50053, 1982).

Albums

Wednesday Morning 3 A.M. (Columbia CS 9049, 1964); *Hit Sounds Of Simon And Garfunkel* (Pickwick SPC 3059, 1966); *The Sounds Of Silence* (Columbia CS 9269, 1966); *Parsley, Sage, Rosemary And Thyme* (Columbia CS 9363, 1966); *Bookends* (Columbia KCS 9529, 1968); *Bridge Over Troubled Water* (Columbia CS 9914, 1970); *Simon And Garfunkel's Greatest Hits* (Columbia KC 31350, 1972); *The Concert In Central Park* (Warner Brothers 2BSK 3654, 1982).

I Got You, Babe

Sonny and Cher caught the mood of the moment

IF THE PURITY AND DEPTH of folk-rock is best represented by the Byrds, the essence of its commercialism is found in Sonny and Cher. The songs they sang, the clothes they wore, the image of trendy marital love they projected, all put over a sanitised version of the folk-rockers' Los Angeles bohemianism. Their homely-camp outfits saw them ejected from restaurants and bars, establishing their youth credibility; thereafter they were courted by society gossip columnists. And Cher's cover of Bob Dylan's 'All I Really Want To Do' bettered the Byrds' version by reaching Number 15 in the US charts, prompting Dylan's bitter comment to Roger McGuinn: 'They beat you, man'.

Sonny Bono – born Salvatore Philip Bono on 16 February 1935 in Detroit, Michigan – began his musical career working as an A&R man for Specialty Records from 1957 to 1959. The son of Italian immigrant parents, he was bright and ambitious. A former truck driver and waiter, he familiarised himself with every aspect of the music industry, taking every chance that offered itself.

He wrote and produced releases for artists like Don and Dewey and Roddy Jackson, and co-wrote 'High School Dance' and 'You Bug Me Baby', which were recorded by Larry Williams. He also began to write under the pseudonym 'Don Christy'; 'Don' from his wife Donna, and 'Christy' from their daughter. (The marriage, however, was not to last.) It was under this name that he co-wrote 'She Said Yeah' – later to be covered by the Rolling Stones – for Larry Williams, and cut his first solo sides for Specialty. This period also saw Bono meeting up with Jack Nitzsche, then an untried arranger; the two would later write 'Needles and Pins', which became a smash hit for both Jackie DeShannon and the Searchers.

Bono left Specialty at the turn of the decade, and after a series of failed singles on obscure independent labels, Bono re-established contact with Nitzsche in 1963, which resulted in his time with Phil Spector, for whom Nitzsche was then working. Bono played on several sessions – usually percussion – as well as assisting with some of the arrangements. He also took time out to begin his own independent label, Rush Records, but after only four releases it folded.

It was during this period, while his marriage was falling apart, that Bono met Cherilyn Sarkasian Lapiere in a restaurant. Born in El Centro, California on 20 May 1946 of Armenian and Cherokee extraction, Cher was an aspiring actress. Sonny, however, had other ambitions for her. He tried to get Spector to record her, but Spector was unimpressed. She got to record backing vocals for the Crystals, however, and also for the Ronettes.

Carry on Cleo

Sonny and Cher crossed the border to Tijuana in 1964 for a 'quickie' marriage, and on their return became Caesar and Cleo. This singing duo recorded 'The Letter' for Vault, but it met with little success. Bono's persistence also led to Spector's agreeing to produce Cher's solo single, 'Ringo I Love You'. Released on Annette, a subsidiary of Spector's Philles label, it bombed. Cher was later to explain its failure by saying: 'I sounded too much like a boy. Everyone thought it was a faggot song.'

Caesar and Cleo then put in another appearance with 'Love Is Strange' on Reprise. The follow-up, 'Baby Don't Go', went out under the name Sonny and Cher on the same day. It had originally been intended as a solo single for Cher, but nerves got the better of her and Sonny provided back-up vocals. 'Baby Don't Go' was enough of a regional hit to attract an Atco/Atlantic contract for the duo, and an Imperial/Liberty deal for Cher solo.

In 1965 Sonny began to find his feet as a producer and arranger; his time with Spector was beginning to pay dividends, and the techniques he had learned were displayed on the twin releases 'Dream Baby' by Cherilyn and 'Just You' by Sonny and Cher. Sonny had also teamed up with producer and arranger Harold Battiste to form a production company, Progress Records, to sell material to Atlantic. Battiste was to contribute his superb arrangements to many of Sonny and Cher's hits, but didn't get to see the rewards. Sonny had given him the impression they were 50/50 partners in

Progress, but when Battiste pressed him to see the papers he found that he was not a partner, but had been hired simply as a producer at two cents on an album. 'I always admired Sonny's abilities to deal with all these people and determine what was best for *him*,' Battiste said later. 'Never any guilt about loyalty and that kind of stuff.'

Harold Battiste's arrangement was a vital ingredient of Sonny and Cher's first smash hit, 'I Got You Babe', in 1965. Written and produced by Sonny, the single sounded riveting; the two voices traded perfectly, weaving in and out of Battiste's flutes and oboe over a dense background of strings and horns. With its convincing aura of innocence it was an immediate success, reaching Number 1 in both the US and UK charts.

Bohemian image

In the wake of the Byrds, Sonny and Cher's Los Angeles bohemianism proved to be just right for the times, playing to the preoccupations of the newly vocal teenage generation and confirming their potential as a commercially exploitable market. The press seized upon Sonny and Cher as representatives of protest.

Cher's solo single, a cover of Bob Dylan's 'All I Really Want To Do' – which had been issued the month before 'I Got You Babe' – made the charts soon afterwards, consolidating Sonny and Cher's success. Although it came second in Britain, it swamped the Byrds' version in the US, prompting Dylan's acidic remark. If Cher's version was true to the expectations of folk-rock, it lacked the innovation that the Byrds had brought to the song.

Sonny and Cher arrived in Britain in 1965 to promote both singles and to oversee Sonny's solo release, 'Laugh At Me', which became a Top Ten hit both in Britain and the US. It confirmed the duo's commercial appeal and ensured that one or the other (or both of them) could be seen almost every week on 'Top Of The Pops'. Reprise re-released 'Baby Don't Go', which reached Number 8 in the US and Number 11 in Britain.

The duo's debut album *Look At Us* followed quickly. It was slightly disappointing; the singles easily outdistanced the other tracks, cover versions of 'And Then He Kissed Me', 'Let It Be Me', 'You Really Got A Hold On Me' and others. Cher's solo LP *All I Really Want To Do* was much better. Sonny's production techniques were let loose among some excellent interpretations of 'Girl Don't Come', 'I Go To Sleep', 'Come And Stay With Me', 'The Bells Of Rhymney' and more; all, of course, featuring the requisite 12-strings-meet-Spector sound.

But the allure suddenly began to fade. Folk-rock was sinking fast, and the tone of acts like P. F. Sloan, Barry McGuire, the Turtles and others was getting harder as the hits stopped coming. The next Sonny and Cher single, 'But You're Mine', crawled to Number 15 in America and

Home on the range; Sonny and Cher with their daughter Chastity (above). Their outlandish – but clean – clothes and exotic sets (left) cornered the teen market. Below: Sonny directs his band.

Number 17 in the UK, reflecting perhaps its lack of a real hook-line, despite its full arrangement. Sonny's solo career was nosediving too. 'The Revolution Kind' failed to make much headway and his solo album *Inner Views* was rather poor.

The hits didn't dry up entirely; their version of 'What Now My Love' reached Number 14 in the US charts in January 1966, but it lacked the sparkle of their earlier hits. 'Little Man' and 'The Beat Goes On' were hits in 1966 and 1967 respectively for Sonny and Cher, and Cher's solo career carried on through 'Bang Bang' and 'You Better Sit Down Kids', a tearjerker about a marriage on the rocks, which reflected the switch in their concerns from adolescent rebellion to adult traumas.

Surpassed by bands like the Mamas and the Papas in distinctive style – both musical and sartorial – Sonny and Cher's innate conservatism came to the fore and left them out of touch with the age group who had originally bought their records. Their 1968 appearance in a US government anti-drugs film did nothing to improve their street-credibility, nor did Sonny's foray into politics at the 1968 Democratic Convention in Chicago. While Mayor Daley's police were brutalising the student demonstrators outside, Sonny Bono got a party platform passed calling for a Youth Commission in government to represent the views of people aged 18 to 25. Sonny went down to the park, Cher recalled, 'to tell the kids to cool it. They didn't care. They said, "*oh yeah . . .*"'

The road to Vegas

The couple had moved into films in 1966 with *Good Times*, directed by William Friedkin, following that with an appearance in an episode of 'The Man From U.N.C.L.E.'. Their second movie *Chastity* (1968) lost them two million dollars, and by the end of the Sixties Sonny and Cher were deeply in debt. The early Seventies, however, saw them making an arduous comeback and a return to financial solvency. They built up a solid reputation on the Las Vegas cabaret circuit, got their own show on CBS-TV, and Cher began modelling for Vogue magazine. They had a couple of hits with 'All I Ever Need Is You' in 1971 and 'A Cowboy's Work Is Never Done' in 1972. Cher's solo career in particular took off; 'Gypsys, Tramps and Thieves' (1971), 'Half Breed' (1973) and 'Dark Lady' (1974) all reached Number 1 in the US charts and 'Gypsys' made Number 4 in the UK.

After a row erupted at a Las Vegas niterie when Cher allegedly flirted with a member of Sonny's band, their marital difficulties were splashed across the tabloid press. The couple soldiered on, but in 1974 they embarked upon bitter and protracted divorce proceedings.

After the divorce, Sonny and Cher had their own separate TV shows; Sonny's flopped, Cher's took off. She signed to Warner Brothers, for whom she recorded an album *Stars* – produced by Jim Webb – in 1975, and continued to have modest hits on the label throughout the Seventies. She went on to record in a variety of styles and on different labels, from the rock of *Allman And Woman* (with her then-husband Greg Allman) to her reunion with Phil Spector and the tense excellence of 'A Woman's Story', as well as her duet with Harry Nilsson, 'A Love Like Yours'. Since then Cher has fronted a band, Black Rose, and worked with Meatloaf. Sonny, meanwhile, was spending his time appearing in TV movies. Their moment of fame may have been short and contrived, but for a brief while in 1965, Sonny and Cher mixed fashion, image and sound in a way that irresistibly caught the mood of a generation. BRIAN HOGG

Sonny and Cher
Recommended Listening

The Very Best Of Sonny And Cher (Hallmark SHM 3036) (Includes: I Got You Babe, Just You, But You're Mine, Sing C'est La Vie, The Beat Goes On, What Now My Love, Little Man).

DAYDREAM
BELIEVERS

The Monkees: puppets or real performers?

NEVER WAS A GROUP so derided, misunderstood and maligned as the Monkees. Fabricated by Hollywood for prime-time TV, the band comprised four fresh-faced actors who didn't even play their own instruments. Critics could ignore the fact that Brian Wilson employed session players to make Beach Boys records, that the Mamas and the Papas contributed only their voices to their lush hits, and even that the forbiddingly cool Byrds were absent from the studio when 'Mr Tambourine Man' was laid down. What they could not ignore or tolerate was that a group of middle-aged Hollywood businessmen had assembled their concept of a profitable rock group and foisted it upon the world.

It mattered not that the chosen participants proved to be as musically able as any number of British beat ensembles who had stormed the United States in the wake of the Beatles, or that the manipulators were, in the main, finely-pedigreed practitioners of their respective crafts. What mattered was that the Monkees had success handed to them on a silver plate.

Caged Monkees: Bob Rafelson surveys his TV creation. Clockwise from left: Micky Dolenz, Mike Nesmith, Davy Jones and Peter Tork.

During 1962, while working as associate producer of such television series as 'The Wackiest Ship In The Army' and 'Channing', young American writer/producer Bob Rafelson began to give thought to a dramatic series based around a folk-singing group. By 1965, when he had formed a partnership with Bert Schneider, son of the president of Columbia Pictures, the idea had germinated into a fully-fledged concept – encouraged by Beatlemania and the cinema success of *A Hard Day's Night* – and was being funded by former child actor Jackie Cooper, head of Screen Gems television.

Natural charm

Rafelson and his colleagues were not interested in giving the public another dose of 'My Three Sons', the typical TV format in which teenagers were presented as basically conservative and subservient: they wanted to achieve the same natural charm that Richard Lester had showcased so expertly in the Beatles film. They were looking for four unknowns who could not command large salaries and would not rock the boat with their own self-interest. So an advertisement was placed in *Daily Variety* and a casting call was sent out to agents, managers and Columbia film and television production offices. Some 437 hopefuls submitted applications and were summarily auditioned by Schneider and Rafelson.

Don Kirshner helped conceive a saturation launching campaign which set RCA back 100,000 dollars – exactly twice the amount Capitol had spent to launch the Beatles in the American market two years previously. A task force of 76 advance 'Monkeemen' criss-crossed the country to announce the group's impending arrival. Six thousand disc jockeys were furnished with preview records, and bumper stickers proclaiming 'Everybody Is Going Ape For The Monkees' and 'Monkee Business Is Big Business' were strewn from coast to coast in bundles of 100,000.

On 29 October 1966 the Monkees' first single, Boyce and Hart's 'Last Train To Clarksville', hit Number 1 in the US Hot Hundred; at the same time, the group's debut album, *The Monkees,* was at Number 1 in the album charts and the biggest musical phenomenon since the Beatles was washing across the States.

Too much Monkee business

Screen Gems and Colgems, the associated record company, expertly maximised the profits from their sudden windfall. Franchises were allotted for 50 Monkee products, including bracelets, lunch pails, pencil cases, shirts, wristwatches, chewing gum and dolls electronically wired to reproduce each member's voice. Mike's familiar green wool hat was rolled out of the mills at 1 dollar 98 cents, 48 cents more than he paid for the original; by the end of 1966, Monkee merchandising had brought in 20 million dollars. The 'Monkeemobile' car used in the series was earning 3000 dollars an appearance at supermarkets, 1600 department stores had opened 'Monkeewear' sections and 'Monkee Nightclubs' (selling soft drinks only) were opening across the country.

Then, on 3 December 1966, the Monkees made their first live appearance in Hawaii. The concert erupted into near-violent riots as 50 club-wielding cops waded into the hysterical crowd. From the moment the four leapt through papier mâché speakers on to the stage, peak Beatlemania was resurrected. By February 1967, a second album, *More Of The Monkees,* was being kept off the Number 1 spot by the first while the new single, Neil Diamond's 'I'm A Believer', had gone to the top of both the US and UK charts.

Not one of the four individuals finally chosen to be part of this phenomenon could have been considered lacking in talent. Micky Dolenz (born 8 March 1946) had been the star of the successful 1956 TV series 'Circus Boy' under his stage name of Braddock. Englishman Davy Jones (born 30 December 1945), who had once had a role in Granada TV's 'Coronation Street', was a Tony Award nominee for his Broadway stage work and had a 12,000-strong fan club. Mike Nesmith (born 30 December 1943), who recorded under the name Michael Blessing, was a songwriter of some reputation. Peter Thorkelson (born 13 February 1945), or Peter Tork as he now became, was an accomplished multi-instrumentalist with considerable Greenwich Village-based performing experience. Once chosen, the four young actors were given definable and recognisable characters: Dolenz was to play the crazy wit, Tork was to be the dumb one, Nesmith the thinker and Jones the cute baby-face.

The Monkees were, initially, given the opportunity to generate the musical content of the show but, as Tork later admitted, their own efforts were 'directionless and musically unproductive'. Besides, acting lessons, photo sessions, costume fittings and various advance promotional activities left the four little time to rehearse as a band. 'All of a sudden the music became an area nobody wanted to talk about,' Mike later explained. 'It all just slipped away from our grip while we were being groomed to become big television stars.'

Supervision of musical aspects of the project was handed to former Brill Building king Don Kirshner, the head of Screen Gems Music publishing company. Kirshner appointed two of his writers, Tommy Boyce and Bobby Hart, as producers of the initial sessions. With just seven weeks to countdown, Boyce and Hart had no time for pleasantries. Each Monkee was given an audition which amounted to an assessment of rudimentary vocal talent.

'We sat them around a piano,' explained Boyce, 'and had them sing all the songs we had written for them. It was obvious that Micky had the Paul McCartney voice, he could really sing. Davy had a passable ballad voice, Michael thought he was Merle Haggard and Peter had no voice at all. Now when you put all that together it wasn't the rock image that the show was supposed to have, so I told them that the truth of the matter was that they were hired as actors and that there wasn't much we could do with all their peculiar talents.' By this point the four Monkees, with varying degrees of graciousness, had accepted that professional session musicians would create the backings for the records.

Monkee recordings were being deftly churned out on the Kirshner assembly line, with the creative assistance of Gerry Goffin and Carole King, Neil Diamond, David Gates, Neil Sedaka, Carole Bayer, Jeff Barry, Jack Keller and other professional pop purveyors. With dollar signs flashing in their eyes, every songwriter or producer associated in any way with Screen Gems made a mad scramble for a piece of the Monkees action.

This situation was intolerable for the temperamental Texan Mike Nesmith. He had come to mistrust, dislike and publicly malign Don Kirshner, whom he saw as a barrier on his path to musical creativity and credibility. During December, with the Monkees radiating an innocent, cheeky charm over mass America, a bitter and resentful Nesmith told the *Saturday Evening Post,* 'The music has nothing to do with us. It is totally dishonest. Do you know how debilitating it is to sit up and have to duplicate somebody else's records? That's really what we are doing. The music happens in spite of the Monkees. It's what Kirshner wants to do. Our records are not our forte. I don't care if we never sell another record.'

Nesmith invited Bert Schneider to hear the band perform as a unit and when Schneider confessed that the group were 'not bad at all', Mike delivered an ultimatum: either Kirshner went or *he* did. The lid finally blew off late in January 1967 at Kirshner's private bungalow at the Beverly Hills Hotel. The four Monkees attended a gold record (and royalty cheque) presentation ceremony there, posing for trade photographs with their musical puppeteer. When the formalities were over, the Monkees were presented with acetates of four new songs, from which the third single was to be chosen. Mike exploded in anger and told Kirshner in blunt fashion that he was no longer prepared to have his name put on other people's music. When Kirshner, flanked by Lester Sill and Screen Gems executive Herb Moelis (whom Nesmith particularly disliked), insisted that he had every right to select whatever song he considered would be the most successful, Mike bellowed, 'Donny, we could sing "Happy Birthday" with a beat and it would sell a million records. Your argument is no longer valid because *we* are the Monkees, we have incredible TV exposure and now we

have all this power. Either we play or I quit.'

When Herb Moelis curtly growled, 'You'd better read your contract', whatever restraint Mike had left evaporated. White and trembling with rage, he smashed his fist into the wall of the 150 dollars-a-day bungalow, screamed 'That could have been your head!', and stormed out.

Kirshner would not entertain the idea of placing the Monkees-performed 'The Girl I Knew Somewhere' on the flipside of 'A Little Bit Me, A Little Bit You'. He went ahead and scheduled 'She Hangs Out' as a flip and was subsequently dismissed as head of Colgems Records by Abraham Schneider, president of Columbia Pictures, on the grounds that he had issued an unauthorised disc, generated 'self-adulatory publicity which was demeaning to the Monkees' and allegedly taped telephone conversations. Kirshner immediately sued for 35 million dollars' damages, the single was withdrawn in that form and the Monkees announced that they would be playing on all future Monkee recordings with Chip Douglas producing.

Monkeemania exploded in Britain at the beginning of 1967 with five million viewers tuning in every Saturday evening to view their antics. To fan the flames, they flew into England at staggered intervals during early February on what were officially described as 'holidays'. While the music press devoted saturation coverage to these visits, Fleet Street was less supportive, Jack Bentley of the *Sunday Mirror* describing the group in a banner headline as 'A Disgrace To The Pop World! . . . a bunch of kids trading on other people's talents and cashing in on millions.'

Aquarius and asthma

Back home, there were more problems. Having won the battle to work together in the studio, the Monkees found that that was exactly what they couldn't do; their tastes were simply too diverse. Gradually they separated into different camps, recording their own style of repertoire – country-rock from Mike, folk-bluegrass and social comment from Peter, straightahead pop-rock from Micky and cutesy-pie ballads and cabaret croons from Davy. The music that emerged from this jumble of activity, though often impressive and occasionally excellent, resulted in two very uneven albums, *Headquarters* and *Pisces, Aquarius, Capricorn And Jones Ltd.*

In June 1967, the Monkees embarked on their first fully-fledged tour, beginning with five riotous concerts at London's Empire Pool, Wembley, where they delivered a fiercely entertaining show that stunned even the harshest critics. The American leg of the tour commenced on 7 July in Atlanta, Georgia. It was prefaced by the group's first official press conference, at New York's Warwick Hotel, location of similar events with the Beatles. Screen Gems had finally backed down and allowed their million-dollar property to face the American press, after a similar exercise in London went well.

Playing it safe, Jackie Cooper stacked the room with Screen Gems staff journalists. Mike was warned, 'If they ask you about drugs, talk about asthma'. As Micky recalled, 'They were afraid we'd say, "Well we're bigger than the Beatles, which means we're bigger than Jesus, and we shoot Drano!".' Micky and Davy had no objections at all to the carefully-controlled conditions. Still the half of the group that considered themselves actors before musicians, they wanted to transfer the fantasy of the television series to real life, with loony lines and cheeky cavorting. Peter didn't care much one way or another and Mike grudgingly agreed to curb his tongue.

From their dramatic entrance in psychedelic garb hoisting a giant garbage can aloft, the Monkees proved themselves every bit as adept at promotion as the Beatles before them. Did they plan to put their music into the psychedelic bag, asked a 16-year-old girl reporter. 'Yes, we're going to give the tape recorder LSD,' assured Micky, earnestly. 'Is it true that the group is breaking up?' 'Sure,' they chimed in unison, walking away from each other.

Expectant silence descended when the questions switched to drugs. 'Have any of you ever taken LSD?' asked one keen young writer. 'I haven't,' said Davy, 'have you?' 'Yes,' he shot back. 'Would you recommend it?' returned Davy, receiving no reply. Asked if they really sang on their records, Davy instructed 'Right, everybody sing', and the four squawked as tunelessly as possible. After emphatically asserting that they played all their own music, on records and stage, the four merry pranksters left the room, having greatly impressed the Big Apple's cynical press corps.

The American concert dates featured the Jimi Hendrix Experience as support. Turned on to him by the Beatles during his first London visit, Micky had become an avid fan and had offered the tour stint as soon as Jimi left the stage at Monterey. Promoter

Far left: An early promotional shot of the Monkees; from left Davy Jones, the 'cute' one, Peter Tork, the 'dumb' one, Micky Dolenz, the 'crazy' one, and Mike Nesmith, the 'thinker', in ever-present woolly hat. Below, left to right: The Monkees' TV show combined polished pop, zany antics and fantasy sequences to win the hearts of millions.

Dick Clark reluctantly agreed. The Monkees had hoped to use Hendrix to break out of the sub-teen market, appeal to older teenagers and gain acceptance in the rock establishment. It was also, as Tommy Boyce pointed out, 'A personal trip. They wanted to watch Jimi Hendrix every night, they didn't care if he didn't fit.'

With just five dates completed, crisis struck. Halfway through his set Jimi Hendrix gave the audience the finger, uttered an expletive and stormed offstage, announcing that he was quitting the tour. This came as no surprise to those who had watched the psychedelic purveyor die a death at every show. What was surprising was that he had actually been booked in the first place, something Mike Nesmith conceded later: 'His type of music and guitar playing was inextricably interwoven with the drug culture and the whole Haight Ashbury thing and the Monkees had nothing whatsoever to do with any of that. We may have looked similar but we were two very different animals. When Jimi was on the same stage as the Monkees it was like having your mouth all set for pineapple and getting lemon. Jimi, rightly so, had no desire to play in front of a bunch of 10-14 year olds waving their arms, so he quit.' This incident brought home to the Monkees the futility of seeking recognition by the rock cognoscenti.

Following well-deserved hits with Goffin and King's 'Pleasant Valley Sunday' and John Stewart's 'Daydream Believer', the Monkees phenomenon began to run out of steam in early 1968. 'Valleri', issued without the group's knowledge, prompted Nesmith to publicly declare: 'The Monkees are dead! . . . "Valleri" is the worst record I have ever heard in my life.' Nonetheless, the record went to Number 3. The next, however – a remake of the Coasters' 'D. W. Washburn' – could only struggle to 19 and no single after that even cracked the Top Thirty. The second series of the TV show ceased at Christmas 1967 and Screen Gems opted out of a third. The Monkees feigned delight and announced an ambitious series of TV specials and feature films.

Immediately after recording the self-indulgent *The Birds, The Bees And The Monkees* album, they commenced work on a film project. *Head,* as the feature was eventually titled, was a bizarre affair indeed, far removed from the mild corn and gentle humour of the TV series. Live concert footage was intercut with shots of Vietnam atrocities and a scene featuring the four as dandruff in the hair of a gigantic Victor Mature. Cameo appearances from Annette Funicello, Sonny Liston and Frank Zappa with a talking cow compounded the film's strangeness and it bombed badly at the box office. The kids were totally confused and adults weren't interested in seeing a 'pop group' film.

Now in their death throes, the four recorded the first and last of what was intended to be a series of three television specials – '33⅓ Revolutions Per Monkee'. As in *Head,* they took perverse delight in puncturing, deflating and ridiculing what remaining shreds there were of their popular image. This was unfortunate, as the special was a commendable effort, featuring exciting guest appearances from the Buddy Miles Express, Julie Driscoll, Brian Auger and the Trinity, Little Richard, Jerry Lee Lewis and Fats Domino. Screened opposite the 1969 Academy Awards telecast, it rated disastrously.

Good clean fun

Both the film and television special made plain the vast social, musical and professional gulfs between the four Monkees, who had been thrown together as a temporary acting ensemble rather than a close musical unit. Peter Tork was the first to concede the obvious and quit the group on 30 December 1968, claiming he was musically frustrated. Surprisingly, Mike Nesmith did not follow, but actually closed ranks with the others to keep the group operating. The new threesome hooked up with a black seven-piece outfit, Sam and the Goodtimers, and concocted an impressive two-and-a-half-hour concert 'revue'. Reviews were strong but attendance was poor and the show was pulled off the road mid-tour. After the dreary Boyce and Hart-penned 'Tear Drop City', from the patchy *Instant Replay* album, had flopped as a single, Nesmith finally won his first self-penned A-side with 'Listen To The Band' in July 1969. Recorded in Nashville with the country-rock musicians who would later become Area Code 615, it was one of the finest Monkees singles of all. However, in the US it reached a new chart low – Number 63.

In the UK market, Paul Williams' 'Someday Man' scraped into the Top Fifty at Number 47 while another country-folk single, 'Good Clean Fun', completely bypassed the charts in both countries. After another album as a trio, *The Monkees Present,* the line-up was reduced once more by the inevitable departure of Nesmith. Micky and Davy carried on as the Monkees from his exit in March 1970, recording the ninth and final album, *Changes.* For a time there was a joke around the industry that Colgems Records would end up issuing an album called *The Monkee.*

After the final split, each Monkee was battered and torn by the experience. Mike surfaced first with a string of highly-acclaimed country-rock albums and, in the Eighties, took a leading role in the field of rock video manufacturing and production. Micky and Davy got back on the road quite successfully in 1975 with Tommy Boyce and Bobby Hart for a 'Golden Great Hits Of The Monkees' show; Micky subsequently pursued a career as a television producer/director in England, while Davy continued a sporadic theatrical career. Peter suffered the worst; his immediate post-Monkees group, Release, didn't even record and in 1972 he spent four months in prison after

Below: In the Seventies, Nesmith turned to country rock, forming the First National Band. Below left: In 1975, Jones and Dolenz teamed up with Monkees' songwriters Boyce and Hart to perform and record. Above: Peter Tork goes hippie, 1969. Right: Mike Monkee on stage.

conviction on drugs charges. In the Eighties, however, he was back where he had started, playing in the folk dives of Greenwich Village – arguably the best survivor of the whole phenomenon.

By the late Seventies, the much-maligned Monkees had at last shaken off much of the prejudice which had accompanied their rise and fall. The advent of punk and new wave saw their songs adopted by young bands and their original records – particularly the *Head* soundtrack album – often assume immense value on the collectors' market. With hindsight, the Monkees appear as credible as any other rock sensation of the era, as a fresh listen to their better recordings will doubtless attest.

GLENN BAKER

THE MONKEES
Discography

Singles

Last Train To Clarksville/Take A Giant Step (Colgems 1001, 1966); I'm A Believer/(I'm Not Your) Steppin' Stone (Colgems 1002, 1966); A Little Bit Me, A Little Bit You/The Girl I Knew Somewhere (Colgems 1004, 1967); Pleasant Valley Sunday/Words (Colgems 1007, 1967); Daydream Believer/Goin' Down (Colgems 1012, 1967); Valleri/Tapioca Tundra (Colgems 1019, 1968); D. W. Washburn/It's Nice To Be With You (Colgems 1023, 1968); Porpoise Song/As We Go Along (Colgems 1031, 1968); Tear Drop City/A Man Without A Dream (Colgems 5000, 1969); Listen To The Band/Someday Man (Colgems 5004, 1969); Mommy And Daddy/Good Clean Fun (Colgems 5005, 1969); Oh My My/I Love You Better (Colgems 5011, 1970); Daydream Believer/Monkee's Theme (Arista 0201, 1976).

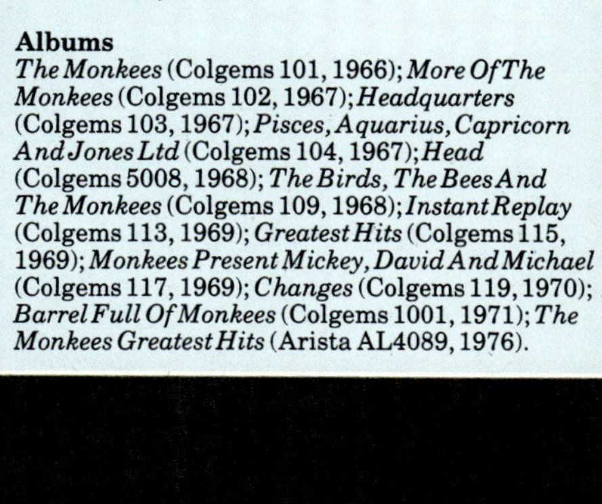

Albums

The Monkees (Colgems 101, 1966); *More Of The Monkees* (Colgems 102, 1967); *Headquarters* (Colgems 103, 1967); *Pisces, Aquarius, Capricorn And Jones Ltd* (Colgems 104, 1967); *Head* (Colgems 5008, 1968); *The Birds, The Bees And The Monkees* (Colgems 109, 1968); *Instant Replay* (Colgems 113, 1969); *Greatest Hits* (Colgems 115, 1969); *Monkees Present Mickey, David And Michael* (Colgems 117, 1969); *Changes* (Colgems 119, 1970); *Barrel Full Of Monkees* (Colgems 1001, 1971); *The Monkees Greatest Hits* (Arista AL4089, 1976).

MONTEREY POP

The first large-scale rock festival of the Sixties

IT IS RARELY POSSIBLE to pinpoint a moment or event at which a new style of music or a new attitude towards music-making becomes public property. Elvis Presley's appearance on Ed Sullivan's television show in 1956 may be accounted one such moment; perhaps the arrival of the Beatles in the United States in February 1964 was another. On these terms, the Monterey Pop Festival of June 1967 was the next comparable event in the history of rock music.

Monterey was significant for several reasons. It emphasised the peak of musical activity in the Bay Area; it telescoped the hippie cult of the West Coast and projected it to the outside world; it encompassed both the origins of rock music – and its future – in its line-up; and it began a whole era of rock festivals.

The initial concept – conceived by LA concert promoter Alan Pariser – was of a cross between the San Remo Song Festival (with its emphasis on unknown acts) and the Newport Jazz Festival. Pariser took the idea to Ben Shapiro, a big-name booker since the Fifties, who thought the idea would work but didn't agree with Pariser's non profit-making concept. It was decided to hold the festival at Monterey, partly because it was the home of the annual jazz festival, and partly as it was situated on the coast between Los Angeles and San Francisco, the cities from which many of the bands and much of the audience would be coming.

Money matters

The agreement to lease the site was signed in April 1967 and the festival was scheduled for June, which meant that the organisers had to move fast. The Mamas and the Papas were the first group approached, and John Phillips also became involved in the festival organisation; the singer, however, refused to be associated with it as a profit-making venture. Shapiro, realising that his vision of a fast million was slipping away, agreed to be bought out by a combination of Phillips, entrepreneur Lou Adler (Phillips' manager) and Paul Simon. Pariser stayed on as producer of the festival, and Phillips and Adler became joint directors. Adler had served as manager of Jan and Dean and Johnny Rivers for years and Scott McKenzie's chart-topping 'San Francisco (Be Sure To Wear Flowers In Your Hair)' had been recorded for his newly-formed Ode label.

Monterey was LA's answer to the SF music scene which had spawned the Trips Festival, Acid Tests and January 1967's Human Be-In at Golden Gate Park. LA was more commercially-minded than SF in its attitude to flower power and, although Monterey was not itself intended to show a profit, its organisers were far from slow in exploiting all the commercial avenues of such an event's offshoots. The film and TV rights were sold in advance and record company executives were invited to the festival to scout for new talent. Hollywood's groovy people were enlisted to make the festival a success – designer Tom Wilkes created the posters (metallic ink on silver foil), publicity was put in the skilful hands of former Beatles press officer Derek

Taylor, and D. A. Pennebaker was brought in to record the happening on film.

An advisory panel was assembled to put forward suggestions for performers, and included Paul McCartney, Brian Wilson, Brian Jones, Paul Simon and Art Garfunkel. Artists were to receive expenses only for their appearance at Monterey, but the problem of what to do with the profits had yet to be solved. There were rumours, early on, that it was to be given to the Diggers in San Francisco, an anarchic organisation of 'hippie Robin Hoods'. This, together with concern at the number of people who might attend, worried the citizens of Monterey; Adler finally convinced the City Council on 15 May that the money would only go to recognised charities. He also stated that the festival was unlikely to attract more than the 7,000 ticket holders (he was wrong, but probably unwittingly, about that). After the assurances, the festival was given the go-ahead.

Getting the acts together

With less than a month to go, finalising the acts the organisers wanted was no easy task; somehow they got most of them. Those they failed to get included the Beatles (who couldn't have played without temporarily doubling the population of Monterey); the Stones (Jagger and Richards had just been busted; Brian Jones attended as a guest); Cream, the Young Rascals and the Lovin' Spoonful (and a few others) were already booked elsewhere, while the Beach Boys were going to play but Carl Wilson had to appear in court to justify his desire to stay out of the US Army.

The name of the event was expanded to the First Annual International Pop Festival: the 'annual' part never materialised, while the 'international' label was stretching it rather. Most of the 'imported' acts were from Britain – the Who, Jimi Hendrix (who was living in Britain at the time and was put on the bill at the insistence of Paul McCartney), Eric Burdon and the Animals and Beverley. The latter was perhaps the most obscure performer on the bill, achieving greater fame after her subsequent marriage to John Martyn. Canada supplied the Paupers, while Ravi Shankar from India and black South African Hugh Masakela also appeared.

The original idea had been to present a broad cross-section of current pop music but things didn't quite work out that way. For one thing there were hardly any US black acts on the bill; only Otis Redding, Booker T. and the MGs and Lou Rawls appeared, although the Impressions and Dionne Warwick had originally agreed to appear. And, despite being on the board of directors, Smokey Robinson didn't play. It has since been suggested that the black community felt that Monterey was set up by whites for whites and that any black acts that played there would be selling out.

Of the American acts, at least 14 were from California (not even counting the Electric Flag who had virtually settled in San Francisco). Thus the majority of the bands played new-style West Coast acid rock and it was they (plus the Who and Hendrix, who both played a form of acid rock, anyway) who made the festival so famous. Not that all was love and peace in the Californian camp; the festival highlighted the fact that there were two distinct Californias, LA and SF.

Absence of Love

The SF contingent, especially the Grateful Dead, bitched about what they considered to be the LA music-biz style administration of the event, especially the high cost of the tickets. They would have preferred a much more loosely structured affair along the lines of the free concerts in Golden Gate Park or a stoned night at the Family Dog. They also felt that most LA bands were pretty unhip, for although the festival featured Buffalo Springfield, LA bands like Love, the Doors and Kaleidoscope had not been booked.

The organisers, of course, saw it differently. Although they wanted the event to be 'super-groovy', they argued that unless it was properly organised the town council would never have permitted it. They realised that Monterey was going to be held up as the model for any future festivals; they had to do it right or no one would be allowed to put one on again. Being the first of its kind, problems were still being dealt with right up until the 3-day festival opened on 16 June. By the first afternoon all the tickets had been sold and at least 30,000 extra bodies had arrived. To reduce the numbers of gate-crashers, speakers were put up outside the gates so those outside could at least hear. Some anticipated problems never arose; the townspeople, terrified of potential rape and pillage, were amazed by the beatific smiles and general good vibes. The police, for their part, chose to ignore the rampant dope smoking.

The festival consisted of five performances: Friday night, Saturday afternoon and evening, and Sunday afternoon and evening. Friday night proved to be something of a dry run; the talented but misplaced Association opened the show, followed by the Paupers, a relatively obscure Canadian band who were greeted with mild enthusiasm. After them came the essentially nightclub-orientated Lou Rawls; he was followed by Beverley, who left as obscure as she arrived. After her came Johnny Rivers, a pop star managed by Lou Adler. Next up were the highlight of the evening, Eric Burdon and his newly-reformed Animals. Gone was 'House Of The Rising Sun', in was a storming version of 'Paint It Black' with John Weider on violin. Last up were Simon and Garfunkel, probably the only non-rock act to get much out of Monterey.

Blues without blacks

Saturday afternoon was blues time, although lacking any black acts. Canned Heat opened with Bob 'the Bear' Hite lumbering around the stage; what they lacked in drama, they made up for in authenticity and knowledge of the blues. They were followed by *the* success of the festival, Big Brother and the Holding Company with Janis Joplin on vocals. The sound was raw, brash and exciting and the crowd loved it. Their success led to rave reviews, a deal with Columbia Records and, as an immediate bonus, a slot in the

Super-groovy! Hendrix brought the gift of fire to Monterey (below). The Beatles couldn't be there but sent a card instead (inset opposite), while their compatriots the Who provided a showstopping performance (opposite).

Above left: The Mamas and the Papas, whose John Phillips helped organise the festival. Above right: Janis Joplin casts aside ball and chain. Below: Monkee Peter Tork (centre, sitting) and Jimi Hendrix (far left) look on.

Sunday-night show. They proved to be a hard act to follow; although fellow Bay Area bands Country Joe and the Fish, Quicksilver Messenger Service and Steve Miller attempted it, none were on their best form.

During the afternoon, in a football field over the hill, the Grateful Dead were playing some of the best music of the weekend, free; they also refused to sign a release for the projected film of the festival. The Grateful Dead simply couldn't deal with 'the LA bureacracy'. Saturday night was a mixed bag – more SF bands in Moby Grape and Jefferson Airplane, the Byrds, Hugh Masakela (a total flop) and singer-songwriter Laura Nyro, who was totally out of place on a festival bill. But the evening culminated in a stunning performance by Otis Redding.

Sunday afternoon was totally given over to Ravi Shankar and proved to be an opportunity for the fans to 'mellow out a little'. Sunday night turned out to be a grand climax to the festival. After the Grateful Dead and the Blues Project, the Who proceeded to amaze the audience with a performance both visually and aurally riveting; the sight of Pete Townshend letting off smoke bombs and smashing his guitar was beyond most of the audience. Following the Who, and going one better, Jimi Hendrix actually set fire to his guitar. Buffalo Springfield had no hope after that performance. In fact it wasn't until the Mamas and the Papas came on to close the festival that the audience were able to give the artists on stage their full attention again.

The festival proved a success on most levels. Its motto had been 'music, love and flowers' and it was a sort of Garden of Eden for the Sixties' hippies. The festival netted 200,000 dollars for charity; there were no reports of arrests or injuries, which overshadowed later festivals subsequently staged on ever-grander scales.

Monterey the festival was immortalised in *Monterey*, the film which was released in 1968. The highlights of the movie are undoubtedly the performances of the Who and Hendrix and Janis Joplin's rendition of 'Ball And Chain', but there is also some excellent footage of Jefferson Airplane, Otis Redding and Country Joe and the Fish. The film captures the feeling of an event which was the first large-scale showcase of its kind and may be described as the moment the rock generation became aware of itself.

JOHN PLATT

GOIN' TO CALIFORNIA

To the rest of the world, music appeared to burst from the West coast of America without warning, but in fact, in districts like Haight Ashbury and the Bay Area, there was a long tradition of bohemian life-styles and fluid musical associations. The uncompromising improvisation of the Grateful Dead, the hedonistic nihilism of Jim Morrison's Doors and the more reflective musings of Joni Mitchell all took the West Coast heritage in hitherto unexplored directions, and extended its influence all round the world and into the present day

STREET LIFE

How love went sour on Haight Ashbury

The Haight Ashbury community in San Francisco did not, as is sometimes believed, appear suddenly at the drop of an acid tab. Its roots went back a long way. San Francisco's long tradition of bohemianism stretched back to the founding of the modern city in the mid-nineteenth century. What made that tradition unique was its fusion of outrageous self-indulgence with serious, and often radical, intellectualism.

SF grew up as a goldrush town full of brothels, gambling halls and opium dens – particularly in an area known as the Barbary Coast, which was destroyed in the 1906 earthquake. There already existed communites in the Bay Area that catered for all persuasions – theosophists, word reform freaks, occult dabblers *et al*. By the turn of the century the city had gained a reputation as a haven for anyone who felt out-of-step with conventional society.

Above left: The Haight Ashbury intersection, where all roads led to freedom. Left: Allen Ginsberg preaches the legalisation of marijuana to the converted.

Breath of fresh air

By the mid Fifties, SF had its own Beat community, centred on North Beach, which was full of artists, poets, musicians and craftsmen. North Beach was awash with people living a completely new style of life. There were bars like the Place featuring a 'Blabbermouth Night', when people could sound off on whatever subject they wanted, and bookshops like City Lights, which was run by Lawrence Ferlinghetti, who was busted for publishing Allen Ginsberg's *Howl*. Freedom was the key word and drugs became fashionable. Smoking marijuana had been accepted in the jazz world for years – now middle-class white kids were starting to indulge.

While preserving its very individual identity, the North Beach community attracted numerous outsiders; Jack Kerouac and Allen Ginsberg both lived in the area, on and off, for years. After the conformist pressures of the McCarthy years and in the midst of America's booming consumer society, the Beats seemed like a breath of fresh air to many young people.

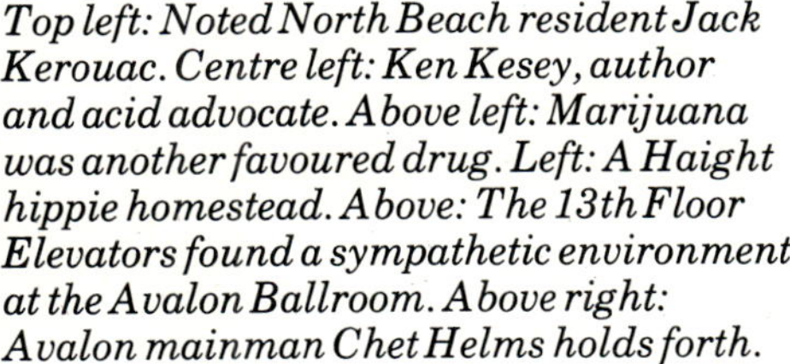

Top left: Noted North Beach resident Jack Kerouac. Centre left: Ken Kesey, author and acid advocate. Above left: Marijuana was another favoured drug. Left: A Haight hippie homestead. Above: The 13th Floor Elevators found a sympathetic environment at the Avalon Ballroom. Above right: Avalon mainman Chet Helms holds forth.

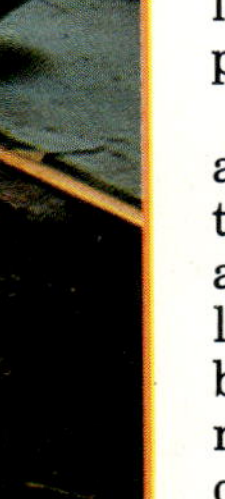

North Beach lasted as an entity until about 1960, when the community started to crack under the twin pressures of police activity – not even San Francisco was *that* liberal – and commercialisation. The area became SF's strip-club centre, although many of the old haunts survived by putting on folk music: places like the Coffee Gallery and the Fox and Hounds which, within a couple of years, provided a stage for Janis Joplin and Dino Valente.

Kids growing up in the suburbs and down the peninsula in towns like Palo Alto were discovering a Beatnik lifestyle for themselves – growing their hair, abandoning suits and ties and discovering marijuana. Many of them moved into folk music, and at places like the Tangent in Palo Alto and the Boar's Head in San Mateo in 1962 you could have heard people like Jerry Garcia and Pigpen (later of the Grateful Dead) and Peter Albin (later in Big Brother and the Holding Company).

Around the same time, writer Ken Kesey, author of *One Flew Over The Cuckoo's Nest,* was taking part in Government investigations into the effects of LSD. Afterwards he started throwing parties with acid as the chief attraction. In 1965 these events evolved into the notorious Acid Tests, organised by his entourage, the Merry Pranksters, in hired bars and night clubs, sometimes beneath the gaze of the bemused proprietors. The Grateful Dead were the house band, and the music mingled freely with tape, slide and performance shows. Quite often, several things would be going on at once; 'there was this incredible cross interference and weirdness,' Jerry Garcia of the Grateful Dead recalled later.

A new community was simultaneously growing up in another part of the city – the old Haight Ashbury district, an area full of crumbling, but elegant, Victorian houses. For years it had been a working-class area, housing mainly Polish and other European immigrants. By the early Sixties its cheap rents were attracting new inhabitants, many from North Beach.

Links between the Beatnik days and Haight Ashbury were strong. One of the first new residents in the Haight was Beat poet Michael McClure, whose play *The Beard* won him notoriety in 1966 and who helped organise the first Human Be-In, along with Allen Ginsberg.

Although the hippies, as they were to be known, had attitudes similar to those of the Beatniks, times had changed. The McCarthy era had passed, civil rights and the Vietnam War were becoming contentious and there were different things to enjoy – in particular rock music and acid. Local rock music started to emerge as the folk musicians began to go electric. By the late summer of 1965 the pioneers of the new breed were getting together.

The Charlatans, in their Wild West gambling outfits, played probably the first real SF rock music that summer – ironically in Virginia City, Nevada. They were loosely associated with an outfit called the Family Dogg who lived in a commune on Pine Street, a couple of blocks from the Haight. Later that year they hired the Longshoremen's Hall in downtown SF and put on three dances that are acknowledged as being the first rock dance-concerts in the city. Most of Haight Ashbury turned out in all manner of bizarre costumes as cowboys, Indians, riverboat gamblers.

The Family Dogg helped organise a three-day Trips Festival in the New Year of 1967 at the Fillmore Auditorium in the black ghetto that bordered Haight Ashbury. Drawing on the experience of the Acid Tests, the Trips Festival attempted to re-create the aural and visual effects of LSD through music and light shows.

One man who recognised the money-making potential of these new ventures was Bill Graham, who began organising dances at the Fillmore Auditorium. But it was the Avalon Ballroom, run by the Family Dog, under the guidance of Chet Helms, that became the real music centre of the community, drawing in bands like the 13th Floor Elevators from Texas, Kaleidoscope from LA and the Youngbloods from New York, as well as local bands. Just down the road was Golden Gate Park, which became a venue for free rock concerts; its offshoot, the Panhandle, was used as a base from which the Diggers – a kind of underground Good Samaritans – could distribute free food.

One long carnival

Life in Haight Ashbury was, as far as possible, one long carnival. People worked – but mainly at things they enjoyed doing and which they considered to benefit the community. Places like the Psychedelic Shop at 1535 Haight Street, selling drugs paraphernalia and psychedelic posters, was also a meeting place and information centre. As the community began to attract more and more media attention, runaways from all over flocked to the Haight in the search for drugs and free love. The city fathers and the police were growing worried and the previously-flaunted freedoms of the hippies became threatened.

In many ways, 1967's Summer of Love was both the climax and the end of the Haight Ashbury community. Events like the Human Be-In, held in Golden Gate Park in January 1967, had been a big success and the music was getting better and better. But the intensity of the media coverage of Haight Ashbury caused such an influx of young hopefuls that the community – both the informal networks like the Diggers, and the official social services – could no longer support them. The influx also brought with it a commercialisation of the drug scene and, according to Jerry Garcia, an injection of old, hard-nosed East Coast values which were antipathetic to the hippie lifestyle and philosophy: 'The inability of not being able to say, "Get out, go away" . . . tells us something about what innocence is. It's that which allows itself to become no longer innocent.'

Sensing the change, the original freaks moved out. Behind them they left the casualties of the heavily adulterated acid that had become widespread. Murder, rape, prostitution reached alarming proportions. The public health authorities could not cope, and disease became widespread; there were even rumours of bubonic plague. By mid 1968, Haight Ashbury had become a ghetto for speed freaks and muggers.

JOHN PLATT

By mid 1967, the writing was on the Haight Street wall for the hippie ideal: commercial interests had moved in.

S·F·FANTASIES

Beach parties gave way to San Francisco's counter-culture in the summer of 1967

IN THE LATE FIFTIES and early Sixties, California was the Mecca of the American Dream. It was the Golden Land of endless summers and surf-pounded beaches; and the city of Los Angeles stood for everything that was modern and go-ahead. By the late Sixties, however, the hippest city in California was undoubtedly San Francisco. This change in emphasis marked a definite shift in rock music. Popular music was part of established business in LA; but San Francisco represented something else – rock as counter-culture, as a lifestyle, and as music outside the corporate business structure.

Ever since Hollywood had become the entertainment centre of the world in the Twenties there had been people in Southern California with an awful lot of money and a lot of time in which to spend it. Leisure took on a whole new meaning. As Kenneth Anger's book *Hollywood Babylon* makes clear, the excesses of the Sixties were nothing new. Whatever you wanted – drugs or sex, or booze during the Prohibition era – someone could provide it; and if it was legal someone would package it and serve it up to the masses.

The film industry expanded rapidly in the Thirties and Forties and moved into the newer areas of radio, records and TV. By the early Sixties all the major labels were centred on LA, some such as Columbia and Warner Bros being offshoots of film companies. Success, other than on a local level, meant a move to LA.

Beach party romps

A whole new lifestyle grew up around the beaches and was adopted by teenagers who had access to parental wealth, enjoyed long summer vacations and were seemingly blessed (particularly the girls) with almost supernatural beauty. To the outsider it all seemed very enviable, especially as portrayed by Hollywood exploitation movies that featured Annette Funicello in endless beach party romps. It wasn't just the beaches, either: the whole business of going to drive-ins and cruising for burgers in huge sports cars seemed a million miles away for most teenagers.

It was perhaps inevitable that a musical style should grow up alongside this pleasureable way of life. Dick Dale was the first to play music that reflected surfing, but when Dennis Wilson suggested to his brothers that they should write songs about it, a new musical genre came into being.

As the Sixties progressed, the image of Californian youth changed; suntans and beach buggies gave way to long hair and brightly-painted, psychedelically-patterned trucks (below). Suddenly it was in to opt out; drugs had long been a part of San Francisco's jazz and beatnik scene, but now – to the consternation of their parents – middle-class teenagers were experimenting too. A new lifestyle, with its own music, was born.

The traditional Hollywood role had been to market myths, and now they had found, on their own doorstep, one they could sell to the world. Teenagers, even if they were 1000 miles from the nearest beach, dreamed of surf as those beautiful harmonies washed over them. By late 1963 the surf-sound had swept the States and by the end of 1964 the Beach Boys were popular worldwide.

But fads fade, and by late 1964 America was in the grip of Beatlemania, which was followed by the British invasion. Suddenly, pallid, hairy British groups became far more appealing, both visually and musically, than sun-bronzed blond Californians. Anxious to be first with a new trend, LA welcomed the new styles with open arms. The British Mod look – or America's somewhat bizarre variant of it – was perfect for fun-loving LA.

New kicks

The other new musical style was folk-protest. Bob Dylan was starting to break out of the purist market, civil rights was becoming a burning issue and agitation over the Vietnam War was growing. With the Beatles showing that rock could be fun, a marriage of socially-conscious lyrics and 'the English sound' proved irresistible.

Initially, the new movement was spontaneous – even as successful a group as the Byrds were nothing less than sincere. But by the end of 1965 the LA record industry was sucking in anybody that could be turned into a protest singer, provided they could make money: the 'message' was all. In the process some great records were made – Barry McGuire's 'Eve Of Destruction', many by the Turtles, even Sonny and Cher.

By mid 1966 the protest genre began to wane, however, splitting roughly two ways. On the one hand were the Mamas and the Papas, Spanky and Our Gang, and Harper's Bizarre who, with smooth harmonies, trod an uneasy path between beautifully-crafted soft-rock and mawkish MOR. The second strand were folk-oriented bands who moved further towards rock and pioneered the LA psychedelic scene that was to attract media attention.

Initially, the LA psychedelic scene was traditional Hollywood decadence with new trappings. The early clubs like Ciro's and the Whiskey were full of well-heeled young movie-types looking for new kicks. The Peter Fonda film *The Trip* accurately portrays the period that produced some amazing music by bands of the calibre of Buffalo Springfield, Love and Kaleidoscope.

Although most of these bands were folk-based, a few weren't – notably the Doors and the Mothers of Invention. Jim Morrison's persona and lifestyle are pure Hollywood and Zappa's music, on certain levels, portrayed perfectly LA trash culture.

LA has produced the ultimate pre-packaged, disposable society. The flip-side of Dream City is that it is one of the ugliest, most polluted places on earth. Despite the fact that so much innovative music came out of it in the Sixties, LA tended to follow trends, not make them. By 1967 the psychedelic scene in LA was largely a copy of what was happening 400 miles up the coast in San Francisco. Previously LA had always managed to become the centre of trends even though it hadn't started them; but with the growth of the San Francisco sound and culture, it failed to do so. The big companies suddenly became aware that things were happening in San Francisco, and that the groups there represented not just the local eccentricities of a small community, but were making music that struck home to an audience on a worldwide scale.

Rock turns acid

The San Francisco scene did not just appear overnight, of course. Like the Liverpool sound before it, this musical phenomenon had a particular history. Most of the San Francisco bands had been in existence for well over a year when the great surge of interest began in 1967 and the majority of the musicians had been involved in music (mainly folk) since the beginning of the decade.

Whether there was a genuine San Francisco sound is a moot point. Most groups played a bastardised, but very electric, folk-rock with plenty of added ingredients gleaned from jazz, blues, Eastern and even classical music. Unlike their LA counterparts who generally sounded better in the studio, live performance was more important to the San Francisco bands. Their music was spontaneous and free-flowing, often featuring long improvisations. It

The new Californian music took different forms, from the smooth, folk-rock harmonies and wholesome image of bands like the Mamas and the Papas (above left) and Spanky and Our Gang (above) to the bizarre acid-rock experiments and free improvisation of Jefferson Airplane (above right) and the Grateful Dead (right, in Golden Gate Park, San Francisco).

was dubbed acid rock because most of the bands indulged in drugs. More important than the music itself was what it represented: a new set of relationships between performer and audience; a new idea of the possibilities of rock.

The great LA-SF meeting occurred at the Monterey Pop Festival in June 1967. Although it was organised almost entirely from LA, and despite the presence of the Byrds and Buffalo Springfield, San Francisco groups like the Grateful Dead, Jefferson Airplane and Big Brother and the Holding Co (with Janis Joplin) showed themselves to be the real stars. Monterey was a watershed. A&R men swamped San Francisco in the subsequent months, attempting to sign up every long-haired band in sight. The Summer of Love in San Francisco had arrived and, for a while at least, the city was the musical centre of California and the world.

JOHN PLATT

QUICKSILVER MESSENGERS

The bands that made music in the Bay Area

During the Fifties and early Sixties, the United States was the breeding-ground for every genre and progression in popular music and the San Francisco Bay Area, as a hotbed of bohemianism, played a major part in this development. A singularly European city in terms of scale and atmosphere, San Francisco thrummed with bebop and beatnik jazz – based around the local independent Fantasy label – and, later, with the sound of young folkies preaching civil rights and nuclear disarmament in song. In 1964, the Beatles burst into the American media, ending Stateside pop dominance, and the young inhabitants of the Bay Area were immediately won over to the new sounds.

The British invasion had an immediate effect on the American pop scene as hordes of groups formed and attempted to emulate the musical feats of the Beatles, Stones *et al.* The Bay Area witnessed a particular flurry of such activity and by 1967, with flower power in full bloom, San Francisco had taken over as the rock capital of the world. 'Merseybeat' was long passé – it was now the age of the San Francisco sound.

Incense and peppermints

The first bull's-eye for San Franciscan rock had come from a group whose devotion to Merseybeat was total – the Beau Brummels; their first national hit, 'Laugh Laugh' in January 1965, was a direct copy of the Beatles' sound, while on later recordings, such as 'Don't Talk To Strangers', they aped the Searchers. Meanwhile, at upmarket clubs like Mother's and the Peppermint Tree, imports such as New York's Lovin' Spoonful and the Byrds from Los Angeles were wowing the hip vanguard. Rock was becoming more hedonistic, more erotic, more of a confrontation as technology and drugs (particularly LSD) were thrown into the melting pot. Although no distinct 'sound', as such, existed among the bands of San Francisco, there was a recipe of sorts, the ingredients of which included American rock'n'roll (as subverted by the energy of the British invasion), jazz, folk and country. And running through the diversity of the hundreds of bands that seethed through the area during the boom years of hippiedom was a shared spirit, an exultation in community.

Typical of the hippie bands were the Great Society – young, bedraggled, and intense; they were fronted by guitarist Darby Slick and his ex-model sister-in-law Grace who in 1966 wrote and sang a dervish hymn called 'White Rabbit' in praise of LSD. The Great Society galvanised the scene and Tom Donahue, pioneer of FM rock, took them under his wing and along to his own Autumn label, where they recorded under the canny eye of Sly Stewart – the Sly Stone of later years.

Suddenly there was spontaneous combustion, a breakout on several levels as musicians and street performers began to swarm around the intersection of Haight and Ashbury streets. LSD was readily available and still legal, and outright weirdness was *de rigeur*. New venues opened, hosting 'dance-concerts' with wildly eclectic bills and liquid and luminous 'psychedelic' lightshows. One such hall was the Avalon, where the Grateful Dead conducted their Acid Tests. Another was the Matrix where a polite folk-rock outfit, quaintly named Jefferson Airplane, seduced Grace Slick and her repertoire from the Great Society and became the first Bay band to achieve national stardom. Be-Ins in the park demonstrated that a new movement was being born, and the establishment was frankly baffled.

As the disgruntled young flotsam of affluent America began to make tracks for the celebrated Haight, with them came myriad bands, particularly from Texas and the South. Such diverse groupings as the flashy Steve Miller Blues Band, the down-home Sir Douglas Quintet, Mother Earth and the punky Other Half migrated to escape the redneck belt. Others, like Salvation, Mad River and Melting Pot, just showed up looking for receptive ears. By the end of 1966 there were hundreds of groups working in the area, from the spacey HP Lovecraft to the true originators of Bay Edwardian chic the Charlatans; from the poppy Sopwith Camel to drug-oriented heavies like Loading Zone, Little John, Second Coming and the brass-augmented Sons of Champlin. Loose aggregations with exotic names like William Penn and His Pals, the Only Alternative and His Other Possibilities, and Walter Wart and the Pickledish swarmed fruitlessly. The radical intellectuals of the university district of Berkeley contributed the lilting feminism of Joy of Cooking and the psychedelic folk of Country Joe and the Fish. North of the city, Sausalito countered with the musclebound funk of Tower of Power.

Through 1966, the hippies – as they had, essentially sarcastically, come to be called

– never had it so good. But the dreams soon faded. Acid was legislated off the streets and would-be hippies began to litter the Haight as the glare of worldwide media attention focused on the lifestyle of the 'now generation'. And with the media came the record companies, who began signing SF acts with abandon. Quicksilver Messenger Service and the Steve Miller Band went to Capitol, the latter with an enormous advance, while Columbia picked up Moby Grape – potentially the greatest of them all – then proceeded to destroy them under a heap of hype and gimmick such as the simultaneous release of five singles, all culled from the group's debut album. Columbia also grabbed the loud and gutsy Big Brother and the Holding Company, fronted by Janis Joplin.

In their frenzy to cash in on the hippie boom, less astute companies continued to sign up any gaggle of longhairs with little regard for their musical qualities. The sublime and the ridiculous mingled as Vanguard signed the excellent Notes from the Underground and the pompous Serpent Power, Mercury snaffled Morning Glory, Savage Resurrection and Linn County, while Dot got the dubious Womb and the frightful Mount Rushmore. Yes, even total turkeys like the twee and silly Columbia signings Gale Garnett and the Gentle Reign got a look-in.

Woodstock withers

Like all constructs of fashion and media, the blooming fascination of the Bay Area had eventually to fade as the Haight became ugly with squalor and desperation and the nucleus of intellectual activity left town in resignation. The positive exhilaration of Country Joe, the Airplane and their contemporaries gave way to gloomy confrontation as Vietnam came to the forefront of public consciousness and a chain of sad circumstance led from the euphoric bravado of Monterey and Woodstock Nation, through the Kent State slayings to Altamont, where the Dead and the Airplane stood in the wings and watched the hippie dream sour in an orgy of violence. By the end of the decade, people were using their kaftans to wash the car and the Bay Area beat boom had withered and died.

In the appendix of his book *The Jefferson Airplane And The San Francisco Sound* the journalist devotee of SF rock, the late Ralph J. Gleason, listed the many hundreds of groups active in the Bay Area during the Sixties. Their stylistic diversity was astonishing and their abilities infinitely variable, but their Utopian fantasies were seductively consistent and drastically mobilised rock's potential as a vehicle for communication and social evolution. In the final analysis, the San Francisco sound existed in the spirit of the city and the political stance of its musicians.

'White Rabbit' was the anthem for a generation, and the legacy of San Francisco remains a loud, proud affirmation of love, life and laughter through electric music for mind and body. STEVE BURGESS

Opposite: Quicksilver Messenger Service. Above: Salvation hit the road.

Above: Moby Grape – spoiled by success? Below: The Beau Brummels – an SF Merseybeat group.

BOTH SIDES OF *Joni*

Joni Mitchell: from folk to jazz-rock fusion

OF ALL the singer-songwriters who emerged at the beginning of the Seventies, only Joni Mitchell has been able to build significantly on the music which first made her name. While many of her peers were finding it increasingly difficult to follow up their first success, Mitchell was developing from a gifted, folksy songwriter into a popular artist of unusual breadth and originality. Always innovative, Mitchell never ceased to absorb new influences. She cast the traditional rock devices aside in favour of the less-structured framework of jazz. To describe her work as jazz-rock, however, would be to do it an injustice, for whatever Mitchell turned her attention to she made her own.

She was born Roberta Joan Anderson on 7 November 1943 and brought up in the Canadian prairies of Alberta by her middle-class family. Her first instrument was the ukelele, learnt from a Pete Seeger instructional record. She discovered folk just as it was enjoying its largest revival, one which would have enormous implications for popular music. As Mitchell later put it: 'Rock'n'roll went through a really dumb vanilla period. And during that period, folk came in to fill the hole.'

After visiting the Mariposa Folk Festival in 1964, she abandoned her art-school course and began singing in the coffee bars of Toronto's Yorktown folk scene. In 1965 she married fellow folkie Chuck Mitchell, with whom she worked together for a while in a duo. But the marriage was short-lived. After moving to Detroit, from where they hoped to conquer the eastern states folk circuit, the couple went their separate ways. (In 1983 she was married again, to bassist Larry Klein.) Mitchell based herself in New York, booking her own tours and handling her own finances.

Rush for stardom

In Detroit, the Mitchells had met Tom Rush, one of the more adventurous new folk-singers. Rush tried to get Judy Collins to cover one of Joni Mitchell's songs, 'Urge For Going', in 1966. Collins demurred, so Rush recorded it himself and scored a local hit with it. Mitchell herself did not record the song until 1972.

Tom Rush's next LP, the commercially and critically successful *The Circle Game*, contained two of Mitchell's songs, including the title track. That same year, 1967, Judy Collins featured two Mitchell tunes on her LP *Wildflowers*. One was 'Michael From Mountains'; the other, 'Both Sides Now', which made the US Top Ten and established Mitchell as a major songwriter. By this time, Mitchell had got herself a record deal with Warner-Reprise. Originally Frank Sinatra's label, Reprise was in need of some hip credibility by 1967; that year, the label signed Jimi Hendrix, Randy Newman, Arlo Guthrie and Joni Mitchell herself. Elliot Roberts, who was responsible for the signing, remained Mitchell's manager into the Eighties, a role he also fulfilled for her fellow countryman Neil Young.

Joni Mitchell's self-titled debut album, produced by former Byrd David Crosby, was released in the summer of 1968. Like her songs for Rush and Collins, *Joni Mitchell* and its successor, *Clouds* (1969), displayed her obvious way with words and flair for melody. But neither album suggested that Mitchell was anything more than another folksy 'poet' whose main function would be to furnish more gifted vocalists with the occasional song, and she herself was later to call *Clouds* her artistic nadir. Her phrasing was locked firmly within the folk tradition, and she sounded uncomfortably self-conscious in the recording studio. Her songs tended to be dour; her portrait of her ex-husband, 'I Had A King', was, despite its vitriol, too solemn to make the impact of, say, Dylan's epistle to rejected love, 'Positively Fourth Street'. Many of her songs indulged in fanciful imagery inspired by the natural world, a tendency that was reinforced by her move to California during the last phase of flower-power.

The artistic development of Joni Mitchell (above) took her from idealistic youth to confident maturity. Inset opposite: The young folk singer at Newport Folk Festival in 1967. Opposite: The assured rock star of the mid Seventies, stunning packed houses.

By this time, Mitchell had become part of the Los Angeles Laurel Canyon rock-star community, a predicament reflected in the title of her third LP, *Ladies Of The Canyon* (1970). She was also living with former Hollies star Graham Nash; in case the public didn't get the message, Nash and Mitchell wrote their respective ditties about it. CSN&Y recorded 'Our House', while the somewhat slight 'Willy' was included on *Ladies Of The Canyon*.

Not all the songs on the album were so disposable, fortunately. Mitchell was beginning to take musical chances. Piano now shared the limelight with Joni's acoustic guitar, and the feel of the music was closer to rock. Jim Horn's exuberant sax playing made a fitting coda to 'For Free'. This song introduced one of Mitchell's recurrent concerns, the paradoxes of making a living out of self-expression. As time went by, she would address herself more and more to the problem of her relationship with her audience.

Yellow and blue

Ladies Of The Canyon also included 'Big Yellow Taxi', which became her first UK hit single. A great little plug for ecology, the song was a vocal *tour de force*, delicately poised between exuberance and regret. 'The Circle Game', which Rush had recorded earlier, saw Mitchell breathing new life into the traditional folk metaphor of the seasons as a symbol for ageing. And, despite its naivety, 'Woodstock' was a landmark for Mitchell. While Crosby, Stills, Nash and Young never shook off their identification with the song – their frenzied electric arrangement appeared on their album *Déjà Vu* (1970) – Mitchell was only briefly associated with that myth, in spite of having written its theme tune.

By the end of 1970, Joni Mitchell had established herself as a recording artist in her own right. Commercial logic would have suggested a world tour to consolidate her success, but Mitchell was uncomfortable with the role of rock star. Instead, she decided to withdraw from the limelight, travelling in Europe and sailing from Jamaica to California with David Crosby and Graham Nash. It was a time of re-assessment: 'Like falling to earth,' she

tended to writing telling songs about other people's experiences as well as her own, such as 'Cold Blue Steel And Sweet Fire' and her 'Beethoven' number 'Judgement Of The Moon And Stars (Ludwig's Tune)'.

Mitchell's fans had to wait until 1974 for another album. With *Court And Spark* and the live double album *Miles Of Aisles* – and an extensive tour including two visits to Britain – they were amply rewarded. Working with Tom Scott's elegant jazz-rock combo, the LA Express, Mitchell was now projecting an image closer to night-club chic than folksy hippie. Scott's bright, immaculate arrangements, deftly executed by the band, propelled Mitchell's music to new heights of expressiveness.

Richly melodic and featuring some singularly sharp songs of observation, *Court And Spark* gave Mitchell an unprecedented commercial success. She still used her songs to reveal her own inner struggles, although a kind of giddy humour now underlay some of the material. This was most noticeable on 'Twisted', an Annie Ross song – the first time Mitchell had sung a song by another writer on her albums, and proof of her increasing desire to jettison rock for jazz.

Summer sophistication

The Hissing Of Summer Lawns (1975) confirmed this change of direction. Exceptional for its dearth of confessional material, it was even more elaborately arranged than its predecessor. It touched levels of sophistication rare in pop, both musically and in terms of its subject matter, for the most part a commentary on middle-class American suburbia.

Mitchell carried off this ambitious experiment with remarkable aplomb. Unfortunately much of her trailblazing fell on deaf ears, particularly in America where the critics sharpened their knives for a ritual shredding.

Undaunted, Mitchell's next work, *Hejira* (1976) was just as adventurous. In sharp contrast to the luxuriant textures of *The Hissing Of Summer Lawns*, *Hejira* echoed the stark beauty of *Blue*, only this time Mitchell's rhythms derived from jazz and not rock. Named after Muhammad's flight from Mecca to Medina, the LP sprang out of Mitchell's own flight from a relationship. Filled with the restless imagery of travel, the songs indicated an acceptance of the impossibility of reconciling the demands of love and freedom.

In five years Mitchell had made as many great albums. She'd assimilated rock and jazz influences in a unique way. She'd written about a range of subjects and situations with an incisiveness and wit unprecedented in rock. Her more recent work

said. 'It felt almost as if I'd had my head in the clouds long enough . . . Shortly after that time, everything began to change. There were fewer adjectives in my poetry. Fewer curlicues to my drawing. Everything began to get more bold and solid in a way.'

That year's sabbatical produced the album *Blue* (1971). Where Mitchell's idealism has previously got the better of her, she now told the story from the other side, taking a wry and anti-sentimental look at both personal relationships and public affairs. 'California' saw the author of 'Woodstock' admit, 'That was just a dream some of us had'. Despite this new mood, *Blue* was an international success, and established Mitchell at quite a different level. The generation that had been told it could have everything – the world included – responded to her mood of disillusionment.

Instrumentally, too, the LP was a breakthrough. Apart from Joni Mitchell's acoustic guitar work, the contributions of Stephen Stills, James Taylor and Sneaky Pete of the Flying Burrito Brothers (on pedal steel guitar) all formed a supple and rhythmic backdrop. And, for the first time, Mitchell was using her full vocal range, singing with passion and skill.

After an extensive American and European tour, accompanied by the then-unknown Jackson Browne, she retired to Canada to contemplate her next move. The hippie in Mitchell had taken a battering on *Blue*, but she was still trying to put some of the dream into practice: 'I actually tried to move back to Canada, into the bush. My idea was to follow my advice and get back to nature.'

In contrast to the restrained arrangements of *Blue*, the subsequent *For The Roses* (1972) featured the elaborate horn and woodwind arrangements of Tom Scott, though there was still room for Mitchell's doleful piano. Much of the LP dealt with the ambiguities of exploiting one's personal history for fame and fortune. Mitchell's new maturity, however, ex-

Above left: Joni Mitchell jams with B.B. King at the Bread and Roses Festival in Berkeley, California in 1980. Right: Playing at Wembley, September 1974. Far right: On stage with Tom Scott, whose LA Express backed Mitchell live and on record in the mid Seventies.

had taken on a mystical quality as her desire for musical progress seemed to mirror an inner search.

A reckless release?

It was only on *Don Juan's Reckless Daughter* (1977) that Mitchell began to show signs of losing her sustained creative momentum. Yet there was much to applaud on the record, particularly the playing of Wayne Shorter and Jaco Pastorius from Weather Report. And Mitchell's poetic consciousness had lost none of its edge, even if she over-reached herself musically on the autobiographical 'Paprika Plains' which occupied an entire side of the album.

In 1979, Joni Mitchell took her preoccupation with jazz to its logical conclusion, collaborating with that giant of post-war jazz, Charles Mingus. The resulting LP, *Mingus*, her most ambitious yet, proved a critical success but a commercial failure. If Mitchell was to be admired for her audacity in making the album, in truth it failed to match her previous triumphs.

Mingus was followed by a pregnant silence. In 1982 Mitchell returned with *Wild Things Run Free*, a hollowish resumé of what had gone before. For once Mitchell was not, as she had remarked in 1979, 'pushing the limits . . . or the perimeters of what entails a popular song'. For once Mitchell had stopped searching. But who knows where her restless spirit will take her next? It is difficult to imagine Joni Mitchell merely reiterating past glories just to satisfy the platinum demands of the record industry. STEVE CLARKE

Joni Mitchell
Recommended Listening

Blue (Reprise K44128) (Includes: All I Want, A Case Of You, This Flight Tonight, Carey, Little Green); *Court And Spark* (Asylum SYLA8756) (Includes: Free Man In Paris, Car On A Hill, Raised On Robbery, Twisted, People's Parties).

Arthur Lee's brand of LA progressive pop

LOVE WERE A LEGEND – the quintessence of Hollywood, simultaneously seedy and transcendental, pure but scandalous. Arthur Lee – a young Memphis black – injected rock with the soul of a hack nightclub singer. On Love's best records Lee shifts from Jaggerish venom to Mathis-like mawkishness, producing music that is at once opaque and yet exotic. Love were the thinking man's flower-power popsters. And they were five weird dudes.

Arthur Lee was born in Memphis, Tennessee, in 1944. His family moved to Los Angeles when Arthur was in his early teens and he instantly set about forming numerous *ad hoc* combos that reflected his grounding in Southern blues and soul. One of these groups – Arthur Lee and the LAGs (Los Angeles Group) – cut a single for Capitol. Love were born out of the Grass Roots, assembled in 1964, with Memphis-born John Echols on lead guitar, Don Conka on drums, Ken Forssi (formerly of the Surfaris of 'Wipe Out' fame) on bass and classically-trained ex-Byrds roadie Bryan Maclean, from LA, on second guitar.

Above: Love on stage in 1970, with Arthur Lee on acoustic guitar. Insets: EP sleeves from the group's earlier days.

The group changed their name after the materialisation of a commercially successful band also named the Grass Roots. Originally Maclean alternated with Lee in the spotlight, but by the time Love debuted at a rundown joint called Brave New World in early 1965 Lee was very much the boss. The band also played at Ciro's on Sunset Strip and later had a residency at Bido Lito's in Hollywood.

They were spotted by Jac Holzman,

whose folk-rooted independent Elektra label was scouting around for quality rock acts. Signed later that year, they immediately debuted on disc with one of the definitive albums of the folk-rock era.

Love was peppered with pilfering from other highflyers in the field: the Turtles, the Byrds, the Leaves, Jagger and Dylan, but its music was more real than the usual confectionery. There was the ballad 'Signed D.C.' ('D.C.' being Don Conka, kicked out for his heroin habit and replaced with the Swiss-born Alban 'Snoopy' Pfisterer), a ferocious reading of the Bacharach-David number 'My Little Red Book' originally penned for the movie *What's New Pussycat?* and a controversial version of the LA circuit standard 'Hey Joe' which was filched from the Leaves or the Byrds.

But while the album sold 150,000 copies, Lee was losing patience with Snoopy's inability to cope with some of the stampeding, firecracker drumming demanded; the singer thus drafted in Michael Stuart from the ruins of local band the Sons of Adam, and jazz reedman Tjay Cantrelli. Snoopy was transferred to keyboards.

It was this line-up that, in early 1967, caught the tempo of the times and guaranteed Love a place in rock history with the LP *Da Capo*. Side one featured six blazing classics, from the roaring, bucking hit single 'Seven And Seven Is' to the intricate, percussive fantasia of 'The Castle' and the spaced-out crooning of 'She Comes In Colours'. The track 'Stephanie Knows Who' was later covered by the Move. Side two consisted of one continuous opus, 'Revelation' – an adventurous, if unsuccessful, experiment that made side two as self-indulgent as side one was concise. Snoopy and Cantrelli left the band later that year.

Communal chateau

The group, already installed in seedy isolation in a peculiar Gothic mausoleum in the desert, began to withdraw from the world and live dates became scarce. Lee eventually refused to travel more than a few miles to a gig. Despite rumours that his mental state was suffering because of his continuous experiments with drugs, Lee's creative powers were at their height, and it was barely six months after *Da Capo* that Love cut perhaps their most characteristic album – *Forever Changes*. The LP was intricate and delicate but with an unsettling undercurrent of paranoia and decay – 'Oh the snot has caked against my pants/It has turned to crystal' sang Lee. Acoustic-based, with formal washes of strings and horns arranged by David Angel, *Forever Changes* included the tracks 'Alone Again Or' and 'Andmoreagain'. The album was an influential one.

Things appeared to be getting out of hand at the communal chateau, and gossip about groupies, drugs and gay liaisons between members of the band were rife. The story goes that the band, spurred on by critical acclaim and the excellent sales of *Forever Changes*, then disappeared into the studio, running up colossal bills and emerging some time later with the master-tape of an album that they had failed to grasp was totally appalling (some say because they were so stoned). The only Love product during 1968 was a single – 'Laughing Stock'/'Your Mind And We Belong Together' – salvaged from the tape. After this fiasco, the band split up, and Lee went on to form yet another Love line-up in late 1968.

The new Love comprised his old friend Frank Fayad (bass), George Suranovitch (drums) and guitarist Jay Donellan (real name Lewis), and this band made two albums in 1969 – *Four Sail* and *Out Here*. *Four Sail* pointed towards the disintegration of the characteristic Love sound, the intricate acoustic base being usurped by a bone-crunching Hendrix-style flamboyance which worked with a vengeance on 'Autumn' but for the most part only succeeded in stripping the lyrics of their mystique and making the product clumsy.

This was followed by the patchy double album *Out Here*, on Blue Thumb Records which sounded like a sloppy demo tape. Guest musicians were employed, notably English drummer Drachen Theaker (formerly of the Crazy World of Arthur Brown) and guitarist Gary Rowles, whose buzzbomb histrionics sprawled across a couple of sides. Rowles then formally replaced Donellan. The band made a rare sortie from LA in 1970 to tour Britain. While in London, Lee bumped into his old friend Jimi Hendrix; they embarked upon a short and ill-fated album project which was scrapped because of copyright problems. One track, 'The Everlasting First', saw the light of day on the 1971 Love album *False Start*, after which Love again disbanded.

Lee wasn't quiet for long, however. In 1972 he re-emerged with a turgid heavy-metal album *Vindicator*, credited to Arthur Lee and Band Aid (an ensemble which included Fayad). It was high on energy, if low in ingenuity. There was a lull after *Vindicator*, during which time there were reports of Lee living wild in the woods on the West Coast, but he surfaced again in 1973 when he signed for, and recorded an album for, Paul Rothchild's new Buffalo Records. Buffalo ran into financial difficulties and the album was never released. Yet another version of Love was forged in 1974 with Melvan Whittington and John Sterling (guitars), Sherwood Akuna/Robert Rozelle (bass) and Joe Blocker (drums), plus guests Harvey Mandel and Buzzy Feiten (guitars). They cut the lack-lustre *Reel To Real* album on the RSO label and visited Britain again.

Lee refused to go under, however. Towards the end of the decade a self-financed independent EP showed a return to the earlier Love sound, but when a solo album entitled *Arthur Lee* was released on Beggar's Banquet in 1981, the four EP tracks proved the best of a rather poor lot.

Love's records continued to sell steadily and their influence could be seen in bands of the early Eighties such as Scotland's Orange Juice and Liverpool's Pale Fountains, only two of a number of groups who have sought to recreate the distinctive acoustic/electric blur that Lee pioneered.

STEVE BURGESS

Love
Recommended Listening

Love (Elektra EKL 4001) (Includes: My Flash On You, Emotions, Mushroom Clouds, No Matter What You Do, Coloured Balls Falling, Signed D.C.); *Love Masters* (Elektra K32002) (Includes: Seven And Seven Is, Alone Again Or, Hey Joe, My Little Red Book, Orange Skies, She Comes In Colours).

LONG STRANGE TRIP

Inspired improvisation from the Grateful Dead

Of the major American rock bands formed during the mid Sixties, only the Grateful Dead had the staying power to survive both that decade and the next with its nucleus intact. They outlasted the faddishness of the era in which they established their reputation – a feat in itself, especially when contrasted with their West Coast peers like the Charlatans, the Jefferson Airplane, Big Brother and the Holding Company or Country Joe and the Fish. That they came through a chaos of inept financial management and drug busts relatively unshaken may be attributed to the Dead's unique sense of family, purpose and solidarity.

Those virtues alone, while laudable, would not have been enough to safeguard survival; closing ranks is only a tactic in survival. What set the Grateful Dead apart was their music, which came to represent the quintessence of the San Franciscan scene. Their prowess at extemporisation became legendary and their wrongheaded intractability a by-word; they were the last major Bay group to sign a record contract. They created a myth, they fed it; and yet somehow they were never swallowed up by it, despite the overwhelming zealousness of their audience, for whom the term 'Dead Heads' was coined.

In live performance the Dead will offer a wide range of American music ranging from fairly tightly-arranged numbers to free-flowing jams. Their repertoire, as their live albums evince, draws on such apparently random sources as Obray Ramsey, Elmore James, Chuck Berry, Gus Cannon's Jug Stompers, Jesse Fuller, the Reverend Gary Davis, Elizabeth Cotten, Merle Haggard, Harry Belafonte and a host of others, while in the throes of jamming they may quote from inspirations as diverse as Miles Davis' *Sketches Of Spain* and the theme from *Close Encounters Of The Third Kind*. Their own songwriting abilities have become renowned, largely due to the skill of their lyricist, Robert Hunter (who wrote for, but did not actually perform with the band); later they owed much to lyricists such as John Barlow and Robert Petersen. By fusing these disparate elements into a whole, the Dead achieved something truly remarkable.

Left: The Warlocks, from left Jerry Garcia, Bill Kreutzmann, Bob Weir, Phil Lesh and Pigpen. Below: Dead at Monterey. Above right: Lyricist Robert Hunter plays solo. Right: Standing from left Weir, Lesh, Kreutzmann, Pigpen; seated are Garcia (left) and Mickey Hart.

The Grateful Dead's origins were similar to those of the other major San Franciscan groups who came to the fore in the so-called Summer of Love. Other Bay area groups like Country Joe and the Fish, the Airplane and Quicksilver Messenger Service all had roots in folk music and blues to some degree. The Dead were no exception. Jerry Garcia (born San Francisco, 1 August 1942), the group's lead guitarist, nursed a deep and burning ambition to be a bluegrass banjoist – it is his banjo in Philip Kaufman's remake of *Invasion Of The Bodysnatchers*. His travels, as a fan, with the Californian bluegrass band the Kentucky Colonels introduced him to many of the young musicians with the same interests, and playing with die-hard folkies like Jody Stecher and Eric Thompson was part of this formative period.

Invasion of the tub-thumpers

Fresh out of the US Army, Garcia chanced to meet Bob Hunter, another folk music admirer. Small folk or jug bands with constantly-changing line-ups and weird names – the Wildwood Boys, the Hart Valley Drifters, the Thunder Mountain Tub-Thumpers and the Black Mountain Boys – fell together, disbanded and then coalesced into fresh groups over the years until 1964, by which time Mother McCree's Uptown Jug Champions had become the top dog.

Based in Palo Alto, this jug band was one of the immediate forerunners of the Grateful Dead; among its members were Garcia, Bob Weir, Ron 'Pigpen' McKernan, John Dawson and Bob Matthews, all five of whom would be associated with the Dead in various capacities. However, this was still acoustic music played on guitars, banjo, harmonica, jug and occasional piano and it was not until – at Pigpen's prompting – the band found someone with the money to pay for amplifiers that they went electric.

The old name was jettisoned and, as the Warlocks, they added drums and electric bass to become a fully-fledged electric band. Drummer Bill Kreutzmann (alias Bill Sommers, born 7 May 1946) and bassist Phil Lesh (born 15 March 1940) turned them into something quite different: no longer were they fundamentally an upgraded jug band, although they still played numbers like Noah Lewis' 'Viola Lee Blues' and blues like 'Good Morning Little Schoolgirl' and 'I Know You Rider' alongside R&B and rock'n'roll standards.

Of the new recruits, Phil Lesh was the least likely in many ways. Trained in contemporary classical music and with an abiding love of modern jazz, especially John Coltrane, he had studied trumpet; his scholarship and appreciation of musical theory added an extra dimension to the group. The final ingredient was the scene in San Francisco, and in particular the availability of a variety of psychotropic substances.

Experimentation with narcotics had been a characteristic of the bohemian scene during the Beat era (and before that of the jazz scene). The drugs used, however, had consisted largely of marijuana, speed and various tinctures, extracts and proprietary medicines which lent themselves to abuse; peyote and other naturally occurring mind-altering substances had played only a small part. The catalyst for the burgeoning scene which rejected old values in favour of a new, barely-articulated consciousness was, albeit unwittingly, the establishment itself.

At Stanford University, not far from Palo Alto, behavioural trials were being held observing paid volunteer guinea pigs while under the influence of varying dosages and combinations of psychotropic drugs, among which were peyote, mescaline and a synthetic hallucinogen called LSD-25. Among the volunteers who slipped through the screening process designed to weed out the unstable and undesirable were the author Ken Kesey and Robert Hunter, whose accounts of their experiences whetted the appetites of their circles of friends. Tom Wolfe's *The Electric Kool-Aid Acid Test* gives a pen picture of some escapades from this time. The stage was lit for the entrance of the 'psychedelic movement', and until October 1966, when legislation proscribing its use was passed, LSD was legal.

The Warlocks changed their name to the altogether more mysterious and forbidding Grateful Dead and in 1966 released a single ('Stealin''/'Don't Ease Me In') on the independent Scorpio label, although they spurned the approaches of larger companies wanting their slice of profit from the Summer of Love. The first, clinically-controlled experiments with psychedelics gave way to gatherings of friends in rather more congenial surroundings which were known as the Acid Tests, at which the Dead found themselves the court minstrels. Recordings from these events can only hint at how unstructured and spontaneous they were.

Succumbing to the lure of a record contract from Warner Bros, the group made a frenetic first LP *The Grateful Dead* (1967) before producing two of the finest artefacts of the era in *Anthem Of The Sun* (1968) and *Aoxomoxoa* (1969). The basic quintet of Garcia, Kreutzmann, Lesh, McKernan (born 8 September 1945) and Weir (born 16 October 1947) was augmented by keyboardist Tom 'T.C.' Constanten and percussionist Mickey Hart for both albums. The transformation was revelatory: Constanten, with a similar classical background to Lesh, added fresh textural layers, while Hart, a former jazz drummer, pushed Kreutzmann to ever-ascending rhythmic heights.

Their reputation was still primarily a West Coast one, and non-believers scoffed at their meandering renditions of 'In The Midnight Hour' and 'Dancing In The Street'. The Dead would be the first to concede that at times their jaming would fail to connect and resolve itself into any discernible shape; far more often, however, they would majestically resolve their snaking explorations and, as one man, pivot on an intuitively-grasped axis. Controlled feedback became a forte, as extemporisations called 'Feedback' and 'Space' illustrate. A live double album, *Live Dead* (1970) demonstrated that the septet could be fearsomely brilliant, compositions like 'St Stephen', 'The Eleven' and 'Dark Star' being reshaped into vehicles for dynamic, intense and startling live improvisations.

Tom Constanten left and, after involvement with the Incredible String Band and the play *Tarot*, emerged in the Eighties as a composer of modern classical works like 'Heretic Strut' (1981) and 'Alaric's Premonition' (1980), commissioned by the Kronos Quartet, an Oakland-based string quartet. T.C.'s departure coincided with a decision to shift the music's focus, and a pair of albums, *Workingman's Dead* and *American Beauty*, resulted in 1970. A simpler, acoustic framework carried songs of captivating beauty which were lyrically less opaque, with Hunter's surreal word games less in evidence.

Although the group were moving out of debt, the Dead discovered that they had been the victims of embezzlement and, embarrassingly, the culprit was Mickey Hart's father. Hart decided to take a sabbatical in order to study drumming techniques and to produce some of the most spellbinding music of any of the Dead's offshoots. His *Rolling Thunder* (1972) was an artistic triumph but commercially a spit in the ocean, and neither his *Fire On The Mountain* nor *The Silent Flute* were considered worthy of release. *Diga Rhythm Band* (1976), by Hart's group of the same name, showed the influence of his studying under Indian musician Ali Akbar Khan.

Pig funk

With Hart gone, the extended percussion exchanges were no longer possible. They released their second live double album in 1971. It was the second to bear the title *Grateful Dead*. Although it contained some good material, the fire was in short supply. Pigpen, seriously ill with a liver complaint, was unable to handle the required keyboard work and a pianist, Keith Godchaux, joined the band with his wife, ex-Muscle Shoals vocalist Donna.

The band took on a new lease of life, with *Europe '72* and Bob Weir's *Ace* (both 1972) showing that they were still a force to be reckoned with. The Garcia-Hunter songwriting team had shown itself to be both exceptional and prolific; the combination of Weir and lyricist John Barlow also produced a bumper crop. The musicians' penchant for unusual time signatures, implied in the title of 'The Eleven', was reinforced by the Weir-Hunter number 'Playing In The Band', the time signature of which was more apparent in its working title of 'The Seven'. Their ability to embrace such unconventional rhythms singled them out;

Above right: Ron 'Pigpen' McKernan. His death in 1973 from cirrhosis of the liver marked an end of an era for the band; his raw, bluesy vocals and harp work especially were sadly missed. Above far right: Programme for the group's 1978 pyramid concerts. Right and above centre: The Grateful Dead in action.

GRATEFUL DEAD
GRATEFUL DEAD
PRESENTS THREE CONCERTS
At the Sound & Light Theatre, Gizeh
on Thursday, Friday and Saturday
14, 15, and 16 September 1978
at 9:30 PM
Special Guest: HAMZA EL-DIN
فرقة "جريتفل ديد"
تقدم
على مسرح أبي الهول بالهرم ،
ثلاثة عروض للموسيقى أيام
الخميس والجمعة والسبت في
١٤ و ١٥ و ١٦ سبتمبر ١٩٧٨
الساعة التاسعة والنصف مساء
ضيف الفرقة الموسيقار حمزه الدين

such experiments were rare in rock.

The death of Pigpen was the end of an era. His bluesy vocals on 'Smokestack Lightnin'' or 'Mr Charlie' had been a distinctive feature of their music; his death in 1973 severed that link, but the posthumous *Bear's Choice* (1973) serves as a testament to Pig funk.

Again it was a time of reassessment for the Dead. Garcia had become involved in a bluegrass outfit called Old And In The Way which, in its lifespan, included musicians of the calibre of violinists Vassar Clements and Richard Greene, mandolin player David Grisman, bassist John Kahn and guitarist Peter Rowan; an eponymous LP culled from live tapes was issued on Round Records, an offshoot label associated with the Dead. Other projects included the Dead's own *Wake Of The Flood* (1973) on their own (short-lived) label, Lesh and Ned Lagin's electronic *Seastones* (1973), Garcia's second solo (1974), two solo albums by Robert Hunter – the band's lyricist – entitled *Tales Of The Great Rum Runners* (1974) and *Tiger Rose* (1975), plus assorted spin-off bands.

It was a time of stupendous creativity; the surge carried the Grateful Dead through to *From The Mars Hotel* (1974), on which tracks such as 'Unbroken Chain', 'Pride Of Cucamonga' and 'China Doll' attested to their virtuosity. In concert, as on 'Unbroken Chain', Ned Lagin would occasionally add weird electronics, but this had petered out by the time that Hart returned to the fold. He unleashed an outpouring of energy and restored the trinity of Hart, Kreutzmann and Lesh to its rightful place as possibly the finest rock rhythm section. The combination of Lesh's idiosyncratic bass and the two drummers remains the linchpin of the Dead into the Eighties; on LPs as varied as *Blues For*

Above: 'They're not the best at what they do, they're the only ones that do what they do' claimed this 1980 Dead poster. Below: Garcia (left) with Old And In The Way.

Allah (1975) and *Dead Set* (1981), the trio's sense of dynamics underpins the whole.

However, financial instability still dogged them; *Steal Your Face* (1976), an attempt to recover something from a financially disastrous concert film, was a washout, while *Terrapin Station* (1977) and *Shakedown Street* (1978) hardly seemed up to scratch. The firing of the Godchauxs had looked imminent for some while, and after leaving, Keith Godchaux was fatally injured in 1979. Brent Mydland took over on keyboards, making his debut on *Go To*

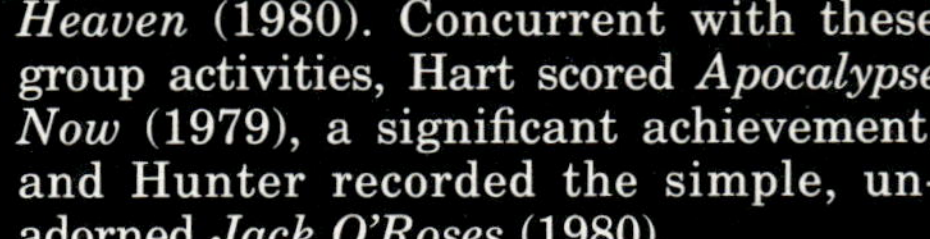

Heaven (1980). Concurrent with these group activities, Hart scored *Apocalypse Now* (1979), a significant achievement, and Hunter recorded the simple, unadorned *Jack O'Roses* (1980).

The turmoil of 15 years has left its scars, yet the Grateful Dead still maintain that aura of the unorthodox about them in the Eighties. Their 1978 concerts at the Pyramids of Giza, climaxing with a performance timed to coincide with the total eclipse of the moon, may have cost them dear, but it was the stuff of dreams; it may have been an accountant's nightmare, but it was also a supreme *gesture*.

They have retained a sense of objectivity, however. They still play benefits for causes they consider deserving, examples being the Vietnam Veterans and Cambodia. The cornerstone of their work remains the live performance (both as the Dead, and as members of satellite groups such as Bobby and the Midnites, High Noon and the Jerry Garcia Band). *Reckoning* and *Dead Set* (1981) serve to reaffirm this, also reconfirming the group's abiding interest in traditional and folk music with songs such as 'Samson And Delilah' and 'Jack-A-Roe'. Acutely conscious of the Myth, the Grateful Dead have still not succumbed to it, continuing to make challenging, inventive and often highly experimental music into the Eighties. KEN HUNT

THE GRATEFUL DEAD
Discography

Singles
Stealin'/Don't Ease Me In (Scorpio 201, 1966); Golden Road (To Unlimited Devotion)/Cream Puff War (Warner Bros 7016, 1967); Dark Star/Born Cross-Eyed (Warner Bros 7186, 1968); Dupree's Diamond Blues/Cosmic Charlie (Warner Bros 7324, 1969); Uncle John's Band/New Speedway Boogie (Warner Bros 7410, 1970); Truckin'/Ripple (Warner Bros 7464, 1971); Johnny B. Goode/ Truckin' (Warner Bros 7653, 1972); Sugar Magnolia/Mr Charlie (Warner Bros 7667, 1973); Let Me Sing Your Blues Away/Here Comes Sunshine (Grateful Dead 01, 1973); Eyes Of The World/Weather Report Pt 1 (Grateful Dead 02, 1974); US Blues/Loose Lucy (Grateful Dead 03, 1974); The Music Never Stopped/Help On The Way (Grateful Dead 718, 1975); Franklin's Tower/Help On The Way (Grateful Dead 782, 1975); Dancin' In The Street/Terrapin Station (Arista 0276, 1977); Passenger/Terrapin Station (Arista 0291, 1977); Good Lovin'/Stagger Lee (Arista 0383, 1978); Shakedown Street/France (Arista 0410, 1979); Alabama Getaway/Far From Me (Arista 0519, 1980).

Albums
The Grateful Dead (Warner Bros 1689, 1967); *Anthem Of The Sun* (Warner Bros 1749, 1968); *Aoxomoxoa* (Warner Bros 1790, 1969); *Live Dead* (Warner Bros 1830, 1970); *Workingman's Dead* (Warner Bros 1869, 1970); *Vintage Dead* (Sunflower 5001, 1970); *American Beauty* (Warner Bros 1893, 1970); *Historic Dead* (Sunflower 5004, 1971); *The Grateful Dead* (Warner Bros 1935, 1971); *Europe '72* (Warner Bros 2668, 1972); *History Of The Grateful Dead* (Pride 016, 1973); *History Of The Grateful Dead* (Warner Bros 2721, 1973); *Wake Of The Flood* (Grateful Dead 101, 1973); *Skeletons From The Closet* (Warner Bros 2764, 1974); *From The Mars Hotel* (Grateful Dead 102, 1974); *Blues For Allah* (Grateful Dead LA 494, 1975); *Steal Your Face* (Grateful Dead LA 620, 1976); *Terrapin Station* (Arista 7001, 1977); *What A Long, Strange Trip It's Been* (Warner Bros 3091, 1977); *Shakedown Street* (Arista 4198, 1978); *Go To Heaven* (Arista 9508, 1980); *Reckoning* (Arista 8604, 1981); *Dead Set* (Arista 8606, 1981).

Airplanes & Starships

West Coast rock with Grace Slick and friends

Top: Jefferson Airplane at the Monterey Festival. Above: The original line-up with Signe Anderson (second from right).

EARLY IN 1965, no one would have predicted that San Francisco, like Liverpool a couple of years earlier, would become the world's focal point for rock music. The local style was beatnik, with the emphasis on folk music. It was against this background that Marty Balin (born in Cincinnati, Ohio, 30 January 1941), then singing with the Town Criers, decided to try some musical experiments. First he found Paul Kantner (born in San Francisco, 12 March 1942), an itinerant folkie and bosom buddy of Byrd David Crosby. Encouraged by Crosby's success, Kantner jumped at the chance and recommended Jorma Kaukonen (born Washington DC, 23 December 1940), an accomplished blues guitarist playing the folk circuit – often with a singer by the name of Janis Joplin, whose powerful voice led Kaukonen to trade his acoustic guitar for an electric model so he could be heard. The original Jefferson Airplane was completed by folk songstress Signe Toly Anderson, drummer Jerry Peloquin and string-bass player Bob Harvey.

This grouping was short-lived. Peloquin was the first casualty – Jorma detested his bossa nova drums on 'Kansas City Blues'. Alexander 'Skip' Spence, whose drumming experience was limited to a school marching band, was his replacement. Jorma was similarly dissatisfied with Bob Harvey. Harvey had bluegrass roots and, despite switching to electric bass, was not a rock player. Jorma recommended his old school pal and musical sparring-partner, Jack Casady (born in Washington DC, 13 April 1944), who completed the line-up which recorded the debut album *Jefferson Airplane Takes Off*, released in September 1966. They had already released a single entitled 'It's No Secret' in the previous February. It was backed by 'Runnin' Round This World', which included the line 'The nights I've spent with you have been fantastic trips.' The implied drug connotation led to RCA insisting it be omitted from the essentially folk-rock *Takes Off*.

As part of his master plan, Marty Balin had taken over a club called the Honeybucket, which he restyled and relaunched as the Matrix, a vehicle for the Airplane. Seeing the publicity for the opening, local fashion model Grace Slick (born in Chicago, 30 October 1943) and her husband Jerry went along and were impressed, not so much with the Airplane, but more with the possibilities. Realising that anyone could start a rock band, they formed the Great Society, with Grace writing the songs. They recorded an album's worth of material under Sly Stone's direction and a single, entitled 'Someone To Love', was released in limited numbers.

Lift-off

The major record labels were now sniffing around San Francisco, anxious to get a slice of the new action. The Airplane had signed to RCA in late 1965, and the Great Society secured a deal with Columbia in the following year. But Signe Anderson had a baby and the band, now touring nationwide, kicked her out. Paul Kantner had been particularly impressed by Grace Slick, and Jack Casady asked her to join. She agreed, and the Great Society folded, cancelling the Columbia contract. The label acquired some live tapes, however, and released two albums after the group's demise.

When Grace joined in October 1966, *Takes Off* had brought the Airplane national fame; Skip Spence had found the drumseat increasingly difficult to fill, however, and had left to play guitar with Moby Grape. Spencer Dryden replaced him.

Top Ten turns

With initial personnel problems overcome, the Airplane, with the guidance of the Grateful Dead's Jerry Garcia, cut their second album, *Surrealistic Pillow*. Grace supplied two Great Society songs, her 'White Rabbit' and Darby Slick's 'Somebody To Love'. Her fierce, metallic vocals were to become a prominent feature of the Airplane's music. A single, 'My Best Friend', was released in December, followed by the album and another single, 'Somebody To Love' in February 1967. 'Somebody To Love' and its follow-up, 'White Rabbit' – ironically the two Great Society songs – both reached the US Top Ten. The Airplane never again achieved such success with a single, but they now qualified for a UK release. (The English *Surrealistic Pillow* was a compilation of the first two albums, containing tracks recorded by both line-ups.)

Surrealistic Pillow showed the group veering away from their folk roots but the follow-up, *After Bathing At Baxter's* (1967), took their development to the limit. Casady and Kaukonen criticised Balin's 'soft' love songs; Marty backed off and only had one co-credit on the new album. *Baxter's* – the very title, according to Kantner, being synonymous with 'after taking LSD' – was an iconoclastic assault on the established format of the rock album; a raging torrent of musical ferocity and distorted images, simultaneously quirky and brutally exciting. Casady developed a pattern of bass-playing that threatened to move continents; Kantner slashed out the rhythm; Kaukonen's guitar screamed; Grace wailed.

The album sounds like a soundtrack to a lunatic nightmare, the lyrics a dimension away from Balin's love songs. In fact, Kantner and Slick's lyrics were largely borrowed from elsewhere. Grace's 'Rejoyce', while not a direct steal, was heavily based on James Joyce's novel *Ulysses*, while Kantner purloined whole chunks from a Ralph Gleason review of a free concert for 'Saturday Afternoon', and lifted extensively from A. A. Milne for 'Ballad Of You And Me And Pooneil'.

Baxter's also introduced the record buyer to a new phenomenon – the art of the inner sleeve – and it became an Airplane trademark to include special inner sleeves and/ or booklets or inserts with their records, on

Star Wars: Marty Balin (right) hated the strident vocals of Grace Slick (left); Jack and Jorma (bottom centre) thought Marty's love songs 'wet', and fell out with Grace and Paul Kantner (bottom left). Spencer Dryden (bottom right) quit to join the New Riders of the Purple Sage.

US copies at least. This inner sleeve also caused the group's second confrontation with RCA; a collection of doodles done during idle moments in the studio assumed grotesque proportions when the corporation decided the outline of an empty cupcake wrapper was obscene.

Crown Of Creation (1968), the fourth album, saw the group's energy channelled into slightly more established forms, evidence of how the commercial failure of *Baxter's* had shaken them. Side one, mainly gentle and relaxed in contrast to their high-energy live performances at the time, included David Crosby's 'Triad', rejected by the Byrds, and Grace Slick's 'Lather', inspired by the birthday of her lover, Spencer Dryden. Side two is arguably the most relentless the Airplane ever produced, culminating in 'Greasy Heart', and 'The House At Pooneil Corner'. Kantner's lyrics for the title track were lifted from John Wyndham's *The Chrysalids*.

Blessed little head

The Airplane were turning in exceptionally potent stage performances at this time, and a live album was inevitable. It came in the shape of *Bless Its Pointed Little Head* (1969). Recorded at the Fillmore West, it opens with the end of the film that preceded the Airplane's performance, *King Kong*: 'Oh no, it wasn't the airplane, it was beauty killed the beast,' echoed the soundtrack as Dryden's drum flurry burst into '3/5 Of A Mile In 10 Seconds'. The record has tremendous dynamics, contrasting raw power with the floating beauty of Donovan's 'Fat Angel', a longtime live favourite, undoubtedly in the set on account of its lyric, 'Fly Jefferson Airplane, gets you there on time.' Also displayed is the group's improvisational ability, from their interpretation of 'Rock Me Baby' to the strange 'Bear Melt'.

Meanwhile, the Airplane turned down various movie offers, but made a New York rooftop appearance in Jean Luc Godard's unfinished *One American Movie*, eventually released as *One PM* (1970). The movie is tedious political cinéma verité, only relieved when the group crank it up, Marty shouting 'Wake up, New York'. They also appear in *Monterey Pop* (1968), performing 'High Flying Bird' and 'Today', the latter showing Grace mouthing the words while Marty sings off-camera.

This kind of thing was beginning to cause friction behind the scenes. Marty disliked Grace's free-form wailing and Grace was toying with the idea of signing to Elektra as a solo artist. Recording sessions were getting less cohesive – nobody was interested in what anyone else was doing. Group members were recording their tracks independently and there are many lurid stories of couples making love on the floor and Jorma riding a motorcycle round the studio. Furthermore, Jack and Jorma were jamming together in clubs, exploring their love of the blues.

Nevertheless, the group bought a mansion. It was initially intended as offices,

The Airplane metamorphosed into the Starship (above) after Casady and Kaukonen had floated off to form Hot Tuna (right). Below: Casady's later band, SVT.

but when they returned from a tour to find the building where Spencer, Grace, Jorma and his wife lived burned down, they all gradually moved into the big house. This was the catalyst for another regrouping within the ranks as Grace, having had a passing dalliance with Jack during the *Surrealistic Pillow* sessions before moving on to Spencer, now began to fall for Paul . . .

Call to arms

The summer of 1969 brought the Woodstock Festival, where the Airplane appeared early in the morning, previewing material from their forthcoming album. They never made it into the movie, but 'Volunteers' appeared on the triple album and 'Eskimo Blue Day' was on the subsequent double, along with 'Won't You Try'/ 'Saturday Afternoon'. These recordings hardly show the group at their best, however. The new album, *Volunteers*, was released late that year; many fans regard it as the group's finest, showing a political perspective that was to permeate their work for some time. Kantner and Slick became the driving force in the band – Paul's call-to-arms 'We Can Be Together' and Grace's sexual-imagery-laden 'Hey Frederick' were highlights of a consistently good offering.

A single, 'Mexico'/'Have You Seen The Saucers', was recorded in February 1970, following which Spencer Dryden married and left, joining the New Riders of the Purple Sage and eventually becoming their manager. His replacement, Joey Covington, a barely adequate and uninspired drummer, even admitted that he disliked the band's music. The end was now in sight; Paul and Grace were one faction, Jack and Jorma the other; fed up with the infrequency of Airplane live performances, the latter were gigging as Hot Tuna, sometimes with Marty, who seemed happy with either faction but not with both simultaneously. Tracks were laid down but most were eventually discarded, and a compilation album, *The Worst Of The Jefferson Airplane*, was eventually released to fulfil their RCA contract in November.

However, the lack of new Airplane material that year was mitigated by the release of the first Hot Tuna album, a live acoustic set, and Paul Kantner's *Blows Against The Empire*, a collection of demos Paul did for the Airplane and which he worked up into an album when it became apparent there would be no Airplane LP. Side one was a collection of personal and political statements, while side two was based around the concept of hijacking a starship to get off the planet. Both Hot Tuna and the Airplane gained a member when Joey Covington introduced the black violinist Papa John Creach (born May 1917) in October 1970.

Meanwhile Grace, having announced to Paul that she wanted his baby, was pregnant. When a girl arrived and a nurse asked for her name, Grace replied, 'God with a small g, I want her to be humble.' The nurse told the papers the story, but the birth certificate said 'China'. A couple of months later, Marty Balin quit the Airplane, initially helping out Grootna before recording with his own band, Bodacious. Despite their previous head-on clashes, the Airplane re-signed to RCA as Grunt Records, a vehicle for Airplane, Tuna, solo projects and anything else that took their fancy.

Mid-1971 to the end of 1974 was a period of hyperactivity; *Bark*, the first Grunt release, had some excellent material sandwiched between the mediocre and the dire. This was swiftly followed by Grace and Paul's *Sunfighter*, a more consistent effort. Joey Covington left early in 1972; his replacement, on David Crosby's recommendation, was John Barbata. *Long John Silver*, released that July, less than a year after *Bark*, had few redeeming features and despite the group's supposed autonomy, provided the most unholy row with RCA over 'Son Of Jesus'. Previous printed lyrics had been at variance with the recordings ('Bulsht' on *Crown Of Creation* and 'Up against the wall, Fred' – in place of 'motherfuckers' – on *Volunteers*) and here the printed lyric read, 'So you think Jesus Christ never a lady', while the recording is 'Never smiled a lady'.

The Airplane's recording career wound up in April 1973 with *Thirty Seconds Over Winterland*, recorded on their final tour in 1972 with David Freiberg (formerly of Quicksilver Messenger Service) filling the gap left in the vocal ranks by Balin's absence. While a distinct improvement on their last two studio albums, it couldn't hold a candle to *Bless Its Pointed Little Head*. *Early Flight*, a compilation of outtakes and non-album single sides was released in April 1974.

The sublime to the ridiculous

Following the last Airplane tour, Kantner, Slick and Freiberg recorded the excellent *Baron Von Tollbooth And The Chrome Nun* (named after Freiberg's nicknames

JEFFERSON AIRPLANE
Discography

Singles
It's No Secret/Runnin' Round This World (RCA 8769, 1966); Come Up The Years/Blues From An Airplane (RCA 8848, 1966); Bringing Me Down/Let Me In (RCA 8967, 1966); My Best Friend/How Do You Feel (RCA 9063, 1966); Somebody To Love/She Has Funny Cars (RCA 9140, 1967); White Rabbit/Plastic Fantastic Lover (RCA 9248, 1967); Ballad Of You And Me And Pooneil/Two Heads (RCA 9297, 1967); Martha/Watch Her Ride (RCA 9389, 1967); Greasy Heart/Share A Little Joke (With The World) (RCA 9496, 1968); Lather/Crown Of Creation (RCA 9644, 1968); Plastic Fantastic Lover/Other Side Of This Life (RCA 74-0150, 1969); Volunteers/We Can Be Together (RCA 74-0245, 1969); Mexico/Have You Seen The Saucers (RCA 74-0343, 1970); Pretty As You Feel/Wild Turkey (RCA/Grunt 74-0500, 1972); Milk Train/Long John Silver (RCA/Grunt 74-0506, 1972); Twilight Double Leader/Trial By Fire (RCA/Grunt 74-0511, 1972).

Albums
Jefferson Airplane Takes Off (RCA LSP 3584, 1966); *Surrealistic Pillow* (RCA LSP 3766, 1967); *After Bathing At Baxter's* (RCA LSP 4545, 1967); *Crown Of Creation* (RCA LSP 4058, 1968); *Bless Its Pointed Little Head* (RCA LSP 4133, 1969); *Volunteers* (RCA LSP 4238, 1969; APD1-0320, quadrophonic version); *The Worst Of The Jefferson Airplane* (RCA LSP 4459, 1970); *Bark* (Grunt FTR 1001, 1971); *Long John Silver* (Grunt FTR 1007, 1972); *Thirty Seconds Over Winterland* (Grunt BFL 1-0147, 1973); *Early Flight* (Grunt CYL 1-0437, 1974).

JEFFERSON STARSHIP

Singles
Ballad Of The Chrome Nun/Sketches Of China (RCA/Grunt APBO 0094, 1974); Devil's Den/Ride The Tiger (RCA/Grunt PB 10080, 1974); Be Young You/Caroline (RCA/Grunt PB 10206, 1975); Miracles/Al Garimisa (RCA/Grunt PB 10367, 1975); Play On Love/I Want To See Another World (RCA/Grunt PB 10465, 1975); Switchblade/With Your Love (RCA/Grunt PB 10746, 1976); St Charles/Love Lovely Love (RCA/Grunt PB 10791, 1976); Miracles/With Your Love (RCA/Grunt PB 10941, 1977); Count On Me/Show Yourself (RCA/Grunt PB 11196, 1978); Runaway/Hot Water (RCA/Grunt PB 11274, 1978); Crazy Feelin'/Love Too Good (RCA/Grunt PB 11374, 1978); Light The Sky On Fire/Hyperdrive (RCA/Grunt PB 11426, 1978); Jane/Freedom At Point Zero (RCA/Grunt PB 11750, 1979); Girl With The Hungry Eyes/Just The Same (RCA/Grunt PB 11921, 1980); Rock Music/Lightning Rose (RCA/Grunt PB 11961, 1980); Find Your Way Back/Modern Times (RCA/Grunt PB 12213, 1981); Stranger/Free (RCA/Grunt PB 12275, 1981); Save Your Love/Wild Eyes (RCA/Grunt PB 12332, 1981).

Albums
Dragonfly (Grunt BFL 1-0717, 1974); *Red Octopus* (Grunt BFL 1-0999, 1975); *Spitfire* (Grunt BFL 1-1557, 1976); *Earth* (Grunt BXL 1-2515, 1978); *Gold* (Grunt BLZ 1-3247, 1979); *Freedom At Point Zero* (Grunt BLZ 1-3452, 1979); *Modern Times* (Grunt BLZ 1-3848, 1981).

for his two collaborators). The most consistent of the solo efforts, it also featured the guitar talents of Craig Chaquico and the resulting line-up, plus Englishman Pete Sears, also worked on Grace Slick's solo LP *Manhole*.

Meanwhile, Grunt Records was in financial trouble; most of its releases (including one Joey Covington and three Papa John Creach solo efforts) had sold poorly, and they were forced to renegotiate with RCA, who applied pressure for them to concentrate on just two main bands: Hot Tuna and – the logical choice since *Blows Against The Empire* – Jefferson Starship. They toured as such in April 1974, with Peter Kaukonen on bass, Pete Sears joining later. They then recorded *Dragonfly*, persuading Marty Balin to sing on one track, 'Caroline'. But the gem on this consistently fine album was the Slick-Sears album closer, 'Hyperdrive'.

Marty Balin rejoined in time to record *Red Octopus* in 1975; his 'Miracles', culled from the album, went to Number 1 in the States and the album hit the top spot no less than four times. Artistically, however, it showed a drift towards middle of the road rock. While on tour promoting the LP, Grace drifted away from Paul to lighting man Skip Johnson, whom she eventually married. Before sessions began on the next album, Papa John Creach left.

The third Starship LP, *Spitfire* (1976), showed some improvement and was a great commercial success, but they plumbed the depths artistically with *Earth*, released in March 1978. Later that year they toured Europe. Grace, whose drinking problem was worsening, couldn't go on stage at a German festival; the band wouldn't play without her and the stage with all their equipment was burned down by irate fans. They played one more gig where Grace, according to one report, put her hand up the dresses of three girls in the front row. Grace quit, the Starship played in England without her and things fell apart.

But all was not lost; the Starship regrouped with Mickey Thomas (ex-Elvin Bishop Group) on vocals and Aynsley Dunbar (most recently of Journey) on drums. This line-up, with uncredited assistance from Grace, recorded *Freedom At Point Zero* (1979), their best effort since *Dragonfly*. 'Jane', the opening track, was even a Top Thirty hit in the UK. But this promise was unfulfilled, as their 1981 offering, *Modern Times*, rarely rose above mediocrity. Grace, who in the meantime went from the sublime (*Dreams*, 1980) to the ridiculous with *Welcome To The Wrecking Ball* (1981), eventually returned to the band. And so, San Francisco's most controversial rock group lurches on through failure and success. NICK RALPH

Psychedelic Wallflowers

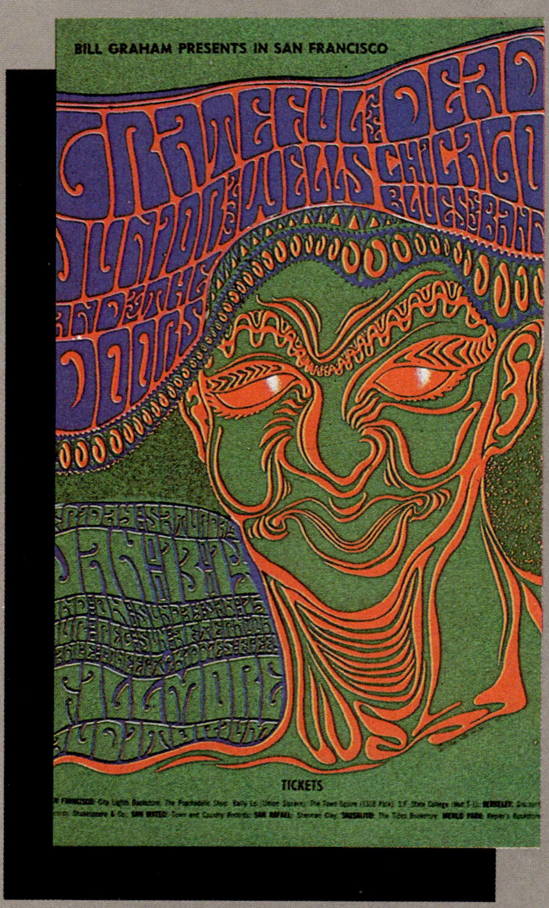

Poster power: the art of blowing your mind

Until the arrival of psychedelia in the mid Sixties, rock posters were purely informative. Visually, they were very dull; the headline artist appeared at the top in the largest lettering, the opening act at the bottom in the smallest. The type was uniform, usually black on white, with maybe a dash of red for good measure. Such posters have no artistic value, and any interest in them is either in the names of the artists or the venues at which they played.

By 1964 there was some attempt to make the rock poster look less like an estate agent's auction list, but it was usually restricted to the use of dark-coloured paper and white ink. In the UK, one or two clubs started to experiment with lettering – notably the Crawdaddy, which adopted similar lettering to the famous Yardbirds logo.

Acid art

The rock poster as an art form dates from the beginning of the 'acid days' and comes, not surprisingly, from San Francisco. The first poster in the new style advertised a now-famous gig – the Charlatans at the Red Dog Saloon in Nevada in the summer of 1965. The Charlatans drew their style of dress from a combination of Wild West cowboys and Mississippi gamblers, and they felt that an appropriate poster was required to reflect their image. Band members George Hunter and Michael Ferguson therefore came up with a marvellously dense design, full of different lettering, caricature drawings of the band members and all manner of little eye-catching devices. Like the band's image, it combined the consciously archaic with the boldly original and fresh. Aspects of this

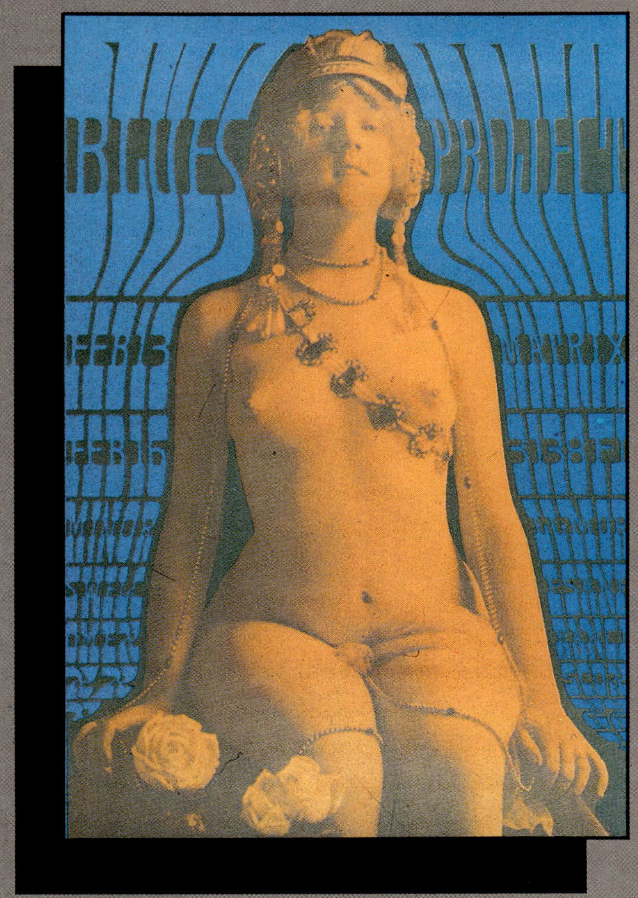

Above, left to right: George Hunter and Michael Ferguson's eclectic pioneering poster for the Charlatans; swirling acid-trip colours from Wes Wilson; movie, Americana and flower-power images boldly used in a poster from the Mouse Studios; sex and Dayglo mysticism make a brilliant effect in one of Victor Moscoso's posters.

poster influenced the San Francisco artists who became famous in the following year.

By early 1966, when the Family Dog and Bill Graham's organisation were running weekly dances at the Fillmore, the idea of having an exotic poster to advertise the gigs and reflect the nature of the music had taken hold. The first regular artist they employed was Wes Wilson, who became well-known for his original style. His work rapidly became stylised, however – he generally used only two heavily contrasting colours in a central design, surrounded by the group's name in standard lettering.

When the Family Dog moved to the Avalon, Chet Helms started to employ a variety of artists, notably Stanley 'Mouse' Miller and Alton Kelley of Mouse Studios. Their work combined Mouse's undeniable draughtsmanship with Kelley's predilection for collage, and both artists would, as Mouse puts it, 'raid the image bank', getting their inspiration for a central image from books on art and photography.

Towards the end of 1966, the Avalon added another name to the list – Victor Moscoso, a highly accomplished SF artist. He specialised in the hypnotic effects created by weird colour combinations, which made his posters difficult to read but stunning to look at. Moscoso's series for the Matrix Club in early 1967 are among the highspots of the era. Another artist who was commissioned by Avalon was Rick Griffin, who is perhaps best known for the

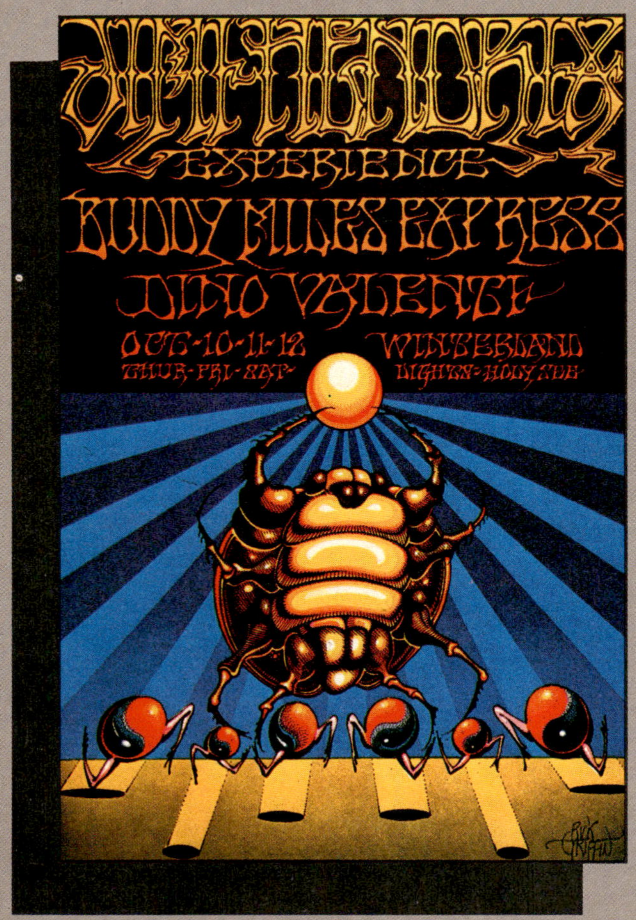

cover of the Grateful Dead's *Aoxomoxoa*, originally an Avalon poster. Less prolific than the others, he was arguably the most talented and witty.

In July 1967 an exhibition by Mouse, Kelley, Griffin and Moscoso was held at a gallery in San Francisco; the posters were no longer merely a by-product of rock, they had become works of art in their own right. In the next three years, these four artists and others almost equally talented, including Randy Tuten and Bob Fried, produced many hundreds of posters for the Avalon Ballroom, the Fillmore and dozens of other smaller venues and one-off benefits; a high proportion of these subsequently became collectors' items. Although they became increasingly sophisticated, they never lost the earthy yet mind-bending quality of the early designs.

San Francisco posters disappeared with the passing of the hippie era. They were intrinsically connected with it and inseparable from groups whose names conjured up psychedelic images, such as Country Joe and the Fish or Kaleidoscope. Mouse and Kelley continued to work closely with the Grateful Dead, the group most evocative of the era, but like the music itself, the style of these posters is a thing of the past.

Other artists in different parts of the United States took their inspiration from the posters produced in San Francisco. In Detroit, Gary Grimshaw produced an excellent set of posters for the Grande and Aragon Ballrooms to rival the best work of Mouse or Griffin. Los Angeles, too, produced some good examples, notably a set of nearly 30 round posters by various artists for the Kaleidoscope Club. In Texas Jim Franklin and Fabulous Furry Freak Bros.

Above, left to right: Resplendent lettering and surreal creatures in a Rick Griffin poster; self-conscious psychedelia from Bob Fried; simpler images and starker colours dramatically employed by Randy Tuten; flowing lines, bird-like images, flowers, stars and a nude poetically combined by Michael English and Nigel Weymouth.

artist Gilbert Shelton designed fine posters for the Vulcan Gas Company venue.

Some of the best of the era came from Britain, from Hapshash and the Coloured Coat, the collective name of artists Michael English and Nigel Weymouth. They produced a series of beautiful silk-screen posters for UFO and the Savile Theatre, as well as promotion material for various bands. Their style was generally more lyrical than that of their American counterparts, but at times maybe just a little too fey and sentimental. Martin Sharp was another truly original British designer, whose swirling Dayglo images also enlivened many early covers of *Oz* magazine, as well as Cream's *Disraeli Gears* and *Wheels Of Fire* album sleeves.

Psychedelic posters vanished even faster in England than in America, largely because the media-inspired 'flower-power' image had become a national joke by the autumn of 1967. Michael English moved on to advertising, and his development parallels the road that rock art took in the early Seventies; posters became slick, sophisticated and very glossy.

Like so much that was good about the mid Sixties, poster art was a naive blend of imagination and talent. The talent may still be there, but the naivety and imagination seem, on the whole, long gone.

JOHN PLATT

FUGGING AROUND

Bottom, from left: Ed Sanders, Ken Weaver and Tuli Kupferberg. Left and below: Onstage antics.

Poetry and obscenity from New York's Fugs

WIDESPREAD COMMERCIAL APPEAL was never high on the Fugs' list of priorities. Their music and lyrics – described by Richard Neville in his 1970 book on underground culture, *Playpower*, as 'clowning decibelic anarchy', and by the group themselves as 'atonal masochism and moral-less mumblings' – were designed to amuse radical hippies and to shock and outrage everyone else. Through the band's cynical satires on such topics as the drug culture, warmongers, the peace movement and (most often) sex, they brought acerbic humour, offensiveness and out-and-out obscenity to rock music for the first time.

Contact high

The Fugs were formed in New York in December 1964 by two 'alternative' journalists and Beat poets, Ed Sanders, editor of *Fuck You – A Magazine Of The Arts*, and Tuli Kupferberg. With drummer Ken Weaver, bassist John Anderson, keyboard player Lee Crabtree and guitarist Vinny Leary, the Fugs began appearing at New York underground dives like the Folklore Centre and the American Poets Theatre. The group took their name from a word invented by Norman Mailer in *The Naked And The Dead* to denote sexual activity.

Though none of the band were particularly musically adept, their theatrical and energetic performances, combined with songs such as Kupferberg's 'Nothing' and Weaver's 'I Couldn't Get High', quickly gained them a cult following and a residency at the Plymouth Theatre in Greenwich Village. Kupferberg described 'Nothing' as 'an immortal masterpiece, a milestone in the reality of the last part of the twentieth century' – the lyric ran 'Monday, nothing. Tuesday, nothing. Wednesday, Thursday, nothing. Friday, for a change, a little more nothing. Saturday, once more nothing . . .' – and the punky 'I Couldn't Get High' told of a party at which the singer takes vast quantities of various narcotics, yet sadly remains unaffected.

By this time, the Fugs had been joined by a pair of anarchic folk singers, guitarist Steve Weber and banjo and fiddle player Peter Stampfel; the duo had been playing the New York folk circuit since 1963 as the Holy Modal Rounders (and before that, Fast Lightning Kumquat and Rinky Dink Steve The Tinhorn). Years later, Stampfel gave a colourful account of the duo's recruitment to the Fugs: 'One day Weber came round and said "Sanders is starting a group and they're doing dirty songs like 'Bull Tongue Clit' and 'Coca Cola Douche'." So I went down to the bookstore and none of them were playing any real instruments. Sanders had a nine dollar 98 cent toy organ, Ken Weaver did have a set of drums but they'd been stolen. He ended up with these African hand drums which he was relieved of in a spectacular manner by two enormous Puerto Ricans with a hammer. Anyway, Weber and I ended up playing with them.'

In mid-1965, the group recorded a limited edition album, *The Village Fugs*, for the Broadside label. Though it contained versions of stage favourites like 'Slum Goddess', 'I Couldn't Get High' and Steve Weber's bawdy 'Boobs A Lot', the LP barely hinted at the group's raucous and frenzied live sound. However, it did lead to a contract with the New York-based independent label ESP; the record was reissued as *First Album*, with a beefed-up mix.

ESP seemed the ideal label for the Fugs, for its product was avant-garde in the extreme; the company had a seeming regard for such non-commercial offerings as *Contact High With The Godz*, an album by New York quartet the Godz that consisted of defiantly anti-musical, tuneless squawkings and wailings with titles like 'Na Na Naa', 'Squeak' and '1 + 1 = ?'. But even ESP balked at the obscenities and downright filth that the Fugs produced for a second album, and the band were compelled to come up with a less crude collection. Despite the clean-up job, *The Fugs* (1966) captured the essence of the group magnificently, from Kupferberg's jolly Vietnamese romp, 'Kill For Peace' ('The only gook an American can trust/Is a gook that's got his yellow head bust') through the babbling 11-minute sprawl of the surrealistic 'Virgin Forest' to Sanders' hilarious send-up of US teen idols, 'Frenzy', and his vicious debunking of LSD-inspired lyricists on 'Skin Flowers' ('I believe that golden lizards fly somewhere in sunshine').

Golden filth

The Fugs sold healthily enough in underground circles to tempt the major companies, and in 1967 the group signed to Reprise. By this time, however, Weber, Stampfel, Crabtree, Leary and Anderson had all left. (Weber and Stampfel, with assistance from Crabtree, resurrected the Holy Modal Rounders and produced the bizarre psychedelic-folk 'concept' album *Indian War Whoop* (1967) for ESP and later savoured a brief moment of glory when their 'If You Want To Be A Bird' was included on the soundtrack of *Easy Rider*.) Fresh Fugs were recruited – Charles Larkey (bass and future husband of Carole King) and Kenny Pine (guitar and future founder of the Quinaimes Band) – in time to record *Tenderness Junction* (1968).

The new members were highly accomplished players and added a touch of sophistication to the music which, at times – particularly on Kupferberg's enchanting folk-rock number, 'The Garden Is Open' – suggested that the Fugs were becoming an orthodox rock band. But harsh satire and jaded visions were still in evidence: there was the brash, noisy 'Turn On/Tune In/ Drop Out', and there was 'War Song', a further grotesque prod at America's involvement in Vietnam. Sex got its habitual look-in on the lewd doo-wop of Sanders' 'Wet Dream', the anti-war chant, 'Out Demons Out', received an airing on 'Exorcising The Evil Spirits From The Pentagon October 21, 1967', and even old Beat guru Allen Ginsberg got to sing (and contribute some excruciating harmonica playing).

Tenderness Junction was released in the UK on the Transatlantic label, and late in 1968 the Fugs arrived in England to promote it. Their staggeringly fast and loud performance of 'Turn On/Tune In/Drop Out' on BBC-TV's 'How It Is' failed to enhance sales, however – and bemused the show's host, Angela Huth, judging from her expression once the din had subsided. Back home, too, the album flopped and the follow up, *It Crawled Into My Hand, Honest*, died a similar commercial death.

By the time the tame and fragmented *The Belle Of Avenue A* was released in 1969, it was clear that the Fugs had lost their bite. The fact was that the group had never really been designed for the studio: it was on stage, where Sanders, Kupferberg and Weaver could unleash their acidic barbs, howl their dirty inter-song raps and jig about like demonic dervishes, that they excelled – as *Golden Filth*, a live set issued in 1970, proved. The album had been recorded at the Fillmore East on 1 June 1968 and contained high-energy versions of their very best material – 'Slum Goddess', 'Nothing', 'I Couldn't Get High' *et al.*

By the time *Golden Filth* was released, the Fugs were no more. Ed Sanders had returned to writing, coming up with a best-selling book in *The Family* (1971), a brilliantly-written, horrifying account of Charles Manson's murderous antics. Tuli Kupferberg, who had edited the underground paper *East Village Other* while simultaneously Fugging in the mid Sixties, reverted to journalism too, and made a brief foray into films when he appeared as a manic, street-stalking urban guerrilla in Dusan Makavejev's 1971 celebration of sexual liberation, *WR: Mysteries Of The Organism*.

By the Seventies, offensiveness and deliberate outrage had become accepted and fashionable elements of rock. At Woodstock, the hordes had responded vociferously to Country Joe MacDonald's plea: 'Give me an 'F' . . . give me a 'U' . . . give me a 'C' . . . give me a 'K'', while up in Detroit, the MC5, and manager John Sinclair's White Panther party, were demanding the right to copulate in the streets. And these new satirists and purveyors of 'filth', whether they knew it or not, owed an enormous debt to the Fugs. As Richard Neville, again in *Playpower*, had written: 'A tradition of conscious cultural subversion had been long established by the Fugs. The Fugs have always been identified with marijuana, pacifism, satire and sexual adventure. They were the fathers of the Mothers Of Invention who with Frank Zappa extended the possibilities of rock way beyond its logical inconclusions.'

TOM HIBBERT

THE FISH CHEER

Country Joe: spelling out his politics in song

'I DON'T KNOW how you can expect to stop the war if you don't sing any better than that! There are about 300,000 of you fuckers out there!' Thus began Country Joe McDonald's classic address to the crowd at Woodstock. The song he wanted them to sing louder was the 'I-Feel-Like-I'm-Fixin'-To-Die Rag', probably *the* definitive anti-Vietnam war anthem. The Woodstock festival took place in August 1969 at the height of the fighting in Asia, but the song in question dated back to the formation of Country Joe and the Fish four years previously when the group had first started to blend forms of folk and protest with psychedelic experimentation to create a unique whole.

Joe McDonald was born on 1 January 1942 in El Monte, California, the son of Communist Party workers (he was named after Joseph Stalin). His father encouraged Joe's musical interests, and by the time he was 14 the youngster was playing guitar in local folk groups. He later ran away from home, however, and joined the US Navy for three years because, as he later confessed, 'I wanted to see the world and have sex.' After leaving the service, McDonald went to college but soon dropped out: 'I went to San Francisco to become a beatnik and start giving up structured lives.' During this period, he performed as a folk singer in various clubs along the West Coast, and in 1964 recorded his first album *The Goodbye Blues* (re-released in 1977 on the Fantasy label) with fellow folk artist Blair Hardman. Moving to Berkeley later that year, he joined the Berkeley String Quartet and later the Instant Action Jug Band, with which he performed as guitarist, vocalist and harmonica player. Then, in September 1965, he decided to form a band of his own, feeling the need to develop the jug band and protest forms further. For this project, McDonald recruited three members of the 13-piece Instant Action Jug Band in guitarist Barry Melton, Richard Saunders (washtub bass) and Carl Shrager (washboard, bells); together with bass player Bob Steele, they comprised Country Joe and the Fish.

The Fish were to go through a number of personnel changes before signing to Vanguard in 1966 and by the time they recorded their first album, *Electric Music For The Mind And Body*, the group's line-up was McDonald and Melton with David Cohen (keyboards), Chicken Hirsch (drums) and Bruce Barthol (bass, harmonium). The record, released in April 1967, documented perfectly their unique conglomeration of folk, blues, country and rock; it also gave evidence of their involvement with the San Francisco drug and hippie scene on the one hand and the radical political movement on the other. The album featured hippie classics like 'Flying High' and 'Bass Strings' (which Joe claimed to be the first song with an overt drug reference) alongside political songs like 'Superbird'.

Despite their enormous popularity in Berkeley, particularly among the students and leftists, Country Joe and the Fish had to fight hard against the elitist attitude of San Francisco's 'in crowd'. Because of their Berkeley origins they were considered to be 'provincial' with the consequence, as Joe put it, that, 'in our quest to be recognised as a true psychedelic band, we must've taken more acid than all the others put together!' They were more than just a psychedelic band, however; for whereas the Grateful Dead were, on the whole, non-political, concerning themselves with 'cosmic', psychedelic excursions and the Jefferson Airplane's ideology changed from project to project and thus seemed somewhat spurious, Joe McDonald appeared sincere in his attempts to unite the hippies and the radicals.

The group's popularity on campus was largely due to their extravagant stage act; dressed up in fancy costumes, they performed slapstick acts, hilarious acid 'commercials' and football-style cheers like the famous 'Fish Cheer': 'Gimme an 'F' . . . Gimme an 'I' . . . Gimme an 'S' . . . Gimme an 'H' . . . What's that spell?' This often turned into a 'F-U-C-K' cheer, much to the disgust of the college authorities.

Fish in the ocean

Seven months after the release of *Electric Music*, a second Fish album was issued. *I-Feel-Like-I'm-Fixin'-To-Die* was another quality product which included stage favourites like 'Who Am I', 'Thought Dream' and the title song, as well as 'Eastern Jam', an Indian-inspired piece which was carried by Melton's fluid, floating guitar patterns. Although the album was well received by hippies and politicos alike, McDonald was by now becoming frustrated with the band and he briefly walked out during the recording of a third album, *Together*, before relenting and returning to the fold. 'I was responsible for seeing that the performances were pretty good, the records were made, the arrangements were okay, we got to gigs on time,' he said later. 'At the same time nobody wanted to rehearse, nobody wanted to work up new ideas, everybody was stoned the whole time.' *Together* continued the psychedelic/political themes of previous work – particularly in the stark and sinister imagery of 'An Untitled Protest' – but was the last album to be met with anything like unanimous praise.

In January 1969, Cohen, Hirsch and Barthol left the band and were replaced by Mark Kapner (keyboards) and ex-Big Brother and the Holding Company members Peter Albin (bass) and David Getz (drums). The new line-up recorded the album *Here We Go Again*, on which the optimism and experiment of previous recordings seemed to be replaced by desolation and resigned despair. This was exemplified by 'Crystal Blues', a song of a woman destroyed by drugs, and 'Here I Go Again', on which McDonald confessed: 'Here I am again/Singing my songs again/Thinking and dreaming/I feel like I could die.'

In June 1970 came the final break-up. McDonald had already released two solo albums, including a tribute to one of his heroes, Woody Guthrie, on *Thinking Of Woody* (1969), and carried on performing and recording as a solo artist. He had become interested and involved in feminism through his wife Robin Mencken, editor of *Women In Film*, and he frequently double-billed with her theatre group for performances.

Gimme an F . . . Country Joe McDonald (second from left), up against the wall with his Fish (above) and on stage (opposite), with his second LP (inset).

It was with a largely female backing crew that McDonald was to record *Paris Session*, released in 1973. Apart from displaying the singer's growing interest in the feminist cause on songs like 'Sexist Pig', it also showed how disillusioned he had become with hippie ideology. One song, 'Zombies In The House Of Madness', was an account of the American prison system spoken over a caterwauling electronic wall of sound. McDonald later explained the motivation behind this unnerving number: 'When I did "Zombies In The House Of Madness", I was hoping people would be stoned when they heard it and get completely bummed out. Because I wanted to destroy that fantasy that life is groovy in 1974.'

Although *Paris Sessions* proved to be McDonald's strongest solo work to date, his career became increasingly erratic following its release. He joined Bruce Barthol's Berkeley band the Energy Crisis for a few months in 1975 then signed to the Fantasy label to record *Paradise With An Ocean View*, an undistinguished effort despite its mild chart success in the States. Then in 1977, Country Joe and the Fish came together once more to record an album, *Reunion*, which was a limp, uninspired and ill-conceived affair. After three further solo albums on Fantasy, McDonald started his own record label with Texan singer-songwriter Butch Hancock. But by now it seemed that Joe McDonald, who had soured of radical politics, hippie ethics and even feminism (his former wife had sued him for alimony in 1975) had become a spent musical force. MARIANNE EBERTOWSKI

Country Joe and the Fish Recommended Listening

I-Feel-Like-I'm-Fixin'-To-Die (Vanguard VSD 79266) (Includes: Eastern Jam, Janis, Who Am I?, Pat's Song, Rock Coast Blues, Magoo); *Electric Music For The Mind And Body* (Vanguard VSD 79244) (Includes: Flying High, Death Sound Blues, Section 43, Superbird, The Masked Marauder).

Vanilla Fudge, Steppenwolf and Iron Butterfly

IN THE WAKE of Jimi Hendrix and Cream, a whole new approach entered popular music. Volume and power combined to produce 'hard rock', an approach that culminated in the heavy metal of the early Seventies. In the USA there were dozens of groups moving in this direction during the late Sixties. They came from a variety of backgrounds and responded to diverse influences – but they all had a commitment to the new sounds. The most notable were Vanilla Fudge, Iron Butterfly and Steppenwolf.

The Fudge were the perfect example of technique over talent. They took recognised songs like 'You Keep Me Hangin' On', 'Eleanor Rigby' and 'Ticket To Ride', radically slashed their tempo, added pseudo-classical overtones, massive production and then turned the volume up high.

The band consisted of Carmine Appice (drums and vocals), Tim Bogert (bass and vocals), Vince Martell (lead guitar and vocals) and Mark Stein (keyboards and vocals). Formed in December 1966, they set out to play 'psychedelic-symphonic rock'. Appice, a New York boy who was 20 when the Fudge gelled, had been playing drums for seven years, three of them under formal tuition. Bogert, two years older than Appice, had been playing sax for nine years and bass for two. Martell, born in 1945, began his music lessons at the age of 13. He played in local bands before meeting up with Stein and Bogert in New York in January 1966.

Stein was very much the showbiz kid. Born in New Jersey in 1947, he was on TV at the age of four. He picked up the guitar at the age of 12, and started his own high school band, releasing his first record in 1959 on Neil Bogart's Cameo Records, and was back on TV at the age of 13. In 1966 he was in a band called Rick Martin and the Showmen, in which he met Tim Bogert. Together they quit the band, along with the drummer whom they ditched in favour of Appice, wheeling in Martell in New York.

Appice of the action

Vanilla Fudge played their first major date in New York on 22 July 1967 at the Village Theatre, on the same bill as the Seeds and the Byrds. By all accounts they went down a storm. They were signed by Atlantic in 1967, and began work on an album called *Vanilla Fudge,* which received considerable airplay on the East Coast. Their grandiose cover of the Supremes' 'You Keep Me Hangin' On', originally released as a single in the summer of 1967, reached Number 6 in the charts on its re-release a year later.

The album, which featured Fudged-up versions of 'Eleanor Rigby', 'People Get Ready', 'Bang Bang' and 'Ticket To Ride' was hugely successful; unfortunately for the Fudge, it was downhill from then on

They released four more albums up to 1970, including the ambitious *The Beat Goes On* (1968), which attempted to present a history of the world and of music in the space of one LP.

While the new wave of heavy-metal bands like Led Zeppelin was going from strength to strength, the Fudge folded in 1970. Mark Stein formed a band called Boomerang which fell to earth soon after, Martell disappeared and Bogert and Appice formed Cactus, later becoming two thirds of Beck, Bogert and Appice; the drummer later played with Rod Stewart.

Insect rock

Iron Butterfly's career was similar to that of Vanilla Fudge, peaking early and then fading away. A West Coast band, their original line up was Doug Ingle (keyboards), Ron Bushy (drums), Danny Weiss (guitar), Jerry Penrod (bass) and Darryl DeLoach (guitar). They signed with Atlantic and recorded their first album, *Heavy* in 1968. Problems within the band, however, led to the departure of Weiss, Penrod and DeLoach soon after its release.

To replace the departing three, Ingle and Bushy recruited Erik Brann on guitars and vocals and Lee Dorman, who was primarily a bassist, but also played a multiplicity of other instruments. The four-piece Butterfly cut an album called *In-A-Gadda-Da-Vida*, which took its title from an 18-minute track written by Doug Ingle.

The sheer length and pretention of that track – remember this was when people were considering underground music as the classical music of the Sixties – earned the Butterfly the most enormous critical praise. The record bulleted into the American charts and stayed there for well over two years.

To get some idea of the importance of the Butterfly at the time it's worth quoting American writer William York who says in his *Who's Who In Rock Music:* 'In 1968 the definitive sound of heavy metal was not the Cream or the new English group Led Zeppelin: it was the Butterfly'.

In September 1969 the Butterfly came to the UK for a tour which opened at the Marquee on 9 September. Their musical approach might be illuminated by a quote from Lee Dorman: 'We have one number, "The Iron Butterfly Theme", which depicts the life of an Iron Butterfly. At the end it crashes and we hit all the amplifiers to make the crash and we use four electronic fires to create a visual ending'.

Despite the dubious delights of that particular number, it was obvious to the band that the only thing their audiences really wanted to hear was 'In-A-Gadda-Da-Vida'. Disenchanted, Eric Brann left to be replaced by guitarists Mike Pinera and Larry Reinhardt in 1969. The new line-up recorded *Iron Butterfly Live* and *Meta-*

Top: Steppenwolf go for the jugular. Inset left: Iron Butterfly. Inset far left: Fudge drummer Carmine Appice playing in Rod Stewart's band in the late Seventies.

Above left: Steppenwolf, with lead singer John Kay looking mean in shades. Above right: Vanilla Fudge model a range of Renaissance to Regency costume against a tasteful matching wallpaper.

morphosis, neither of which came anywhere close to the platinum status of *In-A-Gadda-Da-Vida* or even the gold status of *Heavy* and their third album *Ball.* The band, faced with increasing indifference in the record market and the touring circuit, folded midway through 1971.

Fangs for the memory

Steppenwolf took themselves very seriously. They performed the singular trick of being, at one and the same time, a heavy duty macho biker's band and one of America's most overtly political outfits.

To a large extent, Steppenwolf was John Kay, a charismatic and articulate front man and lead singer. He had more than a hint of dramatic and political chic on his side too, having started life in East Germany and having been brought to the West in 1949.

In Toronto, Kay formed a blues band called Sparrow with drummer Jerry Edmonton and keyboard player Goldy McJohn. The band moved to New York and then to California, where Kay added Michael Monarch on guitar and John Russell Morgan on bass to make up the first line-up of Steppenwolf. Interestingly, none of the band had heard of Herman Hesse's novel of the same name – the band's name was suggested by their first producer, Gabriel Mekler.

They took off immediately after the release of their first album *Steppenwolf,* which included 'Born To Be Wild' and 'The Pusher'. 'Born To Be Wild' went to Number 2 in the American charts in September of 1968, followed by 'Magic Carpet Ride' which made Number 3 that November.

'Magic Carpet Ride' was taken from *Steppenwolf The Second,* which was as successful in the album charts as 'Carpet' in the singles. In addition the band was featured in the film *Easy Rider,* which did them no harm whatsoever in either the credibility or the financial success stakes.

Their radical credibility was enhanced by playing benefit gigs for the Vietnam Moratorium Day and by the outspoken political comments of John Kay: 'We are centralising the thoughts and direction of our generation through music,' he said. 'We are a reflection of what is happening today. We could be called the "thinking man's rebel with a cause".'

Curiously enough, they were quite a conservative band, if truth be known. They were anti-drugs, pro-America, and favoured evolution rather than revolution. Kay announced his intention of running for political office, seeking change from within the political structure of America rather than bombarding it from the outside.

Albums like *At Your Birthday Party, Monster* and *Early Steppenwolf* kept them in the charts, and the band showed no sign of any diminution in popularity even though they underwent personnel changes in 1969 and 1970. Monarch and Morgan left in 1969 to be replaced by Larry Byrom on guitar and Nick St Nicholas on bass. The latter left in 1970 with George Biondo coming in in his stead. Later Kent Henry replaced Byrom.

No doubt these changes were part of the band's decision to dissolve in 1972 – a move which Kay, Edmonton and McJohn announced at a press conference in Hollywood. Steppenwolf was revived in 1974 by Kay, Edmonton, McJohn, Biondo and guitarist Bobby Cochran, but they were never to repeat their earlier successes.

Vanilla Fudge, Iron Butterfly and Steppenwolf all represented a changing mood in America in the late Sixties. People seemed to want more 'meaning' in their songs and they got it in three different ways from these bands: Vanilla Fudge attempted, albeit in a hamfisted sort of fashion, to demonstrate that 'pop' songs could be serious. Butterfly tried to be a modern 'classical' band – serious and portentous – and Steppenwolf were one of the first major successful bands to use rock music as a vehicle for political comment.

All three were fortunate to come along at a time when underground music went overground, and when the major record companies realised that 'underground' was synonymous with good business; and all three demonstrate a fundamental change in terminology. For they could never have been described as 'pop' groups. They were 'rock', and for rock fans, pop was now a pejorative term.

BRIAN HARRIGAN

Vanilla Fudge
Recommended Listening

Vanilla Fudge (Atlantic 587086) (Includes: You Keep Me Hangin' On, Eleanor Rigby, People Get Ready, She's Not There, Ticket To Ride).

Steppenwolf
Recommended Listening

Gold (MCA MCL 1619) (Includes: Magic Carpet Ride, The Pusher, Born To Be Wild, Sookie Sookie, It's Never Too Late, Hey Lawdy Mama).

Iron Butterfly
Recommended Listening

Sun And Steel (MCA MCF 2738) (Includes: Lightnin', Sun And Steel, Free, Watch The World Goin' By, Get It Out); *In-A-Gadda-Da-Vida* (Atlantic K40022) (Includes: Most Anything You Want, Flowers And Beads, My Mirage, Termination).

Strange days

Jim Morrison opened the Doors to perception

THE DOORS were just one of the musically exploratory new bands to emerge from California during the turbulent mid Sixties. But while most of their contemporaries were busy celebrating the joys of LSD and the 'summer of love', the music of the Doors dwelt in altogether darker and bleaker waters; others sang of freedom and togetherness but the Doors sang of violence and guilt. This music, coupled with the mystique surrounding Jim Morrison – a poet seemingly obsessed with sex and death and a man possessed of finally-realised self-destructive urges – has ensured that the sound of the Doors continues to gain new devotees and influence fresh generations of musicians over a decade later.

Breaking on through

James Douglas Morrison was born on 8 December 1943 in Melbourne, Florida and, after graduating from high school, moved to California in 1964 to study film technique at UCLA. The following year, on a stretch of beach at Venice, Los Angeles, Morrison encountered fellow student Ray Manzarek (born 12 February 1935) to whom he recited the lyrics of a song he had written – 'Moonlight Drive'. 'Those are the greatest song lyrics I've ever heard,' enthused Manzarek. 'Let's start a rock'n'roll band and make a million dollars.'

Although he had never played an instrument or sung into a microphone in his life, Morrison had – or so he was to claim later – started to hear songs in his head: 'I heard in my head a whole concert situation,' he was to say, 'with a band and singing and an audience – a large audience. Those first five or six songs I wrote, I was just taking notes at a fantastic rock concert that was going on inside my head. And once I had written the songs, I had to sing them.'

Manzarek, a classically-trained pianist, was already playing part-time in an R&B group, Rick and the Ravens, with his brothers, harpist Rick and guitarist Jim. By September 1965, Morrison was singing with them, and John Densmore (born 1 December 1945), who had played with local band the Psychedelic Rangers, had come in on drums. In addition, the group boasted a girl bass-player, whose name has since been forgotten. In the autumn, the

Shaman's Blues: addicted to alcohol and downers, Jim Morrison moved rapidly from being a lithe, reptilian youth to a heavy, bearded figure (right).

group went to World Pacific Studios and recorded a six-track acetate of Morrison originals – including 'Moonlight Drive', 'Summer's Almost Gone' and 'Break On Through' – which Jim took around the companies of LA. Eventually these recordings came to the attention of Billy James, head of talent research and development at Columbia Records, who signed the band to a six-month contract.

By now Manzarek's brothers had left the band (along with the mysterious female bassist) regarding Morrison's songs as 'too far out'; Robby Krieger (born 8 January 1946), a bottleneck guitarist from a local jug band, had been brought in to the fold, and Rick and the Ravens had become the Doors. The new name, chosen by Morrison, had been inspired by a line from the poetry of William Blake: 'There are things that are known and things that are unknown; in between are the doors,' and by Aldous Huxley's *The Doors Of Perception*. (Huxley's book had acquired a cult readership among Californian youth by the mid Sixties; it described the writer's experiences under the influence of the drug mescaline.)

By early 1966, although the Columbia contract had come to nothing – 'No one was interested in producing us', said Morrison – the Doors were playing five sets per night, six nights a week at the London Fog, a tiny club on Sunset Boulevard. The band's reputation grew rapidly and Jim Morrison – whose features proved irresistible to a large percentage of the female audience – was soon an LA sex symbol. By the end of the year, they had moved up from the London Fog to the Whisky A-Go-Go where they were spotted by Arthur Lee, the leader of Love. Lee urged Jac Holzman, president of Elektra Records, to check out the Doors and having done so, Holzman signed the group. (Arthur Lee was soon to regret his move as the Doors quickly overtook Love in terms of popularity.)

Strange days

Late 1966 saw the group in the studios to record an album under the auspices of producer Paul Rothchild. Released early the next year, *The Doors* exceeded all expectations in terms of quality; doom-laden songs were caressed by Krieger's bluesy guitar, Manzarek's hypnotic organ and Densmore's jazzy, scattershot drumming while Morrison delivered the lyrics, crammed with imagery, in stark, theatrically-urgent manner. The climax of the album was 'The End', an intense, dramatic opus that clocked in at 11 minutes. (This song had earlier got the Doors banned from the Whisky A-Go-Go because of its subject matter which encompassed patricide and incest – the Freudian Oedipus complex.)

Also included on the LP was a Krieger composition, 'Light My Fire', which was dominated by Manzarek's instantly seductive, spiralling organ patterns. Trimmed down from over six minutes to two-and-a-half, 'Light My Fire' went to Number 1 in the US in April and, through repeated radio play, became the anthem of a generation. The Doors had emerged from the underground to become a top mainstream attraction.

A second album, *Strange Days*, was released later that year in a bizarre cover that carried a photograph of carnival performers, and was in very much the same style as the first. It contained further songs of alienation in 'People Are Strange' and the apocalyptic, raging closing track 'When The Music's Over'. 'Horse Latitudes', meanwhile, was a cacophonous orgy of sound over which Morrison intoned a poem which detailed how horses were jettisoned from Spanish galleons in the doldrums. Two singles, 'People Are Strange' and 'Love Me Two Times', were culled from the album and both made the US Top Thirty.

> 'The thing they call rock, what used to be called rock'n'roll – it got decadent. And then there was a rock revival sparked by the English. That went very far. It was articulate. Then it became self-conscious, which I think is the death of any movement. It became self-conscious, involuted and kind of incestuous. The energy is gone. There is no longer a belief.'
>
> **Jim Morrison, 1969**

By now, Morrison had been heralded as rock idol and teen Messiah; he had adopted his tight black leather suit and was grooming his 'lizard king' image. In earlier days, the singer had clung, crouching, to his microphone, exuding a sense of menacing debilitation. But now he began to indulge in stage theatrics, writhing and contorting and often executing an 'accidental' fall into the audience to wild screams from the teenyboppers in the front rows. Such dramatics, however, although they delighted the younger pop audience, drew derision from the group's early 'underground' admirers.

In America, 1968 was a year of political unease as youth's awareness of the escalation of the war in Vietnam manifested itself in demonstrations and confrontations with authority. And the Doors were to reflect this unease on their third album, *Waiting For The Sun*, in songs such as 'The Unknown Soldier' and 'Five To One' which included the line: 'They got the guns but we got the numbers'. Underground fans found the group's political pose shallow and unconvincing, however; promotional film for 'The Unknown Soldier' showed Morrison being blindfolded, shot and spewing blood from his mouth and seemed to say more about the singer's preoccupation with death than the horrors of war. Another song from the album, 'Hello, I Love You', which appeared to be based on the Kinks' 'All Day And All Of The Night', gave the band their second US Number 1 (and their highest UK chart placing at Number 15), further establishing the 'angel in leather' as more of a teen idol than a political poet.

The lascivious lizard

Morrison himself claimed dissatisfaction at the idea that critics and fans separated him from the rest of the group and paid more attention to describing him in such cliches as 'The Lizard King' and 'The King of Orgasmic Rock' than they did to the music. By 1968, Morrison's diet of alcohol and 'downers' was begining to take its toll. The mythology that surrounded him cast him as a heavy drinker and he did nothing to play down the role, stating in an interview: 'I love drinking but I can't see drinking just milk or water or Coca-Cola. It just ruins it for me. Getting drunk, you're in complete control up to a point.' But he was passing that point with increasing frequency.

On 9 December 1967, the Doors played a concert at the New Haven Arena in Connecticut. During the group's performance

Right: Jim Morrison enlists the support of a mike-stand in a typical stage pose. Below and bottom: The singer's blatantly sexual antics cause him to be led off stage during a concert at Cleveland, Ohio.

of 'Back Door Man', Morrison launched into an obscene tirade against the police in the auditorium; the police responded by jumping the stage, spraying the singer with 'Mace' (tear gas) and charging him with breach of the peace and resisting arrest. Worse was to follow. Another concert, in Miami on 2 March 1969, resulted in six arrest warrants – two for indecent exposure, two for open public profanity, one for public drunkenness and a felony charge of 'Lewd and lascivious behaviour in public

Below: The Doors in their heyday – Ray Manzarek (keyboards), Jim Morrison (vocals), John Densmore (drums) and Robbie Krieger (guitar). Left: The remaining Doors soldier on without Morrison. Opposite: The final delusions of grandeur?

by exposing his private parts and by simulating masturbation and oral copulation.'

The Doors now began to withdraw from the concert platform, partly because few promoters were willing to risk Morrison's drunken antics and partly because of Morrison's growing disillusionment. 'I think I was just fed up with the image that had been created around me,' he later said of the Miami incident, 'which I sometimes consciously, most of the time unconsciously, cooperated with. It was just too much for me to really stomach and so I just put an end to it in one glorious evening.'

The weariness of the group was displayed on the 1969 album *The Soft Parade* which lacked energy and direction, traits accentuated by the fact that many session musicians augmented the band. Similarly the double *Absolutely Live* which appeared in the following year, captured a group in the throes of boredom going through the motions. With *Morrison Hotel* (1970), however, the group returned to a more crude, basic R&B style and garnered the first favourable reviews for years. *LA Woman* the following year was, again, the work of a mature and confident band. Produced jointly by the Doors and engineer Bruce Botnick, it showed, particularly on 'The Wasp (Texas Radio And The Big Beat)', that Morrison had rediscovered his gift for rich, mysterious imagery. It also provided the band's last hit with the melodic, atmospheric 'Riders On The Storm' which reached the US Number 14 position in August 1971. By this time, however, Jim Morrison was dead.

The music's over

Morrison had announced his temporary departure from the group some months before the final hit and had gone to live in Paris with his wife Pamela to concentrate on poetry. On Saturday 3 July he had a heart attack in his bathtub. The details of his death remain cloaked in mystery. The corpse was seen only by Pamela, who died from a heroin overdose in 1974, and an anonymous doctor, thus allowing fans to speculate that Morrison had, in fact, faked his own death in order to escape from public life forever. The man, himself, would have probably derided the fans' fantasies; as he had once said: 'I wonder why people like to believe I'm high all the time. I guess maybe they think someone else can take their trip for them.'

Stripped of their focal point, the three remaining Doors carried on regardless, producing two albums, *Other Voices* (1971) and *Full Circle* (1972) which displayed mastery of instrumentation but a lack of composing inspiration and a total inability to sing on the part of Manzarek. In 1973 the Doors finally parted company though Krieger and Densmore stuck together and in 1974 joined the Butts Band, a group fronted by throaty British vocalist Jess Roden. In 1977, Krieger turned to jazz-rock, producing an unremarkable album, *Robbie Krieger And Friends*, to which Densmore contributed the drumming. Manzarek, meanwhile, attempted to pursue a solo career and released three albums, *The Golden Scarab* (1975), *The Whole Thing Started With Rock'n'Roll, Now It's Out Of Control* (1975), and *Nite City* (1977) all of which were characterised by self-indulgence and an abundance of session musicians. In 1980, he resurfaced as producer and occasional keyboard player with the LA punk combo X.

The three surviving Doors were to reunite on one occasion, however. On 8 December 1970, Jim Morrison had recorded several hours of poetry readings and in 1975, Krieger, Densmore and Manzarek began to add music to his words. The project, which took some 30 months to complete, resulted in *An American Prayer* (1978), an album that served to remind that Morrison had always viewed himself first and foremost as a poet, whatever his public image may have been.

The underground audience and critics, initially seduced by his enormous charisma and unusual articulacy, thought he had descended to the level of a fat, drunken circus clown by 1969. They dismissed him as irrelevant, a narcissistic egomaniac. Authority saw Morrison, if not as a threat, at least as a minor nuisance. And the younger pop audience saw only the mystery of sex in leather. 'I'm interested in anything about revolt, disorder, chaos, especially activity that seems to have no meaning,' he was once quoted as saying. 'It seems to me to be the road to freedom.' For James Douglas Morrison, it proved, instead, to be the road to oblivion.

DAVID PROCKTER

THE DOORS
Discography

Singles
Break On Through/End Of The Night (Elektra 45611, 1967); Light My Fire/The Crystal Ship (Elektra 45615, 1967); People Are Strange/Unhappy Girl (Elektra 45621, 1967); Love Me Two Times/Moonlight Drive (Elektra 45624, 1968); The Unknown Soldier/We Could Be So Good Together (Elektra 45628, 1968); Hello, I Love You/Love Street (Elektra 45635, 1968); Touch Me/Wild Child (Elektra 45646, 1968); Wishful Sinful/Who Scared You (Elektra 45656, 1969); Tell All The People/Easy Ride (Elektra 45663, 1969); Runnin' Blue/Do It (Elektra 45675, 1969); You Make Me Real/Roadhouse Blues (Elektra 45685, 1970); Love Her Madly/Don't Go No Further (Elektra 45726, 1971); Riders On The Storm/Changeling (Elektra 45738, 1971); Tightrope Ride/Variety Is The Spice Of Life (Elektra 45757, 1971).

Albums
The Doors (Elektra 74007, 1967); *Strange Days* (Elektra 74014, 1967); *Waiting For The Sun* (Elektra 74024, 1968); *The Soft Parade* (Elektra 75005, 1969); *Morrison Hotel* (Elektra 75007, 1970); *Absolutely Live* (Elektra 2-9002, 1970); *LA Woman* (Elektra 75011, 1971); *Other Voices* (Elektra 75017, 1971); *Full Circle* (Elektra 75038, 1972); *An American Prayer* (Elektra 5E-502, 1978).

FLOWERS IN THEIR HAIR

The era of psychedelia brought with it a new kind of consumer, eager to buy from the alternative market in 'groovy' ideas as well as commodities. In contrast to the colourful innocence of flower-power, there was the sordidness of drug abuse, the groupie culture and the manipulation of the hippie ideal for the financial gain of a few perceptive entrepreneurs

Turn on, Tune in, Drop out

Rock music and LSD were the opiates of the West's new young consumers

The early Sixties saw two or three years of spectacular economic growth in the West. In particular, the increase in world trade at the beginning of the decade was unprecedented in modern times, more than matching the increase which marked the great days of Empire in the first dozen years of the twentieth century.

Inevitably, the mood of the period reflected the changed circumstance of economic expansion. A new liberalism spread across Europe and America as more money, more leisure time and a greater variety of goods and services became available to people. The relatively narrow horizons encouraged by austerity and Cold War paranoia in the Fifties broadened under the influence of cheap travel, new and powerful communications technologies and the pressure of industries seeking new markets.

In Britain, the satire boom, the Profumo affair, the popularity of the Beatles and a revolution in fashion, spreading from small boutiques in Carnaby Street and the King's Road, all heralded profound changes in mass society. Old attitudes and stale traditions were being swept aside as rampant consumerism encouraged a sense of experimentation and freedom in sexual morality, clothes, hairstyles, music, art and politics.

In the United States – where conditions were significantly different – the changing mood of the early Sixties was evidenced by the growth of folk-protest music, the increasing acceptance of 'beatnik' ideals, the burgeoning appeal of modern or 'cool' jazz and the birth of the radical student movement. Towering above all these, perhaps, was the fact of John F. Kennedy's election to the presidency in 1960.

High-school autograph hounds surround John F. Kennedy in Milwaukee, 1960. Kennedy's election to the presidency that year seemed to symbolise the changing, youthful and optimistic mood of the times.

In the president's steps

Kennedy was young, good-looking, apparently liberal and – a first for the US presidency – a Catholic. As many commentators have noted, Kennedy's assassination in 1963 provides at least a partial explanation of the Beatles' subsequent success with younger generations in America – they stepped into the vacuum Kennedy left and came to symbolise everything that the president had once symbolised: youthfulness, success, good-humour, good looks, playful boyishness, innocence combined with native cunning, hope for the future and a crucial unconventionality. And if it's argued that the Beatles were a group, then Kennedy had his family, his brother Robert, his elegant wife Jackie, his courtiers and his Camelot.

With Kennedy and the Beatles, the line between politics and showbiz became all but invisible. Both seemed to represent a new and popular urge to democracy and the overthrow of restrictive national boundaries. And rock – accepted as the form of showbiz for the young – was the perfect vehicle for the aspirations of those who were beginning to see themselves as the first settlers in a Brave New World. The possibilities were seemingly endless.

Indeed, rock music's role in the changing mood of the Sixties can hardly be overestimated. The new electronic technologies that shaped rock and grew up on its back helped create new patterns of consumption and new styles of music. Fifties' rock'n'roll was relatively unsophisticated in its aspirations, but, by the time Phil Spector was producing his 'little symphonies for kids' with the Ronettes and the Crystals, rock had developed a sense of its own artistic potential. Developments in broadcasting, recording and amplification technology would help fulfil this potential, while the widespread availability of cheap hi-fi (also made possible by rock's enormous popularity) gave rock artistic credibility by enabling the private consumption of crafted work.

Perhaps even more significant was the way that rock tied in with radical politics, becoming an instrument for stirring the consciences of the young. Consumerism created its own contradictions. In making ideas and technologies widely available for the sake of profit alone, it was unable to discourage more radical ideas and the use of technologies in a struggle against the profit-system.

The key figure in this process in the early Sixties was undeniably Bob Dylan, who had renounced rock'n'roll at the end of the previous decade to pursue a more 'committed' kind of music. Dylan's involvement in the early Sixties' movement for black civil rights made him a political figure. But that movement – like the anti-Vietnam War movement that followed it – was essentially a part of the same general process of liberalisation that lay behind Sixties consumerism.

World of hope?
One of the crucial aspects of this liberalisation was that it confirmed the end of imperialism. From the beginning of the Sixties, Third World cultures were no longer reviled as alien, inferior and merely exploitable. On the contrary, they were promoted (at least, in public) as exotic, interesting, future partners in the worldwide adventure of industrialisation. On a more superficial level, the East was famed as the source of spicy foods, colourful clothes, profound ideas and fascinating art – all of which, in one form or another, could be gainfully exchanged for dollars and pounds.

Although overt imperialism was at an end, this did not deter Western nations continuing to exploit and oppress former colonies and colonised peoples. The American blacks were such a people, and the Civil Rights movement was seen as an essentially anti-imperialist struggle. Blacks became 'Afro-Americans', some converted to Islam and many argued for a future independent of – even separate from – white America. The Vietnam War, too, was seen as an anti-imperialist struggle; as the Sixties progressed, supporters of the struggles of such colonial peoples – whose ideas had been allowed free range in the liberal atmosphere of an expansionary West – began to see that very expansionary West as an ogre.

Dylan and many of his contemporaries turned that message into song. They promoted their vision of a better world in terms that pitted the values of industrial, urbanised societies against the 'more human' values of (a probably imaginary) Third World and rural peasantry. Folk music, country blues, marijuana, Tibetan bells, Indian incense, Islam and Buddhism all became fashionable, as did many other products of Third World and rural societies. These were the overt symbols of opposition to the oppressive technocracy of the West.

Dylan – who turned the Beatles on to marijuana in 1964 and thereby opened at least one set of floodgates – was canny enough to understand technology's contradictory nature. His going electric in 1965 seemed a sell-out to many radicals and folk musicians, but it was, for Dylan, a route to vaster audiences than any traditional folk musicians could previously have dreamed of.

Top: At the court of the acid king – the messiah of LSD, Dr Timothy Leary (centre) holds forth while Yippie activists Abbie Hoffman (left) and Jerry Rubin turn on and tune in. Above: Oz *magazine, launched in London in February 1967 by Australian Richard Neville, was a colourful (and often illegible) mixture of radical politics, hippie philosophy, drugs, music, cartoons, psychedelic graphics and pornography. Along with* IT, *the paper helped give a united voice to the London underground scene until it ceased publication in the early Seventies.*

Into this ferment of new music, political radicalism, colourful clothes and unconventional lifestyles stepped LSD – the most powerful hallucinogenic drug known. Through the patronage of people like the novelist Aldous Huxley and the philosopher of religion Alan Watts – as well as a number of experimentally-inclined psychiatrists and psychologists – LSD had already gained something of reputation as a wonder drug. Huxley and Watts promoted a quasi-religious view of LSD, linking it to mysticism and the ancient ritual use of other hallucinogens such as the psilocybin ('magic') mushroom, mescaline and hashish. Others had investigated the drug's use in more mundane problem-solving or therapeutic contexts. Those who had come across LSD by the onset of the Sixties were inevitably convinced of its potential for changing human awareness on an individual level.

The single most important thing about LSD, however, was that it was a synthetic substance – a technological product which seemed to have profoundly humanising effects. Here was the acute contradiction of Sixties economic expansion embodied and resolved in an odourless, colourless, tasteless liquid: LSD was a mass-produced commodity in the exclusive service of the spiritual and creative lives of human beings.

The drug's messiah, psychologist Timothy Leary, was sacked from Harvard University in 1962 for spreading the LSD gospel. Travelling through California, Mexico and New York, he propounded his philosophy of 'the psychedelic revolution' (the term psychedelic – literally, 'mind manifesting' – was coined by an early LSD-experimenter to describe the drug's effects). Leary left a trail of converts whose attitudes to LSD's 'consciousness-expanding' possibilities varied from the playful to the deadly earnest. Almost everybody who came in touch with LSD in those days did take one of Leary's messages at face value: 'turn on, tune in and drop out' became the slogan of the age.

A common effect of the drug was to heighten the senses and break down the barriers to perception. Colours would glow, sounds would linger and resonate; sometimes one stimulus would provoke quite an unexpected response so

Bottom left: The Magic Bus of Ken Kesey and his Merry Pranksters takes to the streets of New York, June 1964. Left: At the Fillmore East, Procol Harum play before a psychedelic lightshow designed to simulate the visual LSD experience. Below: An ageing hippie peddles underground tracts, London, 1973.

that music would become translated into imagined visions. Rock music – loud, simple, often repetitive and highly rhythmic – became the favoured soundtrack for the LSD 'trip'. New performers emerged in the 'Acid Tests', 'Trips Festivals', 'Be-Ins' and 'Freak-Outs' that started in the mid Sixties as anarchic events to occupy the sensation-hungry tripper through an eight to twelve-hour experience. These performers – notably the Grateful Dead in America and Pink Floyd in Britain – cultivated a style which depended on simple chord structures, massive amplification and much repetitive improvisation. Their performances were often accompanied by light shows using slides, spotlights and bits of film, and audiences were encouraged to dance, wear make-up and flowing clothes and generally pursue as many different stimuli as possible.

By 1967, LSD itself had been made almost universally illegal. Yet the psychedelic lifestyle was in full swing, a rendered-down liquor strained off from the casserole of economic expansion, the resurgence of rock and LSD itself. Indeed, psychedelia was most significant as a popular fashion towards the end of the Sixties, when beads, bells, paisley shirts, cut-rate Eastern religions and flower-power pop finally found their niche in the expanded marketplace.

GARY HERMAN

THE INNER LIGHT?

On the Sixties trail to Eastern enlightenment

'IF YOU APPRECIATE the tuning so much, I hope you'll enjoy the playing more,' said Ravi Shankar at the 1971 Concert for Bangladesh when the audience burst into applause after a couple of minutes warm-up from his Indian band. The incident typified the benign misunderstanding that greeted Eastern music and religion during its excursion to the West in the late Sixties and early Seventies. At the time, however, its influence seemed all-pervading – Eastern concepts like *karma* and *yin/yang* found their way into everyday language. Sitars suddenly appeared on many rock singles, notably the Rolling Stones' 'Paint It Black'. DJ John Peel, sitting in a cramped ship's cabin off the south coast of England, read late night extracts from *The Perfumed Garden* to Radio London listeners. Many young people, particularly at pop festivals, wore colourful, Eastern-influenced clothes, and a group of Hindus, under the name Radha Krishna Temple, took a Hare Krishna chant into the UK Top Twenty.

In retrospect these influences may seem superficial, but in terms of contemporary lifestyle they were revolutionary. Eastern culture, along with hallucinogenic drugs and rock music, became part of a movement that questioned the work ethic, competition and – in rock music – the Top Twenty mentality. It was genuinely believed that it would only be a matter of time before changes in individuals' personalities fostered by this new lifestyle would transform Western capitalist society beyond recognition.

The hippie trail

Travelling, well within the reach of increasingly affluent Western youth, became important, too – not only to get away from a hostile capitalist society but because travelling seemed an important concept in Eastern religion: gurus pointed out that answers often lay in the journey itself rather than in reaching a destination. Young 'seekers after truth' failed to appreciate the metaphorical nature of such pronouncements, and, by the time MP Philip Goodhart pointed out in May 1968 that 'hippies are now, of course, the major British contribution to the Afghan scene', virtually everyone under the age of 25 seemed to be spending part of the year hitching further and further east from Morocco through Istanbul, Ankara and India to Katmandu.

These journeys weren't without difficulties, especially with cash dwindling rapidly on the way back ('And half the blasted idiots are stuck in Yugoslavia/with hardly a dina . . .' chortled Roy Harper on 'Nobody's Got Any Money In The Summer'). Many of the countries concerned, frightened that their tourist industries would be threatened by these scruffy itinerants, began to impose vindictive 30-year jail sentences for trivial drug offences. The travellers pressed on, however, and the further East they went, the greater the resulting influence of Eastern mysticism on Western ideas, music and fashion.

Young Westerners who were unhappy in their own countries tried to settle in Marrakesh, Morocco, wherever took their fancy. A hippy commune in the crumbling villas surrounding Tangier became like Ladbroke Grove in exile, with house-to-house visiting, picking up supplies of locally-grown hashish and taking odd jobs when money was needed. In return, gangs of saffron-robed Hindus came to Europe and danced up and down the city streets chanting and begging, selling religious books and records to the gullible. Neither group of exiles, in the West or the East, ever made much sense to the native population and, with their blithe disregard of local custom and feeling, seemed often to reinforce George Harrison's perspective in 'The Inner Light' that 'the farther one travels, the less one really knows . . .'

Eastern echoes

Harrison, of course, introduced the sitar to rock; it is difficult to realise just how bewildering it first sounded back in 1965 on the Beatles' 'Norwegian Wood' when most people had never even heard of the instrument. Although at this stage Harrison merely strummed the sitar, before long he and other rock musicians were exploring its possibilities further and studying under Indian musicians like Ravi Shankar. Unlike Western music, where the scale forms the basis of both melody and harmony, Indian music is based on the idea of the *raga*. Each *raga* is a brief, modal melody that forms the basis for improvisation over a continuous drone. As a result, Indian classical pieces tend to be fairly long, and since they are devoid of the chord changes that provide tension and climax in much Western music, this has to be achieved by increasingly intricate solo patterns. The rhythmic unit – or *tal* – on which an Indian piece is based is often long and complex, resembling the 7/4 and 13/8 time signatures that had been employed in some jazz and classical music, and which were about to infiltrate rock.

Under this influence, progressive Western records became so long that Radio One DJ John Peel, whose show used to go out live on Saturday afternoons, was able to slip out to listen to the football results and still be back at his turntable before the track he was playing had ended. Gone were the 8-bar guitar solos in the middle of conventionally-structured pop songs. Instead, lead guitar pieces – often improvised – were like long, stoned meditations that assumed an importance all their own. On tracks like the Grateful Dead's 'Dark Star', the listener was supposedly being offered an apparently spontaneous outpouring of guitarist Jerry Garcia's feelings, and the idea consequently arose that, depending on the 'vibes' from the audience or the guitarist's chemical state, no two performances of a piece were ever quite the same.

Since self-expression was now so important, tuning-up on stage became very fashionable – depending on how stoned the musician was, this could sometimes take longer than the song itself – and celebratory jam sessions, as on Harrison's *All Things Must Pass* album, also became common. At the other end of the scale, repetition became a preoccupation of some composers. Soft Machine performed a particularly repetitious piece entitled 'We Did It Again', which deliberately set out to be boring because, according to organist Mike Ratledge: 'If you find something boring, a basic Zen concept, then in the end you find it interesting. If you listen to something repeated in the same way your mind changes the structure of it each time.' This idea was taken up by Mike Oldfield in the repetitive layers of *Tubular Bells*, while John Lennon had used it in a more accessible way with the loop tapes on 'I Want You (She's So Heavy)'. It wasn't always easy to tell just how serious musicians took this, however; Ratledge admitted that 'We Did It Again' was a piece Soft Machine saved especially for when they wanted to annoy their audience.

Lyrically, terms of reference were set by the Beatles' flower-power anthem 'All You Need Is Love'. Its underlying sentiment – that anything is possible for the individual – was somewhat at odds with the self-effacing lifestyle extolled by Eastern religion, but the emphasis, in both Buddhism and

The hippies (opposite) favoured Eastern thought and were hostile to Western materialism, but this was not without its contradictions. After the Beatles discovered the Maharishi (right), George Harrison had his fireplace decorated in oriental style (below).

Hinduism, on intuition had an obvious appeal for a generation that rejected Western rationalism and regarded the entire educational system as misguided. 'We can miss off school', suggested Steve Marriott in the drug-oriented lyrics of 'Itchycoo Park' (1967), 'Why go to learn the words of fools?' There had always been a rebellious streak in rock, but in the late Sixties it began to flirt with a structured, philosophical view of the world.

The Beatles may have set the general parameters – and popularised the East at a stroke with their trip to India to visit the Maharishi Mahesh Yogi – but others gave lyrics a more specific direction. Despite their antiquity and basic passivity, Eastern ideas seemed in tune with a decade that sought instant salvation, in the same way that, a few years earlier, a demand for instant art in Swinging London had made photography fashionable. *Be Here Now*, the title of a book which became a hippie primer, was also an idea that cropped up constantly alongside lyrics that dealt with the psychedelic experience, colours, the illusion of the real world and the knowledge that all truth is within.

Partly due to Indian influences, styles of writing changed too: images were piled up one on top of another in an attempt to express states of mind rather than creating a flowing narrative. This technique was by no means confined to overtly religious lyrics. King Crimson, for instance, offered 'Pictures Of A City': 'Concrete dream flesh broken skull/Lost soul lost trance lost in hell'. Lennon's 'Across The Universe', the lyrics of which forced their way into his head in the middle of the night, was equally typical of the trend.

The dream-like quality captured in many of the songs at this time was often linked to an underlying principle of the Universe. Robin Williamson of the Incredible String Band, describing his writing technique to *Oz* magazine in 1969,

Below: Ravi Shankar was the musician most responsible for popularising Indian classical music in the West. Inset below left: Quintessence emerged from Notting Hill's hippie community to adopt Hindu names and chant mantras.

observed: 'A year ago I'd have said I was in touch with the spirit that wrote all the songs. I would have said I wasn't responsible for their existence, it was just the music. But now I'm starting to take responsibility for actually creating them.' People actually based their lives around such ideas; Quintessence dressed in robes and sandals, adopted Indian names and chanted mantras that they recorded for their albums. Lead vocalist Shiva said: 'What we are trying to put across in the music is that it is within the grasp of everyone to attain infinite knowledge, love and peace.'

Seeing the light
Many aspects of Eastern religion, however, were ignored – like the proscription of sex and drugs – if they were considered inconvenient. The fundamental doctrines of Hinduism were never really followed. In brief, they hold that all phenomena are manifestations of a divine ground and that the only aim in life should be to reach a full, intuitive knowledge of this divine ground and become one with it. Hindus believe that human beings can penetrate to this divine reality by intuition ('You can penetrate any place you go', sang John Lennon on 'Dig A Pony') and that man has a double nature: a phenomenal ego, which should be disregarded, and an eternal self.

These philosophies led to a vaguely benign outlook that fostered ideas about such concepts as communal living. The belief that the human species is one with all nature tended to manifest itself in a fascination for the children's stories of A. A. Milne (*Winnie The Pooh*) and Kenneth Grahame (*The Wind In The Willows*), as well as fostering a vague interest in UFOs and space travellers. Such fantasy – quite the opposite of a Hindu search for a divine *reality* – became entangled with a general worship of the past (Eastern beliefs were ancient as well as distant) that had little significance apart from heavily subsidising the old-age pension of J. R. R. Tolkien, author of *The Hobbit* and *The Lord of the Rings*.

Denial of the personality, in practice, often amounted to self-indulgence: rock stars pretended to be gurus and gurus passed themselves off as rock stars (the Maharishi Mahesh Yogi actually went on a bill-topping tour with the Beach Boys) and people wandered around with a dramatic sense of their own importance. Much importance was placed on drug-induced ecstasy, and this was often linked to Zen Buddhism, a cult that became very popular (especially on the West Coast of America) because its teachings allowed for 'accidental' enlightenment. After years of graft the truth might come like a blinding light at an unexpected moment, so why not jumble up your preconceptions with a little acid and make that state of mind more likely?

It was only a short step, therefore, to Timothy Leary announcing acid as a religious sacrament – despite the fact that the eight-fold path (eight essential conditions to reach Nirvana) excluded drugs, which were believed to work against meditation. People giving up tea, coffee and meat but still dropping acid were not uncommon. True seekers of Nirvana were also required to give up all relationships and family as mere worldly illusions to be stripped away. This idea had a certain romantic appeal to a generation that didn't trust adults, but it rarely went further than a few months away on the Marrakesh Express.

The denial of the world in Buddhism and Hinduism was conveniently taken to mean the Western world only. Eastern religion was used to legitimise the hippie revolution – music, drugs and the non-competitive lifestyle – in much the same way as puritanism had legitimised the English Civil War. It provided a moral authority to throw at old people and politicians. Seen from afar, it appeared to be a very attractive religion. But it seemed attractive *precisely* because it was seen from afar, a standpoint that enabled converts to pick and choose their beliefs. The fact that Eastern religion was outside the Western set-up was a great attraction, encouraging

For the diligent searcher after the One Truth, the only path to follow was the long and hard one of prayer and meditation (bottom). Many hippies found a convenient shortcut through drugs like cannabis (below).

the idea of a freak society in exile. It is also interesting, given the political climate of the time, that America was fighting a war in Asia, and adherence to religions popular in Vietnam was an ideal way of siding with the oppressed.

Nothing lasts

The implications of the fusion between rock and Eastern ideas were largely social rather than directly musical. A few communes survived in the Eighties, leading a ragged existence in the hills of North Wales, but perhaps the most significant result has been the growth of the ecology movement. The migration of hippies to the countryside, in an attempt to love and cultivate the earth, stemmed from the Eastern belief that there is one life in all things. Flowers, for instance, have always been a symbol of the divine in Eastern mandalas. This underlying principle of life also discouraged people from eating meat and made vegetarianism respectable rather than cranky. None of these ideas would have gained prominence had they not been aligned to rock music.

At the time, the religious fascinations of the East may have provoked an opposing response in the work of musicians as diverse as Loudon Wainwright III ('Guru') and Jethro Tull (1971's *Aqualung* album), but in the long term they 'legitimised' the stars' individual beliefs. Rock musicians like Pete Townshend and Carlos Santana stayed with their respective gurus well into the Seventies, while others, like Richard and Linda Thompson and Cat Stevens, were converted to Islam.

There is also an ever-increasing band of born-again Christians, of whom Bob Dylan is the most famous convert. As for the saffron-robed followers of Guru A. C. Bhaktivedanta, heavily subsidised in the past by George Harrison, they still dance up and down city streets on occasion, but no-one takes them very seriously.

Below: Why don't we do it in the road? The hippies' sublime disregard for the material world could prove exasperating to those less enlightened souls intent on getting to work. Bottom: A service at the Krishna Temple.

For a brief period, however, Eastern ideas gave a revolutionary new lifestyle a certain cultural context and moral authority. They helped music expand its frontiers both structurally and lyrically, and, aligned with drugs, forced people to look at the natural world in a new way. The net result of these years was to destroy the illusion that life is ordered on any kind of logical, consecutive plane – something rock'n'roll always instinctively felt but never had the vocabulary to articulate.

But why, in the end, were there no other far-reaching effects? Firstly, the movement was incredibly naive in its belief that the world could be changed simply by changing people. Moreover, combining a social conscience with a world-denying religion was in effect trying to reconcile contradictory aims and, in any case, it wasn't possible to graft one culture on to another by some kind of cerebral sleight of hand. In the end, the two just didn't fit. Westerners were rarely trying to absorb the real thing, and those who eventually took a hard, close look at Eastern culture – like John Lennon – often found they couldn't bear it. The ex-Beatle eventually had to throw out the group of Hare Krishna freaks he'd allowed to live around his house at Tittenhurst Park because, as he pointed out, only half-jokingly: 'I just couldn't get any bloody peace with them walking around chanting and smiling all the time.' COLIN SHEARMAN

Flower Power or Money Power?

Kaftans and compromise abounded as groups and singers cashed in on psychedelia

LIKE BEATLEMANIA and the protest boom, the flower power fad of 1967 offered yet another example of how a minority cult could be transformed by the media and record industry into a craze of international proportions. The blossoming counter-culture of San Francisco gave young America its first real taste of hippie lifestyles and attitudes, yet it was a fundamentally false, over-romanticised version of hippiedom that the newspapers and record companies peddled. Flower power was important for unearthing numerous new bands and for creating a more progressive climate for musicians to work in, but often what passed for flower power music bore little relation to the genuine 'acid-rock' of the original San Francisco groups. For most record labels and even many established pop acts, flower power was just another bandwagon to jump on in pursuit of the youth market.

The bandwagon started to roll even before the historic Monterey Pop Festival of June 1967, when most of the San Francisco bands were signed by the major labels to big-money contracts. Predictably it was the small, independent labels scattered around Los Angeles who first saw the commercial possibilities of flower power, just as they had all but monopolised the surfing and protest pop crazes earlier in the Sixties. Crucial to the appeal of surf and protest had been the *message* in the music, its expression of a particular attitude or mode of living rather than any innovation in style; likewise, Los Angeles flower music appealed mainly because of its celebratory aspects, the ability of groups like the Turtles, the Seeds, the Mamas and the Papas and others to capture on disc the youthful, hedonistic spirit of the time. If there was nothing revolutionary, genuinely counter-cultural or even particularly controversial about their brand of flower-power pop, they nevertheless succeeded in dominating the singles charts of 1967 as none of the San Francisco bands quite could.

Aural architects

The two prime architects of flower power pop were Lou Adler and John Phillips, both of whom combined an astute business sense with a real sympathy for the direction that pop was taking during the mid Sixties. Adler was a veteran of the Los Angeles music scene, a former songwriting partner of Herb Alpert and Sam Cooke and the mastermind behind Barry McGuire's success in the protest field in 1965; he produced hits for dozens of West Coast singers and groups – Johnny Rivers, Jan and Dean, P. F. Sloan and the Grass Roots among them – and ran Dunhill, one of the city's most successful independent labels. Phillips was a

Well-known British flower-power group the Beatles promote one of the Summer of Love's hottest singles in four different languages – well, almost!

founder member of the Mamas and the Papas, who had moved to Hollywood in 1965 at the suggestion of Barry McGuire and, under Adler's shrewd tutelage, developed a gentle, crystalline vocal style closely based on that of Peter, Paul and Mary. They also adopted an engaging if contrived hippie image for themselves which proved to be a highly successful publicity gimmick.

The Mamas and the Papas' 'California Dreamin'', a Number 4 US hit during the spring of 1966, encapsulated all the attractions of life on the sunny West Coast and was, in effect, the first flower power hit: if you're spiritually dead, the song suggested, head out to California where even the winters are warm and the soul can be reborn. Subsequent releases by the group like 'Go Where You Wanna Go' and the autobiographical 'Creeque Alley' – like 'California Dreamin'', a John Phillips composition – carried the same implicit message.

The Mamas and the Papas were Dunhill's leading act, but Adler and Phillips were also responsible for producing the one record that set the seal on the flower power craze – Scott McKenzie's million-selling 'San Francisco (Be Sure To Wear Flowers In Your Hair)'. Written by Phillips and recorded by McKenzie for Adler's newly-launched Ode label – the logo of which, characteristically, incorporated a daffodil – the song had exactly the same exultant, euphoric quality of the Mamas and the Papas' best records, painting a thoroughly beguiling picture of a city bathed in LSD and good vibes. More than this, the record was deliberately conceived as a rallying call to young people everywhere, an invitation to listeners to become part of the 'new generation with a new explanation'. It attracted literally thousands of students and teenagers to San Francisco during what was described ecstatically as the 'Summer of Love', turning the hippie district of Haight Ashbury into a tourist trap and contributing to the eventual dissolution of its community spirit.

The disc was issued just prior to the Monterey Pop Festival (which both Adler and Phillips played key roles in organising) and McKenzie made a triumphant performing debut there. He was instantly adopted by the world's press as spokesman for the whole hippie movement: *Time* magazine profiled him and defined his hippie followers as dedicated to 'altruism, mysticism, honesty, joy and non-violence, finding an almost childlike fascination in beads, blossoms and bells, ear-shattering music, exotic clothing and erotic slogans'. His hippie credentials, in fact, were not that solid: he hailed not from San Francisco or even Los Angeles but from Virginia, and he had been a professional folk singer since the early Sixties. He had met John Phillips during a spell with New York folk group the Journeymen and made a few forgotten records for Capitol before moving to the West Coast in 1967.

After playing the Los Angeles folk clubs as a backing musician, he teamed up with Phillips once more and recorded 'No, No, No, No, No' for Epic before finding his particular niche in flower power. As it happened, he was quite sincere in his belief in the tenets of hippie

'San Francisco', sung by one-hit-wonder Scott McKenzie (above), caught the mood of the moment in highly commercial fashion. Its author John Phillips repeated the formula with his own band the Mamas and the Papas (below right), as did the Strawberry Alarm Clock (top right) with 'Incense And Peppermints'. But were they only in it for the money?

philosophy and tackled his new role of flower power prophet with dignity. By the time the craze had passed, however, he found himself unable to live down his hippie image and was labelled by the record industry as a one-hit wonder. He had only one more minor hit, 'Like An Old Time Movie' in late 1967, before retiring from recording altogether for three years. His flower power connections have conspired to thwart subsequent comeback attempts.

Forever changes

Most Los Angeles-based singers and groups adopted at least some aspects of the flower power cult during 1967, some out of genuine commitment, many simply to stay in fashion. The two long-time leaders of the California group scene, the Byrds and the Beach Boys, had stayed strategically on the fringes of flower power with records that not only sounded suitably avant-garde – the Byrds' 'Eight Miles High' and *Fifth Dimension* album, the Beach Boys' 'Good Vibrations' and *Pet Sounds* – but had definite drug connotations. In common with many of their contemporaries, both bands adopted a public posture on the drug question that was strikingly ambivalent: chart-oriented groups had to maintain a wholesome pop image, yet at the same time cultivate credibility with the more hip sections of the rock audience. Most bands compromised by picking up on the flower power 'look' of floral shirts, kaftans, beads and Jesus sandals, and by making vague statements about 'getting high on life'. Material subtly changed: songs of person-to-person relationships, the stock repertoire of every pop act, were generally dropped in favour of all-embracing message songs about *universal* peace and love.

The Association typified the degree of compromise. Beginning in the Los Angeles area as a straight Beach Boys-influenced group with a particularly neat line in vocal harmonies, this six-piece band made their chart debut in mid-1966 with the provocative 'Along Comes Mary' on the independent Valiant label – the Mary of the title representing, or so the hip cognoscenti had it, marijuana. Despite their adoption of longer haircuts and multi-coloured jackets in the flower power mode, they protested their innocence on any charge of corrupting the nation's youth and recorded the inoffensive 'Cherish', a conventional ballad, as a follow-up. By early 1967, however, they were once again stepping on controversial ground with a brilliantly commercial drug novelty, 'Pandora's Golden Heebie Jeebies', and two concept albums with stereotypically hip titles soon followed in *Renaissance* and *Insight Out*. Finally, unable and unwilling to keep up with all the changes in rock, they dropped their flower power stance completely and returned to recording smooth middle-of-the-road ballads like 'Everything That Touches You' and 'Never My Love'.

Like the Association, the Turtles – who recorded for another independent, White Whale – fitted comfortably into the flower power bag after flirting successfully with folk-rock and a Phil Spector-inspired sound. In terms of image, they came closest to being *the* archetypal flower power group, though their madcap stage act suggested that they didn't intend it to be taken too seriously. Their album tracks revealed some gleaming gems of flowery wisdom, notably 'The Walking Song' (which also appeared on the flipside of 'She'd Rather Be With Me') and the bizarre 'Can't You Hear The Cows'.

Flower power also spawned dozens of new acts with spectacularly florid names, most of whom won the immediate interest of fad-conscious record companies, made one hit and then floundered. One of the first was the Peanut Butter Conspiracy: discovered in Los Angeles by Byrds producer Gary Usher, they were marketed nationally under the ready-made slogan of 'The Peanut Butter Conspiracy Is Spreading'. The presence of an angelic-looking girl singer in Sandi Robinson – her image apparently modelled on Michelle Phillips of the Mamas and the Papas – gave them added promotability, and the group fared fairly well in the period before Grace Slick and Jefferson Airplane (not to mention Janis Joplin and Big Brother and the Holding Company) showed the true potential of a charismatic female lead in a rock band. The Conspiracy had two major hits in America during 1967 with 'It's A Happening Thing' and 'Turn On A Friend (To The Good Life)', both hymns to the hippie way of life.

Other acts to enjoy momentary recognition through flower power included the Strawberry Alarm Clock, a self-styled teenybopper answer to the Jefferson Airplane whose musical mock-psychedelia (best exemplified by their 1967 Number 1, 'Incense And Peppermints') was much copied by

TOP OF THE POPS
BEEGEES

bubblegum groups like the Lemon Pipers; the Seeds, who were actually the already well-known Sky Saxon's Blues Band in another, more contemporary guise and who had a hit in 1967 with 'Pushin' Too Hard'; Circus Maximus, a would-be art-rock band from Los Angeles who included Jerry Jeff Walker in their line-up; and Biff Rose, an eccentric composer, singer and folk-club raconteur whose two albums for the small Tetragrammaton label featured such mood-of-the-moment titles as 'It's Happening', 'Gentle People', 'Spaced Out (I've Got You Covered)' and the awesomely sentimental 'Fill Your Heart' (later recorded by David Bowie on his *Hunky Dory* album).

Beatles and the bandwagon

Most of the more established American groups acknowledged flower power in their music – the Monkees with 'Take A Giant Step', Harpers Bizarre with 'Come To The Sunshine' (written by Van Dyke Parks), the Lovin' Spoonful with 'Only Pretty What A Pity', the Youngbloods with 'Get Together', even the Supremes with 'The Happening' and 'Reflections'. In Britain, too, some of the most regular chart names were quick to associate themselves with the new fad, which arrived via Carnaby Street, the Sunday newspapers' colour supplements, pirate radio and the proselytising efforts of the Beatles, the Who, the Rolling Stones and other UK bands who had heard the sounds of San Francisco at first hand.

The Beatles gave particular encouragement to British psychedelia with the 'Strawberry Fields Forever' single and the *Sgt Pepper* album, before giving the whole movement what amounted to a royal seal of approval with possibly the ultimate in flower power songs – 'All You Need Is Love', recorded before a live television audience of millions the world over, with all four Beatles splendidly adorned in the very latest hippie gear. The Hollies responded with 'King Midas In Reverse' (and achieved their lowest-placed chart hit for years); the Troggs abandoned the rude charm of their earlier hits for a 'sophisticated' paean to love and peace called 'Love Is All Around'; the Move released 'I Can Hear The Grass Grow' and then arguably prophesied the wilting of flower power in 'Flowers In The Rain'; the Bee Gees listened hard to Scott McKenzie and produced a soundalike Number 1 in 'Massachusetts' and Eric Burdon, probably the most enthusiastic of all British converts to flower power, issued a string of aggressively pro-hippie singles with a re-shaped Animals line-up, notably 'San Franciscan Nights', 'Monterey', 'Sky Pilot' and 'Good Times'. Likewise Donovan, always prone to feyness in his music, switched deftly from folk-rock to such acid-soaked singles as 'Sunshine Superman', 'Mellow Yellow', 'Epistle To Dippy' and 'Sunny Goodge Street'. The more naive sections of the British pop press greeted him as the poetic avatar of the new generation.

New groups arrived on the back of flower power. Former boozy bluesman Zoot Money took the Eric Burdon route and donned kaftans and bells to launch Dantalion's Chariot, while whizz-kid manager Simon Napier-Bell recruited budding flower child Marc Bolan into new signings John's Children and promoted them as the UK's first truly home-grown flower-power group. Pop tycoons Ken Howard and Alan Blaikley, still doing well with Dave Dee Dozy Beaky Mick & Tich, groomed the Herd in the same manner and wrote and produced the pseudo-progressive 'From The Underworld' as the group's first chart disc. Also very much in the flower power vein were Warm Sounds, a close-harmony duo who reached the Top Thirty with the self-written 'Birds And Bees'; Floribunda Rose, whose very name was a blatant flower power cash-in; and the new wave of progressive acts first heard on John Peel's 'Perfumed Garden' programme on Radio London, who were labelled flower power for want of a better description. These included Tomorrow, Pink Floyd and Procol Harum.

The Beatles' 'All You Need Is Love' apart, the biggest British-made flower power hit of 1967 was the Flowerpot Men's 'Let's Go To San Francisco'. Arguably the most cynical of all the exploitation records, it was conceived by ex-Ivy League members John Carter and Ken Lewis as a one-off disc in the harmony-based vocal style they themselves had popularised in hits like 'Funny How Love Can Be' and 'Tossing And Turning'. The lyrics of the song, however, were pure tourist brochure copy, describing 'gentle people walking hand in hand' and celebrating the city of love and acid as the place where 'flowers grow so very high'. For television appearances, Carter and Lewis recruited leading session singer Tony Burrows and the success of 'Let's Go To San Francisco' precipitated a rash of similar one-shot hits.

The flowers fade

Flower power pop proved as ephemeral as the summer itself, a passing fashion far too rooted in the mythology of 1967 to endure for long. Many of the ideas that surfaced in the US during the flower power era continued to prevail – the gigantic Woodstock festival of 1969 seemed a living vindication of all that the hippies had originally set out to achieve – but the trend had less lasting impact in the UK. Physically and culturally remote from the conditions that had inspired flower power in the first place, British musicians, record people and fans alike were always more concerned with the superficial trappings of flower power: the clothes, bric-a-brac, the sexual licence it gave.

Flower power pop had its casualties. Just as Scott McKenzie could never live down his status as one-time leader of the world's flower children, so Eric Burdon and Donovan never again enjoyed the same kind of popularity or record sales. The Beatles, recognising the excesses of 1967 that they had partly inspired, eschewed the psychedelia of *Sgt Pepper* for a double-album of back-to-the-roots simplicity in *The Beatles,* the release of which just about ended the flower power era. In the more sober, restrained atmosphere of 1968, true progression in rock was seen as having more to do with musicianship and ideas than paying lip service to some spurious philosophy from across the Atlantic.

STEPHEN BARNARD

Top of the pots: the Flowerpot Men (left). The Bee Gees (inset far left) turned out the lights in Massachusetts, Donovan (inset centre) turned on in Goodge Street, while the Troggs (inset left) turned around to cash in.

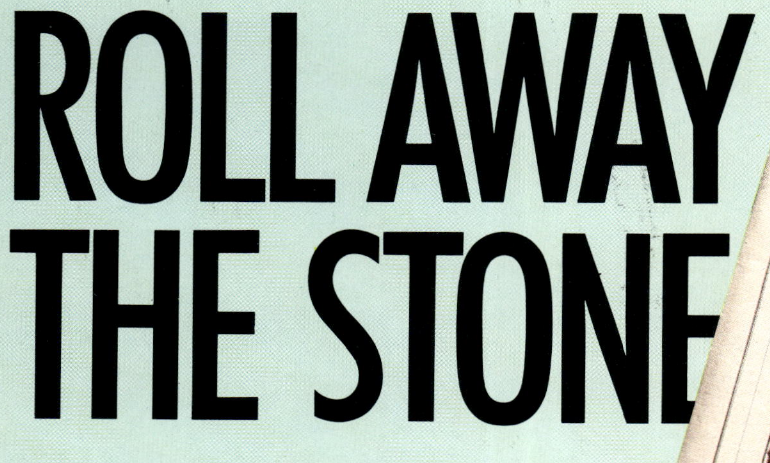

ROLL AWAY THE STONE

ROLLING STONE

15p

GOD IS ANGRY WITH THE WICKED EVERY D

PSALM 7-11

NOW SLY TELLS HIS SIDE OF THE STORY, SORT OF

BY TIMOTHY CROUSE

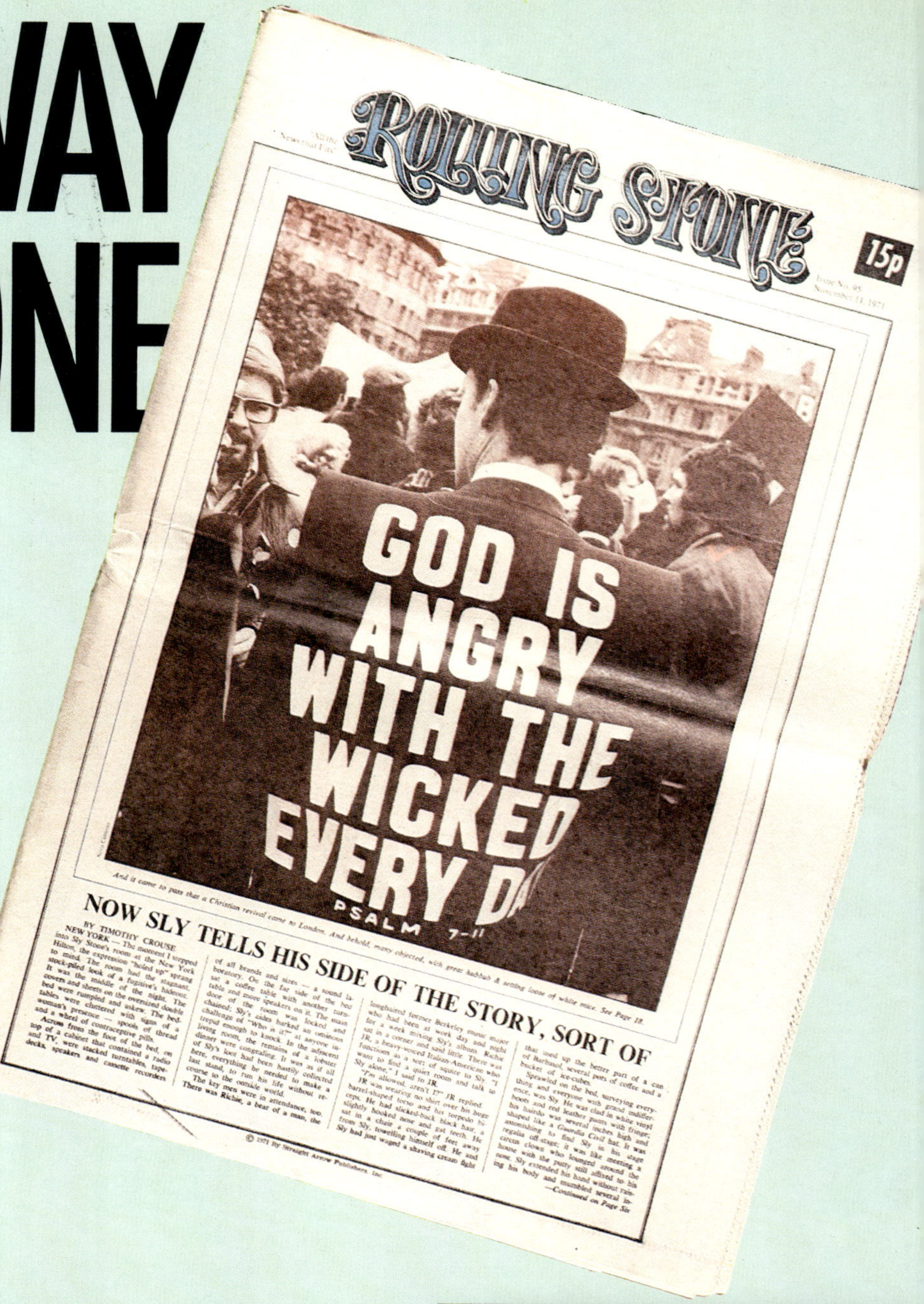

The magazine that opened a new era in rock writing

In 1968 STREET VENDORS were arrested for selling copies of an underground magazine called *Rolling Stone*, which featured a nude picture of John and Yoko on the cover. By 1970, the street-wise journal that spoke the language of the counter-culture was nominated the Columbia Graduate School of Journalism's Magazine Of The Year.

Rolling Stone magazine grew out of a friendship between Jann Wenner and Ralph J. Gleason, who had contributed a jazz/pop column to the *San Francisco Chronicle* since the early Fifties, and also wrote for a radical magazine called *Ramparts*. Gleason encouraged Wenner, then a student at the University of California, to write for its underground offshoot, *Sunday Ramparts*. When that folded, Wenner discussed his plans for his own underground paper with Gleason.

The outcome was *Rolling Stone*, with Wenner as its editor and publisher. His initial efforts were aided by his wife Jane, while Gleason continued to provide encouragement, finance (the remainder was coaxed from Wenner's family and friends) and much practical advice. He suggested that the only feasible way of launching such a paper was to persuade the printers to give it office space; many of *Rolling Stone*'s early editions were put to bed while the presses roared deafeningly below.

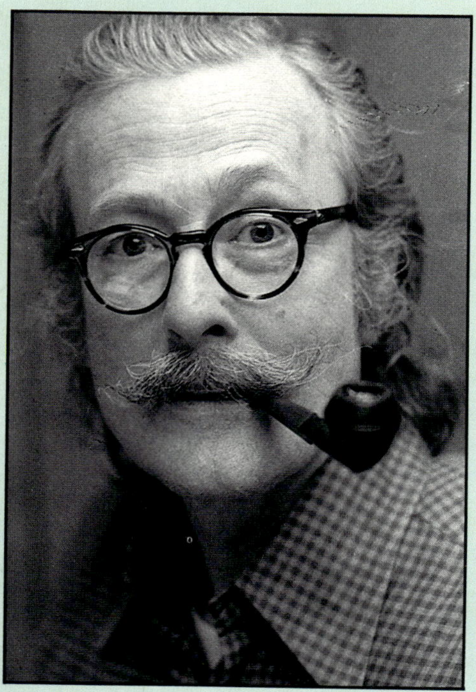

A letter from home

Rolling Stone Number 1 was published on 9 November 1967 in San Francisco, where the underground movement was in full swing. The magazine's two-fold aim reflected this background: to consider rock 'n'roll as an enduring and not an ephemeral music, and to report on the subculture in which it was created.

Being a part of the underground, *Rolling Stone* refused to be shackled by the conventions of professional journalism. Sometimes deadlines were met, and sometimes they weren't. Nevertheless, while similar

Ralph J. Gleason (left), Jann Wenner (right) and the paper they founded (above).

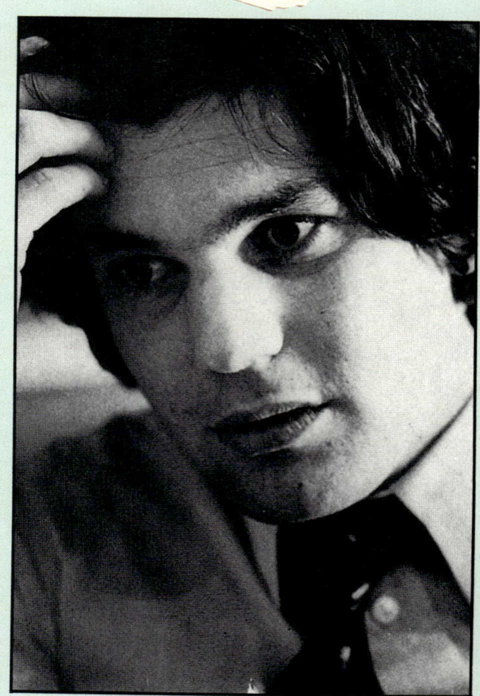

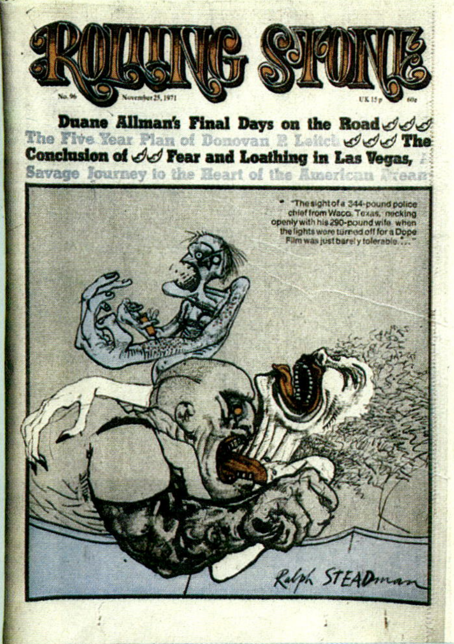

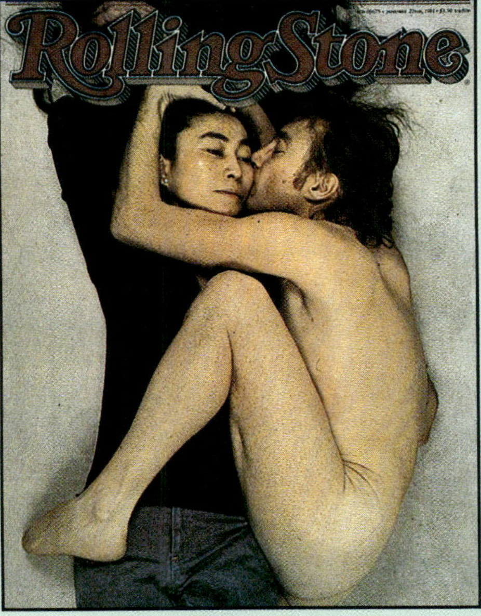

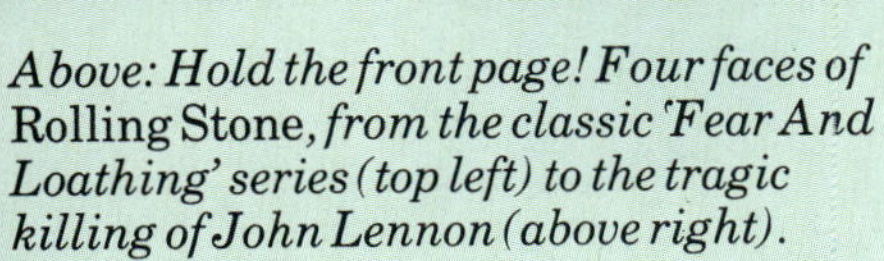

Above: Hold the front page! Four faces of Rolling Stone, *from the classic 'Fear And Loathing' series (top left) to the tragic killing of John Lennon (above right).*

periodicals were undone by a lack of application and a surfeit of drugs, *Rolling Stone*, under Wenner's helmsmanship, struck a balance between alternative lifestyles and publishing practicalities. The paper did espouse the ethics of the underground; but it was also expertly designed, intelligently written and immaculately produced.

Rolling Stone had a ready-made audience. It was, in Gleason's phrase, like a letter from home. Thousands of rock fans across America suddenly discovered that there were others who appreciated the same things they did. No comparable publication existed in the US. *Billboard, Cashbox* and *Record World* were all trade papers, and nothing else pitched between them and the fan magazines. *Rolling Stone* thus survived and prospered simply because there were so many who wanted to read it. The key to its success was its assumption that the views and lifestyles of rock musicians were as interesting as those of politicians or businessmen.

All this came at a time when the music was changing, and rock musicians were taking themselves more seriously. Although the magazine did write appreciatively about such black music stars as Aretha Franklin and Sam and Dave, who regarded themselves primarily as entertainers, it is nevertheless true that its intellectual approach to rock'n'roll often encouraged a self-conscious artistry in performers of very limited abilities. Dr Hook and the Medicine Show satirised the magazine's pre-eminence in 'The Cover Of *Rolling Stone*'.

Beyond that, *Rolling Stone* succeeded simply because there had previously been virtually no informed coverage of rock music. Two aspects of this coverage were of particular significance. The first were the record reviews, which were thorough, literate and (usually) serious. The other was the *Rolling Stone* interview. Rock music celebrities were questioned at length about all aspects of their career, as well as their overall philosophy and aesthetic values. The interviews appeared in question-and-answer form – a device that newspapers had traditionally reserved only for the most erudite subjects.

The apogee of this approach came with the John Lennon interviews, conducted by Wenner himself in New York in December 1970. Lennon took the opportunity to demolish a number of popular myths surrounding the Beatles. The interviews, which appeared in *Rolling Stone* Numbers 74 and 75, were duly turned into a book, *Lennon Remembers*. Annie Leibovitz took the pictures, and she never looked back.

Rolling Stone made headlines itself across the US in October 1975 with its Patty Hearst revelations. Meanwhile its assiduous reporters had proved of incomparable benefit to Lennon in his battle with the US Immigration authorities; likewise, the magazine remained commendably persistent in its pursuit of the case of Karen Silkwood, the nuclear worker who died in suspicious circumstances in 1974 after secretly investigating irregularities in industry.

Stone rolls east

In 1977 *Rolling Stone* moved to New York. There were fears that such an upheaval would jeopardise the magazine's unique character. While such fears have not proved justified, the magazine has long since achieved journalistic respectability, and with sales of over 800,000 has ceased to be an 'alternative' newspaper.

One of *Rolling Stone*'s abiding strengths has been its consistently impressive design, which was totally revised in January 1981. This last change was accompanied by an editorial shake-up. The music section was put into the back half of the paper, with the longer articles, interviews and political commentary occupying the front half. *Rolling Stone* thus continued its drift away from music; film stars have since been awarded cover stories more regularly than rock performers.

Critics chided *Rolling Stone* for deserting the music; it could equally be argued that the music deserted *Rolling Stone*. Although the magazine has played its part in helping to establish new acts like the Clash and Elvis Costello in the US charts, it was all too obvious that American rock lost much of its excitement in the late Seventies and after.

Rolling Stone, though, will always be criticised – precisely because it is in many ways a peerless publication. Ralph Gleason, who died in 1975 but is still affectionately remembered on the staff-list, told Wenner at the outset that the magazine could become established if someone devoted a year of his life to it. Wenner has since devoted many years of his life to it, and it is impossible to conceive of the magazine without him.

BOB WOFFINDEN

HIGH TIMES

How important have drugs been in rock?

BY THE TIME the Beatles ushered in a new musical era with their first recordings in 1962, music and drugs had long had a special relationship. Jazz musicians had habitually smoked cannabis for half a century and many also took heroin, in some cases with tragic results. The reasons for this connection lay partly in the social circumstances of the jazz musicians, and partly in the fact that drugs have been used for inspirational purposes since the dawn of history. In the 1790s, Samuel Taylor Coleridge's visions induced by laudanum, a solution of opium in alcohol then commonly available as a proprietary medicine, stimulated his famous mystical poem 'Kubla Khan'.

The many attempts to classify types of drug according to their effects, however, have come to grief on the fact that people will use almost any drug to achieve almost any effect. Opium and its derivatives, morphine and heroin, traditionally regarded as painkillers open to abuse as a destructive escape from everyday problems, can be used to induce visions. Cannabis can be used as anything from a sedative to a hallucinogen, depending on how, why and by whom it is ingested. LSD, much-praised by hippies and mystics as a gateway to other forms of consciousness, is often used as a stimulant, or again as a form of escape . . . the functions seem endlessly interchangeable.

Reefer madness

In spite, or perhaps because, of this interchangeability of their functions, different drugs have been popular at different periods in the history of rock and have become associated with different lifestyles, philosophies and types of music. During the Fifties, the most modish incarnation of jazz bohemianism, the Beats, did much to popularise the use of an essentially harmless recreational herb which they called 'pot', 'tea', 'reefer' and fifty other euphemistic things. It tended to make people relaxed, receptive and increased one's empathy for the nuances of music like nobody's business. This mild but captivating plant, *cannabis sativa,* came in two main forms, the dried leaves and flowering tops (grass) and a sticky or powdery resin (hashish). It had been used as an intoxicant since time immemorial, particularly in the Middle East where alcohol was forbidden by Islamic law, but in this century it had also been used by many American blacks.

This latter use had been an important factor behind the prohibition of the drug in the US in 1937; anti-cannabis laws were a convenient instrument for the harassment of black people. It was feared that consumption of the drug might lead to increased contact between young blacks and whites, as was indeed happening in the jazz clubs. An absurd smear campaign was orchestrated, largely by Harry Anslinger of the Federal Bureau of Narcotics, with the aid of a press eager for lurid scare stories. A series of propaganda films such as *Reefer Madness* depicted upstanding youths turning into crazed zombies after one puff on a 'reefer'; these movies are still enjoyed today for their unintentional humour.

The anti-cannabis laws were forced through both in Britain and the US in spite of the fact that virtually every government-commissioned enquiry, like the US La Guardia Report of 1939, found that the drug was not intrinsically addictive and did not produce negative personality changes. The Wootton Report, commissioned in the UK in 1967 by then-Home Secretary Roy Jenkins, concluded that cannabis is 'very much less dangerous than the opiates, barbiturates, amphetamines, and also less dangerous than alcohol . . . it is the personality of the user, rather than the properties of the drug, that is likely to cause a progression to other drugs.' Jenkins' successor, James Callaghan, ignored the report's findings on its publication in 1969 on the grounds that the committee had been 'got at' by the cannabis lobby.

As pop music turned into rock and alternative lifestyles flourished in the mid Sixties, more and more young white people in all walks of life took to using cannabis. And although its use among musicians seems to have declined slightly with the changes in musical fashion, it is still true that where you find any form of rock music you will almost certainly find cannabis. In a sense one can argue that the Beatles, by turning on, perverted pop and invented rock as we know it.

By the time a serious interest in drugs had entered the Moptops' muse – around the time of *Help!* – another drug, with a unique power to alter perception, had entered the arena: LSD-25, or 'acid', a chemical originally synthesised during the war years by a Swiss chemist, Dr Albert Hofman. His account of the effects the drug had on him – 'vertigo, visual disturbances – the faces around me appeared as grotesque, coloured masks . . . occasionally I felt as if I were out of my body' – remains a classic description of the kind of state induced by LSD.

Since LSD was not made illegal by Congress until 6 October 1966, it was perfectly OK for the Haight Ashbury hippies to dump vast quantities of the drug into dustbinfuls of soft drink and distribute it at the legendary 'Acid Tests, at which the Grateful Dead improvised and unearthly light shows pulsed. The visions the drug induced, whether heavenly, bizarre or downright hellish, were held to be revelatory. Not surprisingly, the perky, chirruping pop of the Merseybeat years emerged from this gleeful, dayglo decadence as a distant, alien mutation in which hypnotic modal patterns, feedback and random noise replaced neat verses, choruses and bridges; the Grateful Dead's own double album *Live Dead* is a fine example of 'acid rock'.

This tradition of radical experimentation became an integral part of the social upheavals of the Sixties; in songs like 'Mexico', Jefferson Airplane sang of drugs as an overtly revolutionary force. But, as the musicians became more successful and affluent, both rock music and the drug scene shifted away from psychedelics and confrontational politics. Imperceptibly, the saccharine offerings of bands like Crosby Stills and Nash opened the floodgates to a Seventies cloud-cuckooland of close-harmony emotional placebos, handbuilt in Los Angeles by craftsmen whose preferred drug was a powdery white pharmaceutical called cocaine.

Known to its aficionados as 'the champagne of drugs', cocaine has much in common with that drink in that it costs the earth and does little to justify the investment. Indeed, its aura of exclusivity seems to be its main attraction, and far more people have suffered cocaine abuse through being fed homogenised, 'progressive' pap during the Seventies than have ever taken the drug itself – one of its long-term effects, incidentally, being chronic paranoia.

Uppers and downers

Amphetamines and barbiturates – uppers and downers – have been prescribed by doctors since the Thirties to restore lost energy or ensure a good night's sleep respectively. Although their widespread abuse has led to a more responsible attitude towards their prescription among the medical profession, for a long time they were handed out like sweets, a practice satirised by the Rolling Stones in 'Mother's Little Helper'.

Amphetamines – or 'speed' – have always been popular among musicians whose music and lifestyle was self-consciously fast, loud and energetic: rockabillies in the Fifties, Mods in the Sixties and punks in the Seventies. The drugs were cheap and easily available; what could be more natural for a young Mod who, after a week of dull, unfulfilling work, wanted to cram as much as possible into the weekend, than to take a handful of mum's pick-me-up from the bathroom cabinet? Powdered, diluted and injected into the bloodstream, speed causes intense bouts of euphoria; unfortunately it also destroys your bones, liver and stomach lining, and is extremely addictive.

Barbiturates and other, milder, downers like quaaludes and mandrax have remained popular among oblivion seekers and heavy-metal freaks lost in a Valhalla of plodding rhythms and tortured guitar feedback. Barbiturates, again, can be fatal, especially when taken in conjunction with alcohol, and are particularly nasty when injected.

Left: cannabis sativa, *the Indian hemp plant, in cultivation. Inset left: Cocaine, extracted from the coca plant, on sale in Colombia.*

The ultimate downer is heroin. Ironically, the drug was originally derived from opium in 1898 as a non-addictive substitute for morphine; but by the end of the First World War there were already an alarming number of addicts in major American cities. The Harrison Narcotics Act of 1914 had made it illegal, but – far from stamping out the drug – prohibition only forced up prices and created a flourishing black market. For the simple reason that the drug is physically so addictive – when its effects wear off, the extremely unpleasant withdrawal symptoms last for days and can only be alleviated by a further dose – prohibition merely criminalises addicts without discouraging them. Given this policy, and the fact that the economies of many US-backed right-wing regimes such as Turkey and Taiwan depend on opium production – not to mention the influence of the drug's main importers, the Mafia – it seems unlikely that this epidemic will be stamped out in the near future.

Among the rock musicians who took heroin and lived to tell the tale were John Lennon, whose 'Cold Turkey' is a harrowing description of the drug's after-effects, and Lou Reed, whose 'I'm Waiting For The Man' and 'Heroin' conveyed the despair and desire for oblivion of the addict. The death of Neil Young's close friends Danny Whitten and Bruce Berry inspired him to unleash the horrifying *Tonight's The Night* album. In contrast, Eric Clapton took the detox cure, stayed clean and never produced a truly emotional noise again.

One for the road

There's one more drug, and a particularly nasty one at that; it is highly addictive, unlike cannabis or LSD, the tissue it poisons can never regenerate, and its abuse commonly results in destructive and antisocial behaviour. It's available almost everywhere and to almost everyone, and is called alcohol. But, apart from being cited as causing the deaths of Pigpen of the Grateful Dead and Bon Scott of AC/DC, this noxious stuff has never had a heyday in the history of rock culture; it has existed, rather, as a kind of low undercurrent, and was debatably only a catalyst in English 'pub-rock' of the mid Seventies.

Rock culture has today fragmented into numerous self-sustaining cults, each with its own music, dress, ideology and drugs. Just as cannabis and LSD were part of the hippie ideology, so speed became part of punk, in reaction to what had gone before. Hippies were – or aspired to be – gentle, meditative, mystical, and they smoked a lot of dope to help induce such states. In contrast, punks wanted to be hard, realistic, in touch with the 'real' world of the streets, so they took speed.

Meanwhile, the general, 'straight' public, fed with a diet of *News Of The World* scare stories, remains wary of the Sex'n'Drugs'n'Rock'n'Roll triad and reaches for potentially the most lethal drug of all, the one in the bottle. It's true, of course, that the history of rock is littered with the corpses of great and obscure musicians; but often the causes lay in their psychology or circumstances as much as in the drugs they took. Janis Joplin died because she took anything, anytime, indiscriminately. Sid Vicious died because he was a masochist with a deathwish as much as because he was a junkie. While rock deaths make headlines, nobody ever splashes the awful truth about the death rate among alcoholic commercial travellers over the front page of the *Sun*. Rock has always bellowed for freedom from the constraints of 'correct' social behaviour, and freedom means the power to choose – seeing drugs for what they are, and not treating them as the answer to all problems or an undifferentiated threat to youth.

JOHN DENNIS

Below: Smoking cannabis was an intrinsic part of the hippie lifestyle.

'Let me take you higher,' sang Sly and the Family Stone (below). Sure enough, the assembled 500,000 at Woodstock got higher, even if they had to climb the scaffolding (inset right). Some chose to disport themselves au naturel *(inset left).*

Peace, love and a movie moneyspinner

THE CELEBRATION that took place on Max Yasgur's farm near Bethel in upstate New York over the weekend of August 15, 16 and 17 1969 represented the spirit of the decade probably better than any other single event in the Sixties. On closer examination, 'Woodstock Nation' proves to be as ephemeral and insubstantial as one would expect from a weekend gathering of hippies, even if it briefly transformed the sleepy hamlet of Bethel into the third largest city in New York State. But as a symbol of the contradictory and confused hopes the burgeoning counter-culture brought forth from the underground ghettoes of San Francisco and London, Woodstock reigns supreme.

Unlimited capital

The festival, its gates long since trampled down and any attempt to charge admission given up, began at 5.00 on the Friday afternoon when Richie Havens ambled to the stage to perform for the 200,000 strong crowd. It came to life an hour later when Country Joe McDonald chanted his alternative version of the 'Fish Cheer' – 'Give me an "F", give me a "U", give me a "C", give me a "K"! What's that spell?...'. It ended at 9.30 am on the following Monday when Jimi Hendrix played 'Purple Haze' to the 30,000 who stayed on until the very last. In between, the attendance briefly touched the half-million mark and, in conditions that veered from balmy sunshine to torrential rain, the festival-goers survived the failure of essential sanitary services and the lack of food (both a regular feature of festivals) and still maintained an atmosphere that for the most part was indeed characterised by 'peace and love'.

The festival – or the 'Woodstock Music and Arts Fair: an Aquarian Exposition', to give it its full title – grew directly out of a meeting on 6 February between John Roberts, Joel Rosenman, Artie Kornfeld and Michael Lang. Roberts and Rosenman were Ivy League graduates who had turned their backs on law and Wall Street respectively for careers as would-be television writers. They hit on the idea of having a couple of trouble-shooter financiers as the linch-pin of a TV series, but then couldn't think of ideas for their fictional duo to explore. To find odd projects they placed an ad in the *Wall Street Journal* with the intention of borrowing the ideas presented to them and no more: 'Young Men with Unlimited Capital looking for interesting, legitimate, investment opportunities and business propositions.'

Most of the ideas they received were ridiculous, but a few were intriguing

Above: Director Mike Wadleigh won the 1970 Oscar for Best Feature Length Documentary for his film Woodstock. *Below: Joe Cocker gave a characteristically sweaty performance. Above right: David Crosby (left) and Graham Nash later sang the theme song for Wadleigh's film with CSN&Y.*

enough to make them quit their prospective careers as TV writers to try out the role of financiers; in this they were greatly aided by Roberts' family fortune which meant that they really could invest in unusual projects. One of the first such ventures they attempted was Media Sounds, a new recording studio complex in New York. It was an immediate success and brought Challenge International to the attention of Lang and Kornfeld, who were promoting a studio complex in the Woodstock area. Lang, who would quickly become the guiding force of the festival, was a street hustler who had made it to the fringes of the music business when he had persuaded Kornfeld, Capitol's head of East Coast A&R, to sign Train, a band that Lang managed.

Festive fun

Lang and Kornfeld's first meeting with Rosenman and Roberts was unfruitful, but at the next one Lang suggested an open-air concert to publicise the studio, mindful of the stars like Bob Dylan and the Band who lived in the vicinity. And so was born the Woodstock Festival – out of the desire of Lang and Kornfeld to make their mark in the rock business and of Rosenman and Roberts to put on the largest festival ever.

Lang would always remain the prime mover, the man whose energy and boundless enthusiasm for the project in the early months kept it alive. But if Lang was the moving force, as the festival lurched closer and closer to actuality it seemed as if it was being willed into being by the people it was put on for. As Roberts' resources were stretched to the limit and the original half-million dollar budget was exceeded (any prospect of a profit disappearing with it), only the immensity of the project kept it alive.

What everyone thought was going to be the hardest problem, getting performers, was easily overcome in a manner that suggested how each subsequent problem could be solved – overpayment. Creedence Clearwater Revival were the first to sign up on 10 April when they agreed to play for the (then) grossly inflated sum of 10,000 dollars. With a major band on the books and big money in the offing, an impressive roster was quickly assembled; the week beginning 21 April alone saw the signing of Canned Heat (13,000 dollars), Johnny Winter (7,500 dollars) and Janis Joplin (15,000 dollars). Dealing with the underground politicos wasn't quite as easy. Eventually, at a meeting of students and radicals, it was voted that the festival be a weekend of fun rather than a political event, much to the relief of Roberts and Rosenman – but not before Abbie Hoffman, leader of the extreme-left Yippies organisation, had demanded and obtained 10,000 dollars (in small bills, of course) after threatening to denounce the festival as a 'capitalist rip-off'. The organisers paid up because their investment was so great and their fear of losing 'street credibility' – and thus an audience – was equally great.

Down Dope Alley

However, the major problem was obtaining a suitably large site. That seemed solved when Howard Mills agreed to lease land and the town council of Wallkill agreed to host the festival after being misled by Lang as to its size and character. But as the preparations got underway and the inhabitants of Wallkill began to realise the true nature of the plans, a rising tide of animosity against hippies finally resulted in a new town ordinance that made it impossible to hold the festival there. With 31 days to go, the gates of Wallkill had been padlocked against peace and love. (Woodstock had its revenge on Mills and Jack Schloser, Wallkill's town supervisor who had led the anti-festival fight: Arnold Skolnick's poster to publicise the change of venue featured two stereotype hillbilly characters who bore an uncanny resemblance to Mills and Schloser.)

The festival was rescued by Max Yasgur, who a week later, over several gallons of chocolate milk (his favourite tipple), negotiated himself a tidy sum for the use of his farm and a place in rock history. The festival had a new home and, with the assistance of some two hundred assorted hippies, the real preparations began in earnest. By now the profit motive had fallen by the wayside of Happy Avenue (the aptly-named road that led to the festival). Thus, on the advice of Wes Pomeroy – a policeman in charge of security, who was keen to try passive policing with smiles replacing guns – the planned fence along the festival perimeter was not erected; in its place was a string of youngsters asking people to pay to get in. Similarly, although hamburgers and such were available from the ill-named Food For Love (the company that won the food concession), an alternative company – the Hog Farmers – were also flown in to produce more appropriate counter-cultural fare. The result, as one New York dietician put it, was 'enough macrobiotic food to wipe out the entire US Olympic team'.

Now unstoppable, the festival took on a life of its own as its dimensions began to be appreciated by the likes of the telephone company, sanitary engineers and the Highway Patrol, who had previously turned a deaf ear to appeals for help. One by one the remaining wrinkles were ironed out, with money – as ever – smoothing the way. All that remained was for the audience to trek to Bethel and the performers to be flown in by helicopter. A few problems would occur: the burning of the Food For Love stands, a near-electrical failure, the demand of the Who (and, uncharacteristically, the Grateful Dead) for cash in hand before they would play, and three deaths among the audience. But despite the fears of those who importuned Governor Rockefeller to declare the festival a disaster area, it was Max Yasgur who was proved right. On stage he enthusiastically delivered his verdict on the weekend's events: 'This is the largest group of people ever to have assembled in one place . . . I think you people have proven something to the world – that a half a million kids can get together and have fun and music and nothing but fun and music. And I God bless you for it!'

Standing by Dope Alley (where the dealers congregated) and listening to the big numbers being discussed, the hordes must have found Yasgur's comments naive; by the free stage where the likes of Joan Baez had been regular performers, his remarks seemed commonplace. But then, as the film *Woodstock* demonstrates, Woodstock was all things to all comers, a glorious bash on the world's village green and hippiedom's greatest hour. PHIL HARDY

Woodstock: The Performers

Joan Baez
The Band
Blood, Sweat and Tears
The Butterfield Blues Band
Canned Heat
Joe Cocker
Country Joe and the Fish
Creedence Clearwater Revival
Crosby, Stills and Nash
The Grateful Dead
Arlo Guthrie
Tim Hardin
The Keef Hartley Band
Richie Havens
Jimi Hendrix
The Incredible String Band
Jefferson Airplane
Janis Joplin
The Joshua Light Show
Melanie
Quill
Santana
John Sebastian
Sha Na Na
Ravi Shankar
Sly and the Family Stone
Bert Sommer
Sweetwater
Ten Years After
The Who

GROUPIES

Cream cheese and warm vibes with bitter aftertaste

STAR PERFORMERS in all fields have long been the object of their audience's sexual fantasies; and male performers, as the embodiment of power and success, have proved particularly attractive to women in an age when it often seemed that the only way they could identify with these attributes was sexually. It's not a new phenomenon; Beethoven and Liszt had their groupies, aristocratic ladies who saw in their artistic 'temperaments' a rebel machismo that flaunted the polite constraints of nineteenth-century society. The same is true of influential and charismatic politicians; Oswald Mosley, even when he was a member of the Labour Party, enjoyed the sexual favours of London society hostesses, while Hitler was pursued by besotted fans like Unity Mitford. Power, as Henry Kissinger has said, is a great aphrodisiac.

Leaders of the pack

The fact that the entanglement of sex with power and success became so prevalent – and so public – in the rock music industry in the Sixties resulted from a number of coinciding circumstances. Never before had artists been offered so much power, prestige and adulation, and never before had they been so predominantly young and groomed for their looks. Paradoxically, many were powerless in the hands of their managers and record companies, so that to be offered power over women was a compensation for their own impotence over their destinies. At the same time, the youth movements of the time were fostering ideas of sexual liberation, of freedom from the puritanism of the previous generation; this was an idea all too often interpreted as a crude equation of promiscuity with freedom.

In an intensely competitive society, where status is everything, sex itself becomes a status symbol. At school, both boys

Inset: A scene from the film Groupies. *Stars like Jagger (left) were objects of sexual fascination; those who made it into their beds were envied by their peers.*

and girls boast of (often fictitious) sexual conquests, and some conquests – the captain of the football team, for instance – are worth more than others. As Eric Clapton once said, 'You were at school, you were pimply and no-one wanted to know you. You get into a group and you've got thousands of chicks there.' Schoolgirl sexual competitiveness was immortalised in the songs of the early Sixties, like the Shangri-Las' 'Leader Of The Pack'. 'Is she *really* going out with him?', one of the vocalists asks breathlessly, as the lead singer answers eager questions about the boyfriend's virtues: 'How does he dance?' 'Close . . . real *close*.'

From there, it was only a step to the sexual idolisation of the pop stars whose posters lined the bedroom wall. These boys were emaciated, pale and sullen and Pa thought they looked like girls or fairies with their stringy cascades of hair – not at all like the boys of school with their short hair and their creepy ways. The decibels and curiously sinister electric guitars made rock stars seem beautiful prophets of truth and freedom. And fantasies were fed by the apparent unattainability of the stars.

For most adolescent female pop fans, fantasies went no further than watching their idols, spellbound, from the back row of the Hammersmith Odeon. But some decided to take it further. As one groupie recalled in *Oz* magazine, 'It was evident that there was a pop conspiracy to blow the mind of my generation. I was interested but not involved. I only began to understand the group symbol when I met Simon Dupree and the Big Sound in a TV studio . . . they were all looking at me . . . With a kind of hot innocence, I suddenly realised that groupiedom was possible'.

For most, the road to the stars involved bribing doormen, security guards and roadies with sex. This achieved, they found themselves in a twilight world of intense competition, abuse and brutalisation. The wave of British rock stars who made it in America – the Dave Clark Five, Herman's Hermits, the Stones and, of course, the Beatles – became virtual prisoners in their plush and impersonal gilded suites, trapped in a cage of noise and boredom. Escaping the trap of industrial England with its bus queues and numbing drabness, the popsters found themselves exhibited as in a zoo. Appropriately, they behaved like animals. So what for the rows of figures marching across the accountants' calculators; there was nothing but gigs – no monitors, couldn't hear yourself play – and the endless platitudes, boorish media and hotel room after hotel room: 'We had to do something,' John Lennon recalled, 'and what do you do when the pill doesn't wear off? If we couldn't get groupies we would have whores and everything, whatever was going.'

Mick Jagger once said, 'There's no reason to have women on a tour unless they've got a job to do. The only other reason is to screw. Otherwise they get bored. They just sit around and moan.' Bands treated groupies as a mere convenience – Jimi Hendrix, who wasn't averse to beating them up when they didn't show the required degree of servility, called them 'band aids' – and, because of fear of venereal disease and because they were really there to act as a symbol of the musician's power, they were almost invariably required to perform oral sex; an unreleased documentary by Robert Frank about the 1972 Rolling Stones tour of America was titled *Cocksucker Blues*. Jimmy Page expressed the stars' callous attitude towards groupies succinctly when he said, 'If you humiliate them a bit they tend to come on alright after that.'

Below: Frank Zappa was a well-known observer and patron of the groupie subculture. 'Sociologically, it's really heavy', he said.

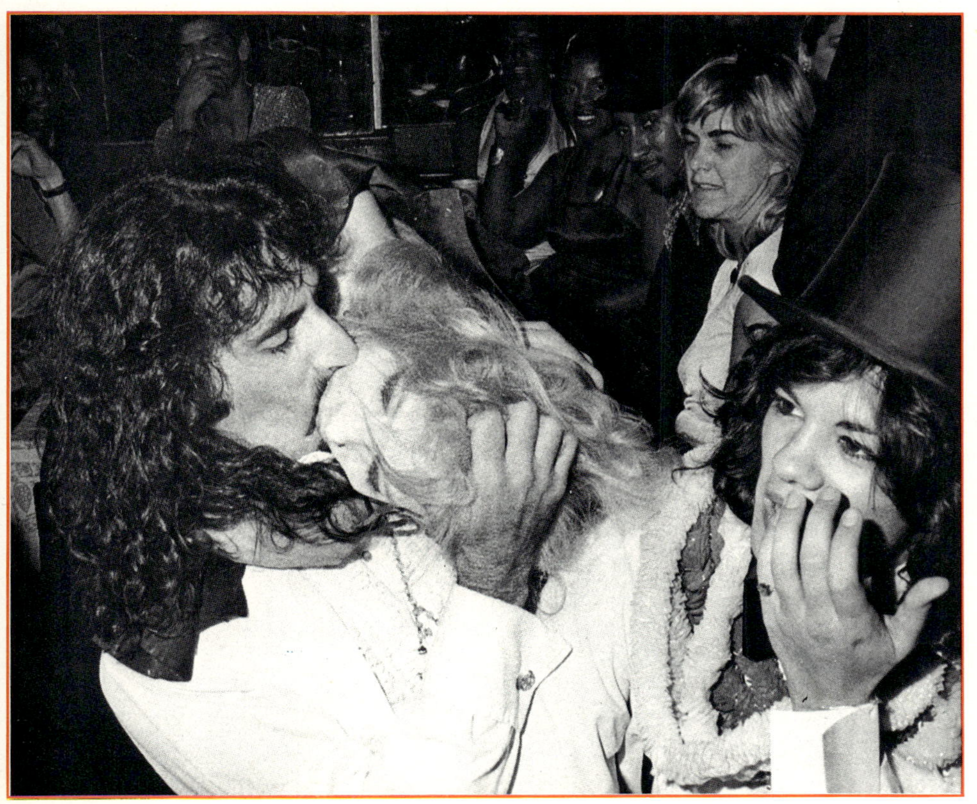

The new hierarchy

Pretty soon these squalid little encounters blossomed into a whole dusk-to-dawn society with its own hierarchy, philosophy and language in which, for example, the sexual act became, in groupie argot, 'making piggies'. As one groupie acutely observed, 'All this anti-establishment has led to an establishment of its own'. Being a groupie was a full-time job, and a look and a lifestyle had evolved by 1970. The look was assembled of very long hair and a gypsy wardrobe made up of layers of silk, velvet, muslin, cotton, paisley, leather and lace, assorted bangles and a pint or two of patchouli oil.

The wardrobe of clothes was expressly designed to establish a groupie's place in the pecking order and her position as a feminine, submissive accessory to the rock-star lifestyle. While their peer group regarded their groupie sisters as intensely liberated, groupies actually dressed the part of slaves. And the pecking order was fierce; at the top were 'supergroupies' like Devon, a frequent companion of Jimi Hendrix, who overdosed two years after his death and whose attentions were prized by other rock stars. Another such 'supergroupie', Suzy Creamcheese, was immortalised in song by Frank Zappa. At the bottom, groupies were openly despised by the groups who exploited them. Bobby Colomby, the drummer in Blood Sweat And Tears, once said: 'We're the ugliest band ever born. We have the funniest groupies in the world – real bottom-of-the-barrel stuff.'

The Earth Records album *The Groupies*, compiled by Alan Lorber from hours of tapes of four groupies comparing notes, provides a document of the groupie world-view. Stars were simultaneously adored and condemned as misogynists, relentlessly pursued and regarded as inconveniences: 'These guys are making so much bread it doesn't matter *what* they do . . . They really drag you through the mud, you end up a whore . . . Music is all my life and that means all the cute boys . . . They're just dying to give money to girls for nothing, they just want a pretty girl to be their friend . . . They bullshit all night, you know what's coming . . . I couldn't go with anyone that wasn't a musician . . . I got better things to do than be with them . . .'

For a period of time in the late Sixties, the phenomenon of groupiedom was dignified with all kinds of liberationist rhetoric. The 'sexual revolution' of the hippies, which all too often entailed men telling women that they were frigid and unliberated if they didn't go to bed with them, provided an ideal cloak for this kind of activity. 'Groupies are beautiful,' Country Joe McDonald, self-professed supporter of women's liberation, once said: 'They come to hear you play, they throw flowers and underpants, they give you kisses and love, they come to bed with you.'

The Plaster Casters of Chicago, who made casts of pop stars' penises, felt that what they were doing was of profound sociological importance. 'I think every girl should be a plaster caster,' Cynthia Plaster Caster once said. 'Try it at least once. It's going to be a significant element in the revolution.' Frank Zappa agreed with her: 'I appreciate what they're doing, both artistically and sociologically. Sociologically it's really heavy.' Underneath the vacuity of Zappa and the sentimentality of McDonald lay a reality of exploitation unintentionally hinted at by Eric Clapton: 'As a rule, they're incredibly warm people. If making love to you was going to make you happy, they'd make love. If you were tired and didn't want to make it, they'd cook you a meal and make you feel at home. They were really ports of call.'

As the idealism of the Sixties faded, such romanticisation gave way to the harsh realism of the Stones tours and *Cocksucker Blues*. And if groupies have become less common, especially after the advent of the essentially asexual punk movement and with the increase in the number of women musicians, the phenomenon has never faded away. In a society which creates stars and lavishes adulation on them, and in which women are seen as sexually submissive, groupies will remain a feature of the rock industry. The Sex Pistols were pursued by them on their American tours; the bisexual Sid Vicious, desperate to prove himself, once pushed his way past the security guards holding them at bay, screaming 'I don't want to fuck them all, I just want to fuck one of them.' He eventually lived with a groupie, Nancy Spungen, in New York's Chelsea Hotel, stabbing her to death a couple of months before he himself OD'd on heroin. And in the early Eighties, New Romantics Spandau Ballet were proving themselves part of the rock hierarchy they had claimed to despise by boasting of their conquests in the toilets on a tour of Italy.

But, although groupies are still around, and although male performers continue to exploit them, this particularly nasty form of sexual slavery does seem to be on the wane. There are more mixed-sex bands, for a start, which tends to inhibit the worst excesses of the 'boys on the road' behaviour so common in the Sixties and Seventies. The increasing number of women performers has shown that a woman doesn't have to sleep with a musician to be a part of the music scene; she can be a musician herself.

JOHN DENNIS

Top right: Sid Vicious with his groupie girlfriend Nancy Spungen. Right: The career of Deborah Harry marks a turning point. A former groupie, she has become a star in her own right.

THE DREAM GOES SOUR

The Beatles' split amidst rancorous financial wrangling; the untimely deaths of Jimi Hendrix and Janis Joplin; violence and murder at the Altamont Festival. These events seemed to pull the music business out of a dream-like state, to be superseded by a concern with bleaker themes as predicted in the musical obsessions of the Velvet Underground and the sparse, dark lyricism of Leonard Cohen

All Things Must Pass

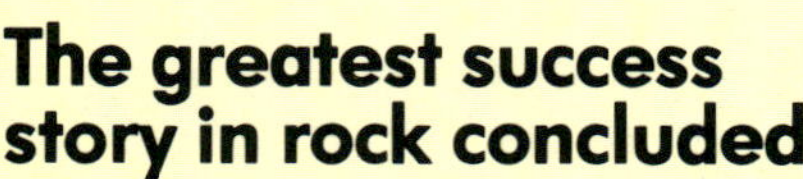

The greatest success story in rock concluded

As 'The Beatles Christmas Show', a three-week stint at London's Hammersmith Odeon, ushered in 1965, the astounding success of the previous two years showed no outward signs of abating. London was now 'Swinging London', the London of David Bailey and Jean Shrimpton, of Mary Quant and Carnaby Street. The worlds of art, photography and fashion had come into contact with the world of pop, and were flourishing. What was more, British pop – for so long the poor relation of its American cousin – now found the situation reversed. In the wake of the Beatles, almost any act sporting guitars, nice smiles and English accents were welcomed with open arms and wallets across the Atlantic.

Despite all killjoy predictions that the phenomenon couldn't last, and despite a string of young pretenders to their crown, the Beatles still ruled. Their work-rate never flagged as they went from concert tour to recording studio to film set with scarcely a break in-between. Incredibly, in view of this cruel schedule, their music was still growing . . . each single a step forward from the last, each album exploring new directions for others to follow. And, although the media insanity of Beatlemania had inevitably assumed a slightly less frenetic pitch, the Fab Four were still the prime objects of public curiosity.

A kind of loving

Filming of *Help!*, the second Beatles movie, was constantly hindered by fans and onlookers, whether in the Bahamas, the Austrian Alps or on Salisbury Plain. Tours, like the nine-date run round France, Italy and Spain at the end of June, were a predictable routine of huge crowds – the largest, 32,000, in Milan – and oppres-

sive hysteria. For the public, the obligatory Beatles image of four fun-loving lads without a care in the world, who actually enjoyed all the madness, was maintained. The truth was actually less palatable. The Beatles were no longer enjoying being Beatles. 'The bigger we got, the more unreality we had to face, the more we were expected to do,' John recalled years later. 'It was always the police chief's daughter or the Lord Mayor's daughter, all the most obnoxious kids – because they had the most obnoxious parents – that we were forced to see all the time. We had these people thrust upon us.'

The pressures had their rewards, of course. Although the deals made by the inexperienced Brian Epstein meant that they only saw a fraction of the money generated by their records and the huge array of merchandising spin-offs, that fraction still allowed them to live in the manner of which they had dreamed with flashy cars, bungalows for their parents and expensive residences in upmarket areas for themselves. Appreciation of their efforts had also been expressed in another way. On 12 June 1965 it was announced that the Beatles were each to be honoured with the award of the MBE. This caused a mild flurry of controversy and the return of medals by some outraged members of the order, but generally reflected the place held by the Beatles in the heart of the nation.

This place was further cemented during the summer months by the release of *Help!*, the film, which saw them hailed as modern Marx Brothers, and *Help!*, the album, which maintained their tradition of filling LPs with great songs when most

Far left: The four Beatles show off their walrus moustaches. Below left: At San Francisco's Cow Palace in September 1965, a frenzied fan is bundled from the stage. Left: Same tour – different gig. Below: Backstage with the Beatles and manager Brian Epstein (left).

Below left: Ringo on the set of Candy *and (bottom) with son Zak and wife Maureen. Their marriage ended in divorce, as did that of John and Cynthia Lennon (far left) and George and Pattie Harrison (below right). Paul McCartney's relationship with fiancée Jane Asher (left) also went awry.*

groups were still padding out a couple of hit singles with mediocre cover versions. And 'Help!', the single, released in July, gave the group their eighth consecutive UK Number 1 (and their ninth US chart-topper).

On 13 August, the Beatles set off on their third American tour. By recent standards, and indeed by their own standards, it was quite a short tour – just 16 concerts in 10 cities. But it included the historic Shea Stadium concerts, where the Beatles played to record audiences of 56,000, the Hollywood Bowl appearance that made up the majority of the Beatles' only official live album, and another coast-to-coast TV appearance on the 'Ed Sullivan Show'. In two weeks, over 300,000 people saw them in person, millions more on TV and at the cinema.

Away from the relentless public gaze, however, once again things seem to have been rather different. By this stage, all four Beatles were tiring rapidly of their Jekyll-and-Hyde existence and the frantic pace they were having to maintain. Privately, they intended to give films and records priority over live work. Indeed, throughout the second half of 1965 plans, which finally came to nothing, were being made for a third Beatles film, based on the novel *A Kind Of Loving*. And the next album, *Rubber Soul*, was the result of several weeks in the studio – much longer than had been spent on any of its predecessors.

Their personal lives were also beginning to take increasingly divergent paths, as the time they had to themselves between group commitments began to lengthen. The four boys who had shared – and had now achieved – the single goal of being rich and famous, were now four very different individuals with different ambitions.

Cleave and the Klan

None of this was obvious to the public at the time, however. *Rubber Soul* came out as the by-now-traditional Christmas album, coinciding with the by-now-traditional pre-Christmas tour of Britain, and it seemed like business as usual. Admittedly the early months of 1966 had been very quiet while the group worked on *Revolver*, with the TV premiere of 'The Beatles At Shea Stadium' the only notable event, but the summer months were as hectic as ever. First the group did a two-week sprint round Germany and the Far East before *Revolver* came out, then they played a three-week, 14-city tour of the States. By the end of the summer, they were confirmed as the most popular, most creative group ever – and finished as a live act.

During the tour of the Far East, the Beatles had had a particularly unpleasant stop-off in the Philippines when they fell foul of local officialdom – the President's wife claimed that they had snubbed an invitation to the palace in Manila and officers of the law kicked and jostled the group members for this supposed act of discourtesy. The American tour, too, had been overshadowed by the threat of violence when citizens in the South's Bible Belt began burning Beatles records as well as effigies of the four stars. Their anger had been caused by a remark of John Lennon's when he told London journalist Maureen Cleave in an *Evening Standard* interview that the Beatles 'were now more popular than Christ'. The pious communities of the Southern States – including members of the Ku Klux Klan – had been incensed and Brian Epstein had considered pulling out of several concerts in the South: 'I didn't want any chance of the boys being harmed,' he said. But cancelling performances would have angered fans and possibly prompted *them* to violence, so the appearances had gone ahead after a somewhat half-hearted retraction from Lennon.

With their music maturing and the novelty of mass adulation long worn off, the dubious pleasure of going out to play 30-minute sets, rendered inaudible by screams, was simply not worth the pressures and indignities involved. For a while, it seemed the Beatles might disintegrate completely as the various members began to pursue individual projects. John Lennon went off to Germany and Spain, playing the part of Private Gripweed in *How I Won The War*, a film directed by Richard Lester, who had also directed the two Beatles movies. Paul went on an African holiday, composed the soundtrack music for the Boulting brothers' film *The Family Way*, and began producing Peter and Gordon and Cliff Bennett. George disappeared to India for two months, studying the sitar with Ravi Shankar and pursuing his interest in Indian mysticism, while Ringo became the perfect family man with his wife Maureen and baby son, Zak.

Second to one

Not surprisingly, rumours began to circulate about the Beatles' possible future, or lack of it, especially when they failed to release any record, single or album, for the Christmas market. In fact, the Beatles had been back together in the studios since November, and three months' work finally resulted in the release of a double A-sided single, 'Penny Lane'/'Strawberry Fields Forever'.

As if to celebrate their new deal with EMI, which saw them taking a 10-15 per cent royalty in place of the very small change they had been getting, the new record was a masterpiece. As if to mock them, however, fate decreed it should stop short of Number 1 as Engelbert Humperdinck's 'Release Me' refused to yield its chart-topping position.

Originally the two songs were meant to be part of the next Beatles album, which was to have their Liverpool childhood as a theme. When the album came out in June 1967, however, neither song was included and the theme had been altered somewhat. The result was *Sgt Pepper's Lonely Hearts Club Band*.

In retrospect the album did have its weak moments, but the highpoints (most notably 'A Day In The Life') were towering indeed, and the effect of the record's release cannot be overestimated. Its surreal, druggy aura was in perfect keeping with the mood of the times and its breadth of musical and lyrical imagination, its assimilation of influences and its exploitation of increasingly sophisticated studio technology made it a key point in the development of rock music.

On top of the world

Once again, the Beatles were looking down on the rest of the rock world and their position was emphasised by the group's appearance later in June on 'Our World', the first round-the-world satellite TV link-up, when an audience of 400 million in 24 countries saw them recording their new single 'All You Need Is Love'. They were also going through a phase of renewed togetherness, which had its most public manifestation when, at the instigation of George's wife Pattie, they all went to a lecture by the Maharishi Mahesh Yogi at the London Hilton.

The Maharishi – never one to scorn a bit of free publicity – invited them to join his weekend meditation course at Bangor University, but on their second day there, 27 August, Brian Epstein was found dead in his London flat. 'After Brian died, we collapsed,' John was to state later. 'Paul took over and supposedly led us. But what is leading us, when we went round in circles? We broke up then. That was the disintegration.'

The management contract which Epstein's NEMS organisation had with the Beatles was due to expire in the coming October and, since the Beatles' plans for group activities were quite limited, they decided not to replace him. Instead they set up their own business organisation, run by various ex-NEMS and Beatles employees, but with themselves as decision-makers. In view of their financial situation (which was complex then, and soon became quite labyrinthine) and the chaos which was to ensue, it could be argued that they made a mistake.

Their first post-Epstein move, however, was an artistic (rather than a business) misjudgement. 'Magical Mystery Tour', which started out as a song written by Paul for the *Sgt Pepper* album, was expanded into an EP and film. Partly inspired by the travels of Ken Kesey's Merry Pranksters in America, the idea was to load the Beatles, friends, freaks and film crew onto a bus and set off round England, shooting a few pre-planned sequences and whatever else happened along the way.

What happened, however, was far from magical. The bus was hounded from start to finish by the media and the fans, the mood was ill-tempered and the organisation was a shambles. Not surprisingly, the finished product, which was screened – in black and white – by the BBC on Boxing Day 1967 amid much ballyhoo, was a long way short of impressive. The critics loathed it, and even staunch Beatle fans experienced misgivings. The general reaction was so unfavourable, in fact, that plans to show the film in the United States were scrapped.

On the brighter side, the Beatles managed a Christmas single that year, 'Hello Goodbye', which stayed at Number 1 for seven weeks over the festive season, with the double EP from the much-maligned film reaching Number 2. What was more, the new Apple empire was sprouting in all directions during early 1968, fertilised by good intentions and infectious enthusiasm, and the Beatles themselves were apparently finding tranquility and oneness on a three-month course at the Maharishi's ashram in Rishikesh. This togetherness didn't last, however; Ringo came home after just 10 days, complaining of homesickness and stomachache. Paul stayed for nine weeks before getting disenchanted and returning to England; John and George followed shortly afterwards.

Their mutual rejection of the Maharishi could be seen as their last gesture of real group unity. Back home again, rather than bringing them together, Apple tended to emphasise their differences. Ringo was actually involved very little, preferring to concentrate on launching a solo film career via appearances in *Candy* and *The Magic Christian*, and being with his family. Paul was mainly responsible for the 'family entertainment' end of the Apple roster, working with the likes of Mary Hopkin and

Below: The Beatles pause during filming of 'Magical Mystery Tour' to act silly in flower-power regalia. Left: Paul McCartney attempts to purloin camera from his photographer bride Linda. Above right: Yoko Ono nods off as the group mix Let It Be, *their last release.*

the Black Dyke Mills Band, while George indulged his more esoteric bent, producing Jackie Lomax and the Radha Krishna Temple, and making his own albums, *Wonderwall Music* (a film soundtrack LP) and *Electronic Sound*.

Hello... goodbye

John, meanwhile, was by now living with Yoko Ono, whom he had first met at the end of 1966, and was entering a strange world of avant-garde art, totally uncommercial musical experimentation and quasi-political campaigning. At the time, and often since, Yoko was blamed for breaking up the Beatles by influencing John and alienating the others. But, at worst, it seems her arrival in John's life merely accelerated a process of decay that had begun some years previously.

The double LP *The Beatles* (the 'White Album'), recorded over a period of five months during the summer of 1968 and released just in time for the Christmas market, emphasised what had been suspected for some time – that the Lennon-McCartney songwriting partnership existed now in name only. Group morale during recordings for the album was so low that Ringo resigned at one point, only to return a week later. And when they next met in the studio, on 2 January 1969, to start work on their next film and record, things were little better.

The original intention was to rehearse for a performance to be given to a specially-invited audience of about 1500 people and to film both rehearsals and performance. The scheme was devised as a substitute for normal live work and the working title for the project, 'Get Back', was indicative of the desire (largely motivated by Paul) to turn back the clock.

A fitting epitaph

Sadly, the atmosphere at these sessions was tense, to say the least. George actually quit nine days into the enterprise, and though he was persuaded to come back, the idea of the big live show was dropped. Instead, the recordings moved from the huge studios at Twickenham to the more intimate surroundings of the Apple basement, and they were climaxed by the famous rooftop set played to an audience of Apple employees and bemused passers-by.

The cans of film and reels of tape then lay untouched for several months until, in early 1970, the film was completed for cinema release and the album was put together with existing tape and some overdubbing of strings, horns and choirs by Phil Spector. That they finally bore the *laissez-faire* title *Let It Be* instead of the more positive *Get Back* is symbolic, if not intentional.

Though *Let It Be* was the last Beatle recording to be released, the last recording to be made was *Abbey Road*, which was recorded between July and September 1969. This, in fact, *could* just as appropriately have been titled *Get Back*; recorded between John's tireless peace campaigning, George's own recordings, Ringo's film commitments and amid the collapse of Apple, it was conceived by Paul as a last attempt to make an album with George Martin 'the way we used to do it'.

Musically, it was a fitting epitaph for the Beatles. A week before its release, John Lennon had told the others that he was leaving. No announcement was made, because business manager Allen Klein didn't want to jeopardise the deals he was making on behalf of Apple and the Beatles but on 13 September, 1969, the Beatles effectively passed away, making way for years of wrangling over the estate, and half-hearted and fruitless attempts to exhume the remains.

PAUL KENDALL

THE BEATLES
Discography (from 1964)

Singles

Can't Buy Me Love/You Can't Do That (Parlophone R5114, 1964); I Feel Fine/She's A Woman (Parlophone R5200, 1964); Ticket To Ride/Yes It Is (Parlophone R5265, 1965); Help!/I'm Down (Parlophone R5305, 1965); Paperback Writer/Rain (Parlophone R5452, 1966); Eleanor Rigby/Yellow Submarine (Parlophone R5493, 1966); Penny Lane/Strawberry Fields Forever (Parlophone R5570, 1967); All You Need Is Love/Baby You're A Rich Man (Parlophone R5620, 1967); Hello Goodbye/I Am The Walrus (Parlophone R5655, 1967); Lady Madonna/The Inner Light (Parlophone R5675, 1968); Hey Jude/Revolution (Apple R5722, 1968); Get Back/Don't Let Me Down (Apple R5777, 1969); The Ballad Of John And Yoko/Old Brown Shoe (Apple R5786, 1969); Something/Come Together (Apple R5814, 1969); Let It Be/You Know My Name (Look Up The Number) (Apple R5833, 1970); Yesterday/I Should Have Known Better (Apple R6013, 1976); Back In The USSR/Twist And Shout (Parlophone R6016, 1976); Sgt Pepper's Lonely Hearts Club Band/With A Little Help From My Friends/A Day In The Life (Parlophone R6022, 1978); The Beatles Movie Medley/I'm Happy Just To Dance With You (Parlophone R6055, 1982).

EPs

All My Loving (Parlophone GEP 8891, 1964); *Long Tall Sally* (Parlophone GEP 8913, 1964); *Extracts From The Film 'A Hard Day's Night'* (Parlophone GEP 8920, 1964); *Extracts From The Album 'A Hard Day's Night'* (Parlophone GEP 8924, 1964); *Beatles For Sale* (Parlophone GEP 8931, 1965); *Beatles For Sale (No 2)* (Parlophone GEP 8938, 1965); *The Beatles' Million Sellers* (Parlophone GEP 8946, 1965); *Yesterday* (Parlophone GEP 8948, 1966); *Nowhere Man* (Parlophone GEP 8952, 1966); *Magical Mystery Tour* (Parlophone SMMT 1/2, 1967).

Albums

A Hard Day's Night (Parlophone PCS 3058, 1964); *Beatles For Sale* (Parlophone PCS 3062, 1964); *Help!* (Parlophone PCS 3071, 1965); *Rubber Soul* (Parlophone, PCS 3075, 1965); *Revolver* (Parlophone PCS 7009, 1966); *A Collection Of Beatles Oldies (But Goldies)* (Parlophone PCS 7016, 1966); *Sgt Pepper's Lonely Hearts Club Band* (Parlophone PCS 7027, 1967); *The Beatles* (Apple PCS 7067/8, 1968); *Yellow Submarine* (Apple PCS 7070, 1969); *Abbey Road* (Apple PCS 7088, 1969); *Let It Be* (Apple PCS 7096, 1970); *The Beatles 1962-1966* (Parlophone PCSP 717, 1973); *The Beatles 1967-1970* (Parlophone PCSP 718, 1973); *Rock'n'Roll Music* (Parlophone PCSP 719, 1976); *Magical Mystery Tour* (Parlophone PCTC 255, 1976); *The Beatles At The Hollywood Bowl* (Parlophone EMTV 4, 1977); *Love Songs* (Parlophone PCSP 721, 1977); *Hey Jude* (Parlophone PCS 7184, 1979); *Rarities* (Parlophone PCM 1001, 1979); *The Beatles Ballads* (Parlophone PCS 7214); *Reel Music* (Parlophone PCS 7218, 1982).

The brief, brilliant career of Janis Joplin

JANIS JOPLIN was one of the most remarkable vocalists to emerge from the United States during the Sixties and even though her fame and success was based as much on her public image – the dope, sex and cheap thrills – as it was on her vocal abilities, her status as a singer will endure. For the generation who witnessed her at her peak her status remains assured, while her legend has continued to grow since her death, fed by several biographies but more importantly fed by a continuing trickle of recordings and the film *Janis*. That the greater proportion of her recorded legacy has come out posthumously is as indicative of continued public interest in her as of the commercial interest in her sales potential.

Watching Big Brother

Janis Joplin was born on 19 January 1943 and raised in Port Arthur, a typical Texas oil town. A shy, retiring girl, she was 17 before she developed a love for the music of Leadbelly, Rose Maddox, Woody Guthrie, Odetta and her main idol, Bessie Smith – 'She's the reason I started singing,' Joplin confessed years later. After leaving school, she started performing in local clubs (either on her own or with local folk group the Waller Creek Boys) and made her recording debut in 1962 with an advertising jingle for a local bank sung to the tune of 'This Land Is Your Land'. Material recorded between 1963 and 1965 and subsequently released as part of the *Janis/Early Performances* (1975) package consisted, by and large, of country-blues and folk standards such as 'Silver Threads And Golden Needles', 'Walk Right In', 'Careless Love' and 'Stealin''. These early performances were unremarkable, Joplin's voice barely hinting at the powerful and emotional delivery of later years; the majority of these songs were recorded before audiences in Austin, Texas, although some were made with the Dick Oxtot Jazz Band in San Francisco.

Janis had come to California in the early Sixties at the instigation of Chet Helms, poet and entrepreneur who, while on a visit to his home state of Texas, had heard her singing in Austin club Threadgill's. But although she obtained occasional work singing in San Francisco, she spent more time acquiring an appetite for hard liquor and drugs. After a spell in hospital, where she was weaned off methedrine and heroin (for a time, at least), Joplin returned to Texas.

By late 1965 the Bay Area's music scene was coalescing; the first dances featuring the likes of the Charlatans, the Great Society, the nascent Jefferson Airplane and the Marbles had been held at the Longshoreman's Hall. Chet Helms was by now running one of San Francisco's prime venues, the Avalon Ballroom, and was also managing a band, Big Brother and the Holding Company. By the summer of 1966, the group – Peter Albin (bass), Sam Andrew (guitar), James Gurley (guitar) and Dave Getz (drums) – were struggling and Helms, taking a leaf out of the book of the Great Society (who were fronted by Grace Slick) and Jefferson Airplane (who then featured Signe Anderson), decided that they might fare better with a female vocalist. Still impressed with Joplin's talents, he despatched a compatriot to Texas to recall her to San Francisco.

Balls and chains

It was the first time Janis had sung with amplified accompaniment, and a combination of having to cope with drums and electric guitars and the continuing diet of drugs and alcohol that had already brought a somewhat ravaged timbre to her voice led to the evolution of her gravelly, hoarse and bluesy style. Big Brother were, in fact, a rather undisciplined band, prone to playing out of tune and out of time, but fronted by Joplin – who would pound the stage with unparalleled (for a female singer, anyway) energy and deliver each number with a rasping, husky yet subtle performance – they soon became one of San Francisco's major draws, along with the Grateful Dead, Country Joe and the Fish, and Quicksilver Messenger Service.

Early in 1967, the group signed to the Chicago-based Mainstream label and recorded a debut album, *Big Brother And The Holding Company*. This was not released until after the Monterey Pop Festival in June, an event at which Joplin and the group truly established themselves, capturing the hearts of the audience with a raw and impassioned performance. The album itself, however, was rather a patchy effort, with only a handful of tracks ('All Is Loneliness', 'Light Is Faster Than Sound' and 'Bye Bye Baby') hinting at the band's potential. But by January 1968, Albert Grossman – Bob Dylan's manager – had taken over the handling of the group from Helms and persuaded Columbia Records to buy out Big Brother's Mainstream contract for some 250,000 dollars.

A second album, *Cheap Thrills*, emerged in September and showed the group in their true light for the first time on record. Joplin's voice had taken on an even harsher gutsy intensity and meshed perfectly with the raw, primitive sound of the group. Gershwin's 'Summertime', and the Andrew-Joplin number 'I Need A Man To Love' oozed passion, but it was on 'Ball And Chain' and 'Piece Of My Heart', that she really displayed her astonishing talent; Joplin bared her soul and revealed her vulnerability and desperate need for affection in truly expressive and emotional performances. *Cheap Thrills*, with its eye-catching Robert Crumb artwork, sold a million, but Joplin departed to form a new backing band soon after its release, having been elevated by media

attention to star status and feeling that she had outgrown the group.

Retaining the services of Sam Andrew, she assembled an outfit that comprised Bill King (organ), Brad Campbell (bass) and Ron Markowitz (drums) augmented by a horn section – Terry Clements (sax) and Marcus Doubleday (trumpet). The group, the Kozmic Blues Band, however, replaced the raunchiness of Big Brother with a pale sort of Stax impersonation in which the unfocused hotch-potch of brass was used with little notion of delicacy or finesse. The group gave their debut live performance on 21 December 1968 at the Stax-Volt Convention in Memphis and they flopped. Although they tightened their sound considerably after personnel changes, they still lacked power and unity by the time they appeared at the Woodstock Festival on 16 August 1969; their album *I Got Dem Ol' Kozmic Blues Again Mama*, released in November, laid bare their inadequacies further.

The record compared most unfavourably with *Cheap Thrills*; its arrangements were mostly uninspired and its mix cluttered – yet in spite of the extraneous noise, it contained some noteworthy Joplin vocal performances, particularly the heartrending 'Little Girl Blue', 'To Love Somebody' and 'Work Me Lord'. Her voice was tougher than ever, more liquor-soaked – she was presented with an expensive fur coat for her sterling work in championing Southern Comfort – and absolutely distinctive. Even with a voice as strong as hers, however, it must have often been a battle competing with the horns, so it was a relief for many fans when the band folded in December 1969.

Farewell songs

Her last band, the Full Tilt Boogie Band, rose phoenix-like out of the ashes. Only bassist Brad Campbell and guitarist John Till (who replaced Sam Andrew after *Kozmic Blues*) remained from its immediate predecessor; they were joined by Richard Bell (piano), Ken Pearson (organ) and Clark Pierson (drums). For the first time in her career Joplin felt that she had a tight backing band whose skills backed her to the hilt. The material being worked up prior to the sessions for *Pearl* (1971) was painstakingly thought-out. The arrangements were sympathetic and the more limited instrumentation better suited her needs. The posthumous album *In Concert* (1972) and 'Tell Mama' from *Farewell Song* (1982) testified to the FTBB's prowess, whether handling older material like 'Try' and 'Ball And Chain' or the newer 'Half Moon' and 'Move Over'.

On 4 October 1970, during the sessions for *Pearl*, Janis Joplin died of a heroin overdose and the popular press was quite ghoulish in its coverage. She had dabbled

Janis Joplin cut a flamboyant figure on stage (left and right), singing with style and passion. Inset right: Relaxing with Big Brother and the Holding Company.

with various hard drugs for many years and her alcohol intake was notorious. Jimi Hendrix had already died and rock fatalities were news. With the death of Jim Morrison that trio of mortalities was complete, provoking such 'tributes' as the Righteous Brothers' 'Rock'n'Roll Heaven', a supremely tasteless release. In the wake of her passing the team put the finishing touches to *Pearl*, and the tragedy of her loss was made all the more evident when the album came out.

The songs *Pearl* contained were direct statements, superbly sung with all of Janis's vocal mannerisms, style and gusto, completely devoid of excess. Whether singing the mournful 'A Woman Left Lonely', her song of 'great social and political significance' 'Mercedes Benz', the uptempo 'Move Over' or Kris Kristofferson's 'Me And Bobby McGee' (a US Number 1), Janis Joplin's voice was at its prime.

Sadly, the legend of Janis Joplin was built more on her public image than on her inimitable vocal prowess. The media had built her into a larger-than-life figure – a boozy, druggy, promiscuous bisexual who really craved only loving and tenderness, a Judy Garland of the rock world. And in living up to that image or, at any rate, doing nothing to live it down, Joplin ultimately destroyed herself.

Nonetheless, her place in the annals of rock is assured. Listening to Janis tear into 'Piece Of My Heart', wail out 'A Woman Left Lonely' or whoop through 'Half Moon' serves to confirm her ranking as one of rock's truly great female vocalists.

KEN HUNT

Janis Joplin
Recommended Listening

Cheap Thrills (CBS 67241, 1968) (Includes: I Need A Man To Love, Combination Of The Two, Summertime, Turtle Blues, O Sweet Mary); *In Concert* (CBS 67241, 1972) (Includes: Bye Bye Baby, Ego Rock, Kozmic Blues, Ball And Chain, Flower In The Sun, Move Over).

Hendrix

The man and the myth

Jimi Hendrix was, without doubt, the most innovative guitarist of his, or any other, era. During a sadly brief career, he extended the possibilities of the instrument, taking the art of electric guitar into areas previously undreamed-of. And although many since have attempted to emulate Hendrix's feats, none have been able to enlarge on, or even match, his incredible achievements.

James Marshall Hendrix was born on 27 November 1942 in Seattle, Washington. He started playing guitar at the age of 11, acquiring his first electric instrument the following year, and spent many hours listening to Southern-born blues greats such as Muddy Waters, Howling Wolf and B.B. King on the radio and on record. While still at school, he began playing with R&B groups, performing in parks and recreation centres for teenage dances. At the age of seventeen, he enlisted in the 101st Airborne Paratroopers where he stayed for fourteen months and made 25 successful jumps. On his 26th jump, however, he broke his ankle and was invalided out of the US Army.

Jimi now went on the road and played guitar on many star-studded package tours. During this spell he played behind his old hero B.B. King, Sam Cooke, Solomon Burke, Chuck Jackson, and Jackie Wilson. He then joined Little Richard's band and went on to play with Ike and Tina Turner. However, whilst these were all top flight bands in which Hendrix was able to learn much of his stagecraft, and gain valuable experience, he became increasingly frustrated at being required to adhere strictly to somebody else's musical and visual ideas. In 1964 he arrived in New York where he recorded with Curtis Knight, the Isley Brothers, and Lonnie Youngblood. The following year he set up his own group called Jimmy James and the Blue Flames. They were playing in the Cafe Wha, Greenwich Village in 1966 when Chas Chandler, formerly bassist with the original Animals, first saw him.

London calling

Chandler simply could not believe that Hendrix was languishing in such obscurity and persuaded the guitarist to accompany him back to London where they arrived in September 1966. Chandler, now manager, and Hendrix agreed that the ideal group set-up would be a trio, with bass and drums, to allow the guitarist optimum space for his ideas and novel experimentation. With this in mind, they recruited Mitch Mitchell, an energetic, Elvin Jones-influenced drummer, who had previously played with the Pretty Things, the Riot Squad and Georgie Fame and the Blue Flames. For a bass player, they picked Noel Redding, a six-stringed guitarist of little professional experience who had just failed an audition with Eric Burdon's new Animals. Redding was selected precisely *because* of his lack of experience – Hendrix would be able to tell him exactly what to play on the bass and Redding would not, it was hoped, get ideas above his station. The new three-piece – the Jimi Hendrix Experience – rehearsed for three days before making their debut at Evreux, France on 13 October 1966.

The trio returned to London for more rehearsals and a string of club gigs that started a tremendous groundswell of support. Every time they played, it seemed as if the entire audience from the previous gig had turned up with all their friends in attendance. In addition, a friendship developed between the previously unassociated Eric Clapton and Pete Townshend as they stood in awe of the young black guitarist at almost every gig he played.

Holocaustic haze

Hendrix combined a host of talents. Onstage he had all of Jagger's assured sexuality and arrogant elegance of movement; his negroid features framed by an outrageous halo of long frizzed hair, clothed in wildly colourful Regency stage gear, he was magnetic. He sang in a wry American drawl and often half-spoke his lyrics in a type of stoned slur that was peculiarly expressive and suggestive. And he played the guitar in a way that no one had seen before. Just as a starting point, he had all of Beck's speed and ingenuity, all of Clapton's blues technique and emotional depth, and all Townshend's manic auto-destructive energy. On top of this he added an uncanny ability to wrench noises and effects from his guitar in a way that has never been fully understood.

Using the tremolo arm, a device ignored by rock guitarists since Hank Marvin, Hendrix bent and shaped all sorts of configurations of feedback, harmonic distortion and plain electronic noise coaxed from amplification set-ups cranked up far beyond the maximum levels for which they were designed. He played the guitar behind his back, between his legs, with his teeth, against his speakers, along the microphone stand, and often, when he had tired of these activities, he would smash the instrument to pieces, or set fire to it, or both. Holding fast throughout this holocaust were bassist Noel Redding and drummer Mitch Mitchell. Musically, Redding was the anchor man; under Hendrix's tuition, he had quickly become a steady, solid player who was allowed little deviation from the bass lines he had learned. Mitchell, meanwhile, was a wild and anarchic drummer who had been chosen for his free-flowing playing and technical skill, and he proved to be the perfect partner for the genius of Hendrix's guitar.

In early November, the group recorded two tracks for a potential single, 'Hey Joe', a number that had been a hit in America for the Leaves in July, and Hendrix's own 'Stone Free'. They approached Decca with the recordings but, 'I don't think he's got anything' was their A&R man's response to Hendrix's sound. Through the efforts of another of the group's admirers, Kit Lambert, manager of the Who, the record was released on Polydor in December 1966. Word was by this time filtering back to the public at large through the music press. The stir created by Jimi's club appearances and the attention of a press who had been quick to realise what good copy his 'wild man' antics made, were now consolidated by a television appearance on the pen-

Full circle: Hendrix served his apprenticeship with the Isley Brothers (below), while his subsequent guitar pyrotechnics (opposite) influenced Ernie Isley on the band's later records.

ultimate edition of 'Ready Steady Go!'. 'Hey Joe' entered the charts on 5 January 1967 and reached Number 6 during its ten-week run.

On 31 March, the Experience set off on a 25-day round-Britain package tour, one of the last of its kind. They were bottom of a bill that included the Walker Brothers, Engelbert Humperdinck and Cat Stevens – an incongruous mixture of talents. 'Purple Haze', the second single, released on Kit Lambert's own Track Records label, had just entered the charts, and Hendrix was in the headlines from the first gig when he set fire to his guitar. His show was branded as obscene and dangerous and he was frequently told to clean up his act. He never did, and it is doubtful whether the little girls who came to see the Walker Brothers ever found his act anything but an amusing prelude to the appearance of their heart-throbs anyway, but by the end of the tour Jimi Hendrix had been propelled into the nation's consciousness. A third single, 'The Wind Cries Mary' entered the charts in May while 'Purple Haze' was still in the Top Ten. A wistful lilting ballad, very much influenced by Dylan in terms of vocal delivery, 'The Wind Cries Mary' revealed a more subtle and sensitive Hendrix.

Axis of experience

Are You Experienced?, the first album, was released on 20 May 1967. Produced by Chas Chandler, it contained eleven brand new Hendrix originals, and was an album of astonishing range and innovation. The songs dipped and swerved, the guitar and drums surging with an impatient power. The dive-bombing nightmare gloom of 'I Don't Live Today' was matched against the light-hearted blues of 'Red House'; an apocalyptic vision of Earth through the eyes of an alien visitor in 'Third Stone From The Sun' contrasted with the gentle ballad 'May This Be Love'. *Are You Experienced?* raced up the charts, reaching Number 2 and firmly establishing Hendrix's position in Britain.

The Jimi Hendrix Experience still meant very little in America but on 16 June they appeared at the Monterey Festival for which they had been booked on Paul McCartney's recommendation. The set was devastating, ending up with another charred guitar, and establishing Hendrix as a cult hero. Another mismatched tour, this time supporting the Monkees, followed, causing parental outrage and sufficient press attention to make the guitarist a household name in his native country. The Monkees' teen fans paid little attention to Hendrix's music, however, and on the fifth date he stormed off stage in frustration and quit the tour. Replacement dates were set up and in August the Experience played to more adult crowds in Central Park (supporting the Young Rascals), at the Whisky A Go Go, at the Hollywood Bowl and at Bill Graham's Fillmore West before flying back to Britain on the 25th.

As with their great friends and rivals, Cream, the Jimi Hendrix Experience had by now become spearheads of the psychedelic 'revolution'. Hendrix, with his penchant for garishly coloured clothes, beads, bracelets and bangles and floppy hats, his American drawl and hip language, came to personify the 'freak' image. But although his stage act was aggressive and violent, and his image to many quite frighteningly wild, there was not a reporter or close friend of Hendrix's who did not describe him as a shy, considerate and courteous man, offstage. There is no doubt that he really believed in the hippie ideals of love,

Hendrix's shows were often outrageous displays of virtuosity and bravado, driving his amplifiers to the limit (left), playing the guitar on his back (below), with his teeth (right) or even rubbing it against a microphone stand (far right).

peace, freedom and brotherhood and that when he made a peace sign it was no empty gesture. And, of course, he was no innocent in the freaks' world of other stimulants and no stranger to the delights of groupies – 'chicks' or 'foxes' as he called them.

The second Jimi Hendrix Experience album, *Axis: Bold As Love*, was released in December 1967 and brought Hendrix the composer more to the forefront, and reflected the gentler side of his character, whilst the cover with its mystical Indian overtones was a classic piece of psychedelic art. 'Up From The Skies' and 'Spanish Castle Magic' were both stoned voyages to strange places, and the title track was a kaleidoscopic account of emotional upheavals and rivalries, revolving round the all-powerful, eternal Axis of Love. (For a man not especially associated with love songs, it is surprising how often the word crops up in his work.) There were less guitar histrionics, though plenty of especially lyrical guitar passages, as in the introduction to 'Little Wing'. This was another side of Hendrix's playing style, often overshadowed by his more explosive outbursts. Subsequent live versions of 'Little Wing', and Dylan's 'Like A Rolling Stone' feature his adept and fluent use of brief flurries of melodic breaks thrown in between the vocal line with a deceptively casual ease.

Naked ladyland

At the end of January 1968, the group began their second tour of America, a long, gruelling affair that took its toll on the Experience and Hendrix as a musician. Noel Redding had been allowed to write, sing and play guitar on one track of *Axis: Bold As Love* (the resulting 'She's So Fine' was the album's low point), but this was not enough for him; he resented his lack of musical freedom. A man of strong will with a distorted view of his own talents, he had begun to question Hendrix's demands that he play the bass patterns exactly as written and the pair had several serious arguments. Earlier in the month, while on a short Scandinavian tour, Hendrix had spent the night in jail after destroying a Gothenberg hotel room during the course of one of these bitter disputes.

At the same time, Hendrix began to feel boxed in and trapped by his audience's expectations of him as a performer. The wilder extremes of showmanship that had at first brought him such attention now became a burden. He couldn't perform his dramatic stage antics to order, and now that the initial burst of excitement was over, he just wanted to play music for the music's sake. By the time the American tour reached Anaheim Stadium in California in February, he was refusing to indulge in stage gimmickry. He just stood and played his instrument and audiences mistook this for apathy.

This honesty of approach also meant he couldn't disguise a bad night. There were no slick musical arrangments for the group to hide behind. They were completely exposed and too much depended on Hendrix's mood. Schedules such as the one which included 54 concerts in 47 days left them drained and led to increasingly listless and ragged performances. And on top of this the group were criticised in Britain for spending too much time in America.

Criticisms and problems aside, when the Experience's version of Bob Dylan's 'All Along The Watchtower,' was released in October, it went straight into the UK charts, reaching Number 5 in November, the same month that the third and final official Experience album *Electric Lady-*

Brought to England by Chas Chandler (below), Hendrix teamed up with drummer Mitch Mitchell and bassist Noel Redding (above). Bottom: Isle of Wight, 1970.

land was released. An extravagant double set, with a cover littered with somewhat unattractive naked ladies, it featured star guests such as Al Kooper, Stevie Winwood and Jack Casady and was considered by many to be rather self-indulgent. Nevertheless, as well as 'All Along The Watchtower', it contained many essential Hendrix songs, such as 'Crosstown Traffic', '1983 . . .' and two versions of 'Voodoo Chile' – one a long slow blues, the other a scorching track, peppered with wah-wah guitar, which was later to be a posthumous Number 1 single. November 1968 also marked the first announcement of a split in the group.

In February 1969 the Experience played a 'farewell' concert at the Albert Hall. In May they played in Canada, where Hendrix was arrested at Toronto International Airport for possession of hashish and heroin. (When the case came to trial in December, he argued that a fan had given him the packet and he had slipped it into his suitcase without checking to see what it contained. He was acquitted.) After the concert in Toronto, Hendrix based himself in New York, while Redding and Mitchell returned to Britain. Apart from one single, 'Crosstown Traffic', which reached only Number 52 in the US and Number 37 in Britain, there were no official releases in 1969. In June, Redding played with Hendrix for the last time at the Newport Festival, after which an old army buddy, Billy Cox, was recruited on bass and Mitch Mitchell was retained for an appearance at the Woodstock Festival in August. Hendrix's historic appearance at the festival was captured on the film *Woodstock,* in which he performs his savage, feed-back-riddled reading of 'The Star Spangled Banner'.

In December, Hendrix got together with Billy Cox and drummer Buddy Miles, previously with the blues-oriented Electric Flag and his own Buddy Miles Express, to form the Band of Gypsies. On 31 December 1969, this all-black combination played their debut at the Fillmore East and although Bill Graham called it 'the best set of rock and roll music ever performed at the Fillmore East Theatre', the band's set and the audience's reaction to it were mixed. The concert was recorded and in 1970 appeared as a rather patchy and lacklustre album *Band Of Gypsies.* Hendrix's guitar genius was evident on 'Machine Gun' but elsewhere he was out of tune and careless, while Miles' drumming was sluggish and his compositions – three of which were included on the LP – were substandard to say the least.

Hendrix himself was dissatisfied with the gig and was reluctant to play with the Band of Gypsies again but he needed funds to finish building his Electric Lady recording studios in New York, so towards the end of January the group appeared at Madison Square Gardens in front of a crowd of 19,000. The audience failed to get much for their money, however, for during the second number Hendrix stopped playing and spoke into the microphone. 'I'm sorry but we just can't get it together,' he said before putting down his guitar and walking off stage.

For the next few months Hendrix kept a low profile, diverting what energies he had towards the building of his recording studios. In May, however, he started playing again with Cox and Mitchell, performing a concert at the Berkeley Community Theatre, and then departing for Hawaii where the group were filmed for the *Rainbow Bridge* movie. On 26 July 1970 Jimi played his last American concert at his birthplace, Seattle, a sad affair which featured a frustrated Hendrix yelling 'Fuck you! fuck you!' at the dissatisfied audience.

On 25 August his dream studios, Electric Ladyland were officially opened and, following a massive all-night party, Hendrix departed for England where he was to play the Isle of Wight festival.

The Isle of Wight turned out to be his last ever British performance. It was a disappointment to the audience, fuelled by gross over-expectations, three days of booze and drugs, and a keen desire to hear all the old hits. It was a disappointment to the group, overtired, under-rehearsed and keen to try out the new songs. Nevertheless the gig yielded arguably Hendrix's best live album to date, the curiously under-rated *Isle Of Wight*, released in autumn 1971. Hendrix battled against rebellious equipment and the adversities already noted to produce diamond-hard versions of 'Freedom', 'All Along The Watchtower' and 'In From The Storm'.

Jokers and thieves

Hendrix died on Friday 18 September 1970. His girlfriend Monika Danneman, at whose Notting Hill flat he was staying, called an ambulance when she couldn't rouse him from his sleep. He was pronounced dead on arrival at St. Mary Abbott's Hospital, Kensington. It was often suggested, particularly by the more lurid tabloids, that Hendrix had either committed suicide or unintentionally overdosed on drugs. In fact, an open verdict was recorded at his inquest, cause of death being suffocation due to inhalation of vomit.

The posthumous album *Cry Of Love* (1971), which was more or less what he would have released were he still alive, was a vibrant record, alive with fresh ideas and enthusiasm, not the swansong of a burned out casualty. A lot of nonsense has been talked about Hendrix making a 'deliberate' exit at an 'appropriate' time. What seems more likely is that this great artist, with so much still to offer, was simply the victim of tragic carelessness.

The flood of unofficial Hendrix albums that had started in 1968 with *Get That Feeling*, an LP comprised of loose jams with Curtis Knight, grew apace following the guitarist's death. He had always been an insatiable jammer; many sessions had been committed to tape and now a plethora of dubious product featuring Hendrix with everyone from Little Richard to, of all people, Timothy Leary, began to be released. In addition there were many tapes of out-takes, live recordings and even conversations that unscrupulous businessmen saw fit to cash in on. Few of the posthumous releases did Hendrix any justice. For it had been with the Experience, when he had kept his fellow musicians under his direct control and had been able to harness his instrumental mastery within the context of tightly structured rock compositions, that Jimi Hendrix had excelled.

DAVID SINCLAIR

JIMI HENDRIX
Discography

Singles
Hey Joe/Stone Free (Polydor 56 139, 1966); Flashing/Hush Now (with Curtis Knight) (London HL 10060, 1966); Purple Haze/Fifty First Anniversary (Track 604 001, 1967); The Wind Cries Mary/Highway Chile (Track 604 004, 1967); Burning Of The Midnight Lamp/The Stars That Play With Laughing Sam's Dice (Track 604 007, 1967); How Would You Feel/You Don't Want Me (with Curtis Knight) (Track 604 009, 1967); All Along The Watchtower/Long Hot Summer Night (Track 604, 025, 1968); Crosstown Traffic/Gypsy Eyes (Track 604 029, 1968); Burning Of The Midnight Lamp/Let Me Light Your Fire (Track 604, 033, 1969); No Such Animal Parts 1 and 2 (RCA 2033, 1970); Angel/Night Bird Flying (Track 2094 007, 1971); Gypsy Eyes/Remember/Purple Haze/Stone Free (Track 2094 010, 1971); Johnny B. Goode/Little Wing (Polydor 2001 277, 1972); Hear My Train A-Coming/Rock Me Baby (Reprise K14286, 1973).

EP
Jimi Hendrix Memorial (Track 2095 001, 1970, includes Voodoo Chile).

Albums (selective)
Are You Experienced? (Track 612 001, 1967); *Axis: Bold As Love* (Track 613 003, 1967); *Get That Feeling* (with Curtis Knight) (London SH8349, 1968); *Smash Hits* (Track 613 004, 1968); *Strange Things* (with Curtis Knight) (London SH8369, 1968); *Electric Ladyland* (Track 613 008/9, 1968); *Band Of Gypsies* (Track 2406 002, 1970); *Monterey* (Reprise K46430, 1970); *Cry Of Love* (Track 2408 101, 1971); *Original Motion Picture Soundtrack From* Rainbow Bridge (Reprise K44159, 1971); *Jimi Hendrix At The Isle Of Wight* (Track 2302 016, 1971); *Hendrix In The West* (Track 2302 018, 1972); *War Heroes* (Track 2302 020, 1972); *Soundtrack From The Film* Jimi Hendrix (Reprise K64017, 1973); *Loose Ends* (Polydor 2310 301, 1973); *Crash Landing* (Polydor 2310 398, 1975); *Midnight Lightning* (Polydor 2310 415, 1976); *Jimi Hendrix Concerts* (CBS 88592, 1982).

The Velvet Underground

Drugs, trash and art on the wild side of the street

ALTHOUGH THEY WERE virtually ignored by the rock audience during their brief flurry of activity, the Velvet Underground have since proven to be perhaps the most influential American group of the late Sixties, be it in terms of attitude, image or their music. They have inspired such diverse bands as the original Modern Lovers and Roxy Music.

Founder member of the Velvet Underground, Lou Reed was born on 2 March 1944, the son of well-to-do Brooklyn Jews. His first connection with music had been five years spent studying classical piano, but by his early teens he was hooked on rock'n'roll and playing in short-life high-school bands. One of these, the Shades, got as far as recording a single, 'So Blue', on Time Records; 'Our big moment was gonna be when Murray the K played it,' Reed remembered years later. 'But he was off sick that day . . .' Lou's royalty cheque for 'So Blue' came to a massive 78 cents.

With such meagre earnings coming his way, it is hardly surprising that Reed remained at school, finally graduating with honours from Syracuse University. Brief periods studying journalism, theatre and music followed until he eventually landed a job as staff songwriter for Pickwick Records, a company specialising in quickie albums designed to cash in on any current teen craze. 'Four of us would be literally locked in a room writing songs,' Reed later recalled. 'Then when we had enough for an album we'd run down to the studio in the basement and do it as quickly as possible.' This sensible attitude to studio economics was to prove helpful later on – the first two Velvet Underground albums were recorded over less than two days apiece.

Primitive rhythms

In 1964, Reed made the acquaintance of John Cale (born 5 December 1940), the son of a Welsh miner. Success at school had found Cale a place at music college in London, and from there a scholarship had taken him to study in the States. 'By the time I arrived in America I'd just about had it with avant-garde music,' Cale announced years later, but this did not prevent him from diverting the Tanglewood Academy by incorporating an axe into a concert, hacking at a table and a piano in the manner of John Cage.

Having abandoned his studies, Cale joined a group with former Cage disciple and hotshot avant-gardist LaMonte Young, with whom he played electric viola. When Reed offered the Welshman a chance to play on a single he had written – 'The Ostrich' – Cale jumped at the chance, dragging along Scots percussionist Angus MacLise with him. Reed added a singer/guitarist named Sterling Morrison and the Primitives were born. The record came out, the group got a small piece in *Vogue* (Reed's commercial hook for this dance novelty was an ostrich-feather revival he had read was on the way) and that was it. Ostrich feathers didn't come back and 'The Ostrich' went the way of the Dodo – not undeservedly so, for it was a messy concoction featuring what sounds like a bunch of drunks whining over a tinny 'Hang On Sloopy' backing riff. 'First you put your head on the floor/Then you step on it . . .' urged lead drunk Reed.

Following the failure of 'The Ostrich', the Primitives became the Warlocks and the Falling Spikes before a friend suggested borrowing the name of a book of dimestore titillation by Michael Leigh – *The Velvet Underground*. By the time the Velvet Underground made their performing debut at a high school dance in Summit, New Jersey on 11 November 1965, Angus MacLise had been replaced by Maureen 'Mo' Tucker, a diminutive and totally untrained female whose main qualification for joining was the fact she owned a van and no-one else did. Mo often played standing up, and if there wasn't a drum-kit handy, she apparently didn't mind hitting a couple of garbage cans instead. Cale contributed bass and viola.

Left: An uncharacteristically ebullient Velvet Underground enthuse over their new bass guitar; from left Sterling Morrison, Lou Reed, John Cale and Maureen 'Mo' Tucker. Below: Lou Reed; his early songs, which included 'Heroin' and 'Venus In Furs', were out of step with the optimistic hippie times.

Fun in the Factory

From their early days, The Velvet Underground's hard-line support came from the New York artistic community – principally Andy Warhol, NYC's art and fashion Führer by this time. The group improvised

backings for Warhol movies, were filmed in action and became a movie of their own. Soon their numbers were enlarged by Nico, a beautiful German ex-model who had dabbled in cinema before moving to New York, where a spot of night-club chanteuse work had preceded her recruitment to Warhol's entourage. When Nico spoke it was like coffin-lids creaking, when she sang it was like ravens taking off 13 at a time – in short, she was just what the Velvet Underground were missing.

As their live sets progressed, Warhol's multi-media unit, the Factory, helped improvise backings of old films and lightshows to the long improvisations over which Nico just howled wordlessly, like the Bride of Frankenstein hailing a taxicab. The simultaneous act of dancers Gerard Malanga and Mary Woronov heightened the aura of bordello entertainment: their costumes were mainly leather, and whips were their favourite props. 'It was all about shock and being provocative,' Woronov remembers. 'Because then there were still lots of ways that you could be shocking, ways of getting people to react.'

Meanwhile, following a nationwide tour as part of the Warhol circus, the Exploding Plastic Inevitable, the Velvet Underground were at last to get a record of their own out. The Velvets' debut LP had been in the can for a while already after being made in a single breathless day's work; unfortunately their record company, Verve, usually dealt in jazz and had no idea what to do with *The Velvet Underground & Nico* and gave the album scant promotion following its release early in 1967.

Top: Reed (left), Cale (centre) and Nico. The eerie sound produced by Cale's viola and the odd tones of Nico's voice gave the Velvet Underground's first LP its distinctive quality. Above: Nico as femme fatale. Right: Lou Reed solo in the Seventies at Crystal Palace.

'The Velvet Underground Produced By Andy Warhol' said the spine. You had to look there, or on the back, or in the fold-out sleeve because the group wasn't named on the front. Instead there was a large yellow peel-off banana on a white background. Under the banana big letters screamed: Andy Warhol. Inside there were photos of everyone in the group. 'Produced by Andy Warhol', it said again, not bothering to mention that Andy probably couldn't tell a recording studio and a can of sardines apart.

The record itself bowed in with a gentle ballad, 'Sunday Morning'; this innocent introduction soon admitted a party of venomous snakes, however, as Lou Reed took over with a masterful portrait of the agonies of junk addiction in 'I'm Waiting For The Man', the lyric delivered over a distinctly skew-wiff riff that would become the Velvet Underground's trademark.

'Femme Fatale', with its chorus of near-jeers, was displayed back-to-back with its sister in sin, 'Venus In Furs', based on Leopold Von Sacher-Masoch's similarly titled memoir/fantasy. On this track, a langorous Reed gave voice to some of his most precise and lyrical lines; 'Taste the whip, in love not given lightly', he coaxed before switching abruptly to the insistent: 'Kiss the whip! Now bleed . . . for me!' The line closed with a curtly dismissive grunt, leaving the stage wide for the unanaesthetised sawings of John Cale's electric viola. By comparison, 'Run Run Run', a solid rock number with a middle section pilfered wholesale from Marvin Gaye's R&B hit 'Hitch Hike', and even the Nico-fronted wail of 'All Tomorrow's Parties' were rather mellow.

But the Velvets expanded their basic palette as the record progressed, taking tentative steps with structure and length. 'Heroin', the astonishing drama that opened the record's second side, was spread across seven minutes in which Reed's protagonist ran the gamut of joy, ecstasy, agony and the realisation that addiction would kill him in the end – the whole thing delivered in an ambiguous deadpan that was impossible to pin down. Was he advocating drug abuse or warning people against it? Thereafter a more placid and familiar period intervened as the jolly 'There She Goes' gave way to Reed's brilliant breakdown of the Warhol philosophy, 'I'll Be Your Mirror'.

Finally the group let themselves go for the last two items, 'Black Angel's Death Song' and 'European Son To Delmore Schwartz'. But where the cacophonies of sound that resulted were among the most exciting moments on the album, Reed's reaction to being given a free rein for his voice and lyrics wasn't so productive. Instead, spewing a stream of barely coherent words, he frequently sounded like a man who had swallowed too much Dylan.

A peep into hell

One way and another, the Velvet Underground's debut LP was primarily a record that reinforced the overall impression that, for all the brouhaha, the group were really a rather orthodox rock band whose staple diet of dance rhythms and ballads was overlaid by one or two gimmicks: there was the odd sound John Cale's viola provided, the even odder sounds the lovely Nico made without any external help and there were some songs that touched on relatively taboo subjects.

But with their second album, released later that same year, a new Velvet Underground emerged. Nico had, by now, departed to pursue a solo career and with her, it appeared, all commercial considerations had gone too. Having created a fairly normal debut album which, for all the good reviews, the public chose to ignore, the group unleashed *White Light/White Heat* which, from the contemptuous opening title cut inwards, was far from orthodox. The second track, 'The Gift', was an accompanied short story, related by Cale, which seemed to come straight from the pages of some horror comic from start to ultra-slick conclusion.

From there, it was straight into 'Lady Godiva's Operation' and its genuinely spooky surgeries; the record seemed to grind on, the drumming more funereal and mechanical by turns, the various instruments and voices suggesting all manner of vices suddenly exposed to the light. Finally, in the ceaseless torture chambers of 'Sister Ray', the words and music achieved a dark apotheosis and Reed, Cale and cohorts hit a peak in their collective careers. Here all the eccentrics of the Warhol crowd came to life, part of a nightmare as distinctive and vivid as anything envisioned by William Burroughs. 'Sister Ray' was a dark world that somehow sums up New York as well today as when it was recorded. And it gave a peep into hell as well.

On the album, the Velvets set themselves apart forever from the so-called psychedelic groups of the West Coast. If there was any solace for hippies in *White Light/White Heat*, it was certainly well hidden. Instead of the big-eyed optimism the country's youth was so keen to celebrate as they ransacked the theatrical costumiers for outfits for the fancy dress ball that life apparently became when one 'turned on' . . . instead of the naïve dream-palaces being sold by the exploiters of the hippie idea, the Velvets offered nothing less than the keys to hell.

The album was, to a great extent, self-indulgent; nonetheless, the Velvet Underground had come up with something more sturdily resonant than much of the music of their contemporaries. By the Eighties, the Beatles' *Sgt Pepper*, for instance, sounded heavily dated – naïve, innocent, dreaming its pot-and-pipe dreams forever. The self-indulgence of the Velvet Underground, however, had become more like the soundtrack for the current time than ever before.

By the time the Velvet Underground's eponymous third LP arrived in 1969, John Cale was gone, embarked on a ceaseless chain of extremes of his own to be replaced by Doug Yule on bass, guitar and keyboards. This time, the angry thumpings and the wild and desperate scenarios of *White Light/White Heat* were traded for a selection of songs that were melodic, relaxed and beautifully crafted – so many plain, strong, simple songs at last. Even the single hint of 'experiment', the multiple-voiced 'The Murder Mystery', lacked anything remotely akin to the barbs which characterised 'Sister Ray' or even most of the first LP.

Lou gets loaded

But the Velvets triumphed again, even with the old barriers re-erected, as if the period of catharsis leading up to *White Light/White Heat* was over and the freedom to do anything had made the group want to start back from square one. Hence 'Pale Blue Eyes', one of Reed's most beautiful love songs, the bridled rock energy of the brilliantly-understated 'What Goes On?', the delicate sketchings of 'Candy Says' and the quiet resignation of 'Jesus'. These, together with the quiet, sure optimism of 'I'm Set Free' or 'Beginning To See The Light' (another great rocker, again masterfully subdued), presented a rarely-seen side of Lou Reed: the tender, gentle alter ego to the more frequent opposite extremes he has portrayed throughout his career.

The Velvet Underground closed with 'Afterhours', an irresistible pastiche of cooing jazz with a token hint of perversion provided by Maureen Tucker's little girl delivery – at times totally innocent, at others assuming the grotesque disproportions of Bette Davis dressed up in her dolly clothes in *Whatever Happened to Baby Jane?*

There was one more studio LP to come, however. *Loaded* (1970), of which Reed has spoken so often with more than a little rancour, was apparently remixed and edited after he'd resigned from the group, with Reed's name being dropped down the credits so that he appears to be a mere contributor when, in fact, he wrote all the songs himself. The title, said Reed, was meant to say the album was 'loaded with hits', though many thought otherwise.

Here, with Reed finally tired of being a cult hero who couldn't pay the rent, are his best shots at cutting a commercial long-player. Whatever tamperings may have occurred in Reed's absence, they surely haven't destroyed the album in question. The 'Waiting For The Man' riff Reed and the Velvets had made their own is the keynote to a solidly-written, arranged and played pop long-player. Unadventurous in terms of earlier Velvets records, certainly, *Loaded* still has more than a few solid gold reasons for deserving its place in any record collection worth being walled up with. 'Sweet Jane' and 'Rock & Roll' have become semi-standards, often covered and even more frequently re-written; and 'I Found A Reason' functioned both as a Fifties tribute/pastiche (the glorious doo-wop heart) and as an extremely active example of the more vigorous mid-Seventies rocker. It also reveals the rarely seen humorous side of Lou Reed in all its banal glory: 'As I walk down life's lonely highway/hand in hand with myself . . .'

Enormous fun at the time it certainly was, but *Loaded* has worn less well than its sibling studio long-players. Overall its surface polish and undeniable zip can't disguise the fact that it lacks the distinctiveness of the other records – even Mo Tucker sounds like a pro drummer and there are more than a few out-and-out fillers.

Above: Reed in the Seventies; decadence and ambivalence personified. Below: Nico at the keys of her harmonium.

Beginning a new age

Reed quit the group in 1970, opting for a solo career and leaving behind some live recordings that would resurface later on the albums *Live At Max's Kansas City* and *1969* (both 1972). *Live At Max's* was a documentary-style recording of one of Reed's last concerts with the group as preserved on a small cassette machine, on which the audience were often as audible as the group. *1969 (The Velvet Underground Live)* was a double set containing gritty and ferocious performances.

The remaining Velvet Underground members continued to operate without Reed for a spell, coming up with a bland country-flavoured album, *Squeeze* (1972), and touring Britain to a largely indifferent response with the addition of Boston 'legend' Willie 'Loco' Alexander on guitar.

The Velvet Underground finally ground to a halt in 1973. But though they were finished, their influence was just starting to make itself felt. Their fanatical follower and former Max's busboy Jonathan Richman was soon to become an underground darling with his first-edition Modern Lovers and Reed-inspired songs like 'Pablo Picasso' and 'I'm Straight'. Then the deluge, from the first trickles of Roxy and Bowie's deliberate incorporation of various stages of the dismantled Velvets machine in their own work through to later hordes of skinny people in black like Television, the Stranglers and several hundred other US and UK punk outfits.

Ultimately, more fittingly than anything else, the Velvet Underground were *the* garage band – a bunch of snotty kids having fun making a racket. The fact that they happened to have a smattering of culture and were located in exactly the right place and time for their crazy hodge-podge of noise, art and self-indulgence to be taken seriously was just luck. That was the real message the Velvet Underground left behind them: 'We were lucky; we weren't brilliant, just a row anyone could make.' The same group of people in the Depression would have been . . . what? Labour leaders? Bank robbers?

And in the Eighties? Terrorists, perhaps. Trouble, certainly. GIOVANNI DADOMO

THE VELVET UNDERGROUND
Discography

Singles

Nico and the Velvet Underground
All Tomorrow's Parties/I'll Be Your Mirror (Verve 10427, 1966); Femme Fatale/Sunday Morning (Verve 10466, 1966).
The Velvet Underground
Here She Comes Now/I Heard Her Call My Name (Verve 10560, 1967); Jesus/What Goes On? (MGM 14057, 1969); Oh, Sweet Nuthin'/Who Loves The Sun (Cotillion 44107, 1971).

Albums

The Velvet Underground & Nico (Verve V6-5008, 1967); *White Light/White Heat* (Verve V6-5046, 1967); *The Velvet Underground* (MGM SE 4617, 1969); *Loaded* (Cotillion SD 9034, 1970); *1969 (The Velvet Underground Live)* (Mercury SRM2 7504, 1972); *Live At Max's Kansas City* (Cotillion SD 9500, 1972); *Archetypes* (MGM M3F 4950, 1974).

The Dream Goes Sour

The harsh realities of Altamont and after

Well I'm going down to Yasgur's Farm/ I'm gonna join in a rock and roll band/ I'm gonna camp out on the land/And set my soul free . . .

Idealistic words from Joni Mitchell's 'Woodstock', a song considered by many to express clearly the spirit of the generation that brought new connotations to the 'arts' festival. It reflects, they argue, the atmosphere of relaxed enlightenment that surrounded an aware sub-culture getting to grips with its responsibilities and striving to base an alternative society on mutual trust and understanding.

Although festivals had been in existence since the first stirrings of interest in the performing arts, Woodstock gave strident voice to an idea conceived initially at the 'love-ins', 'be-ins' and 'Trips Festivals' of San Francisco around 1966 and 1967. Here at last was evidence weighty enough to stifle the 'straight' world's snickering accusations of misplaced idealism, a public demonstration of young people's ability to pull together, with *love*, despite it all. Aquarius rising. A new dawn. And so on . . . Here was a generation with a *new* way, embracing radical concerns. The Woodstock Festival was its manifesto.

Yet in many ways Woodstock was a disaster, though most of its bad points got lost in the general backslapping, obscured by sheer relief that no serious calamity occurred during the mud-caked nightmare. Predictably a number of births were claimed; but the most conspicuous offspring was this peculiarly naive myth of loving togetherness, a cosy notion that would have its awful immaturity exposed only months later. Meredith Hunter's murder at Altamont in December 1969 tore gaping holes in the argument and revealed that alternative societies, too, have their darker side.

Left: Woodstock – three days of peace and love. Below: Altamont – one night of hell. The Angels kill while Their Satanic Majesties play on (bottom).

Bring on the clowns

With the benefit of hindsight, it is obvious that the simple matter of scale was a key factor in the decline of the festival. Although comparatively small affairs, Woodstock's forerunners had had their fair share of problems and it should have been obvious that such organisational difficulties would multiply in direct proportion to the size of the audience. As soon as somebody realised that it was possible to construct a stage in a convenient wide-open space, import all available 'superstars' of the time, jack up the ticket prices and entice hordes of footloose young people from one side of a country to another, there was bound to be trouble. Woodstock, it is true, was eventually declared a 'free' festival but only after circumstances made the organisers' task impossible and forced them to abandon most of their administrative control.

Festivals like Woodstock and the Isle of Wight were a strange and confused mixture of intentions. To the faithful they were wonderful celebrations of noble ideals, a chance to revel in a non-materialistic pantomime while behind the scenes the entire organisational edifice relied on massive financial manipulation to keep it from crumbling. Even then, this commercial wizardry seldom proved successful; Woodstock's organisers went bust faster than their idyllic green pasture turned brown, only to be rescued by the phenomenal box-office receipts earned by the subsequent film of the fracas.

The incongruous wheeling and dealing was distasteful to most of the audience, and was hastily obscured in a haze of dope smoke. One of the bitterest pills swallowed by a 1969 Isle of Wight hopeful was the fact that Dylan jetted in, played for his allotted hour and flew out again some 75,000 dollars richer – a vast sum for the times. Out around the campfires with a biting wind howling in the ears, that knowledge did little to warm the bones . . . Commercial interest spawned a chill realisation that, already, the 'beautiful' new ideology had succumbed to the lure of capitalism and had been neatly turned upon its creators as the cornerstone of a hugely lucrative industry.

The impact of commercial humiliation, however, was nothing compared to the body-blow that was delivered at Altamont. It seems ironic that human nature should choose a 'free' festival in the very state that acted as midwife at the birth of the 'Woodstock Generation' less than six months earlier at which to bare its bleaker aspect. The Rolling Stones decided to stage a free concert in San Francisco's Golden Gate Park, the intention being to obtain sufficient footage to complete a movie of their 1969 US tour. It proved impracticable to hold the show at that venue, so the concert was re-scheduled for the Sears Point Raceway; with Jefferson Airplane, Crosby, Stills, Nash and Young, Santana and the Flying Burrito Brothers added to the bill, a suitable end sequence for the Maysles

Right: A hippie surrenders to the arms of the law, Windsor 1974. The free festival held in the Great Park was broken up by 600 policemen. Above: More mud than music at Reading, 1975.

Brothers' film looked assured. Problems arose, however, when the proprietors of the raceway realised how many dollars could be generated by a movie of the Stones playing at *their* venue and demanded a slice of the distribution rights. Equally competent at arithmetic, the Stones refused to surrender any interest in the film and, 20 hours before the planned start time, Sears Point pulled out.

Let it bleed

Just as it began to look *too* late, the enterprising proprietor of the Altamont Speedway successfully tempted the Stones to his venue, a barren track surrounded by scrub-encrusted dirthills that more often bore witness to automobile destruction derbies than other, comparatively genteel, pursuits. Due to the short notice, every aspect of the required organisation proved inadequate – most crucially the provision of back-up medical facilities, food supplies and sanitation. To make matters worse, the Stones attracted a far larger crowd than anticipated. And, though so potent a brew hardly needed a catalyst to trigger the inevitable reaction, the Stones' road manager Sam Cutler chose this moment to make the most ill-advised decision of his career. Basing his judgement upon an alleged suggestion by the Grateful Dead and experience of *British* Hell's Angels at an earlier Hyde Park free concert, he hired a bunch of California's 'one per centers' to police the stage. Stoked by copious quantities of dope and alcohol, a day-long atmosphere of unease hung over the crowd, erupting into periodic bouts of brutality around the front-of-stage area which found the available medical aid wanting long before the Stones even began their set.

Much has been made of the Stones' image during this period, Jagger's apparent flirtation with Lucifer being held in some way responsible for the day's bloodshed. Yet at Altamont Jagger seemed powerless and vulnerable, unable to exert his charismatic control over an audience and keep them teetering on the perilous knife-edge between ecstatic adulation and dangerous abandon. There was nothing 'satanic' about rock's fallen angel here and, in truth, the only thing that can be blamed for the whole disaster is an appalling lack of foresight on the part of everyone concerned. Nevertheless, it *was* during the Stones' set that the luckless Hunter drew a pistol to ward off a Hell's Angel who'd already stabbed him at least once, and was promptly dealt with in the most final of fashions. With him died any belief in the 'Woodstock Generation' as a realistic and potent force for change.

Old contemptibles

The blaze of litigation that followed the killing demonstrated once and for all that the unifying force – music – was prone to the same contemptible considerations as the gladiatorial cut-and-thrust of big business in general. As the squalid fit of buck-passing ushered in the new decade it became painfully obvious that nothing had been achieved, nothing was changed. Only the most blinkered defenders of the cause refused to recognise their failure both to confront those considerations and to organise an effective alternative. After Altamont it was only a matter of time before rigor mortis set in and, although the devout continued to attend similar gatherings well into the Seventies, each passing year saw the accent swing farther and farther from the Woodstock blueprint. By the mid Seventies, the balance had tilted irretrievably towards blatant money-spinners, the British examples of which included the large-scale one-day concerts at Knebworth Park, the annual Reading endurance test or Bob Dylan's second outdoor appearance in the UK at Blackbushe Airfield in 1978.

There were exceptions, nonetheless. Those 'hippies' (by now a disparaging term) who had not tired of beating their heads against immovable conventional mores had to be content with low-key gatherings in the shadow of Glastonbury Tor or, at summer solstices, on the wind-blown plain surrounding Stonehenge. Only at such places was there any real remnant of the earlier determination for more tranquil patterns of existence; but instead of being observed anxiously by the society they sought to subvert, they were largely ignored or, at best, regarded with an amused tolerance. CLIFF ASH

Above right: Reading 1981. A street vendor displays his wares – heavy-metal badges and assorted mementoes. Right: Blackbushe Airfield strewn with litter following Dylan's appearance there on 15th July 1978.

Songs from a ROOM

The inside story of Leonard Cohen

IT WAS IN 1956 that the work of Leonard Cohen first appeared before the general public in book form, an event that marked his transformation from unofficial poet laureate of McGill University to fully-fledged writer. While Anthony Eden grappled with the problems of Suez, the Soviets faced the war of the Hungarian Revolution and General Eisenhower began his last presidential term, the protest era was being cautiously ushered in by the Beat Generation. Although Leonard Cohen was essentially a child of the Fifties, he has come to be regarded as a figure of the Sixties when the poet/singer-songwriter became a new type of idol.

Good guys don't wear white: Leonard Cohen (opposite and above), sardonic singer of sentiment and cynicism.

Poetic licence

Cohen was born in Montreal on 21 September 1934, the son of middle-class Jewish parents. On graduating from high school, he studied English Literature at McGill and Columbia Universities. It was at McGill that Cohen's poetic gift was discovered, and his work was chosen to inaugurate the McGill Poetry Series, a collection of books designed to bring to public notice the work of the university's more outstanding students.

Referring to his anthology *Let Us Compare Mythologies*, written during his teenage years and published in 1956, Cohen has since commented: 'A lot (of the poems) are as good, if not better, than anything I'm doing today in that field.' Reviewing the collection in *The Fiddlehead*, Allan Donaldson noted that Cohen's 'handling of the character and problems of his people strikes one particularly for its imaginativeness and honesty'. His observation is a key to almost all of Cohen's work, including his best-known novel *Beautiful Losers*, published in 1966.

The early Sixties anthology entitled *Parasites of Heaven* assumes a particular historical importance, since it contained five of Cohen's poems that were later to become songs: 'Suzanne', 'Teachers', 'Master Song', 'Avalanche' and 'Fingerprints'. It was a mid-Sixties performance by Judy Collins that had inspired Cohen to write songs. Her renditions of 'Suzanne' and 'Dress Rehearsal Rag' (on her 1966 album *In My Life*) brought Cohen international recognition as a songwriter, turning artistic acclaim into popular success.

Collins continued to champion Cohen's talent in the years that followed, recording a number of his songs. In 1967 she brought him on stage at a concert in New York's Central Park. The poet was almost too frightened to sing, and the late Lillian Roxon wrote that he looked 'diffident, handsome and very vulnerable'. A couple of months later, he debuted in his own right at the Newport Folk Festival. In 1959, the Newport showcase had brought a young Joan Baez into the spotlight; in 1963, Bob Dylan had emerged as 'crown prince'; and in 1967 Leonard Cohen and Joni Mitchell – fellow Canadians – triumphed there. Both owed their success to Judy Collins, who was on the festival's board of directors.

Finally, in 1968, an album appeared: *Songs Of Leonard Cohen*. Within a few months, a Cohen cult of considerable magnitude had grown up, and it became a cliché to spend a night alone with a bottle of burgundy and a Leonard Cohen LP, basking in acute romantic agony. *Songs Of Leonard Cohen* was a powerful first record, including 'Suzanne', 'The Stranger Song', 'Sisters Of Mercy', 'So Long, Marianne' and 'Hey, That's No Way To Say Goodbye'. To quote Lillian Roxon again: 'His thin and diffident voice made for a realism that seemed to bring him right into the room with the listener . . . there is a hypnotic repetitiousness that makes the album a calm antidote for loneliness . . .'

Cohen's emergence as a singer-songwriter at a time when he was a *cause célèbre* of the world's literary establishment did not owe entirely to inspiration, however; it was also an economic necessity. As he later commented: 'I couldn't pay the grocery bills . . . [but] anyone who leaves writing to try to make a living as a singer would have to be a fool. If there's anything chancier than writing, it's singing.'

In 1956, a poet could not have existed in the music scene, for anything beyond three minutes of moon/June rhymes about boy-meets-girl, falls in love and lives happily ever after was considered far too heavy for popular consumption. Bob Dylan made it possible to be a poet *and* a rock star, but even he was well-established before he began to employ the rich allusive imagery that characterised his *Highway 61 Revisited* and *Blonde On Blonde* period. Dylan's achievement enabled Cohen to enter the music scene as a poet first and foremost. Cohen saw no anomaly in his being both a poet and a singer-songwriter. He has said: 'I was always a musician, so I always had a feeling of the closeness between the written lyric and the lyric that is sung. Indeed, they were the same at one point, and they've always been the same for me. Narrative song, lyric expression migrate easily from music to the page.'

Songs Of Leonard Cohen was a runaway best-seller – much to the surprise of the DJs, who hadn't given it needletime. 1969's *Songs From A Room* was similarly successful, although a less consistent album than its predecessor. Attempting to place contemporary despair and violence in relation to the European holocaust, the album's high point was 'Bird On The Wire'. *Songs Of Love And Hate* appeared in 1971, and was a more remarkable opus, containing three of Cohen's best songs: 'Dress Rehearsal Rag', 'Joan Of Arc' and 'Famous Blue Raincoat' – exquisite expressions of anguish, detached objectivity and resignation, respectively. Cohen had also begun to tour and, in 1972, Tony Palmer filmed a *cinéma-vérité*-style movie of his European jaunt, entitled *Bird On A Wire*. An album, *Live Songs*, appeared the following year.

In 1974, with *New Skin For The Old Ceremony*, Cohen leaned heavily toward cabaret-style soft rock and a much fuller sound, with the help of producer/arranger John Lissauer. Cohen's work had always contained a good deal of sardonic self-parody; now the humour was more manifest, as in lines such as 'You were the sensitive woman, I was the Very Reverend Freud/You were the manual orgasm/I was the dirty little poet' (from 'Is This What You Wanted?').

Lost words

1977 saw Cohen in the studio with the legendary Phil Spector to produce *Death Of A Ladies' Man*. The album showed Spector at his most extravagant – as Cohen put it, 'in his Wagnerian phase'. Cohen was far from happy with the end product, although he by no means disavowed the content: 'The songs are very, very good and there are some of my best lyrics on that album . . . (but) the words got lost in the mix, from which I was excluded by both secrecy and armed bodyguards.'

Recent Songs, his 1979 release, was very much a return to the spirit of his early albums, although musically it was much more sophisticated, using some fine instrumental touches – including a Mariachi band and a gypsy violinist. Cohesive, thematic and replete with richly ornate, symbolic imagery and allegorical reflections, it is a fully-fledged romantic album which once again mixes sex with religion – here with a droll sense of the absurd. Cohen's ironic delivery ideally suits the ambiguous emotions expressed in the lyrics.

To call Leonard Cohen a folk-singer is an inaccurate pigeonholing of his talent, for his melodies bear little relation to traditional Anglo-American ballads. He remains an intellectual poet, working mainly on the stage, rather than the page, fusing poetry and music in a very exacting manner. His lyrics are meticulously chosen and, with his scholarly linguistic precision, Cohen has brought to rock music an awareness of the classical themes and formal disciplines of poetry. His word-weaving and imagery can hypnotise, and Cohen punctuates the trance by the juxtaposition of everyday speech and elaborate metaphor.

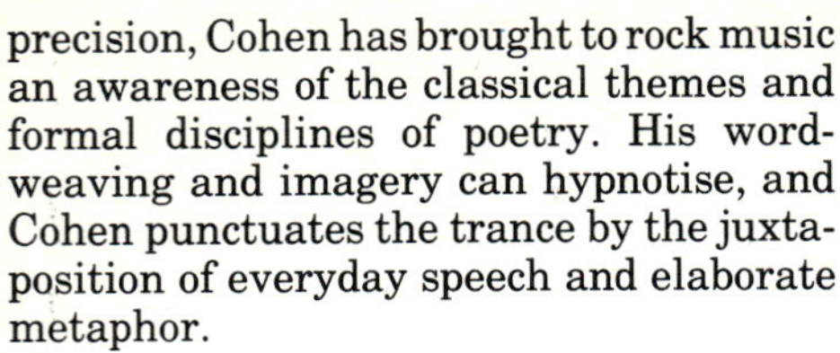

Love in the darkness

Cohen's recurring themes – sex, sexuality, religion, death, myth and mysticism – are frequently interwoven in his songs. Unlike Dylan, Cohen is not concerned with the notion of apocalypse and few of his songs contain any overt social or political commentary beyond an implicit social criticism. Cohen's perceived world is corrupt, sordid and materialistic, and love provides an escape from the ordeal of everyday existence.

Cynics and detractors might say that Cohen appeals only to the professionally depressed and self-consciously tormented aficionados of gloom. True, he can be self-pitying and indulgent, lacing his songs with seconal, razor blades and consuming fires, but to denigrate his talent is to denigrate rock itself. Far from being simply a doom-mongering writer singing in a gloom-laden monotone, Cohen's voice is one of the most intimately expressive sounds in contemporary music.

ELIZABETH M. THOMSON

Right: Poet-balladeer Cohen strums his guitar. Inset above: On stage in France, 1972.

Leonard Cohen
Recommended Listening

Songs Of Leonard Cohen (CBS63241) (Includes: Suzanne, Sisters Of Mercy, Master Song, Teachers, The Stranger Song, So Long Marianne); *Songs From A Room* (CBS32074) (Includes: Tonight Will Be Fine, The Butcher, Story Of Isaac, Lady Midnight, The Partisan, Bird On The Wire).

CHRONICLE OF AN ERA

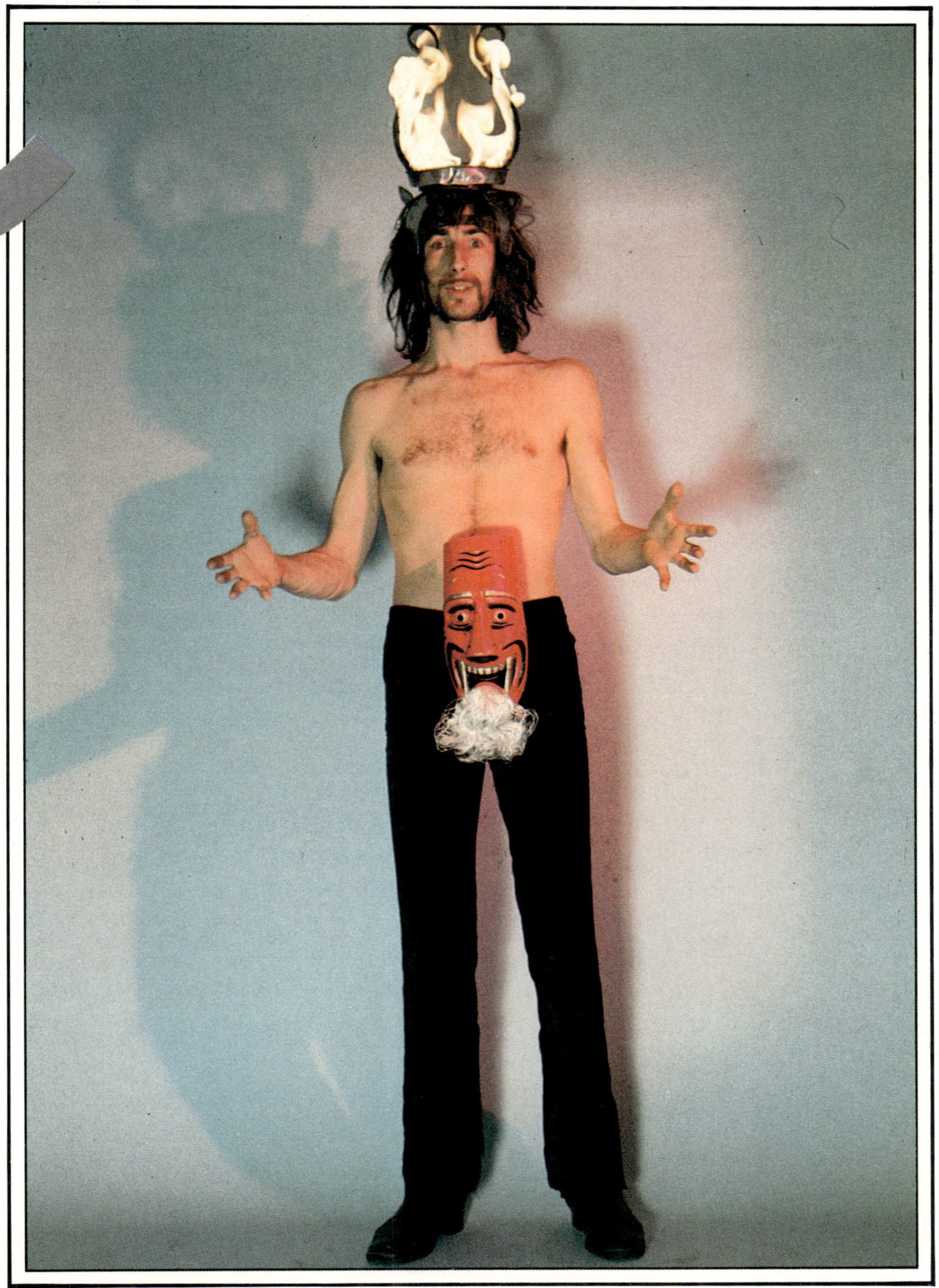

In spite of the diversity of styles that characterised the late-sixties, there is a recognisable spirit of the age which becomes apparent as its chronology unfolds. The beginning and end of an era seem well symbolised by the chart-topping position of the Beatles' 'Day Tripper,' covert drug references and all, in January 1966 and by the premiere in 1970 of *Gimme Shelter*, the Rolling Stones film which dealt with the harrowing tragedy at Altamont

ROCK '66

The great British beat boom that had taken the musical world by storm in 1964 and 1965 had died away by 1966, although groups like the Beatles and the Rolling Stones continued to have regular Number 1 hits on both sides of the Atlantic. The rock world had diversified and the most popular acts of the year were mainly from the pop stream. The most successful chart group in the UK were the virtually unknown Dave Dee, Dozy, Beaky, Mick and Tich, whose four Top Ten hits meant that they were in the UK charts for 50 weeks during 1966. In the United States, 1966 saw the beginnings of another even more famous pop act, the Monkees. Starting off as a pop group manufactured for a television series, their records – released to promote the shows – proved a massive hit with new teen audiences.

While unashamedly pop-oriented groups were in the limelight, 1966 also saw the first stirring of what later was to become 'progressive rock'. In Britain, Eric Clapton, Jack Bruce and Ginger Baker formed Cream in June and in December the Jimi Hendrix Experience came into being. On the West Coast of America, groups as diverse as the Mothers of Invention, Big Brother and the Holding Company, and Jefferson Airplane were being noticed. These groups were to set the style for the future.

January
As the year opens, chart-toppers in the UK are the Beatles with 'Day Tripper'/'We Can Work It Out', and in the US, 'The Sounds of Silence' by Simon and Garfunkel.

January chart-toppers the Spencer Davis Group (above) and Simon and Garfunkel (below left). Below: Power-trio Cream, a major force in progressive rock.

20 The Beatles are removed from the top chart position in the UK by Birmingham R&B band the Spencer Davis Group, who have a Number 1 with 'Keep On Running'.
26 Eric Burdon deputises for Paul Jones when Manfred Mann play at London's Marquee (Jones is recovering from a car crash).
30 Radio Caroline's ship, the *Mi Amigo*, is forced into dry dock in Holland after running aground at Frinton-on-Sea.

February
Midlands-based rock group the Move are formed.
2 Sgt. Barry Sadler's 'The Ballad Of The Green Berets' enters the US pop charts and becomes the surprise Number 1 of the year. In the UK the song reaches Number 24.
14 The Beatles, Herman's Hermits, Petula Clark and Tom Jones are nominated for Grammy awards in the US.
27 The Walker Brothers, Billy J. Kramer and Peter and Gordon star in an edition of 'Ready Steady Go!' broadcast from the La Locomotive Club in Paris and shown live in the UK.

March
American folk-rock band Buffalo Springfield are formed, featuring Neil Young and Steve Stills.
3 The Kinks enter the UK charts with 'Dedicated Follower Of Fashion'.
11 Wilson Pickett plays to enthusiastic audiences at London's premier soul club, the Flamingo.
13 Rod Stewart, vocalist with Steampacket, leaves the group to pursue a solo career.
29 Martha and the Vandellas fly into London to open a British tour.

April
9 Jeff Beck, guitarist with the Yardbirds, collapses on stage at a gig in Marseilles.
14 Chris Andrews' 'Something On My Mind' enters the British charts and becomes his third chart success.
16 Bob Dylan's 'Rainy Day Women Nos 12 & 35' enters *Billboard*'s Hot Hundred and rises to Number 2.
19 David Bowie and his group the Buzz begin afternoon sessions at the Marquee in London.
28 Dusty Springfield has her first Number 1 as 'You Don't Have To Say You Love Me' tops the UK charts.

May
1 The Rolling Stones star at the *New Musical Express* Poll Winner's Concert at the Empire Pool, Wembley.
5 'Pretty Flamingo' by Manfred Mann begins a four-week stint as the UK's chart-topping single.
26 The Rolling Stones top the UK charts with 'Paint It Black', their sixth Number 1 hit single.

June
4 The Beatles create a storm in the US when they dismiss 'The Ballad Of The Green Berets' as 'rubbish'.
8 Roy Orbison's wife, Claudette, is killed riding a motorcycle near Nashville.

10 Janis Joplin joins Big Brother and the Holding Company. They play their first gig at the Avalon Ballroom in San Francisco.
11 Gene Vincent visits a hospital in New Mexico after being informed that his already crippled leg may have to be amputated.
12 The Dave Clark Five make their 12th appearance on the 'Ed Sullivan Show' – a record for an English group.
25 *Melody Maker* announces the formation of the new band Cream, which consists of guitarist Eric Clapton, bass-player Jack Bruce and drummer Ginger Baker.

July
2 The Rolling Stones hire the yacht the SS *Panther*, moored in New York's West 79th Street Marina, after US hoteliers state they are unwelcome guests.
8 Singer Michelle Phillips leaves the Mamas and the Papas.
22 On their North American tour, Mick Jagger of the Stones says: 'One thing I will say about the American Press this time is that, in spite of the rubbish written by the usual idiots who come back to the dressing room and say "which one of you is Ringo", we are getting great reviews.'
28 Chris Farlowe has his only UK Number 1 with the Mick Jagger-Keith Richards composition, 'Out Of Time'.
31 Paul Jones plays his last gig with Manfred Mann at Blackpool's North Pier.

August
West Coast band the Mothers of Invention cut their first album, *Freak Out,* under the direction of leader Frank Zappa.
1 The Who cause a sensation at the National Jazz and Blues Festival at Windsor in a ritual on-stage destruction of their equipment causing thousands of pounds worth of damage. A small section of the audience responds by breaking-up chairs and damaging canvas screens.

Above: Chris Farlowe with Mick Jagger, co-writer of Farlowe's Number 1 hit 'Out Of Time'. Below right: Guitar king Jimi Hendrix formed his Experience in 1966.

3 Bob Dylan is injured in a motor-cycle crash, breaking several vertebrae in his neck. The accident occurred when Dylan was taking his bike to a garage for repairs; the rear wheel locked and tossed him over the handle bars. Following the accident Dylan goes into semi-retirement.
13 British group the Move record a 30-minute live show at the Marquee for American Forces Network; it is to be broadcast to US troops in Vietnam.
20 'They're Coming To Take Me Away Ha-Haaa!', sung by Napoleon XIV, jumps to Number 11 in the UK charts, but is taken off the air by a majority of radio stations in the US following complaints from doctors and psychiatric hospitals.

September
Singer Signe Anderson leaves Jefferson Airplane and is replaced by Grace Slick, late of the Great Society.
12 First screening of the television show starring manufactured pop group the Monkees. The show is an instant success, and a single is released to promote the show. Entitled 'Last Train To Clarksville', it races up the charts to become a Number 1 hit in the US.
15 London Mod group the Small Faces are at the Number 1 spot in the UK with 'All Or Nothing'
23 The Stones open their last British tour for over four years – a 12-day stint with Ike and Tina Turner and the Yardbirds.
30 'I Love My Dog' by Cat Stevens is released by Decca's new Deram label, which is described as a 'hip label for groovy people'.

October
1 Tape cassettes are launched in the UK and retail at £2 each.
7 Johnny Kidd – of Pirates fame – is killed in a car crash in Lancashire, England.
11 Ginger Baker collapses after a 20-minute drum solo at a gig at Sussex University and is said to be suffering from exhaustion and influenza brought on by over-work.
15 The Troggs' 'I Can't Control Myself' is banned in Australia.
28 Cream's first album, *Fresh Cream,* is released in the UK.
29 Diana Ross and the Supremes enter the US charts with 'You Keep Me Hangin' On', which becomes their second Number 1 of the year.

November
3 At a press interview in New York the Yardbirds describe the British music scene as 'reactionary' and claim that the best music is coming from the States. For them, 'the Beach Boys and Lovin' Spoonful are the biggest things happening right now'.
10 Tom Jones' 'Green, Green Grass Of Home' enters the UK charts. One of the most successful records of the year, it remains in the charts for 22 weeks and becomes Jones' first and only Number 1 hit.
17 The Beach Boys top the British charts with the Brian Wilson composition 'Good Vibrations'.

December
3 Ray Charles is fined 10,000 dollars, given a five year suspended prison sentence and put on probation for four years by a Boston court for possession of heroin and marijuana.
10 'I'm A Believer' by the Monkees enters the US charts and becomes their second Number 1 record.
11 Cream release 'I Feel Free' in the UK; it is their most successful chart single and rises to Number 11.
24 Polydor's Track Records makes its first signing, guitarist Jimi Hendrix.
25 The Jimi Hendrix Experience's 'Hey Joe' is released in the UK.

ROCK '67

In 1967, rock's new maturity and sophistication came to the fore as groups and musicians began to view themselves as artists and virtuosos rather than mere pop performers. The Beatles reflected the prevailing drug culture with *Sgt Pepper's Lonely Hearts Club Band,* bringing a greater experimentation to their music, while newer acts, such as the Doors with *The Doors* and Pink Floyd with *The Piper At The Gates Of Dawn,* also explored the potential of the album. A more 'serious' rock audience was emerging, one that demanded more from music than instant accessibility.

But these new 'progressive' trends were scarcely reflected in the singles charts. In Britain, booming middle-of-the-road balladeers held sway; Tom Jones notched up four Top Ten entries and Engelbert Humperdinck reached Number 1 twice. In America, meanwhile, the Monkees dominated.

As the bells and beads of Haight Ashbury stamped themselves on the public consciousness, hippiedom and flower power fell prey to commercialisation and were celebrated in pop hits like Scott McKenzie's 'San Francisco (Be Sure To Wear Flowers In Your Hair)' and Strawberry Alarm Clock's 'Incense And Peppermints'. And by the end of the year, although London's 'underground' scene continued to flourish, San Francisco's original flower children had buried their dream in disgust.

January

1 To see in the New Year, a 'Giant Freak-Out' is held at London's Roundhouse featuring performances by the Pink Floyd, the Who and the Move. Meanwhile, at San Francisco's Winterland, Jefferson Airplane, Grateful Dead and Quicksilver Messenger Service provide the entertainment.

7 Tom Jones tops the UK chart with 'Green Green Grass Of Home' while the Monkees' 'I'm A Believer' holds the US Number 1 spot.

9 Scott Walker receives 4000 cards from fans on his 23rd birthday.

14 The first Human Be-In, held at the Polo Fields in San Francisco's Golden Gate Park, is attended by thousands of hippies. The event is kicked off at 1 pm by Gary Snyder blowing a conch shell while Timothy Leary, with yellow flowers tucked behind his ears, chants 'Turn on, tune in, drop out'.

February

3 Record producer Joe Meek shoots himself dead outside his North London flat.

4 The Move turn down an offer to appear on a BBC-TV show to be broadcast from Birmingham Cathedral after the group's request to burn an effigy of the Devil during their performance has been refused.

11 Lulu has her tonsils removed.

27 The Byrds hold a party at London's Roundhouse in honour of English fans who petitioned the group to come to the UK. Pink Floyd record their first single, 'Arnold Layne'.

In 1967 the divisions between rock and pop became visible. In Britain, ballad singers like Engelbert Humperdinck (above centre) dominated the singles chart while new groups such as Pink Floyd (below left) explored the potential of the album. In America, the Jefferson Airplane (singer Grace Slick, above) and the Doors (singer Jim Morrison, above right) made gold LPs. Below right: Hippies at Woburn, August.

March

4 Promotional film for Cream's single 'I Feel Free' – which shows the band dressed in monks' habits – is banned from US TV.

17 The Stax package tour, featuring Otis Redding, Sam and Dave and others, appears at London's Hammersmith Odeon, while across town the UFO club plays host to an all-night 'perpetual cosmic orgasm'.

24 Jimi Hendrix's 'Purple Haze' is released in the UK.

31 The Walker Brothers, Cat Stevens, Engelbert Humperdinck and the Jimi Hendrix Experience appear at London's Finsbury Park Astoria. Hendrix sustains a burned hand after setting fire to his guitar.

April

1 Manager Larry Page claims he is stopping his band the Troggs from appearing in any London club, saying: 'It has reached the point where if you are in the pop business people think you are going to offer them LSD. I don't want the Troggs involved in that kind of publicity.'

2 Stevie Winwood leaves the Spencer Davis Group to form Traffic.

8 Nancy and Frank Sinatra reach Number 1 in Britain with 'Somethin' Stupid'.

12 America's Greyhound bus company starts running trips for sightseers through San Francisco's hippie areas.

29 The Fourteen Hour Technicolour Dream, a mixed-media event in aid of underground paper *International Times* recently raided by the police, is held at London's Alexandra Palace. 41 groups perform, including Pink Floyd, John's Children, the Move, the Syn, Tomorrow and the Flies, whose lead singer urinates on the audience.

May
1 Elvis Presley marries Priscilla Beaulieu in Las Vegas.
Carl Wilson of the Beach Boys appears before a Los Angeles court on draft evasion charges.
6 Sandie Shaw tops the UK charts with her Eurovision Song Contest winner, 'Puppet On A String'.
12 Jefferson Airplane's 'Somebody To Love' is released in the UK.
27 BBC ban 'A Day In The Life', a track from the Beatles' *Sgt Pepper* album because, the corporation believes, the song contains drug references.

June
10 Procol Harum's 'A Whiter Shade Of Pale' goes to the top of the UK charts.
Jimi Hendrix is refused admission to the botanical gardens at Kew because, according to a spokesman, 'people in fancy dress aren't allowed'.
16 The Monterey Festival opens with performances from Buffalo Springfield, Simon and Garfunkel and the Jimi Hendrix Experience.
19 Paul McCartney admits in an interview to having taken LSD.
30 The Monkees play at London's Empire Pool, Wembley.

July
7 The Monkees embark on an American tour with the Jimi Hendrix Experience providing support. The right-wing Daughters of the American Revolution protest at the guitarist's inclusion on the bill, claiming his act is 'too erotic'.
14 The Who play support to Herman's Hermits in San Diego, California.
23 The Seekers embark on a six-week tour of the States, starting in Atlantic City.
29 The Doors top the US charts with 'Light My Fire'.

August
5 Pink Floyd's first album, *The Piper At The Gates Of Dawn,* is released.
8 George Harrison visits Haight Ashbury.
12 Scott McKenzie's 'San Francisco (Be Sure To Wear Flowers In Your Hair)' reaches Number 1 in Britain.
15 The Marine Offences Act, which outlaws pirate radio stations, takes effect.
26 A three day Festival of the Flower Children opens at Woburn Abbey; groups include the Bee Gees, the Alan Price Set and Marmalade.

September
9 The Flowerpot Men's 'Let's Go To San Francisco' enters the British Top Twenty, while Engelbert Humperdinck is at Number 1 with 'The Last Waltz'.
20 Frankie Vaughan, whose 'There Must Be A Way' is scaling the UK charts, tells the press that love-ins are 'becoming a major menace'.
23 The Mothers of Invention appear at London's Royal Albert Hall.
24 Donovan plays at San Francisco's Cow Palace.
30 The Move's 'Flowers In The Rain' is the first record to be played on the BBC's new pop station, Radio 1.

October
3 Woody Guthrie dies of Huntington's Chorea, aged 55.
6 Hundreds of young San Franciscans, disillusioned with the mass commercialisation of the hippie movement, parade through the city to mark the end of the hippie dream; the event, called 'The Death of Hippie', takes place a year to the day that LSD was made illegal in the States.
9 Windsor Council ban the Windsor Jazz and Blues Festival, stating that the event 'is a big excuse for young people to attend one big love-in'.
28 Lulu tops the US charts for the first (and last) time with 'To Sir With Love'.
29 The rock musical *Hair* opens in New York.

November
9 First issue of *Rolling Stone* published.
17 A two day 'Love-In' commences at the Palais des Sports in Paris; acts include Soft Machine, Dantalion's Chariot and the Exploding Galaxy Ballet.
21 Donovan announces in New York that he has been initiated by the Maharishi Mahesh Yogi.
25 Strawberry Alarm Clock top the US charts with 'Incense And Peppermints'.

December
4 Elvis Presley's 25th film, *Clambake,* is released.
10 Otis Redding is killed when his plane crashes into a frozen lake in Wisconsin.
13 The Monkees head the American charts with 'Daydream Believer'.
25 A children's party is held at London's Roundhouse; Jimi Hendrix appears as Santa Claus.
27 Producer and songwriter Bert Berns dies of a heart attack in New York at the age of 38.

ROCK '68

By 1968, the psychedelic excursions of the previous year were being replaced by more down-to-earth sounds from such American hard rock acts as Steppenwolf and Iron Butterfly, and in Britain by a widespread return to the blues – a boom spearheaded by Fleetwood Mac and John Mayall's Bluesbreakers.

Pop and rock music had by now become two distinct commodities and the needs of the younger singles-buying public were served, in the US, by the bubblegum craze. 1910 Fruitgum Company's 'Simon Says' and Ohio Express's 'Yummy Yummy Yummy' – both million-sellers – paved the way for a mass of similarly catchy and simplistic hits from the Kasenetz-Katz production stable. In the UK, too, fresh-faced popsters such as Love Affair, Dave Dee, Dozy Beaky Mick & Tich and the Herd – whose Peter Frampton was hailed as 'The Face Of '68' – continued to thrive.

Meanwhile, a trend towards more reflective, restrained forms of rock music was signalled by the release of *John Wesley Harding*, Bob Dylan's subdued return to the recording studio following a period of retirement, and the Band's remarkably subtle debut album *Music From Big Pink*.

January
6 The Beatles top both US and UK singles charts with 'Hello Goodbye'.
In a *Melody Maker* interview, Petula Clark dismisses Jimi Hendrix as 'a big hoax', going on to state that 'the fact that he isn't a success with the general public proves something.'
9 John Mayall's Bluesbreakers open an American tour at New York's Café A Go Go.
20 Bob Dylan appears at Carnegie Hall in a tribute to folk pioneer Woody Guthrie, who died the previous October. It is Dylan's first public appearance since his motorcycle accident in August 1966.
28 Ex-Manfred Mann singer Paul Jones, the Who and the Small Faces are thrown off an aeroplane during a tour of Australia, having been accused of 'insulting a passenger, drinking beer and making a hostess cry.'

February
2 Priscilla Presley gives birth to Elvis' first (and only) child, Lisa Marie, at the Baptist Hospital, Memphis.
10 Steve Marriott of the Small Faces, recently returned from Australia, says the group will never go back. 'To the older generation we were a team of pop group rowdies,' he claims. 'They had it in for us so much, it nearly drove me round the twist.'
15 Little Walter, master of the blues harmonica, dies in a knife fight in Chicago.
19 The first European International Pop Festival opens in Rome; acts include Cream, the Who, Donovan, Country Joe and the Fish, Jefferson Airplane and Sopwith Camel.
28 Frankie Lymon, of Teenagers fame, dies in New York from a heroin overdose at the age of 26.

Above: British blues guru John Mayall, who refused to play after his fans were banned from a Wolverhampton ballroom for not wearing ties, sports his own original answer to the problem.

March
1 The Nice release their first album, *The Thoughts Of Emerlist Davjack*.
14 Elvis Presley's 26th feature film, *Stay Away Joe*, is released in US.
16 Esther and Abi Ofarim, a duo from Israel, top the UK singles charts with the novelty song 'Cinderella Rockefella'.
26 Bobby Goldsboro's sentimental ballad, 'Honey', is released in US; the record sells a million copies within three weeks.

April
1 John Mayall refuses to perform at the Top Rank ballroom in Wolverhampton after 30 of his fans have been refused entry for not wearing ties.
6 Syd Barrett finally leaves Pink Floyd. His increasingly erratic behaviour on stage had led the other band members to call in a second guitarist, Dave Gilmour, in February.
27 Louis Armstrong tops the UK chart with 'Wonderful World', which goes on to become the year's top-selling single in Britain.

May
3 The Beach Boys set off on a three-week tour of American colleges with the Maharishi Mahesh Yogi, who opens each concert with a lecture. The tour collapses a week later when only 300 people turn up at New York's Singer Bowl.
5 Buffalo Springfield make their final appearance on stage.
14 Ten Years After play at London's Klooks Kleek club; their performance is recorded for an album titled *Undead*.
24 Sandy Denny replaces Judy Dyble as lead singer of UK folk-rock band Fairport Convention.

June
8 Simon and Garfunkel top the US charts with 'Mrs Robinson', a song featured in the film *The Graduate*.
The Crazy World of Arthur Brown's tour of America grinds to a temporary halt when both drummer Drachen Theaker and organist Vincent Crane collapse from nervous exhaustion.
15 The Jimi Hendrix Experience play at the opening of Majorca's Sergeant Pepper's Club, a venture run by Hendrix's managers Mike Jeffery and Chas Chandler.
21 The Move release Britain's first 33⅓ rpm EP, *Something Else*, which was recorded live at London's Marquee Club and runs for eighteen minutes.
29 A free concert in London's Hyde Park features the talents of Pink Floyd, Tyrannosaurus Rex, Jethro Tull and Roy Harper.

July
13 The Equals go to the top of the UK singles charts for the only time with 'Baby Come Back', a song written by guitarist Eddy Grant.
20 Iron Butterfly's second album, *In-A-Gadda-Da-Vida*, enters the US charts where it stays for 140 weeks, selling over three million copies – all this despite little advance publicity and almost no press coverage.
Singer Keith Relf and drummer Jim McCarty leave the Yardbirds to form a new band, Together.
22 Scott Walker enters a nursing home suffering from psychoneurosis on the day he is to fly to Japan for a concert in Tokyo Stadium.

August
10 The Band's debut album, *Music From Big Pink*, enters the US charts.
17 Canned Heat enter the UK Top Thirty with 'On The Road Again'.
24 Danny Kirwan, a 19-year-old guitarist, makes his performing debut with Fleetwood Mac at Battersea's Blue Horizon Club.

September
6 The Doors perform at London's Roundhouse.
13 The BBC drop Sly and the Family Stone from 'Top Of The Pops' after the

group's bass player Larry Graham is charged with possession of marijuana at Heathrow Airport.
19 Cliff Richard and the Shadows celebrate ten years together in showbiz at the London Palladium.
24 Deep Purple, who have only ever played four gigs in their native Britain, reach Number 4 in the US charts with 'Hush'; the record goes on to sell a million copies, though it fails to chart at all in the UK.

October
18 'All Along The Watchtower' by the Jimi Hendrix Experience is released in UK.
19 The New Yardbirds – Jimmy Page, Robert Plant, John Bonham and John Paul Jones – play their last gig under that name at Liverpool University. The band are thenceforth known as Led Zeppelin.
27 Mary Hopkin, whose 'Those Were The Days' has been at Number 1 in the UK for four weeks and is rapidly scaling the US charts, appears on the 'Ed Sullivan Show'.
31 Tiny Tim makes his first appearance in Britain at the Albert Hall alongside Joe Cocker and the Bonzo Dog Doo-Dah Band.

November
9 Joe Cocker goes to the top of the UK charts with his version of the Beatles' 'With A Little Help From My Friends', while the Beatles themselves are at Number 1 in America with 'Hey Jude'.
26 Cream play their farewell concert at London's Albert Hall.

December
6 Traffic break up for the first time.
14 Fleetwood Mac enter the UK charts at Number 23 with 'Albatross'.
21 Janis Joplin makes her first appearance since leaving Big Brother and the Holding Company at the Stax-Volt Convention in Memphis; she is backed by new group the Kozmic Blues Band.
27 The Jimi Hendrix Experience appear on singer Lulu's BBC-TV show. When the band launch into an unscheduled tribute to Cream, by playing 'Sunshine Of Your Love', the cameras are taken off them.

Danny Kirwan was in the pink after joining Fleetwood Mac (above left). Love Affair (above far left) hit Number 1 in the UK with 'Everlasting Love', as did the Equals (above) with 'Baby Come Back'. Jimi Hendrix (below) appeared on TV.

ROCK '69

If the Monterey Festival in 1967 had hinted at rock's new status and importance, the Woodstock Festival of 1969 confirmed it. Half a million people crowded onto Max Yasgur's farm to listen to the likes of Janis Joplin, Jimi Hendrix, Jefferson Airplane, the Grateful Dead and the Who. But if the hippie ideals of togetherness reached a peak at Woodstock, they suffered severe blows that year with the Manson murders and the fatality at Altamont.

1969 saw new developments in rock music as Led Zeppelin sowed the seeds of British heavy metal, the Who released their 'rock opera' *Tommy* and Crosby, Stills and Nash pointed the way to softer, more introspective forms of rock. The year also marked the end of an era, for it was in February that the Beatles played together in public for the last time.

Although best remembered for Woodstock, 1969 was also a year of novelty acts and one-hit-wonders: Love Sculpture (above) rattled their sabres, while the Scaffold (below) drank a toast to Lily The Pink.

January
4 'Lily The Pink', a novelty song by Liverpool comic trio the Scaffold tops the UK charts while Motown's Marvin Gaye stands at Number 1 in the US with 'I Heard It Through The Grapevine'.
11 'Sabre Dance', a guitar-based instrumental by blues-oriented group Love Sculpture, peaks at Number 5 in the British charts. It is the group's first and only hit, although guitarist Dave Edmunds finds renewed success in the Seventies.
27 'Maybe Tomorrow' by Apple signings the Iveys is released in America. A flop in Britain the previous year, the record reaches Number 67 in the Hot Hundred. The Iveys subsequently become Badfinger.

February
Led Zeppelin's first, eponymous, album is released.
17 Bob Dylan records a duet with country singer Johnny Cash in Nashville; titled 'Girl From The North Country', the song opens Dylan's *Nashville Skyline* album. Released later in the year, the cover of the LP includes a poem, 'Of Bob Dylan', written by Cash.
20 *Candy*, in which Ringo Starr takes his first non-Beatle screen role, opens; the film also boasts the talents of Marlon Brando and Walter Matthau as well as music by the Byrds and Steppenwolf.

March
1 Peter Sarstedt, brother of early Sixties teen idol Eden Kane, makes Number 1 in the UK with 'Where Do You Go To My Lovely'. His chart success proves short-lived, however, for the follow-up, 'Frozen Orange Juice', which reaches Number 10 in June, is his only other hit.
2 The Doors perform in Miami and singer Jim Morrison, accused of exposing himself on stage, is subsequently charged with lewd and lascivious behaviour.
15 'Dizzy' is Tommy Roe's first US chart-topper since 'Sheila' in 1962.

April
The Who's double album *Tommy* – Pete Townshend's 'rock opera' – is released.
16 Elektra Records drop controversial Detroit band the MC5 after the group have insulted a major record store in a newspaper advertisement.
21 Janis Joplin appears at the Royal Albert Hall in London, backed by her Kozmic Blues Band.
25 John Lennon and Yoko Ono's film *Rape* is screened at the Montreux Film Festival.

May
Easy Rider wins award at the Cannes Film Festival.
3 Apple Records hold the top two positions in the UK charts with the Beatles' 'Get Back' (Number 1) and Mary Hopkin's 'Goodbye'.
Frank Sinatra's recording of 'My Way'

enters the British Top Twenty; although it fails to reach Number 1, it is the best-selling single of the year and spends an unprecedented total of 122 weeks in the charts.
16 Guitarist Pete Townshend of the Who spends a night behind bars in New York following an on-stage skirmish with a policeman.

June
9 Brian Jones announces that he is to leave the Rolling Stones. On 3 July he is found dead in the swimming pool of his Sussex home.
11 'Space Oddity' by David Bowie is released in Britain and later gives the singer his first hit.
14 Two stalwarts of the British blues boom, Chicken Shack and Jethro Tull, enjoy their first UK Top Ten hits with 'I'd Rather Go Blind' and 'Living In The Past' respectively.
29 American soul singer Shorty Long, whose hits included 'Function At The Junction' and 'Here Comes The Judge', dies in a boating accident at the age of 29. The Jimi Hendrix Experience play together for the last time in Denver.

July
Crosby, Stills and Nash release their debut album.
12 'Supergroup' Blind Faith play for the first time in America at Madison Square Garden.
18 *Time* magazine describe Zager and Evans' 'In The Year 2525', the record then topping the US charts, as sounding 'as though it were composed by a computer at the Rand Corporation'; the comment fails to affect sales, however, which eventually reach six million worldwide.
25 Neil Young, a recent addition to the ranks of Crosby, Stills and Nash, makes his first live appearance with the group at the Fillmore East.

August
9 The bodies of film actress Sharon Tate and three others are discovered in record producer Terry Melcher's Los Angeles house; would-be recording star Charles Manson is later charged with the murders.
15 The opening day of Woodstock features performances from the Incredible String Band, Joan Baez, Arlo Guthrie, Tim Hardin and others.
22 Elvis Presley performs on stage for the first time in eight years at the International Hotel in Las Vegas.
31 Bob Dylan appears at the Isle of Wight festival.

Tiny Tim and Vicki Budinger (below left) plighted their troth at a State Fair and entered into holy matrimony on live TV; Peter Sarstedt (above) crooned in continental style, while Rolf Harris (below) told of 'Two Little Boys'.

September
6 Jane Birkin and Serge Gainsbourg enter the UK Top Twenty with the highly suggestive 'Je T'Aime . . . Moi Non Plus'.
13 John Lennon's Plastic Ono Band give their debut performance at the Toronto Peace Festival.
18 Tiny Tim announces his engagement to Miss Vicki Budinger at the New Jersey State Fair. The couple's subsequent marriage is televised live on the 'Johnny Carson Show'.

October
3 Blues singer Nehemiah 'Skip' James, whose 'I'm So Glad' was included on Cream's first album, dies at the age of 67.
16 Leonard Chess, the co-founder of the Chicago-based blues label Chess, dies at the age of 52.
22 Paul McCartney officially denies rumours of his death.
25 Elvis Presley tops the US charts with 'Suspicious Minds'.

November
1 'Sugar Sugar' by the Archies stands at Number 1 in the UK, repeating its US summer success.
7 Rolf Harris's 'Two Little Boys' is released. A sentimental song of childhood friendship written in 1903 by Edward Madden and Theodore Morse, the record reaches Number 1 just before Christmas and remains there for five weeks.
27 The Rolling Stones play at New York's Madison Square Garden, the concert being recorded for their *Get Your Ya Ya's Out* album.

December
6 Black youth Meredith Hunter is stabbed to death by Hell's Angels at the Stones' free concert at Altamont.
12 *The Trouble With Girls (And How To Get Into It)*, Elvis Presley's thirtieth film, is released.
14 The Who perform *Tommy* live for the first time at London's Coliseum opera house.
31 Jimi Hendrix's Band of Gypsies make their first appearance at New York's Fillmore East.

ROCK '70

As the Sixties drew to a close, the rebellious, anti-establishment spirit of previous years seemed to fade as a new mood of brooding and introspection took hold. Though loud rock continued to make itself heard – Grand Funk Railroad, Led Zeppelin and Black Sabbath all notched up million-selling albums – 1970 was the year in which singer-songwriters came to the fore. James Taylor (hailed by *Time* magazine as the figurehead of the post-Woodstock generation), Joni Mitchell and Leonard Cohen were among the most successful of this new breed of soul-searching rock artist who put themselves rather than society under the microscope; even John Lennon, on his *Plastic Ono Band* LP, appeared to replace his former political stance with something more personal.

The Jackson Five announced their arrival with a soul-flavoured brand of pop that brought them four US Number 1 hits, but the singles charts on both sides of the Atlantic generally revealed a dearth of teen-oriented acts. The stage was set for the emergence of glam-rock in the early Seventies to attempt an antidote to rock's overt self-consciousness.

January
6 Crosby, Stills, Nash and Young make their first appearance on English soil at London's Albert Hall.
21 *Change Of Habit*, the last film in which Elvis Presley takes an acting role, is released.
31 Singer Carl Wayne leaves the Move to pursue a career on the cabaret circuit. Blues harp-player Slim Harpo dies of a heart attack at the age of 56.

February
11 Arlo Guthrie attends the British premiere of his film *Alice's Restaurant* at the London Pavilion.
13 Black Sabbath's eponymous debut album is released; although the group is relatively unknown, the LP soon charts on both sides of the Atlantic and goes on to sell over a million copies.
28 'Love Grows' by Edison Lighthouse tops the UK charts, while Simon and Garfunkel are Number 1 in the US with 'Bridge Over Troubled Water'.

March
6 Charles Manson, who is on trial for the murder of Sharon Tate and others, releases an album entitled *Lie*.
18 Andrew Loog Oldham's Immediate label goes into liquidation. Its roster had included such acts as the Small Faces, the Nice, Chris Farlowe and P. P. Arnold.
20 Dana wins the Eurovision Song Contest, held in Amsterdam, with 'All Kinds Of Everything'. The Irish chanteuse beats the UK entrant, Mary Hopkin, into second place.
David Bowie marries American Mary Angela Barnett in Bromley, Kent.

Mystic murderer Charles Manson (above) moved into rock with an LP called Lie, *while Fleetwood Mac guitarist Peter Green (right) left rock for the mystic life. Safely back in the mainstream, Dana (below) won the Eurovision Song Contest.*

April
1 Drummer Spencer Dryden leaves Jefferson Airplane, to be replaced by Joey Covington.
4 Simon and Garfunkel hold the UK Number 1 position in both the singles and LP charts with 'Bridge Over Troubled Water' and the album of the same name. The LP remains at the top for 35 weeks.
17 *McCartney*, the first solo album by Paul McCartney, is released. He simultaneously announces in a press release that the Beatles no longer exist.
19 Violence erupts when Hell's Angels run amok at a Who concert at Leicester University; Pete Townshend requires eight stitches for a gash in his head.

May
Woodstock, a triple LP set recorded at the previous year's festival, is released. Despite being the most expensive rock album set ever, it sells over a million copies within four months.
5 Simon and Garfunkel perform at London's Albert Hall before an ecstatic sellout crowd.
16 The England World Cup Squad become the first football team to top the charts when 'Back Home' shoots to Number 1.
25 In the week that Fleetwood Mac's 'The Green Manalishi' enters the UK Top Fifty, Peter Green announces his departure from the group.

June
6 Commenting on Britain's forthcoming General Election, Eric Clapton tells *Melody Maker*: 'I shall vote for B. B. King. The first thing any new MP should do is to apply the mind to producing a self-tuning electric guitar.'
13 The Beatles' 'The Long And Winding Road' reaches Number 1 in the States. It is not released as a single in the UK, however.
14 Derek and the Dominos featuring Eric Clapton make their debut appearance at London's Lyceum.

July
4 The Rattles become the first German group ever to appear in the US charts when 'The Witch' enters the Hot Hundred.
12 Janis Joplin makes her first appearance with her new group, the Full Tilt Boogie Band, in Louisville, Kentucky.

Got My Mojo Working: Arthur Brown (left) was arrested for indecent exposure. The Applejacks (below left) hit the bottom of the barrel and decided to split.

18 Arthur Brown is arrested in Palermo, Sicily, for stripping on stage.
25 Creedence Clearwater Revival's 'Lookin' Out My Back Door' is released; within five weeks the record has sold over a million copies. It becomes the group's seventh consecutive single to go gold.

August
5 Denny Laine (ex-Moody Blues), Trevor Burton (ex-Move) and drummer Alan White join forces to create short-lived Birmingham supergroup Balls.
7 The Popanalia pop festival, held near Nice, France, is abandoned after 12 hours when members of radical group Les Companions de la Route vandalise the stage and equipment.
8 'The Wonder Of You' becomes the last Elvis Presley single to reach the UK Number 1 position during his lifetime. The record, which spends five weeks at the top, is the best-selling single of the year – the only time Presley achieves this feat.
23 Lou Reed performs with the Velvet Underground for the last time at New York's Max's Kansas City.

September
3 Al 'Blind Owl' Wilson, guitarist and harmonica player of Canned Heat, is found dead in a sleeping bag in Topanga Canyon, Los Angeles, at the age of 24.
5 The Applejacks, who have never been able to follow up the success of 'Tell Me When' (a UK Number 7 hit in 1964), finally split up.
18 Jimi Hendrix is found dead in Notting Hill Gate, London.
26 Led Zeppelin play two shows before 24,000 people at New York's Madison Square Garden.

October
1 Jimi Hendrix is buried in his hometown of Seattle, Washington.
2 *After The Goldrush*, Neil Young's third solo album, is released.
4 Janis Joplin is found dead in her Hollywood flat.
9 Donovan marries Linda Lawrence at Windsor registry office.
23 Los Angeles' largest rock auditorium, Winterland, reopens with a bill that includes Jefferson Airplane, the Grateful Dead, Hot Tuna and the New Riders of the Purple Sage.
31 'Woodstock' by Matthews Southern Comfort heads the UK singles charts, while the Jackson Five top the US Hot Hundred with 'I'll Be There'.

November
6 Jim Morrison of the Doors is released on bail of 50,000 dollars pending an appeal against his conviction for indecent exposure in Miami the previous year.
11 Bob Dylan's obscure 'novel' *Tarantula* is published in the US.
16 Grand Funk Railroad's *Live Album* is released; the double LP has advance orders totalling 750,000, and by the end of the year has sold in excess of two million copies.

December
6 *Gimme Shelter*, the film of the Rolling Stones' Altamont concert, is released on the anniversary of the event.
11 John Lennon's *Plastic Ono Band* album, on which the singer avows 'I don't believe in Beatles', is released.
12 Dave Edmunds' revival of 'I Hear You Knocking', a hit in 1955 for Gale Storm and again in 1961 for Fats Domino, is Number 1 in the UK.
20 The Who play a Christmas charity concert at the Roundhouse for the 'needy'; they are joined on stage by Elton John.

INDEX